Planning
Alternative
World Futures

edited by
Louis René Beres
Harry R. Targ

Planning
Alternative
World Futures

Values, Methods, and Models

Praeger Publishers   New York   Washington   London

Library of Congress Cataloging in Publication Data
Main entry under title:

Planning alternative world futures.

(Praeger special studies in international politics and
government)
   Includes index.
   1. International relations—Research—Addresses,
essays, lectures.   2. International organization—
Addresses, essays, lectures.   I. Beres, Louis Rene.
II. Targ, Harry R.
JX1291.P53   327'.07'2   74-33030
ISBN 0-275-05340-7
ISBN 0-275-89420-7 student edition

PRAEGER PUBLISHERS
111 Fourth Avenue, New York, N.Y. 10003, U.S.A.

Published in the United States of America in 1975
by Praeger Publishers, Inc.

© 1975 by Praeger Publishers, Inc.

Printed in the United States of America

To Lisa Alexandra,

    She came, we saw, she conquered

and

To Dena, Rebecca, Genevieve, and Irving Targ

    with much love

The reader of this volume is witnessing a "jailbreak" in process. U.S. scholars of international relations are escaping from the constricting cells in which they had placed themselves. Emphasis on data collection had imprisoned them in the present. Concern about large-scale violence had dimmed their perception of social injustice. Lack of explicit concern for values made them unwitting prisoners of the values of organizations, groups, and classes they served. Focus on a limited set of actors and institutions caused them to believe and propagate the myths of heads of state and foreign ministers about the importance and correctness of their influence in the world. Caught up in the ethnocentric communication system of a large nation state they had lost touch with scholarship around the world that could help to lift them out of their intellectual prison.

While there is overlap in approach in the essays in this anthology, each author tends to take his own route out of jail. This is the great strength of the volume. This provides a key by which the individual reader can relate to this collection of essays. In reading the editors' introduction, I would urge you to select the essays that relate most to your present concerns and read them first. Then work out from there. This will gradually provide bridges to the essays that might initially seem least relevant.

The reader will quickly find that freedom does not make the life of the international relations scholar easier. It is made far more complicated. More explicit attention to values highlights at least five domains that must be simultaneously kept in view: minimization of violence, economic well-being, social justice, ecological balance, and participation. How can one be maximized without infringing on the others? What kinds of global processes of exchange do their interdependencies suggest?

Deepening concern for the future does not release the serious scholar, official, or citizen, from need to know about the present. The essays in this volume make this quite clear. Now that I have explicated my future preferred state, some authors say, how do I get there? Obviously this requires knowledge not only about where we are but also where trends are taking us. This opens up the need for strategies for deflecting trends toward our preferred futures. These are often called transition strategies. The attentiveness to transition strategies distinguishes present work from most earlier proposals for "world order." These often asserted what the world out to be like but usually paid slight attention to how we might get there.

Dialogue between methods developed for the scientific study of international relations of the present over the past two decades or more and efforts to grope toward the delineation and implementation of new global futures is exceedingly important. Such dialogue is to be found throughout this volume. If the futurist wishes to implement his preferred future, he needs reliable information about the present and transition strategies that are grounded in relevant theories of change. On the other hand, feedback from the futurist can help the scholar more attracted to the scientific study of the present to produce knowledge that is useful in the design of alternatives. For example, while scholars have given vast attention to big power confrontations and arms races, they have almost totally ignored the some 3,000 international nongovernmental organizations that link people from different countries in virtually all the occupations and interests of man. Yet knowledge of these "presents" is critical to the design of international "futures." Thus far most systematic inquiry of the present has tended to converge on a very limited number of highly traveled highways rather than illuminate alternative paths that already exist. But this bias is not inevitable.

It is important that a number of scholars writing in this volume draw on the work of colleagues abroad. Indeed, the World Order Models Project, composed of scholars from four continents, has made a significant input into this volume. Transnational dialogue has particularly influenced the broadened value and issue agenda of U.S. scholars. Our focus on war and conflict has been broadened to include economic well-being and social justice through this dialogue. Nevertheless, while the perspectives of this volume are broad indeed, it is still prudent for the reader to remind himself that all authors are living in the United States. The affluent condition of their surroundings makes it possible for them to be a bit more detached and analytic, and manifest a somewhat lesser sense of urgency about economic and social injustice than their Third World colleagues. It is particularly important that readers from the United States and other affluent countries realize that many Third World authors would convey a much greater sense of urgency—and even despair.

It is very significant that some of the authors are concerned with the role of individual citizens in global futures and in transition strategies that lead toward them. The inability of the democracies to extend democratic processes to foreign policy is tragically undermining democratic institutions everywhere. It is very important that some authors discern that greater citizen involvement can include greater direct participation in transnational relations as well as greater participation in the foreign policies of national governments. More thought needs to be given to methods for the development of democratic processes in growing transnational activity lest this activity simply mirror the processes of national governments—or perhaps become even more elitist. This will require broader participation in the development of world futures and transition strategies than we have yet had. We will need much more dialogue between those with a scholarly orientation toward global futures and a diversity of individuals and groups in their own local communities. Not only must the knowledge of the scholar be shared but knowledge must be gained through participation of a diversity of interests and perspectives.

The community of scholarly concern about global futures should reflect the diversity of interests that any world future must serve. Otherwise these futures will be irrelevant to the world at large. This suggests that scholars can only increase their ability to help others to move toward their preferred world future as they are able to create their own world future. This will require more self-conscious planning than we have yet had on transnational relations of scholars and relations between scholars and the public in world futures. The volume you are about to read offers a most provocative milieu in which to ponder these concerns.

ACKNOWLEDGMENTS

We wish to acknowledge our gratitude to each contributor for taking part in the creation of this volume by providing a stimulating essay for our readers to consider and for offering vital criticism of other contributions. As an effort directed toward the improved understanding of world order design processes and methodologies, this volume was conceived and sustained with the help and encouragement of each of these scholars and with the continuing interest of the Institute for World Order in New York City. Without the extraordinary commitment of the Institute to our objective, it is unlikely that a dynamic community of world order scholars would ever have been mobilized or that groundbreaking research and curriculum development in the field would ever have advanced to its present stage of sophistication and attractiveness. Similarly, we wish to add a special note of thanks to our good friend and colleague, Professor Norman Walbek, whose early collaboration on this project provided us with myriad ideas as well as firm intellectual support.

Professor Beres is also grateful to his research assistants, David Cheatham and Carlos Sires, for performing several necessary tasks with dispatch and lively intelligence.

Finally, we wish to acknowledge global citizens everywhere who willingly accept the personal imperative to think more promisingly and productively about the creation of a more humane future for themselves and for their posterity.

CONTENTS

In response to the increasing fragility of man's delicate life-support systems, many students of world politics are now turning their attention to matters of global design. These matters are concerned with the conceptualization of alternative world systems in accordance with certain preselected values and design strategies. Such conceptualization, it is believed, may avert a variety of potentially fateful planetary crises by offering scholars a panoply of suitable models for informed debate and possible implementation.

This sort of model building is not new. Although the current crisis of life on earth is of a uniquely urgent quality (consider the wholly unprecedented constellation of nuclear war, population pressure, resource shortages, and environmental decay), the history of social thought is replete with particular visions or images of alternative world futures. All these visions or images, however, exhibit a very basic flaw. Historic or contemporary, their articulation is uninformed by a sufficient concern for epistemology and methodology.

Yet such concern is necessarily antecedent to the kind of radical system change that is needed. The adequacy of any social alternative is necessarily contingent upon the adequacy of its scholarly foundations. This is true whether the design scope is global, municipal, or even two-person in character.

Recognizing this, the following essays coalesce around the understanding that what is needed now is less a work of specific alternative world future designs than one that deals with ways of studying alternative world futures. How should models of alternative world futures be envisioned and designed? This is the guiding question of our inquiry.

Before embarking upon the primary course of investigating this question, however, a brief perusal of some well-known images will be undertaken. This perusal will serve to concretize the preceding statement that today's developing prescriptions for a new world order are the outgrowth of an ongoing tradition, and it will highlight these prescriptions in their proper intellectual-historical perspective. While certain elements of this tradition are not geared intentionally to the global level, they are nonetheless applicable to world order reform. To fulfill their task creatively, the advocates of such reform must examine speculations and prescriptions about the future at all levels of social organization and spatial comprehensiveness.

THE TRADITION OF SOCIAL THOUGHT AND
ALTERNATIVE WORLD FUTURES

In spite of their extraordinary diversity, prescriptions for an improved world future may be organized into three major categories: community, international-regional, and global. This tripartite division is not meant to imply a condition of mutually exclusive sets of recommendations but only one that reflects varying degrees of emphasis. As the following discussion will reveal, there is in fact often considerable overlap between categories.

The first category reflects the sentiments of theorists who emphasize the creation and maintenance of community in the life of man. Drawing significantly upon the image of the Greek polis, the writings of utopian and anarchist thinkers, and the nineteenth and twentieth centuries' experimentation with communes,[1] these community thinkers plead for self-supporting, participatory political institutions at the immediate or face-to-face level. From the standpoint of world order reform, such institutions become relevant when they are adopted as models for extension to the entire planet.

To understand the guiding spirit of the community orientation, one should turn to the organismic analogy that compares the relationship of human components in any social order to the essential interdependence of individual human parts. Here, each personal sector of social life is judged vital to the health of the whole society. It follows that a breakdown in any such sector constitutes a pathological development that threatens systemic well-being with ills such as war, poverty, and alienation.

Historically, this kind of breakdown is associated with the rise of industrialism, certain forms of technology, and the modern state. These are the villains of the community orientation. Now, it is argued, is the time for a reconstruction of community in the life of man. With such reconstruction, the protracted struggle between what Martin Buber calls "centralistic" political principles and "decentralistic" social principles might be resolved appropriately.

The second category of prescriptions for the world's future reflects a preference for the creation of a strong geographic region (for example, Europe) to superintend the processive development of improved global affairs. In this connection, one may recall Robert Schuman with his design for postwar Europe, as well as the nineteenth-century French utopian thinker Henri de Saint-Simon, whose recommendations entail the establishment of a centrally managed and technocratic European state. Guided in matters of policy by a specially constituted assemblage of prestigious scientists and industrial leaders, Saint-Simon's new political unit is expected not only to end internecine struggles in one part of the world but also to act effectively to fulfill a variety of important welfare needs.[2]

Today the international-regional orientation is very much alive among integration theorists who study the processes of integration and disintegration between states in order to discover the forces that contribute to the former.[3] Implicit in the investigations of these theorists is the assumption that historic struggles between peoples might be ended if the essential dynamics of community building were created in the form of regionwide institutions. Such institutions would be expected to diminish violence and to provide a variety of other human preferences as well. It follows that the international-regional orientation draws importantly upon the community category. In many respects it represents a magnification of the community idea so as to render it more directly compatible with ideas for broad-area reform.

The third category to be described is oriented intentionally toward reform on a global level. Within this general category, a number of more specific types of design or suborientations can be identified: the political-structural, functionalist, and universal-cultural orientations. Once again, individual scholars may find it easy to identify with more than one of these orientations. The points of view expressed by these orientations need not be thought of as mutually exclusive.

Political-structural orientations to global reform emphasize the need to supplant the condition of national sovereignty in world political relationships with strong, systemwide institutions of general authority. By ending the anarchic pattern wherein states coexist without an authority above them, these institutions are expected to deal effectively with the problems of international violence, poverty, hunger, and environmental decay. Cast in the form of a federation, such institutions are expected to replicate the most propitious circumstances of domestic society at the global level.[4]

Functionalist orientations to global reform deliberately skirt political strategies for unification in favor of specially created networks of international cooperation on social, economic, or technical tasks.

The rationale for these networks is essentially that state leaders are unlikely to compromise national sovereignty via federal or political-structural solutions, and that only functional solutions are capable of coming to grips with the problems that demand transnational remedies. Underlying this rationale, of course, is an assumption that is shared with political structuralists: The prevailing state-centric organization of global life is intrinsically dysfunctional.[5]

Universal-cultural orientations to global reform point to consciousness transformation—that is, changes in perceptions, values, and attitudes—as the central precondition of an improved world future. Before people can create viable institutions at the global level, a profound integration of world views, lifestyles, philosophies, values, and religions must occur. This suggests that residents of this endangered planet must establish a certain commonality of perception and existence if they are ever to establish a secure foundation for a satisfactory global alternative. [6]

THE CONTEMPORARY SCHOOLS: PEACE
RESEARCH AND WORLD ORDER

Each of the preceding orientations to inquiry offers a rich body of ideas and reflections pertinent to current research on alternative world futures. Taken together, they form the groundwork upon which today's planetary designer must inevitably build his own set of prescriptions. Presently, these orientations converge into two more or less identifiable contemporary schools of thought about the study of world politics: peace research and world order. While these schools are certainly not mutually exclusive categories of membership, and while a great many scholars would find it easy to identify with both of them, each category has one or more distinctive features that warrant the division.

The first of these schools of thought, peace research, is very much a product of the behavioral revolution in human studies. Arising in the 1950s in the United States, partially in response to the tensions of the cold war and the frightening possibilities of nuclear war, peace research has sought to come to grips with the war problem and more recently problems of social justice via the self-conscious application of empirical-scientific tenets and techniques to inquiry. Its proponents have sought to move their subject as much as possible into the area of "hard" research. But while this has often involved the rather extensive use of quantitative techniques, it has not necessarily meant the demise of qualitative concerns.

Although the peace research orientation is reflected in a number of well-known journals, two stand out for special notice. The Journal of Conflict Resolution, which began publishing articles on conflict and conflict management in 1957, appears to be founded on the understanding that students of peace and war must adhere closely to the same strictures of empirical science as do the practitioners of more "well-developed" fields in the social studies such as economics. The Journal of Peace Research, started in 1964, reflects an essentially similar sentiment with a special measure of concern for policy recommendations and associated value questions. [7]

World order, the school that builds upon the work of Harold Lasswell and Myres McDougal at the Yale Law School, Grenville Clark and Louis Sohn's World Peace Through World Law, and the large body of writings by Richard A. Falk of Princeton and Saul H. Mendlovitz of Rutgers, shares with peace research the preeminent commitment to understanding conflict management and war avoidance, but it also reflects certain basic differences. In the first place, world order—which now has a secure institutional foothold in the form of the Institute for World Order in New York City and its widely known World Order Models Project (see Chapter 5)—embraces a concern for such problem areas as population pressure, resource shortages, ecological spoilation, and dehumanization as well as worldwide poverty and war. In the second place, world order reflects a diminished level of concern for quantitatively directed research and always articulates its own orientation in the accents of "qualitative" scholarship.

Both schools, of course, are deeply committed to the proper pursuit of alternative world futures. After all, such pursuit follows any deeply held concern for profound worldwide change, irrespective of the breadth of problem focus or epistemological/methodological predisposition. The commitment of both schools to alternative world futures also goes beyond studies that seek only to project trends to a given point in time, most commonly the year 2000. And the scholars of both schools are not generally willing to be cast as "social engineers" who are bent upon fostering their ideas upon a pliable and disinterested citizenry. Rather, they are concerned individuals wishing to stimulate broad-based publics around the world to think critically about various world futures they might wish to encourage.

In sum, both schools—peace research and world order—are guided by a number of common inclinations and predilections, but with varying emphases. Both schools are avowedly normative in that they both aim at global transformation along the lines of certain pre-established value hierarchies.

Both schools are demonstrably wholistic in their conceptualization of global interrelatedness, but the world order school extends this characteristic to a veritable plethora of planetary dangers, while the peace research school limits its preeminent concern to war avoidance and social justice.

Finally, both schools are truly interdisciplinary in their use of a broad variety of explanatory variables.

THE SEARCH FOR EPISTEMOLOGICAL/
METHODOLOGICAL FOUNDATIONS

The following collection of essays springs from both the peace research and world order schools. Hence it offers a microcosm of their varying emphases and common orientations. At the same time, it seeks to enlarge upon the contributions of peace research and world order and of the ongoing tradition of alternative futures inquiry from which these schools derive. This enlargement is conceived in terms of a sustained and systematic examination of the epistemological and methodological bases of global design. Each essay is premised on the assumption that only through such an examination can scholars hope to create an adequate theoretical cornerstone for a new and more humane world society.

Until now, the long tradition of social thought concerning alternative world futures has placed little or no emphasis on the essential methodological underpinnings of inquiry. With notably few exceptions,[8] specific proposals for improved planetary systems represent mere assertions of preference—assertions untutored by the benefits of thoughtful analysis and/or the exigencies of implementation. Of course, all prescriptions for new systems of world organization are based upon certain assumptions regarding the nature of man and his various modes of interaction, but these assumptions, whether implicit or explicit, are rarely the starting point for rigorous scrutiny of appropriately formulated hypotheses. Rather, they have regularly led scholarly seekers of a better world future directly to a particular set of conclusions whose acceptability is simply taken for granted. It follows that the central criteria of careful scholarship have been widely ignored.

ESSAYS ON THE STUDY OF ALTERNATIVE WORLD FUTURES: ISSUES OF CONSENSUS AND CONFLICT

The essays in this volume can be grouped along a number of different dimensions. These include (1) the degree of urgency attributed to the current crisis of planetary danger; (2) the breadth of problem focus; (3) the particular kinds of values that are highlighted for fulfillment; (4) the particular sorts of conceptualizations in use; and (5) the particular techniques for the manipulation of data that are favored. Given the relative heterogeneity of the essays on these matters, however, the use of any of these dimensions to supply the principal guidelines for compartmentalization and division in this volume would surely lead to a dysfunctional proliferation of subdivisions and to a fractionation of basic concerns.

But even more important that this, there exists a much more sensible dimension for classifying these essays. This dimension is the level of generality displayed toward epistemological/methodological prescriptions and substantive content. By organizing the presentation of the essays according to this level, the reader is not only apprised of the principal ways of looking at this subject but also encouraged to develop a cumulative and progressive understanding of the study of alternative world futures. Each of the essays, therefore, is grouped into one of three sections representing successive points along a continuum that is defined in terms of this level of generality.

The thrust of the essays in the first part is a very general discussion of epistemological/methodological foundations of inquiry and of proposed modes of analysis for the study of alternative world futures. This discussion proceeds in a manner that deliberately makes no mention of particular values, expectations, or substantive preferences. In effect, Part I is concerned with defining the field in sweeping brushstrokes.

The essays of the second part continue the elaboration of general conceptual Weltanschauungen, but here this elaboration is tutored by a variety of particular substantive concerns. What values in particular ought to guide the study of alternative world futures? Which visions in particular are worthy bases of possible global reform? These are the overarching kinds of questions that distinguish the essays of Part II from those of the preceding category.

The third section of essays is the most specific with reference to the level of its epistemological/methodological prescriptions and to the level of its substantive recommendations. What methods and futures in particular should be endorsed? This is the central question of Part III contributions.

Part I

The five essays that comprise Part I offer an overview of design inquiry from the standpoint of descriptive, predictive, explanatory, and normative investigation of alternative world futures. After pointing to a number of shortcomings of previous efforts in this field of inquiry, each author sets forth some general proposals for improvement. Taken together, these proposals circumscribe the epistemological and methodological bounds of a peculiarly critical area of study.

As its title suggests, the essay by Marvin Soroos presents a methodological overview of the process of designing alternative future worlds. Here, future-oriented research is distinguished from conventional social science, and within future-oriented research, pure forecasting is differentiated from the design of alternative futures. Six potential uses of alternative future designs, some of which do not assume implementation of the design, are briefly discussed. The process of design itself is divided into five stages: value specification, study of the present and projection of current trends into the future, designing alternatives, evaluation of the designs, and drafting transitional strategies. Professor Soroos's discussion of each stage includes questions that may be raised to evaluate a design endeavor.

The essay by George Kent rests upon the twin assumptions that designing the world order of the future is both the most ambitious political design task and the most essential. It suggests that the work of world order scholars must be cumulative as well as constructive and should extend from the production of elegant blueprints to the actual implementation of more desirable configurations of global affairs. The essay concludes with a plea to cultivate the art of all political design so as to demonstrate its possibility, legitimacy, and essential worthiness.

Professor Kent's essay makes certain basic distinctions between prescriptive policy analysts, planners, and designers. The designers are characterized in terms of the weakest tie to extant structures and functions, the greatest amount of imagination in constructing images of future worlds, and the smallest measure of determinism in thinking about alternative world futures. Subsequent to this characterization, there is an examination of the critical phases of the design enterprise itself, with special reference to its processive and open-ended character. Kent argues, in a manner that is contrary to other essays in this volume, that the value clarification phase of world order research may follow the construction of designs. Only a general articulation of values motivating the design enterprise is necessary at the outset. More immediately, states Kent, this enterprise should lead to a listing of functions that particular designs should provide and to the formation of questions about structures that might fulfill these functions.

The essay by Louis Rene Beres suggests that the study of world order may be divided into four basic and successive phases: values, hypotheses, models, and recommendations. Each of these phases is articulated and explored on the assumption that such a fourfold network of inquiry offers an especially promising strategy of world order design. Taken together, argues Professor Beres, these four stages provide scholars with the kind of intellectual guidelines needed to cope with today's planetary crisis.

The essay by A. Michael Washburn rests upon the conviction that all forecasting is normative and that, strictly speaking, any basic distinction between descriptive and normative forecasts is unwarranted. While it is recognized that there is considerable historical justification for such a distinction, the author argues for a characterization of forecasting that is cast in terms of a multistep process wherein statements about the future are produced via the matching of descriptive and normative methods. With this characterization in mind, Washburn outlines a basic, five-step forecasting/planning process as well as a variety of techniques that might be used to enhance its attractiveness and practicability.

Part II

The five essays of Part II continue the exploration of epistemological and methodological underpinnings of alternative futures study, but this time there are also some specific substantive focuses. Here we see not only a general probing of the field's manner of organizing and interpreting knowledge but some suggestion of particular values and visions as well. Taken together, these five pieces transport us several steps farther along the path begun in Part I by anchoring a number of abstract positions and perspectives in concrete sets of preferences and images.

The essay by Davis B. Bobrow, the first piece in Part II, elucidates an approach to global design that highlights performance goals, the operational requirements needed for their realization, and the action instructions needed to meet these requirements. After a critique of what he terms the three most common responses to requests for recommended transition strategies (descriptive utopianism, negative prescription, and macro-modeling), Professor Bobrow applies his approach to global design to an examination of the Institute for World Order's World Order Models Project. The latter parts of his paper offer a number of ideas, findings, and observations that are relevant to the process of global design and serve as a checklist for the production of a blueprint for purposeful action.

The essay by Harry Targ illustrates the expanded concern of Part II by raising four basic questions and offering some tentative responses. These are the questions: (1) What values should a more desirable world future maximize? (2) What are more desirable global futures, and how ought they to be articulated? (3) What national and international processes inhibit the achievement of the values and alternative futures most commonly posited? (4) How can students of alternative world futures structure their thinking about the problem of transition? In responding to these questions, Professor Targ seeks to provide a framework for research and teaching about global design, but he is also careful to emphasize that such a framework is always in need of continual development in conformity with "the best products of substantive and methodological scholarly concerns."

The essay by Saul Mendlovitz and Thomas G. Weiss is founded upon a rejection of "value-free," state-centric orientations to international relations scholarship and seeks to provide a basis for reorienting such scholarship in the direction of greater concern for systemic, normative, and futuristic inquiry. In so doing, it focuses on four essential questions: (1) What are world political and social processes? (2) What are world political and social processes likely to become? (3) What should world political and social processes become? (4) What can these processes become? By raising these questions, the essay goes well beyond the bounds of an earlier sort of international relations inquiry and produces an operational frame of reference for world order study.

Intended as a necessary first step toward creative planetary renewal, this frame of reference is oriented to the minimization of violence and the maximization of economic well-being, social justice, ecological balance, and participation in decision making. Methodologically, it begins with a specification of relevant utopias and culminates in a statement of the investigator's preferred world. To assist in this enterprise, Mendlovitz and Weiss construct a matrix of goals and extant socio/political units and develop a means to score movement toward or away from the desired values over time.

The essay by Francis A. Beer aims at the elucidation of world order inquiry in terms of two dimensions. The first dimension reflects a primary concern for the achievement of peace, justice, prosperity, and liberty. The second dimension centers around regularity and coherence in global relations. It is Professor Beer's contention that the methodology for achieving world order in the first sense is contingent upon one's assumptions about world order in the second sense.

With this contention in mind, the essay goes on to analyze the tasks implied by three such assumptions. For the assumption that order, in the sense of regularity, exists "naturally" in the world, the essay examines orthodox scientific procedures as the appropriate mode of discovery. In this connection, Galtung's morphology of peace and violence is emphasized to help us to define, relate, and measure the phenomena of interest. For the assumption that order exists "artificially" in the world, the essay highlights applied "world engineering" as the contributing methodology. And for the assumption that a coherent set of global relations does not exist at all—the assumption of world disorder—world ethics is cited as the matching methodology.

The essay by Richard A. Falk offers an approach to world order reform that is based upon two orienting imperatives: (1) a methodological imperative and (2) a normative imperative. Emphasizing "the unity of thought and feeling," these imperatives stress the need for reconciling disciplined, systemic inquiry with a continuing awareness of human interdependence and the overall pattern of linkage between man and earth. "It is," says Professor Falk, "the insistence on the coherence of the whole that makes the normative imperative compatible with the methodological imperative and creates the basis for substantive investigations of the present prospects for world order reform." With such insistence as a starting point, the essay is directed to the generation of dynamic equilibrium models of world order that can be accomplished and sustained with the smallest possible measure of trauma and repression.

Part III

The five essays that comprise the third and final section of this book are the most specific with respect to the study of alternative world futures. This characteristic is manifested through the actual application of a particular set of methods to the problem at hand and, as in the preceding two parts, through developmental exposition. As specificity emerges through application, we experience a shift away from an exclusively second-order orientation to global design to one that is also concerned with an examination of the characteristics and consequences of particular designs themselves.

The essay by Charles F. Doran utilizes certain computer simulation techniques to examine some of the outcomes of postgrowth society in world politics. To accomplish this examination, it offers a systematic assessment of a variety of paths to growth equilibrium and their respective implications for developed and Third World societies. In this way, Professor Doran is able to illustrate the application of a particular set of philosophic tendencies and research methods to the activity of global design.

The essay by Michael S. Stohl calls for the recognition of the importance of images (as defined by Kenneth Boulding) for the construction and consideration of alternative world futures. After discussing alternative approaches to system design, Professor Stohl compares anarchist and functionalist images of the future. He concludes that the neofunctionalists have lost sight of the functionalist image of the future because of their concern for institutions rather than for appropriate relationships between and within groups.

The essay by Louis Rene Beres in this section takes as its starting point the argument that prevailing institutional approaches to our planetary crisis must be augmented by behavioral ones. Two basic behavioral strategies are described: (1) a strategy that concerns appropriate changes in individual human beings and (2) a strategy that concerns changes in the characteristic behavior of states. To the extent that students of world order begin to consider these kinds of transformations, argues Professor Beres, they will have created a more auspicious environment for the construction of more satisfactory world futures. The prevailing inclination to define world order reform in entirely structural terms must be reversed accordingly.

The essay by Francis A. Beer in this section offers a look at the manner in which individuals organize their attitudes toward the different levels of "the structure of the world." Examining some of the ways in which identifications with human communities of different scope may be arranged into patterns, Professor Beer focuses on identifications that tend to fall into configurations that are congruent, divergent, and unrelated. The essay goes on to discuss some of the possible reasons for differential development of identifications with different levels and to explore the implications of our knowledge for changes in the structure of world consciousness.

The final essay by W. Warren Wagar presents a study of the possible contributions of the literary and historical imagination to the design of alternative world futures. A rich source of models of the future is the literary genre known as science fiction, which might better be termed future fiction. From H. G. Wells to John Brunner, the writer of every serious scientific romance has been compelled to create a complete future world out of his knowledge and imagination; so also the writers of utopian and dystopian novels. The same fictive arts figure in the work of metabiologists and metahistorians with a futurist bent, such as Spengler, Toynbee, Muller, and Teilhard de Chardin. Creative writers and creative philosophers of history and evolution share a sense of the unique and an empathetic understanding of psychospiritual experience indispensable to a human futurism.

Principal Points of Contention

Upon reviewing the foregoing essays from the standpoint of commonalities and cleavages, four particularly crucial issues emerge. These issues center about both the substance and the methodology of alternative world futures.

The first of these issues concerns values. While each of the authors pleads for an articulation and clarification of the values that must guide futuristic research, there is also considerable disagreement surrounding the specific meaning of these operations. For some, value articulation and clarification represent a uniquely personal sort of task. A necessary implication of this position is that the realization of consensus at any level of the design enterprise is only a remote prospect. For others, the process of articulating and clarifying values is an exercise that yields a common understanding of preferences to be maximized. Here it is believed that sufficient worldwide consensus does exist about several basic values. Typically, these values are described as war avoidance, social justice, and ecological balance.

The second issue concerns the basic objects of transformation. Some of the authors point to a needed change in the cognitive or behavioral orientations of individuals, elites, and/or nonelites, either for its own sake or as an essential precondition of a sought-after configuration of social and political institutions. Others look toward broad-based institutional change, either because such change is valued in its own right or because it is judged the prerequisite for a sought-after change in individual consciousness and behavior. Of course, these differences concern emphases rather than totally conflicting points of view. In one way or another, all of the authors are striving toward an awareness of the optimal mix of behavioral change and institutional change needed to bring about an improved system of world order.

The third issue also concerns the nature of an appropriate mix, but one of a different sort. This is the proper combination of "science" and "imagination" in the study of alternative world futures. What sort of amalgam is most promising? Some of the authors display an uncommon solicitude for the utility of works of art, science fiction, or metapsychological materials to stimulate the design enterprise. Others prefer to highlight the need for greater rigor and for the adoption of presumably sophisticated social science techniques. While there is no logical reason to suppose that these elements are necessarily in conflict with each other or that they cannot be treated as coequal in importance, there is an incontestable tendency among students of alternative world futures to assign a greater weight to one or the other.

Why should this be the case? One answer centers on the assumption that a preoccupation with rigor might have an inhibiting effect on the minds of researchers, thereby foreclosing a number of promising designs prematurely. Another answer, this one stemming from a weighted preference for "science" rather than "imagination," suggests that an inadequate grounding in the basic canons of empirical-scientific inquiry might perpetuate what Bobrow has called "descriptive utopianism."

The fourth and final issue concerns the twin guidelines of desirability and feasibility. Although no one of the contributors would dispute that every world order model must aim at the fulfillment of both of these criteria, there still exists considerable difference of opinion over their relative importance in inquiry. These criteria often tend to vary in opposite directions, compelling scholars to accept certain tradeoffs between them. To be accomplished in accord with the requirements of rational choice, such tradeoffs necessarily must be based upon a predetermined ordering of the two criteria.

Of course, this ordering must always reflect the understanding noted above—that neither one nor the other criterion may be ignored altogether. Scholars who are concerned only with the feasibility of alternative world futures are apt to be locked into configurations that differ only marginally, if at all, from the present. And scholars who are concerned only with the desirability of alternative world futures are apt to construct designs that indicate no discernible awareness of the constraints of the "real" world. The trick, once again, is to settle upon a suitable mix—one that holds out the greatest promise for the preferences in question without straining the limits of probability to their breaking point.

NOTES

1. See, for example, Robert Owen, Report to the County of Lamark: A New View of Society (Baltimore: Pelican, 1969); Mark Poster, ed., Harmonian Man: Selected Writings of Charles Fourier (Garden City, N.Y.: Anchor, 1971); B. F. Skinner, Walden Two (New York: Macmillan, 1948); Aldous Huxley, Island (New York: Bantam, 1962); Paul and Percival Goodman, Communitas (New York: Vintage, 1960). For discussions of utopian thought, see Lewis Mumford, The Story of Utopias (New York: Viking, 1922); Martin Buber, Paths in Utopia (Boston: Beacon, 1949); Louis Rene Beres and Harry Targ, Reordering the Planet: Constructing Alternative World Futures (Boston: Allyn and Bacon, 1974), pp. 63-92.

2. Henri de Saint-Simon, Social Organization, the Science of Man and Other Writings (New York: Harper and Row, 1964).

3. See, for example, Bruce M. Russett, Trends in World Politics (New York: Macmillan, 1965); Ernst B. Haas, The Uniting of Europe (Stanford, Calif.: Stanford University Press, 1965); Leon N. Lindberg, The Political Dynamics of European Economic Integration (Stanford, Calif.: Stanford University Press, 1963); Philip E. Jacob and James V. Toscano, eds., The Integration of Political Communities (Philadelphia: Lippincott, 1964); Joseph S. Nye, Jr., Peace in Parts (Boston: Little, Brown, 1971); Beres and Targ, Reordering the Planet, pp. 92-110.

4. For a useful summary of this literature, see F. H. Hinsley, Power and the Pursuit of Peace (London: Oxford, 1963); Beres and Targ, Reordering the Planet, pp. 111-27; Louis Rene Beres, The Management of World Power: A Theoretical Analysis (Denver: University of Denver Press, 1973).

5. See, for example, David Mitrany, A Working Peace System (Chicago: Quadrangle, 1966); Ernst B. Haas, Beyond the Nation-State (Stanford, Calif.: Stanford University Press, 1964).

6. For an extensive summary of theorists of this approach, see W. Warren Wagar, The City of Man (Baltimore: Pelican, 1963); Louis Rene Beres, "The Errors of Cosmopolis," Philosophy Today, fall 1974.

7. For an expression of the position of the editors of The Journal of Peace Research, see the editorial in no. 1, 1971.

8. See, for example, Beres and Targ, Reordering the Planet; and the set of recommendations in Louis Rene Beres, "On Studying World Order: A Plea for Systematic Inquiry," Policy Sciences 4 (December 1973): 509-21.

Planning
Alternative
World Futures

INTRODUCTION TO
THE INVESTIGATION
OF ALTERNATIVE
WORLD FUTURES

1

**A METHODOLOGICAL
OVERVIEW OF THE
PROCESS OF
DESIGNING
ALTERNATIVE
FUTURE WORLDS**
Marvin S. Soroos

INTRODUCTION

Over the past decade, evidence has been mounting that the quality of life both in the industrial world and in the less developed regions, if not the very survival of large numbers of the world's population, will be increasingly threatened if exponential growth trends in population, the consumption of dwindling reserves of natural resources, and environment-disrupting pollution continue indefinitely into the future. These ecological problems facing mankind are further complicated by widespread poverty and severe inequality and by the increasing danger of warfare following a continued worldwide buildup of conventional and nuclear armaments. The seriousness of mankind's predicament in the last quarter of the twentieth century is suggested by Nobel laureate biologist George Wald:

> Human life is now threatened as never before, not by one but by many perils, each in itself capable of destroying us, but all interrelated, and all coming upon us together. I am one of those scientists who does not see how to bring the human race much past the year 2000. And if we perish, as seems more and more possible, in a nuclear holocaust, that will be the end not only for us but for much of the rest of life on the earth. [1]

Two alternative courses of action appear available to mankind. The first is to allow present growth trends in population, consumption of natural resources, pollution, inequality, and arms development and acquisition to continue in an unplanned, unregulated, and unrestrained fashion. Ultimately, environmental limitations and political and economic problems would apply the brakes to industrial growth. Such an eventuality could take the form of widespread malnutrition and starvation, the collapse of national economic and political systems, and domestic violence and international warfare. Some projections indicate that such a series of developments could occur within the next 25 to 100 years, if not sooner.[2] Technological innovations may, however, postpone the time at which natural limitations become operative. The second option open to mankind would avert such an undesirable turn of events by human design. Such an initiative would include policies designed to constrain growth trends that would otherwise contribute to an exceeding of the carrying capacity of the planet as well as concerted efforts to cope with poverty, inequality, and the threat of war. A prerequisite for progress in this latter, more appealing direction is the envisioning and analysis of alternative futures for mankind that would include not only innovations of a scientific and technological nature but also some fundamental changes in prevailing patterns of thought and the modification or redesigning of existing political, economic, and social institutions.

Most scientific and social scientific research is designed to match theory to empirical observations of previous or current realities. These methods are useful for studying the questions of what is and what has been, and therefore can provide insights and guides for action in systems characterized by relatively slow or repetitive patterns of change, as is the case with many aspects of the physical world studied by the natural scientists and in some of the more static social systems. However, it has been observed by many that the present era is marked by far more rapid social, technological, and ecological change than any previous period of man's history.[3] Past-oriented, data-bound methods of research cannot offer a fully adequate knowledge base for the foresight necessary to manage rapid, irreversible processes and to cope with the distinctively new problems that emerge every year. Likewise these methods are inadequate for the development of visions of alternative future worlds in which a greater degree of human fulfillment may be realized than would be possible in a projection of the existing world into the future.[4]

It is imperative that social scientists develop systematic methods of inquiry that will contribute a knowledge base that is more adequate for anticipating future problems and will facilitate the design and creation of desirable alternative futures.[5] These methods would be developed to answer the questions of what probably will be (under specified conditions), what should be, what could be, and how what should be could be. Considerable efforts toward the development and the utilization of methods of future-oriented research have already been made by some futurists. These endeavors have generally been regarded to be, at best, at the peripheries of social science. Recently, however, increasing recognition has been given to the need for and contributions of future-oriented research. 6 The rigor, objectivity, and utility of existing methods of future-oriented research vary considerably. Relatively sophisticated future-oriented methods have been developed in economics, demography, and the emerging field of technological assessment. Relatively little progress has been made, however, in the application of future-oriented methods in the other social sciences.

The objective of this essay is a contribution to the development of methods of inquiry that can be employed in the designing of more desirable alternative future worlds. In more specific terms, the essay will (1) differentiate the designing of alternative futures from forecasting, another general type of future-oriented research; (2) discuss some potential uses of alternative future formulations; (3) identify the stages in the process of designing alternative futures and describe some methods of investigation that are applicable at each stage; and (4) specify some criteria for validating alternative future designs.

TYPES OF FUTURE-ORIENTED RESEARCH

Within the context of this chapter, future-oriented research is defined loosely as any systematic investigation of which the principal product is a set of images of the future. Future-oriented research and conventional social science can be distinguished on the basis of the relationship of the formulations of the two types of research to real phenomena. The theories of conventional social science describe or explain previously or currently existing realities that can be observed at the time of the inquiry. By contrast, the forecasts and designs developed in future-oriented research describe or explain characteristics of the future that either may or may not take place. Thus, at the time the images of the future are formulated in future-oriented research, they cannot be compared to an observable referent.

Studies of the future can be grouped into two broad categories: pure forecasts and designs of alternative futures. The pure forecaster seeks only to isolate the one image of the future that is most probable from what can be an infinite variety of alternative futures. The designer of alternative futures usually seeks to visualize the future that is most desirable of the perceivable alternatives and to formulate a strategy by which progress can be made toward that desirable alternative. Thus, while the pure forecaster concentrates on the question

of what probably will be, the designer of alternative futures seeks to
answer the questions of what should be, what could be, and how what
should be could be.

In this chapter, a distinction is drawn between forecasts in
general and pure forecasts. In a general sense, a forecast is a response to the question of what probably will be under specified conditions. Forecasts are formulated both by the pure forecaster and by
the designer of alternative futures, but to serve different objectives.
To the pure forecaster, the forecast is the principal product of the
inquiry. By contrast, to the designer, forecasts play an integral role
in the designing and constructing of a desirable future. The role of
forecasts in the process of designing alternative futures will be discussed in more detail below.

A PROFILE OF THE PURE FORECASTER

In asking the question, what probably will be, the pure forecaster
seeks to play a passive, observer role vis-a-vis the forecast developments. In some cases, however, forecasts may provoke adaptive
reactions. For example, a forecast of storms may lead to an increase
in the number of people carrying umbrellas. In other cases, forecasts
may have an impact on the probability of a forecast development. For
example, a forecast of a war can trigger actions that contribute to the
forecast becoming a self-fulfilling prophecy. If the forecast is issued
primarily to influence the probability of an event, it is more appropriately labeled part of a design process than pure forecasting. Moreover, the pure forecaster generally does not explicitly base his work
on values but in many cases takes pains to minimize the extent to
which preferences influence the content of forecasts. In combining a
passive spectator role with an explicitly value-free orientation, the
pure forecaster's approach parallels that of conventional social
scientists.

A future-oriented inquirer may limit his activity to pure forecasting for a variety of reasons. Such a stance may be based on a
deterministic belief that future developments will be governed by
long-term natural processes that are not subject to human intervention,
control, or design. Alternatively, the forecaster may assume that,
while the course of events can in large part be attributed to human
decisions, the momentum of past events as well as the complexity of
existing living and nonliving systems defy significant and effective
human intervention.

A pure forecasting stance also may be taken by a futurist for
reasons other than an assumed inability to intervene significantly in

the evolving turn of events. The pure forecaster may consider his methods of investigation inappropriate for going beyond passive speculation to the design and creation of possibly more desirable future worlds. For example, the forecaster may feel that he has no expertise for making value decisions upon which future worlds may be designed. Alternatively, the futurist may have more confidence in what are perceived to be automatic adaptive processes of the existing system, such as Adam Smith's "invisible hand," than upon planned efforts to modify the system by conscious design. Finally, efforts at social creation may be viewed as unethically manipulative of human beings and therefore contrary to democratic processes and potentially damaging to individual freedom and human dignity.

The following are some implications of an exclusive reliance on the forecasting mode of future-oriented research in view of the planetary problems that have been cited. Forecasts of the severity of emerging problems may encourage adaptive reactions to the situation on the part of individuals or groups. Forecasts alone, however, would be insufficient to stimulate collective action to restructure the more general situation so as to avoid or alleviate the basic problems that are arising. Thus a sole reliance on forecasting is likely to result in mankind following the first general course of action outlined above; that is, unplanned and unrestricted growth until natural limitations become operative.

The stance of the pure forecaster toward technological innovation is at best adaptive. To the pure forecaster, technological innovations that may have a significant impact on global problems are viewed as being almost inevitable, as are the ecological, political, social, and economic implications of widespread adoption of the innovations, which are often investigated only after the technology has been developed. In this way, a reliance on pure forecasting places mankind in the position of reacting and adapting to the technological innovations. Pure forecasting provides an insufficient base for formulating policies that place technology at the service of mankind by allocating research resources toward the development of those technologies that are most likely to serve human needs.

A PROFILE OF THE DESIGNER OF
ALTERNATIVE FUTURES

The designer of alternative futures generally takes a much more action-oriented, interventionalist stance than does the pure forecaster. Visions of the future are formulated that respond to three types of questions: what should be, what could be, and how what should be

could be. The question of what probably will be is not the central
question addressed in the process of designing alternative futures.
Nevertheless, forecasting is integral to the design process both in
evaluating the extent to which a continuation of present trends would
realize the goals of the designer and in assessing the probable effectiveness of transition strategies for accomplishing the desired alternative world. In general, design-related forecasts are more often
based on hypothetical contingencies than are those of pure forecasting
endeavors.

The alternative future designer rejects deterministic assumptions about the future, taking the position that man can and does create
major elements of his future. The elements of the future can evolve
either in a spontaneous, unplanned manner or by conscious human
design. Some designers argue that it is not a question of whether
human beings create their future but of which individuals or groups
are creating the future and for what purposes. Most designers do not
place faith in "automatic" adaptive processes in existing systems,
believing that modifications in systems based on an overall design are
more likely to lead to the satisfaction of human needs and desires and
the avoidance of undesirable developments. While some designers are
reluctant to formulate models for large, encompassing systems,
others have deemed it imperative to tackle the problem of designing
world orders despite the size and complexity of the systems under
consideration. Finally, designers may argue that a coordinated effort
to create a desirable future may contribute to greater realization of
democratic principles if the values underlying the selection of an
alternative future are reflective of the desires of the community in
which it will be implemented. Likewise, it may be argued that personal freedom can be enhanced by designing alternative futures that
preserve or even increase the range of attractive choices available
to human beings.

Designers generally take the position that planetary problems
of population growth, resource supply, pollution, poverty and inequality, and the possible future proliferation of nuclear weapons must be
faced in an active way through attempts to design and implement
future world orders that research indicates are most likely to further
human welfare. Solutions to these problems may necessitate major
changes in existing political, social, and economic systems. Rather
than evaluating technological developments in an after-the-fact fashion,
the designer may formulate research and development priorities and
policies that substantially guide the allocation of research resources
and thereby enhance the likelihood of the most needed technologies becoming operative. The designer will often work with a sense of urgency,
as the sooner efforts are made to confront planetary problems, the
greater the range of alternative courses of action that become possible
for mankind.

Potential Uses of Designs of Alternative Future Worlds

Designs of alternative futures may be developed to fulfill a wide range of objectives. The appropriateness of a variety of criteria of validity of designs is dependent upon the combination of objectives that guided the designer. The following is a brief description of six potential types of contributions of alternative future designs. It may be noted that designing alternative futures can have considerable utility even if a decision has not been made to fully implement a design for a future world, as in the event that it is perceived to lack feasibility at a given time.

Consideration of Values

In asking the question of what should be, the designer raises normative issues that are infrequently faced explicitly but must be explored before rational policies and strategies can be formulated for enhancing the degree of human fulfillment, happiness, and well-being. Failure to confront value questions and to define and redefine goals can result in the retention of value sets and goals that may have been consistent with the knowledge base of a previous era or were appropriate given the problems confronting a particular society at one stage of economic, social, or technological development. However, these value sets may be quite inappropriate for present and future situations in which the problems faced by mankind and by specific societies differ sharply from those of the past and in which scientific and social scientific research and technology have expanded the range of alternatives that are open to individuals and societies.

For example, population growth has been viewed as one means for enhancing the military capability and security of a nation-state. In an era of nuclear weapons and capital-intensive conventional warfare, however, population is likely to have considerably less strategic value. Likewise, there is often a tendency to confuse means to an end or even the quantitative indicators of those means with the ultimate end itself. For example, gross national product per capita, a measure of economic development, has in some contexts become an end unto itself even though the measure fails to take into account the distribution of income and the life conditions of a large proportion of the population that diverges considerably from the mean.

Increased Awareness of Options

Designing alternative futures can increase awareness of the range of options open to mankind. The alternative futures that are

envisioned may be very attractive, in which case they are often labeled
utopias. Alternatively, the futures that are envisioned may describe a
catastrophic series of events. Designs of very undesirable possibilities are often described as apocalyptic futures or dystopias. Awareness of a choice of alternative futures, regardless of whether they are
very probable or improbable given present trends, may stimulate a
broader and more intense interest in the future of mankind and in the
steps necessary to create a more desirable future.

Enhanced Likelihood of a More Desirable Future

Following from the second potential contribution, designing alternative futures may increase the likelihood of a more desirable future
for mankind and decrease the probability of a very unpleasant future
evolving. Such an objective is consistent with Christian Bay's characterization of political activity as "aimed at improving or protecting
conditions for the satisfaction of human needs and demands in a given
society or community, according to some universalistic scheme of
priorities, implicit or explicit."[7] At all levels of human organization,
a carefully planned future would appear to serve the broad-based needs
of a community more effectively than would a future evolving from
spontaneous development or from partial designs incorporating the
private goals of particular individuals or groups.

A decision not to design alternative futures may preclude the
perception of very desirable and feasible alternatives. As a result,
policies designed to realize such desirable futures may never be
undertaken. Such a failure to perceive desirable alternatives is more
likely during periods of rapid change. Even if the more attractive alternatives are eventually envisioned, the irreversibility of many
processes rules out backtracking to a stage at which policies designed
to realize the more desirable alternative can be implemented. A
related possibility is a failure to perceive movement in the direction
of an undesirable, or even catastrophic, alternative future sufficiently
early to promote the initiation of steps to avoid such a turn of events.
In contrast to invention, or creation of the future, the avoidance of
undesirable futures may be considered a process of "preventing a
future."[8]

Perspectives on Present Systems and Policies

Designing alternative future worlds can offer useful perspectives
on existing systems and current potential policy decisions. First, the
design presents an alternative model against which the existing system can be evaluated. In other words, "plans for the future express
what we wish the present were like."[9] Comparing the present system

to a more nearly ideal one can increase awareness of less than desirable features of the current system and trigger a commitment to an altering of the existing system so that it will compare more favorably to the ideal. Second, a design specifying a set of values and contributing a sketch of possible future institutions and processes may offer a sense of direction and consistency to current policy that is lacking when implicit, unexamined, short-term goals serve as a basis for policy. Third, future designs may increase awareness of the impact of current decisions on future developments in the sense of increasing or decreasing the alternatives available to man in the future.

Systematic Evaluation of the Probable Effectiveness of Policies

If a commitment is made to the achievement of specified values, a well-constructed design of an alternative future can enhance the likelihood of formulating policies that will contribute to progress in the direction of these goals. Often the assumptions underlying a policy as to how it will contribute to the achievement of a goal are not made explicit and evaluated systematically. Numerous programs have not had the anticipated results partly because the underlying assumptions were invalid. Constructing an alternative future design can be a technique by which underlying assumptions are made explicit and can be subjected to systematic validation procedures.

Guiding Policies on Technological Research and Assessment

Designs of alternative futures can provide a basis for policies designed to enhance the capacity of science and technology for serving human needs. While there may be a few tasks that science and technology lack the capacity to accomplish, it is apparent that technological resources are insufficient for attacking all the problems facing mankind, much less the overstudying of possibilities that are fashionable, "charismatic" challenges, such as heart transplants, supersonic transport, and manned space flight. [10] The specification of values, goals, and priorities in the designing of alternative futures can offer a sense of direction for policies on research and development that enhances the likelihood of satisfying man's most basic needs.

With regard to the utilization of technologies that already have been developed, designs of alternative futures offer criteria for evaluating the desirability of the social impact of specific potential applications of technology. Too often, the technological capability to do something is translated into the normative position that the technology ought to be applied. Explicit social values and goals are an essential component of any technological assessment endeavor. Moreover, if the range of potentially desirable applications of technologies exceeds available resources, the design can serve as a basis for ranking the technologies in terms of their importance for achieving human goals.

STAGES IN THE DESIGN OF ALTERNATIVE FUTURES

The design of alternative future worlds is a process that can be broken down into five stages: (1) value specification, (2) analysis of the present and forecasting future developments, (3) formulation of designs of alternative futures, (4) evaluation of the designs of alternative futures, and (5) drafting transition strategies. The objectives and some appropriate criteria of validity for each stage are briefly described.

Stage 1: Value Specification

An essential first step in the designing of alternative futures is the specification of values that are to provide a sense of direction for the design process and serve as criteria for evaluating the desirability of the existing world, projections of current trends into the future, and the designs of alternative futures that are formulated. The value formulations normally reflect the designer's conception of human nature and what constitutes the physiological, social, and psychological human potential.

It is assumed in this essay that, while there are some pronounced and cultural differences in the values that are expressed, there are some values and needs that are universal to mankind. Evidence of differences in values is the emphasis placed upon material production, consumption, and competition in societies with capitalistic economic systems in contrast to the primary concern of some Eastern cultures with spiritual values, such as salvation, love, purity, nirvana, and estheticism. Conversely, psychologists Abraham Maslow and William Eckhardt have posited values believed to be applicable across cultures. Maslow suggests that there is a hierarchical ordering of human needs and values. The biological need for food is more basic than the aspiration for safety, which in turn is more vital than the need for love. All these more fundamental values are seen as steps toward "self-actualization," which Maslow defines as "realizing the potentialities of the person; that is to say becoming fully human, everything the human can become."[11] Eckhardt recommends the abstract value of "compassion" in contrast to "compulsion" as a norm for measuring all other human values, scientific theories, empirical fact, and social practices. Eckhardt identifies compassion as being comprised of "a radical faith in human nature, altruistic values, cognitive creativity, justice defined as equality, behavior aimed at actualizing all of these values, and a social structure compatible with and conducive toward their actualization."[12] Eckhardt suggests that values consistent with the compassion criterion contribute to human development and mental health.[13]

Peace theorists and designers of alternative future orders have specified values to be realized in social systems, such as peace defined in terms of the absence of physical violence and exploitation, and the presence of economic welfare, social justice, and freedom. Recently, increasing recognition has been given to the need for present and future social systems living in harmony with the natural environment. Richard Falk set forth the societal goals of (1) peace and equality among men, (2) harmony between mankind and nature, and (3) a due regard for the future of the earth and future generations of men.[14]

Contrasting procedures for formulating and validating goals have been proposed. First, goals may be defined within the academic community in a speculative, deductive fashion and be validated either by a process of dialectical reasoning or by social scientific analysis. A variety of criteria have been suggested for the logical evaluation of values and goals.

Eckhardt proposes five logical criteria that may be applied to evaluate the coherence, or "authenticity," of values, defined as the "will to value for others what we value for ourselves": (1) universality, what is valuable for oneself is good for others as well; (2) eternity, what is good in the short run is good for the long run as well; (3) unity, the values do not contradict but enhance one another; (4) honesty, that the values are actualized as well as verbalized; and (5) the values are freely chosen.[15]

Societal values and goals may be considered valid when they allow for fulfillment of the values and needs of individuals. The systems theorist Ervin Laszlo argues that human institutions and societies function best when they are "spontaneous expressions of freely chosen activities of their interrelated members."[16] Alternatively, there is increasing recognition that individual and societal goals should remain compatible with the functioning of natural, nonhuman systems. Some social scientists argue that the study of values need not be limited to speculation and reason but can be investigated scientifically. For example, Maslow and Eckhardt, in reviewing the extensive psychological reasearch on values and attitudes, have concluded there are relationships between perceptions of human nature and accompanying value sets and the levels of self-actualization and mental health of individuals.[17]

A second method of selection is to seek the opinions of those who would participate in the future world. National or global goal-setting activities may be undertaken by elites, such as selected leaders from governmental, corporate, business, military, technological, and educational communities. Many national governmental and nongovernmental elites have formulated goals for their societies. [18] International conferences, such as the 1972 United Nations Conference on the Environment, have attempted to set global goals and priorities for mankind.

More broadly representative groups of goal selectors have been proposed by some designers. For example, Gerald Feinberg proposes that the search for goals for mankind should involve a sizable portion of the human race. [19] Opinions of a broad spectrum of the population may be gained either by soliciting responses or by scientific sampling procedures.

The opinions from nonacademic circles may be subjected to the same validation criteria that have been suggested above. Elite opinions on goals may not be representative of the entire community and may be inherently conservative, designed to perpetuate the position in society of the goal selectors. A more representative polling may increase perceptions of the legitimacy of a value, but there is serious question whether the average citizen has sufficient knowledge and foresight to make a wise selection between competing goals in a complex and rapidly changing world. Future generations pose an interesting problem for the representative strategy in that they will be living during the era that is the subject of the designer's endeavor but are not as yet able to express their value preferences for consideration in the design process. Implementation of short-run goals to benefit currently politically aware generations may reduce the options or even survival potential of future generations.

Stage 2: Analysis of the Present and Forecasting Future Developments

After specifying the values that are to guide the designing and evaluating of future world orders, an effort may be made to describe and analyze the existing world and to forecast what probably will take place if current trends continue. Evidence of probable discontinuous developments, such as technological innovations or the recent Arab oil embargo also may be incorporated into the future projections. The resulting image of the future becomes one of the alternative futures for mankind that will be given further consideration.

The study of the existing world and the projection of it into the future serves several purposes.

First, by evaluating the present system on the basis of the values specified in stage 1, a judgment can be made on the importance of developing alternatives. Formulating alternative futures may be imperative if the present system and its continuation are likely to lead to dangerous situations in which the survival and well-being of mankind are threatened, as is forecast by a number of scholars and scientists.[20] On the other hand, if no major problems are foreseen and the present system has the capacity for significant progress toward the values specified in stage 1, there may be little need for more than relatively minor adjustments in existing systems.[21]

Second, the analysis of existing systems may be useful for identifying reasons why the present system is less than ideal, knowledge that may be of value for designing models of alternative futures that could eliminate or ameliorate shortcomings of the present system.

Third, the success of strategies for transforming the existing world to a more desirable one, as discussed in stage 5, may be largely dependent upon an adequate understanding of present realities.

Description and analysis of the present system may be undertaken using the methods of theory development and empirical observation commonly used in more conventional social science. These familiar methods need not be reviewed in this essay. The values specified in stage 1 and potential future problems guide the type of research questions that are posed. Additionally, new environmental or social indicators may be formulated to evaluate the conditions of the existing system and research may be undertaken to explain variations in those indicators.[22]

Forecasting may be undertaken using a variety of methods, including historical analogy, trend extrapolation, computer simulation, gaming and man-computer simulations, and individual and group intuition.[23]

Historical analogy assumes that future developments will resemble patterns of phenomena in a historical system that bears a distinct similarity in relevant respects to present and future systems. Historical analogy may be based upon the intuitive interpretation of past systems by a historian or upon theories verified by conventional social scientific methods of inquiry.

Trend extrapolation is the description of characteristics of probable futures by fitting a curve to time series data leading up to the present for purposes of projecting future values, as has been done by Herman Kahn and associates in research on the future.[24]

Computer simulations integrate and extrapolate a number of trends into the future by means of a dynamic formal model in which the interactive effects of the trends will be taken into consideration.[25]

Gaming and man-computer simulations provide for the investigation of the responses of human decision makers to situations in a

laboratory setting that corresponds in relevant respects to characteristics of a probable or possible future world. [26]

Intuitive forecasts are based upon speculations of experts, either
individually or in groups. Group intuitive forecasting can be based on
a variety of procedures, such as brainstorming, polling and structured
interactions. The Delphi method in which experts critique each other's
forecasts in order to increase the convergence toward a group forecast is perhaps the most fully developed and widely used form of intuitive forecasting. [27]

The most obvious procedure for validating forecasts is to wait
for the forecast period to transpire and then compare the forecast to
what actually has taken place. Such a procedure for validating forecasts is inappropriate in the designing of alternative future worlds for
two reasons. First, the forecast loses its utility as a guide for action
as the forecast period is approached and entered. If the forecast includes images of serious problems, the value of the forecast will be
in the stimulation of immediate action to avert the problem. Waiting
to ascertain whether future developments bear out the forecast would
result in too much delay in the undertaking of adaptive strategies or
in a major redesigning of the system. Second, the basic task of the
designer is to formulate and encourage the implementation of an
alternative future and, in so doing, to intervene in such a way that
the future would not correspond to a forecast of an undesirable turn
of events.

Four criteria for evaluating forecasts that are appropriate to
the designer's task are internal validity, reproducibility, interdesign
consensus, and interfield relatedness.

The internal validity of a forecast is a function of how effectively
relevant information is integrated into the development of images of
the future. In general, a forecast with high internal validity would be
characterized by internal consistency and based upon assumed relationships that correspond to those existing in systems comparable to
the one being forecast. The reproducibility of a forecast is the degree
to which the methods used for collecting and synthesizing information
are sufficiently objective and rigorous to allow forecasters using the
same forecast design to derive similar forecasts. Interdesign consensus is the extent of compatibility between forecasts made by forecasters with expertise in diverse disciplines utilizing a variety of
forecasting methods. Interfield relatedness refers to the extent to
which information from diverse but relevant fields is integrated into
the development of a forecast. [28]

Stage 3: Formulation of Designs of Alternative Futures

The task of the third stage is to formulate images of the future that will more fully realize the values set forth in the first stage than does the existing world and a projection of it into the future. The designs that are developed at this stage become instruments for creating the future, not as rigid models but as tentative images of the future that may be evaluated and subsequently modified or discarded. At this stage, the designer is not concerned with the probability of the future that is envisioned but with the questions of what should be and what possibly could be. The designing of alternative futures requires the creative skills of a visionary artist or architect. Becoming critical too soon may close off alternatives that subsequent investigation may reveal are desirable and workable when combined with other ideas. Critical evaluation of the proposals will be undertaken in stage 4.

The designs that are formulated may differ in several fundamental respects. First, the design may contain a variety of mixtures of developmental and transcendent elements.[29] Developmental aspects are present in existing systems but would become more predominant in a proposed future. For example, the design may encourage more widespread acceptance of certain value sets, such as Eckhardt's "compassion," to which some individuals already adhere. Likewise, designs may call for the more widespread adoption of existing national or regional systems, such as that of postwar Europe, which have been relatively successful in achieving economic prosperity and reducing the likelihood of war. Alternatively, the design may specify "obsolescibles," those elements in the existing world that have either become unnecessary for, or even obstacles to, the achievement of desired values.[30] For example, to many peace theorists, the nation-state system and accompanying military establishments would qualify as "obsolescibles" as they are perceived to be institutions that increase the likelihood of war.

Transcendent elements, or what have been labeled "futuribles" by Bertrand de Jouvenel, do not or have not previously existed. Relatively few proposals are clearly transcendent. Inhabiting the moon or other planets to reduce population densities and tap new supplies of resources clearly could be classified as transcendent proposals. Some transcendental designs, such as a peace education proposal, may have specific elements that have existed previously, but a proposed configuration of these elements may never have been previously implemented.

Second, the time dimension within the design may be either a static, "snapshot" end state or a dynamic process that would undergo change indefinitely. The static end state is an ideal world, the achievement of which would constitute the completion of the design process. Time is a much more basic component in the dynamic process variety of design, which generally does not have a specified condition of completion. Paul Smoker suggests that at each succeeding stage of social creation, new perceptions of what constitutes an ideal world may be formulated, which in turn would lead to further designing and creation. [31]

Third, models may vary in scope and variable range. In this context, scope refers to the population size and geographic space for which the alternative is planned. Much of the utopia literature describes relatively small communities of a few hundred or thousand individuals. With the increasing awareness of planetary ecological problems, coupled with step changes in the speed of transportation and communication, more designs of a global scope have been offered. [32] Likewise, the variable range may differ considerably. Some are of a very limited range, focusing on one set of variables, educational processes, and social and economic relationships, whereas other designs are very comprehensive in the range of variables that are incorporated.

Finally, the form of designs differs in very fundamental ways. Robert Boguslaw has offered a typology for classifying designs that includes the following four categories: (1) formalistic, (2) heuristic, (3) operating unit, and (4) ad hoc.

Formalist designs are based upon an explicit or implicit model that specifies how a system operates in foreseeable situations, usually to realize an identified objective. [33] The world dynamics models of Jay W. Forrester and Donella H. Meadows and colleagues are examples of formalistic designs. [34]

Heuristic designs specify the principles and procedures that are to guide action but do not include specific preconceptions of specific problems to be faced. The 26 environmental principles formulated at the United Nations Conference on the Human Environment offer an example of the heuristic mode of design.

The operating unit design focuses upon characteristics of the people, organizations, or machines that perform tasks in the envisioned future rather than upon how the operating units function in specific situations or the principles that guide them. B. F. Skinner's Walden Two and the Charter of the United Nations are, in many respects, operating unit designs.

The ad hoc approach begins with a conception of the existing system and its requirements and entails endeavors to cope with emerging problems in a practical and incremental fashion. The approach does not specify formal models, general principles, or specific operating units.

The formalist approach would appear to be more appropriate in instances in which the problems to be encountered in the future are relatively foreseeable, whereas heuristic, operating unit, and ad hoc designs may be more suitable in less predictable systems.

Validating the designs developed in stage 3 is deferred to the fourth stage in the overall design process. The primary evaluative question to be raised in stage 3 is whether the designer has envisioned a sufficiently wide range of alternatives, such that the potentially most desirable possible future worlds are included in the designs to be given further consideration.

Stage 4: Evaluation of the Designs of Alternative Futures

Whereas creative skills are required in the third stage, stage 4 entails the application of systematic and rigorous methods of critical analysis. The objective of the fourth stage is to assess the relative qualities of the alternative designs formulated in the preceding stage. The following are some questions that may be raised at this step of the design process:

1. What is the potential of the design for contributing to a fuller realization of the values specified in the first stage?

2. How valid are the hypothesized relationships incorporated into the design?

3. How adequately does the design anticipate problems that are likely to emerge in the future?

4. What undesirable consequences could accompany implementation of the design?

5. Are the feedback mechanisms included in the design adequate for providing information essential for continued realization of the values guiding the design process?

6. Is the design consistent with known ecological parameters, such as limitations on the supply of renewable or nonrenewable resources?

These questions are but a few of the many that should be raised in evaluating the tentative designs that have been formulated.

A number of methods of inquiry may be employed in seeking answers to the evaluation questions, even though in most cases the design has not been implemented and cannot be observed directly. First, intuitive evaluations may be made either by individuals or by panels of experts. More confidence may be placed in designs that have been analyzed by specialists representing a wide range of relevant expertise. Cross-impact matrixes, such as those utilized in technological assessment projects, could be employed to assess the impact that components designed to further one value may have on the realization of other goals. Second, empirically testable propositions can be developed from the premises of the alternative future model and be verified or falsified on the basis of previous ongoing social science research.[35] Third, all or part of the design may be expressed in the form of a computer simulation to project the outcome of a complex set of interacting processes.[36] Fourth, man or man-computer simulation models may be developed for studying the behavior of human beings in an environment similar to the alternative future system under consideration.[37] The inclusion of human decision makers may be of particular value if elements of the design are transcendent, that is, do not exist anywhere at the present time such that human responses to the type of situation can be observed only in a simulated milieu. Evaluations of the alternative future may be based both upon the reactions of the participants and upon a systematic analysis of their behavior during the simulation. Fifth, the evaluation may take the form of a public experiment, such as a commune, experimental school, or rock festival.[38] A voluntary reduction in the consumption of a resource in short supply for a trial period to experience an altered lifestyle is another type of public experimentation that can be used to investigate an element of an alternative future.

The range of alternative futures may be narrowed on the basis of the evaluation undertaken at this stage of the design process. A decision on which design to implement may be made at this point or deferred until transition strategies for achieving several alternative designs have been assessed.

Stage 5: Drafting Transitional Strategies

The objective of stage 5 is to define transitional strategies that will transform the existing world into a more desirable alternative future that was designed in stage 3 and evaluated in stage 4. Thus, answers are sought to the question of how what should be could be. Since the transitional strategy may vary greatly depending upon the characteristics of the design, particularly its form, the discussion of methods appropriate to this stage of the design process will by necessity lack specificity.

The formulation of a transition strategy may begin either with the present or with a future point in time at which the design is to become operational. The present-to-future strategy is based on a description of current conditions followed by an outline of a series of policies that will gradually transform the existing system in the desired direction. The future-to-present strategy develops a series of events in a reverse sequence in attempting to unravel a process by which the desired alternative future could develop from the present.[39] The latter process is analogous to the procedure of a historian who seeks to explain how a series of developments came about.

Contrasting assumptions regarding whether social change is best accomplished by initially seeking changes in patterns of human thought and values or, alternatively, commencing with alterations of policies and institutions that impact on human behavior distinguish two basic types of transitional philosophies. The first approach emphasizes socialization and education as a strategy for changes, in particular, the widespread heightening of consciousness of the problems facing mankind and how individuals contribute to those problems and can play a role in creating a more desirable alternative future. An integral element of this philosophy of change is the encouragement of an examination of the currently held values of individuals and the adoption of a modified value set that will serve to guide behavior in desired directions. For example, Christian Bay has called for the realization of a level of political consciousness he labels "militant humanism" and defines as "a commitment to the value of each human life itself, freely evolving."[40] The form of education also can be important. William Eckhardt has proposed a humanist philosophy of education that would encourage insight and independence of thought rather than blind conditioning or indoctrination designed to encourage conformity.[41] Educational programs designed to achieve these ends have been instituted using a variety of rubrics including peace education, world order studies, development education, world studies, global community curriculums, and futures studies.[42]

A second philosophy of change is offered by B. F. Skinner, who argues that "the environment is a more promising point of attack than man himself."[43] Skinner suggests that social problems can be attacked by means of a behavioral technology in which punitive and nonpunitive contingencies are manipulated to encourage desired social behaviors. Similarly, Garrett Hardin, in an essay entitled "The Tragedy of the Commons," warns against relying on conscience or a social sense of responsibility on the part of individuals. Hardin argues that "mutual coercion mutually agreed upon" is necessary to cope with planetary ecological problems.[44] Modification of existing institutions or establishment of new organizations is a related, but usually more fundamental, type of alteration of the individual's environment that has potential for altering human behavior patterns. Such a strategy is exemplified by the establishment of the League of Nations and the United Nations as institutional means for promoting peace.

Institutional changes are an important element in the transitional strategies proposed by Richard A. Falk and Robert L. Heilbroner.[45]

Strategies of change also differ in regard to the agent of change that is identified. Change may be sought by working through representatives of existing governments, as has been attempted in the International Peace Academy in Vienna, which was organized to provide a channel of communication between peace researchers and practitioners, such as high-level diplomats and military officers.[46] Other strategies call for weakening some currently influential elites and look to the emergence of new, enlightened and inventive leadership groups, perhaps drawn from the scientific and social scientific communities, as potentially the most effective agent of change.[47] Robert Theobald and J. M. Scott visualize the possibility of an international "scientists' synergy" becoming a dominant political actor.[48] In contrast to these elite or "top down" strategies, Arthur I. Waskow has outlined a "participation" strategy that calls for the gradual, grassroots construction of elements of a future design without the help, or even the permission or approval, of presently powerful elites.[49]

Finally, transition strategies may differ considerably on the rate and magnitude of the proposed changes. If the ratio of the magnitude of the change to the time designated for achieving the change is high, the plan may be dismissed by potential implementers as lacking feasibility or requiring excessive disruption of the existing society. If the change/time ratio is low, however, the change may not be sufficiently rapid to cope with emerging problems. Moreover, slow rates of initial change may limit later options, thereby necessitating more extreme change further in the future.

In addition to the criteria of validity already suggested in this section, several questions may be posed in the evaluation of transition strategies:

1. Is the strategy based on valid assumptions regarding the characteristics of existing systems?

2. If adopted, is the strategy likely to bring about a future similar to the design and, in so doing, realize progress in the directions of the values specified in stage 1?

3. Does the more desirable alternative world justify the disruptions and costs likely to be entailed in the transition?

4. Have potentially less costly and disruptive strategies been considered?

Answers to the crucial second question above may be sought using the forecast methods described above. The forecasts can be utilized to answer the question of what is probable if a specified step in the transition strategy is implemented. In addition, the hypothesized relationships incorporated into the transition strategy can be investigated using the methods outlined in stage 4 for evaluating the designs of the alternative futures. If the design is actually implemented, continuing observation can ascertain the degree to which the strategy is operating as planned.

A further question that may be raised in considering transition strategies is the very likelihood of a strategy being adopted by appropriate actors. In this respect, the editors of the Journal of Peace Research extend the evaluation process one step further by asking to what extent a proposed strategy has been adopted.[50] This criterion assumes that one measure of a scholar's contribution is the impact his work has on his society.

A CONCLUDING REMARK

The process of designing alternative futures may be described as a peace technology and an applied social science. At the present time, the design methodology is not nearly as well developed as that of pure conventional social science or peace research. It is hoped that this essay has clarified some issues central in the emerging design methodology.

Given the complexity of global social, economic, political, and ecological processes, the design and implementation of a model of an alternative future on a global basis will require a coordinated endeavor by scholars of many disciplines representing a broad range of societies. Each stage of the design process outlined above is potentially a major research endeavor. Unfortunately, trends in the academic community toward specialization and structural isolation of the disciplines pose obstacles to coordinated efforts to design alternative futures.

The need for coordinated efforts does not preclude valuable contributions by small-scale or individual projects. Design endeavors of a modest scale may offer insights pertinent to any one or more of the stages of the design process described above and thereby contribute to a knowledge base for consideration by larger teams in the future.

In efforts to design and implement alternative futures that originate in the academic community, nonacademic participants, such as governmental officials, businessmen, professionals, workers, and the young, must be drawn into the modeling process to enrich the range of perspectives represented by those contributing preferences and insights and to enhance the likelihood of a desirable alternative future being approved and implemented.

NOTES

1. George Wald, "It Is Too Late for Declarations, for Popular Appeals," address to the Twentieth World Conference Against Atomic and Hydrogen Bombs, Tokyo, August 2, 1974, quoted in the New York Times, August 17, 1974, p. 23.

2. Donella H. Meadows et al., The Limits to Growth (New York: Universe Books, 1972), p. 23.

3. See John Platt, "What We Must Do," Science 166, no. 3909 (November 28, 1969): 1115; Alvin Toffler, Future Shock (New York: Bantam, 1970), pp. 9-18.

4. "An Editorial," Journal of Peace Research 8, no. 1 (1971): 3.

5. Harold Guetzkow, "Transcending Data-Bound Methods in the Study of Politics," in A Design for Political Science: Scope, Objectives, and Methods, ed. James C. Charlesworth (Philadelphia: American Academy of Political and Social Sciences, 1966), pp. 185-86.

6. For example, see Alexander L. George, "Some Thoughts on an Agenda for International Studies," presidential address to the 1973 convention of the International Studies Association, ISA Newsletter, June 1973, pp. 8-13; Nazli Choucri and Thomas Robinson, eds., Forecasting in International Relations: Theory, Methods, Problems, Prospects (San Francisco: Freeman, 1974).

7. Christian Bay, "Politics and Pseudopolitics," American Political Science Review 59, no. 1 (March 1965): 40.

8. Paul Davidoff, "Normative Planning," in Planning for Diversity and Choice, ed. Sanford Anderson (Cambridge, Mass.: MIT Press, 1968), pp. 173-78.

9. Ian I. Mitroff and Murray Turoff, "The Whys Behind the Hows," IEEE Spectrum 10, no. 3 (March 1973): 70.

10. Platt, "What We Must Do," p. 1119.

11. Abraham Maslow, Toward a Psychology of Being, 2nd ed. (New York: McGraw-Hill, 1972), p. 153.

12. William Eckhardt, Compassion: Toward a Science of Value (Oakville, Ontario: Canadian Peace Research Institute Press, 1972), p. viii.

13. Ibid.

14. Richard Falk, This Endangered Planet (New York: Random House, 1971), p. xiii.

15. Eckhardt, op. cit., pp. 3-4.

16. Ervin Laszlo, The Systems View of the World (New York: George Braziller, 1972), p. 117.

17. Maslow, op. cit., pp. 149-66; Eckhardt, op. cit., pp. 40-254.

18. For example, see Bernard Cazes, "Long-Range Studies of the Future and Their Role in French Planning," in Planning for Diversity and Choice, ed. Anderson, pp. 45-60; the White House Conference on the Industrial World Ahead, A Look at Business in 1990 (Washington, D.C.: U.S. Government Printing Office, 1972).

19. Gerald Feinberg, The Prometheus Project: Mankind's Search for Long-Range Goals (New York: Doubleday-Anchor, 1969), p. 222.

20. For example, see Falk, This Endangered Planet; Meadows et al., The Limits to Growth; Paul R. Ehrlich and Anne H. Ehrlich, Population, Resources, Environment (San Francisco: Freeman, 1972); Georg Bergstrom, The Hungry Planet (New York: Macmillan, 1972).

21. For example, see John R. Maddox, The Doomsday Syndrome (New York: McGraw-Hill, 1972).

22. For example, see Johan Galtung, "World Indicators Program," Bulletin of Peace Proposals 4, no. 4 (1973): 354-58.

23. For a more extensive discussion of forecasting methods, see Marvin S. Soroos, "Some Methods of Future-Oriented Research for Investigating Problems Related to Global Population, Ecology, and Peace," in Exploring the Limits to Growth, ed. David Orr (Lexington: University of Kentucky Press, forthcoming).

24. Herman Kahn and Anthony J. Weiner, The Year 2000: A Framework for Speculation on the Next Thirty-Three Years (New York: Macmillan, 1972); Herman Kahn and B. Bruce-Briggs, Things to Come: Thinking About the 70's and 80's (New York: Macmillan, 1972).

25. For examples of computer simulations, see the world system models in Jay W. Forrester, World Dynamics (Cambridge, Mass.: Wright-Allen Press, 1971); Meadows et al., The Limits to Growth.

26. For example, see Richard A. Brody, "Some Systemic Effects of the Spread of Nuclear Weapons Technology: A Study Through Simulation of a Multi-Nuclear Future," Journal of Conflict Resolution 7, no. 4 (December 1963): 663-753.

27. Olaf Helmer, Social Technology (New York: Basic Books, 1966); Theodore J. Gordon, "The Current Methods of Futures Research," in The Futurists, ed. Alvin Toffler (New York: Random House, 1972), pp. 164-89.

28. Roy C. Amara and Gerald Salancik, "Forecasting: From Conjectural Art Toward Science," Futurist 6, no. 3 (June 1972): 113.

29. Feinberg, The Prometheus Project, 110-13.

30. Bruce Mazlish, "Obsolescence and 'Obsolescibles' in Planning for the Future," in Planning for Diversity and Choice, ed. Anderson, pp. 155-65.

31. "Anarchism, Peace and Control: Some Ideas for Future Experiment," Peace Research Reviews, 4, no. 4 (February 1972): 67.

32. For example, see Falk, This Endangered Planet, and W. Warren Wagar, Building the City of Man (New York: Grossman, 1971).

33. Robert Boguslaw, The New Utopians: A Study of System Design and Social Change (Englewood Cliffs, N.J.: Prentice-Hall, 1965), pp. 9-28.

34. See Forrester, World Dynamics; Meadows et al., The Limits to Growth.

35. Harry R. Targ, "Social Science and a New Social Order," Journal of Peace Research, 8, nos. 3-4 (1971): 212.

36. For example, see Meadows et al., The Limits to Growth, pp. 156-84.

37. Harold Guetzkow, "Simulations in the Consolidation and Utilization of Knowledge About International Relations," in Theory and Research on Causes of War, eds. Dean G. Pruitt and Richard C. Snyder (Englewood Cliffs, N.J.: Prentice-Hall, 1968), pp. 292-93; Paul Smoker, "Social Research for Social Anticipation," American Behavioral Scientist 12, no. 6 (July-August 1969): 7-13.

38. Smoker, "Anarchism, Peace, and Control," p. 65.

39. An example of the latter is presented in Robert Theobald and J. M. Scott, Teg's 1994: An Anticipation of the Near Future (Chicago: Swallow, 1972).

40. Christian Bay, "Human Development and Political Orientations," Bulletin of Peace Proposals 1, no. 2 (1970): 179.

41. "Research and Education as Approaches to Peace and Justice," Peace Research Reviews 4, no. 4 (February 1972): 91.

42. See Michael Washburn, "Peace Education is Alive—But Unsure Of Itself," War/Peace Report 11, no. 9 (November 1971): 14-18; Magnus Haavelsrud, "Raising Consciousness Through a Global Community Curriculum," Bulletin of Peace Proposals 5, no. 3 (1974): 274-79; Alvin Toffler, ed., Learning for Tomorrow: The Role of the Future in Education (New York: Random House, 1974).

43. B. F. Skinner, Beyond Freedom and Dignity (New York: Bantam, 1971), pp. 138-74.

44. Garrett Hardin, "The Tragedy of the Commons," Science 162, no. 3859 (December 13, 1968): 1243-48.

45. Richard A. Falk, "Reforming World Order: Zones of Consciousness and Domains of Action," in The World System, ed. Ervin Laszlo (New York: Braziller, 1973), pp. 69-93; Robert L. Heilbroner, An Inquiry into the Human Prospect (New York: W. W. Norton, 1974).

46. International Peace Academy Committee, Report from Vienna: An Appraisal of the International Peace Academy Committee's 1970 Pilot Project (New York: IPAC, 1970).

47. John R. Platt, The Step to Man (New York: Wiley, 1966); Gerhard Hirschfield, The People: Growth and Survival (Chicago: Aldine, 1973).

48. Theobald and Scott, Teg's 1994, pp. 67-72.
49. Arthur I. Waskow, "Towards a Democratic Futurism," in The Futurists, ed. Toffler, pp. 85-96.
50. "An Editorial," Journal of Peace Research 8, no. 1 (1971): 2.

POLITICAL DESIGN
George Kent

WHY DESIGN?

New political design means the creation of political forms to fulfill specified political functions. The design perspective contrasts sharply with conventional approaches to the study of politics. Normal political science reinforces passive, noninterventionist observation. Students are taught to analyze, to take things apart, not to synthesize and create. Political scientists claim that they aspire to greater control through increased understanding, but in practice they simply ask how events will evolve, as if their evolution were somehow preordained. Empirical studies most prominently display the constraints and limitations on what can be done. Even the futurists seldom go beyond certifying the gravity of impending social problems.[1]

Charles Hampden-Turner argues that "the projection of present trends into the future represents a vote of temporary approval for such trends."[2] This contention must grate on social scientists who claim with full honesty and the best intentions that their study is motivated by the desire to improve the system, not to reinforce it in its existing state. What, then, is the problem?

The difficulty is that, regardless of the scientist's motivations, his methods, and more important his questions, are conservative. To Oliver Benson, "social science research has a typically conservative cast, in that it is usually research done in the service of the Establishment, or in any event on the 'real world'—on society as it is—or on the status quo rather than on nonexistent alternatives to the status quo."[3] Similarly, in Hampden-Turner's view:

> By concentrating upon the technical and material aspects
> of the trends, the impression is fostered that these
> things "are," like stars and planets around us, so that
> "realistic" men must humbly subordinate their minds
> to these physical "facts." . . .
>   But these projections of existing trends are quite
> <u>unlike</u> the physical universe of dead objects. They are
> <u>cultural</u>, <u>political</u>, and <u>social</u> choices. [4]

Political systems are studied as if they were no different from
biological or solar systems, but systems like the European Economic
Community, the Antarctic Treaty, or the Warsaw Pact are really very
unnatural. Studying political interventions as if they were natural
overlooks the fact that they are deliberately constructed to serve
human purposes. This insight provides the basis for what Herbert
Simon calls the "sciences of the artificial," and thus the science of
design, which he advances as the appropriate alternative to the natural
sciences. [5]

Several strong advocates of formal theory and systematic empirical research now acknowledge that those approaches are not very
helpful in meeting social problems. R. J. Rummel's research led
him to conclude that, within the behavioral-positivistic perspective,
war is inevitable. But now he sees beyond:

> I think the only way to break this iron law of history that
> is war is through the realization (1) that man, not phys-
> ical nature is the center of reality, (2) that man's
> behavior is not subject to the same cause-effect proc-
> esses we ascribe to physical reality, but rather is teleo-
> logically guided by his future goals, (3) that man is
> mainly self determined and morally responsible for his
> actions. To wit: the future lies in his hands and not in
> some causative features of his environment. [6]

Functionalism, in a variety of forms, does try to explain social
systems in terms of meeting goals, purposes, needs. [7] Its usefulness
to the designer is limited, however, precisely because it is totally
concerned with explaining what is. Functionalists examine existing
systems and then speculate on what functions might account for those
forms. They do not create, identifying needs first and then inventing
forms to fulfill those needs.

With few exceptions (such as Johan Galtung and Paul Smoker),
when empiricists theorize and find that their theory does not match
their data, they assume that it is the theory, and not the data of the
empirical world, that is somehow deficient. In Galtung's terms,

they are "data-servile." Emphasizing empirical research or fore-casting or even explaining reinforces the feeling that we are subject to the social system, rather than the reverse. The study of design, in contrast, should be a great liberator. Surely the designer cannot ignore social realities, but he can learn to see them as instruments rather than as crippling constraints. The study of design should free us for effective imagining, for visionary and yet disciplined invention and innovation.

PRESCRIPTIVE POLICY ANALYSIS, DESIGN, AND PLANNING

A quick review of some ways that the terms prescriptive policy analysis, design, and planning are used should help to bring out some conceptually useful differentiations. My purpose here is not to reorganize and purify the language. It is important to make the distinctions, but it does not matter much how they are labeled.

For me, prescriptive policy analyses are systematic studies designed to produce well-reasoned recommendations for action dealing with concrete political problems. The question posed might be: What should Cuba do about the American base at Guantanamo? Or, what should be done about the Middle East conflict? In every case, policy analyses respond to the question of what should be done. [8]

Design, however, is directed toward the creation of new political structures.

Policy analyses generally focus on individual, possibly unique problems. Design, in contrast, is concerned with formulating or altering institutional arrangements, that is, with establishing structures and processes to deal with whole classes of problems. An arms control inspection system, for example, would be designed to cope with violations generally, rather than with some particular violation. This is probably the single feature that best differentiates design from policy analysis. [9]

I think of prescriptive policy analyses as ordinarily referring to situations embedded within stable, ongoing structures, while design does not assume that continuity. This corresponds to the distinction Robert Boguslaw makes between established and emergent situations. [10] The policy analyst ordinarily calls for discrete actions intended to adjust the values of variables within the given system. The political designer, however, wants to invent new relationships among variables. This is why he is not much concerned with careful empirical studies of existing structures. In Saul Mendlovitz's terms, the designer hopes to "free the future from the past." [11] The political designer is bolder, more imaginative, and perhaps a good deal more foolish than the typical policy analyst.

Policy analysis is likely to be reactive, to be concerned with short-term problems, and to deal in ameliorative proposals. Political design, in contrast, is more likely to try to anticipate problems, to focus on the long run, and to try to find deep-rooted solutions.

Policy analyses usually have the key actors selected in advance. That is, the policy analyst is likely to ask what some specified country or organization should do about the problem in hand. The designer, however, would be more likely to begin by asking what should be done, and then let the study itself indicate the most appropriate actors.

There is no reason why it must be so, but the values served by policy analysts are likely to be more limited, narrow, and parochial than those of designers. The policy analyst generally addresses his work to a narrower constituency.

Because of the modesty and close proximity in time and space of the actions he recommends, the policy analyst is concerned with relatively simple implementation procedures, whereas the designer must prepare grand transition strategies. Because of his tendency to formulate specific visions of the future, the designer is likely to make a sharper distinction between means and ends than the policy analyst. Some designers, however, now seem to think more in terms of creating an ongoing process rather than in terms of reaching some relatively fixed and well-defined end.

Design generally begins with the articulation of some desired future end, whether as a condition or a process, and then searches for means to those ends. In policy analyses, however, one can sometimes begin with a survey of the repertoire of possible actions. After the actions are identified, the analyst asks to what end each of them might lead. Confronted with Soviet missiles in Cuba, for example, the United States had only a limited variety of possible actions to consider. Efficiency considerations in such cases suggest beginning with the question: What sorts of things could be done about the problem? It is reasonable to begin with the examination of means rather than ends where the variety of possible means to be examined is small in comparison with the number of possible ends. In thinking about the structure of, say, an International Development Agency, however, the variety of actions that can be considered is, at the outset, too great to contemplate. In design problems it is necessary to explicitly formulate some target, however roughly and tentatively, before it becomes worthwhile to ask what sorts of things could be done to reach the desired end.

There is a great deal of overlap among planning, policy analysis, and design, as is evident from the definition of planning as "the process of preparing a set of decisions for action in the future, directed at achieving goals by optimal means."[12] Another observer says simply that "planning is thinking ahead with a view to action."[13] The differences are differences of emphasis. In my thinking, planning is similar to policy analysis in that it tends to assume the continuation of the existing political system.

Others see this conservatism in planning. To Arthur I. Waskow, planning "is the way for those who presently hold power to project their continuation in power over the period of years ahead."[14] Charles Williams' view is similar to that of Hampden-Turner and other critics of empiricists:

> New visions can form the basis for redirection of our institutions. The lack of such a vision may be attributed, paradoxically, to the desire of planners to be relevant. Seeking relevance, planners base their work on past decisions and projections of current trends, thereby imposing on the future the dominant patterns of the past and making tomorrow a rigid extension of today.[15]

At its core, planning is based on the extrapolation of present trends; it places no great emphasis on creativity. Like policy analysis, planning tends to frame its problems in terms of choices among existing alternatives rather than in terms of creating new alternatives. It is more concerned with tuning variables than with inventing wholly new relationships among variables. The design approach is intended to help break free of the narrow constraints to which planners submit themselves.

In any design problem there are certain aspects or features that are viewed as controllable, as form to be shaped, as resources; and others that are viewed as constraints, as part of the environment, as requirements imposed on the design. In Christopher Alexander's words:

> every design problem begins with an effort to achieve fitness between two entities: the form in question and its context. The form is the solution to the problem; the context defines the problem. In other words, when we speak of design, the real object of discussion is not the form alone, but the ensemble comprising the form and its context . . . .
>
>   The form is a part of the world over which we have control, and which we decide to shape while leaving the rest of the world as it is. The context is that part of the world which puts demands on this form; anything in the world that makes demands of the form is context.[16]

Some writers, like Alexander, use the term "system" to refer to the whole ensemble, both form and context, while others refer to the part of the ensemble that is held constant as the environment and call only the part under adjustment the "system."[17] I will follow Alexander's usage and use the term "system" to refer to the whole ensemble.

There is always some choice in what is to be regarded as manipulable form and what is to be regarded as constraining context. One major difference between the policy analyst and the political designer is that the policy analyst takes much more to be fixed and given than does the designer.

But it is a mistake to draw this distinction too sharply, as if the analyst's and the designer's roles were wholly different. The opportunities for reinterpreting problems should be fully exploited:

There are two sides to this tendency designers have to change the definition of the problem. On the one hand, the impractical idealism of designers who want to redesign entire cities and whole processes of manufacture when they are asked to design simple objects is often only an attempt to loosen difficult constraints by stretching the form-context boundary.

On the other hand, this way in which the good designer keeps an eye on the possible changes at every point of the ensemble is part of his job. He is bound, if he knows what he is doing, to be sensitive to the fit at several boundaries within the ensemble at once. Indeed, this ability to deal with several layers of form context boundaries in concert is an important part of what we often refer to as the designer's sense of organization. The internal coherence of an ensemble depends on a whole net of adaptations. In a perfectly coherent ensemble we should expect the two halves of every possible division of the ensemble to fit one another.[18]

An intergovernmental institution, for example, should have sound internal operations, satisfy the participating countries' foreign policy requirements, meet domestic political demands, and interrelate effectively with other institutions as well. The structure desired in the long term should be sound, and the short-term plans for implementation should fit into current political realities. Any individual trying to develop prescriptions for political action should scan the full spectrum between the idealized prototypes of the policy analyst and the designer, exploring problems from the more conservative perspectives and adapting to the many constraints, and then varying assumptions to explore openings for boldness.

DYNAMIC ENDS AND DYNAMIC MEANS

In our arrogance and shortsightedness, our prescriptions respond to what we view as major problems now. This tendency to ground designs for the future in conditions and views that prevail in the designer's present is plain in the long history of the formulation of utopias. But the consciousness of problems changes rapidly. The poor may always have been with us, but poverty has only recently been discovered as a social problem. Just because nuclear war is high on the agenda now does not mean it will always be a central issue. The spectacular rise of ecological issues in public awareness in the 1960s and 1970s suggests that they, too, can fall away and be replaced.

We must be careful not to fix overly rigid forms on the basis of current priorities. If they are to live, these forms must be given life from the outset. No system will last if it is built to function under only one set of conditions. Any political design should have adaptive mechanisms built into it so that it can adjust to new circumstances and to new problems.

To put this another way, rather than being best for all time, the optimum may be "path dependent" in the sense that the best order at any given period depends on its immediate prehistory. Problems are not simply solved and permanently disposed of. Old problems are traded in on new ones, and what you can get depends in part on what you've got. The designer's job is simply to arrange for the best possible deal.

It is possible to institute continuous adaptation by engaging in and planning for continuous design. Political design should be understood as an endless process, not in the sense of having no goals but in the sense of having no termination. Design should continue until implementation is achieved, and then continue again, beyond that implementation, to deal with the new problems that are inescapably introduced with the eradication of old problems.

Designs should undergo constant revision even before implementation. Arthur I. Waskow portrays the long-term dynamism that he would hope for:

> Sitting in 1967, one cannot expect to draw a 1999 which world society will, in fact, be like 1999. We must expect exactly the opposite: that along the way the processes of imagination and creation will lead one to change his imagination. Hopefully, the process will engage wholly new people in imagining the future who do not now imagine it, and by doing that will engage them in creation of a kind of future which was not imagined by the ones who began

the process. That's one of the major goals. And therefore, one should never expect to achieve that image, one
should expect to move in the direction of it; one should
expect perhaps to move in some quite different direction
after moving part of the way, but never to it . . . this
process never ends; not only is the process itself always
open-ended, but so is the result.

    Thus one starts with a mythical vision, a provi-
sional vision, of the future as an open-ended future: a
future which is free to decide on its own future. [19]

    The process should be dynamic even within the individual
designer's work. Design should be viewed as a continuous process
that, at its core, demands the continuous reeducation of the designer.
This means that he cannot isolate himself. He should go beyond being
open and available and actively seek out new and different perspectives and values. For any given function or any given form, he should
constantly ask: Who does it help and who does it harm? Presumptions
are likely to be wrong; people do not always appreciate what others
regard as good for them. They must be asked. The designer might,
for example, learn to his surprise that not everyone appreciates the
cooling of crises. He might find that the underclass does not see such
functions as politically neutral at all, but rather as counterrevolution-
ary. Such things may not be obvious at first, but the designer should
be prepared to go out and learn them. Information of this sort should
be searched out even though it may mean disturbing or discarding
designs that seemed elegant and took great effort to develop. The
designer must resist closure and he must resist pride of authorship.
He should be restless and always dissatisfied, but he should know how
to use his dissatisfaction constructively, which means that he should
know how to learn.

VALUES

    Having a political design problem means wanting the conceptual
invention and practical innovation of a regularized procedure for dealing with some class of potentially recurring political problems. There
is a feeling that something should be arranged, but it is not clear what.

    This desire is motivated by the anticipation that, if nothing is
done, some important values will go unfulfilled. For example, one
might take up the problem of designing a new health care delivery
system because of the expectation that the old system will not provide
services adequate to the needs of certain classes of people; or one

might propose establishing a system to monitor international arms transfers in the hope and belief that such a system would help to limit what would otherwise be excessive arms traffic.

Values play two different roles in the design process. At the outset, they provide the motivation for engaging in the work and they determine the general sort of design that will be proposed. At this early stage, it is only the major kinds of values to be served that need to be stated. Detailed specifications of priority orderings or of tradeoffs among the different values are not needed.

Explicit values enter once again toward the conclusion of a design task after a number of concrete proposals have been formulated. Values are called upon in the evaluation process where alternative, competing proposals are compared to determine which is preferred and should be selected. Values are brought to bear to decide the relative advantages and disadvantages, the benefits and costs of the different candidate proposals. It is here that relatively precise specifications of the relationships among the different values may be required.

The question of which values will be relevant for guiding the choice among different concrete proposals cannot be answered conclusively until the proposals themselves become visible. Since there is no way to know in advance which particular values will serve to differentiate competing proposals, it is pointless to argue over the relative merits of different value hierarchies before developing concrete designs. In design, the purpose of clarifying values is to help guide choice, and if it is not known what choices need to be made, it cannot be known what values need to be clarified. The most useful debate over values is likely to be that conducted in reference to the relative merits of specific, elaborated design proposals.

The importance of the evaluation process tends to be greatly exaggerated. A good political design is obviously good. If the choice is difficult and controversial, that in itself is an advance warning that each of the alternative proposals contains the seeds of future controversy. Instead of thinking entirely in terms of differentiating proposals and choosing among them, the designer should also think in terms of amalgamating proposals to combine their best features. The analysis of closely competing alternatives should, if possible, lead to their synthesis in a new, clearly superior alternative. The difficult phase of political design is not that of choosing among well-articulated alternatives but that of formulating those alternatives. Difficult evaluation is evidence of bad design; good formulation makes evaluation easy.[20]

The design process should actually be iterative, with some values established to begin the process, some tentative forms suggested, some critical responses made to those forms raising other values to consciousness, revisions or replacements made on the previously proposed forms, and so on. The process should be genuinely dialectic, always tentative, always striving for higher syntheses.

INCOMPATIBILITIES

In the preceding section, the values under discussion were those of the designer. Other distinct sets of values need to be considered, those of the parties who will be affected by the designed structure. In most design work, it is hoped that the designer's values generally will correspond to those of the affected parties. Here, however, the problem is special. An institutional design is specifically political if it is intended to help in managing the claims of parties with incompatible values. A purely technological organization, in contrast, reflects more ordinary design; it does what virtually everyone wants done. The Universal Postal Union is a good example. Often institutions intended as strong political instruments are overwhelmed by the political conflicts in which they are embedded and are reduced to purely technical functions such as calling conferences, issuing innocuous advice, and publishing statistical data. This is what happened to the Food and Agriculture Organization, for example, and on some issues to the United Nations itself. If a political structure is to be adequate to fulfill its designated political functions, it must be based on a clear understanding of the political situation in which it is to operate.[21]

The political designer whould identify the major distinct parties and the ways in which their values are incompatible. To illustrate, the designer formulating arrangements for the future administration of the oceans should be aware that

> Nations with strong navies prefer narrow national coastal jurisdictions (territorial seas), while nations with weak navies prefer wide national coastal jurisdictions.
>
> Many nations which are consumers of minerals hope the seas will be exploited for their mineral resources, while many nations which are now major producers of minerals object to such exploitation (because the shift from scarcity to abundance would depress the prices of these commodities).
>
> Technologically advanced nations prefer freedom of scientific investigation, while less advanced nations tend to oppose this freedom (because they fear the knowledge gained would be used by the advanced nations in their own narrow self-interest).

The designer may ultimately have to make a choice and decide which of these sets of values, and thus which parties, should be favored. It should be recalled, however, that the choice has to be made, not among the abstractly stated values but among alternative concrete designs. Rather than making a prior choice as to which party is to be favored, several designs should be prepared, some favoring one interest and some favoring another. Before choosing, the designs should be restudied to determine whether some satisfactory compromise design could be produced, or even better, if some new design could be proposed that would be preferred by all concerned parties. In any case, one cannot smuggle in a proposal favoring one party with the hope that disadvantaged parties will not take notice. The designer should be very clear and explicit about how he manages the problem of incompatible values.

SPECIFYING FUNCTIONS

A good way to describe the designer's motivating values, and thus to start the design process, is to say what functions the new form is to fulfill. A statement should be drawn up saying what the thing is to do. Although not necessarily detailed at the outset, the statement may be modified as the work proceeds and the designer's understanding of the purposes is progressively refined.

The design problem might, for example, be that of establishing a new international arms control agency. The functions it is to fulfill might be initially specified as follows:

1. Monitoring and reporting large-scale arms flows.
2. Disseminating information on technological advances relating to arms control (e.g., on safety devices or procedures).
3. Providing neutral observation of conflict situations.
4. Serving as "hot line" communications center during crises.
5. Monitoring and reporting plutonium production.
6. Offering services as an inspection agency for new arms control agreements.

Or, as another example, suppose the problem was to establish a peace academy. The functions of the academy might be:

1. Preparing young people to work on behalf of nonviolent conflict resolution.
2. Preparing young people to work for the elimination of structural violence in less developed countries.

3. Providing a center at which global issues can be studied from a variety of perspectives.

4. Promoting the preparation of prescriptive studies to guide the management of global issues.

In the ocean regime proposed by the Center for the Study of Democratic Institutions, functions such as these were enumerated:

1. To regulate, supervise, and control all activities on the high seas and on or under the seabed.

2. To regulate effectively the commercial exploitation of the seabed.

3. To issue licenses.

4. To regulate fishery, fish farming, and aquaculture.

5. To disseminate immediately and effectively information and data received from license owners regarding their activities in ocean space.

6. To issue regulations concerning pollution. [22]

The list of functions for which forms are to be designed should be open-ended and subject to modification throughout the design process. After the initial ideas are stated, the functions should be elaborated in some detail. The designer might begin by focusing his attention on just one or two major functions.

STRUCTURAL DESIGN QUESTIONS

Functions can be fulfilled only through some form: an instrument, a body, a structure, an organ. That function and form are intimately connected is clearly recognized by Elisabeth Mann Borgese:

Functions and organs, certainly, evolve together. It may be useless to peer too far into the future and envision details of organisms that may be doomed to atrophy by lack of appropriate functions, functions that may evolve quite differently from the ways now imaginable. It is equally dangerous, however, to draw up a list of precise functions, and forget about the organs that are to exercise them; for, in this case, either the functions may never be exercised at all—functions without organs are as utopian as organs without functions—or, eventually, they may be exercised very badly, distorted past recognition. [23]

Thus, after the desired functions are outlined, the structural design questions, asking what the particular arrangements for the future should be, must be raised. By what mechanisms and processes can the specified functions be fulfilled? What is it that needs to be decided about the future?[24]

For the creation of an international arms control agency, structural design questions like these might be raised:

1. Should there be a standing organization?
2. Should it operate at one particular site or at a number of dispersed centers?
3. Through what agency should operations be controlled and administered?
4. What should be this executive agency's membership?
5. Under what decision rules should it operate?
6. How are disagreements within the executive agency to be resolved?
7. How is membership to be determined?
8. How should it relate to the United Nations?
9. How should it relate to existing security alliances?

For a peace academy, these are some of the structural questions which come immediately to mind:

1. Is the academy to be national or international?
2. How is it to be funded?
3. How is it to be staffed?
4. Would it be a degree-granting institution?
5. What thematic focus would it have?
6. How would students be selected?

Before trying to find answers the designer should be sure the questions are well formulated. Attention should be given to the quality and scope of the questions, especially with reference to the assumptions hidden within them. The question of whether the peace academy is to be national or international, for example, suggests that a choice needs to be made between these two. But these are really not mutually exclusive and exhaustive alternatives. It is possible to think of a variety of possible blends that mix the features of national and international operations and could incorporate important non-national or supranational features as well.

The designer should make some clear judgments about which of these sorts of structural design questions he wishes to deal with. He can proceed by expanding and refining some of the questions and setting others aside. The questions provide the raw material for planning the

design work. First, broad themes for possible consideration can be
reviewed, with some identified as of core interest, some identified
as interesting because of their association with the core group, and
some deferred or rejected as distractions from the primary objectives.
The design questions that are retained could then be sorted out in a
variety of ways.

Once high-priority design questions are identified, the answering
process should not be hasty. Rather than seize on immediately obvious
and appealing answers, it is important to forcibly defer closure for a
time and instead try to develop a broad variety of tentative possible
answers. On the question of funding a peace academy, for example,
ideas like these might be generated:

1. The academy should be funded by a grant from the U.S.
Congress.

2. The academy should be funded by a grant from the U.N.

3. The academy should be funded by a grant from some
foundation.

4. Nations should be asked to pay in proportion to the numbers
of students they send.

5. Nations should be asked to pay in proportion to the size of
their defense budgets.

6. The academy should be funded by revenues obtained through
exploitation of ocean resources, through a new ocean regime that is
to be developed.

7. Students and faculty members of the academy should charge
fees for services, for consultation, mediation, arbitration, concili-
ation, intervention.

8. Contributions should be solicited from private individuals
without going through governments.

To prevent the stifling of imagination through premature closure,
the task of generating candidate answers should be clearly separated
from the task of choosing among them.

PARTITIONING

In designing a form of any kind, many factors need to be adjusted.
Variables tend to be interconnected with one another so that manipulating one for some advantage may lead to disadvantageous changes in
others. But things are not all connected together equally strongly.
Variables that have strong interconnections among themselves but
weak interconnections with others form separable subsystems, and

thus, separable design tasks. The design of the curriculum for a
peace academy, for example, can be substantially separated from the
task of deciding how it is to be financed.

Alexander makes the important point that these clusters of interdependence may not correspond to common conceptual distinctions:

> These concepts will not help the designer in finding a well-
> adapted solution unless they happen to correspond to the
> system's subsystems. But since the concepts are on the
> whole the result of arbitrary historical accidents, there
> is no reason to expect that they will in fact correspond
> to those subsystems. [25]

It may at first seem sensible to think about staffing and funding
of a peace academy as quite separate issues, but closer examination
is likely to reveal that they are in fact so strongly interdependent that
it would be best to answer those design questions together.

There are several reasons for partitioning design problems.
Some simply could not be handled otherwise. One cannot really design
a whole new political order, for example, any more than one could
sit down and design a machine like a Boeing 747. These things are
literally beyond the comprehension of any one person, and so they
must be divided up into smaller, manageable segments.

Partitioning the larger problem into subsidiary design tasks
permits a division of labor in two ways: in time, through the sequencing of the agenda, and in space through the distribution of assignments
to different simultaneously functioning design teams. One group can
concern itself with the international arms control agency's information-
gathering procedures while another thinks about the problem of
disseminating the information.

The possibilities for dividing and spreading responsibilities
should not create the illusion that unlimited amounts of designing can
be accomplished. Redundancy is valuable in design work. It is probably far better to have three independently operating teams study the
same cluster of questions and then compare their results, than to
have the three teams work on altogether different issues. Similarly,
it is wiser for the individual designer to focus on a small cluster of
design questions and answer them well than to spread his attention
over a very large variety of questions. More resources devoted to
fewer questions helps to assure that those few questions will be
answered well. That is likely to be far more valuable than having a
great many questions answered superficially.

The inescapable limitations on the resources available for any
design task must be taken into account. In addition to allowing for
the division of labor, partitioning allows for the ordering of tasks in

terms of priority. Some design tasks are simply not worth doing. Some are not worth doing until and unless others are completed first. Detailed questions about the peace academy's curriculum may be unimportant until after it is determined that it can somehow be funded and staffed. Early commitments on some parts of the overall design reduce the number of contingencies and alternatives to be examined in later stages. Efficiency is imperative, and efficiency requires the possibility of partitioning off and deferring some parts of the job.

SYSTEMIC THINKING

Subsystems, and thus subsidiary design tasks, can be partitioned off, but even among quite separate clusters some residual interaction will remain. The designer must maintain a keen sensitivity to the ways in which the separate elements fit together to form the whole system.

But how? Admonitions to take whole systems into account tend to be tiresome, especially because they give no advice on how that is to be done. It is not helpful to be told simply to be comprehensive or to somehow take the nonobvious into account. How can one remain alert to larger system considerations while focusing on subproblems of limited scope?

Structural design questions interact, are interdependent, if the choice of which answer is best for one question depends on the answers given to other questions. It is on the basis of these contingent relations among answers that one decides which design questions cluster and should be examined together, and which can be separated from one another.

There will still be some interactions cutting across these separate clusters or subsystems. Decisions for the physical plant for the peace academy may depend in some way on broad decisions about the curriculum, perhaps on whether or not extensive laboratory simulation exercises should be undertaken by students in the academy. One solution would be optimal for a given subproblem if other parts of the larger system were in a given condition, and another solution would be optimal if other parts of the larger system were in some other condition. The designer's sensitivity to the requirements of the system beyond the limited subsystem on which his attention is concentrated can be expressed in the form of conditionals. He can say, if the curriculum designers decide that laboratory simulations should be undertaken, then the building should be designed this way, and if they decide against simulations, then the building should be designed that way. The designer of the building can thus take the possibility of simulations into account without deciding that question himself. Of course, he might take up that question himself at another time, then in the role of curriculum designer rather than in the role of building designer. The subsystem design problems are separate but linked. It is through conditionals that the links are taken into account. The clear specification of contingent relationships of this sort constitutes the essence of systemic thinking.

WORLD ORDER MODELS DESIGN

Designing the world order of the future is the most ambitious political design task of all, and the most essential. The challenge has absorbed the attention of some of the most imaginative minds in history.[26] Their effort has had some effect. Imperfect though they may be, such innovations as federalism or regional economic communities are magnificent inventions. But the greatest legacy of these thinkers is the lesson they teach, not of the futility of the task but of the possibility and value of engaging in world order models design. Can there be any more eloquent way to express hopefulness?

What elements are required in a proposal that is to be counted as a world order model? Must it specify the character (or absence) of, say, a world legislature? Must it describe the character of urban transportation systems? What are the design questions that are raised when we ask for a design of a new world order? Knowing what those essential questions are will help to assure that the designs that are offered are thorough, and will help to assure that different proposed models will be comparable with one another.

No consensus has yet been reached, but after very extensive deliberation and consultation Saul Mendlovitz, the director of the World Order Models Project, has listed six major themes as basic: arms policy, peacekeeping, conflict resolution, economic welfare, the technological and scientific revolution, environment, and social justice. The concrete design questions implied by these terms still remain to be articulated, however.

A study would have to be made of the interactions among the basic design questions to identify the component design tasks. One major partition seems evident even now. While most utopian thinking has been concerned with relationships within communities, the major distinguishing feature of world order models is that they are primarily concerned with intercommunity relations. This provides for a useful division of labor. The general structure of intercommunity relations can be designed without specifying the character of intracommunity relationships in detail.

The variety of different models that have been proposed for the structure of intercommunity relationships is remarkably small. Quincy Wright, for example, lists only four major types: the cosmopolitan world, based on a universal religion or ideology; the imperial world, based on a universal empire or state; the nationalistic world, based on a stable balance of power among states or regions; and the international world, based on some sort of general international organization or federation. 27

On a more abstract level, there are just two basic types of structures of intercommunity relationships, those based on balance and those based on hierarchy.

Balance is maintained through continuous bargaining and negotiation among peers. This is Wright's nationalistic world, like the present one, where the structure is maintained through such means as diplomacy and collective security relationships. The fatal weakness of this model is that the independence and equality of member units is inescapably fictitious, and the idealized balance succumbs to a hierarchical structure in which some small number of superpowers exercise de facto authority. The global balance of power has always been one of domination rather than equality. 28

In a hierarchical system there are dominant-submissive relationships among organizations. There may be one nation exerting power over other nations through a condominium arrangement. Or power may be exerted by some central authority created for that purpose and limited in scope to particular functional sectors, as in Wright's international world. Although limited and controlled, and legitimated by having power vested in it by the consent of the subject nations, the world of international or supranational authority is nevertheless hierarchically organized.

Many specific proposals advocate mixtures of these two forms. Federalist ideas, for example, are based on a formula of balance among units combined with elements of submission to some central authority. There is a call for balance in some functional sectors but for dominance in others.

A third sort of proposal for managing intercommunity relationships is that of amalgamation through a blurring of the distinctions among units. This is the interpenetrated and intermeshed world foreseen by the integrationists and the functionalists and neofunctionalists. 29 It is Wagar's City of Man or Quincy Wright's cosmopolitan world. It is the ultimate socialist/communist world, or the world in which capitalism and communism converge, as envisioned by Academician Sakharov. 30 But amalgamation is not really a form of order; it is rather an absence of structure grounded in a presumed absence of a need for ordering principles. If there are no distinct units whose interrelationships need to be managed, the problem of ordering becomes moot.

World order designers divide over whether this can be a genuine
solution. In my view, amalgamation does not meet the difficulties at
all. Solving the problem of global ordering in this way is no more
useful than abolishing international war by naming the fighting units
something other than nations. Wagar is absurdly wrong when he says
that "only sovereign polities make wars."[31] Amalgamation only trans-
forms the problem from one of ordering intercommunity relationships
to one of ordering intracommunity relationships, a differentiation that
at this level is without substance. The City of Man itself will have to
be divided into boroughs of some sort.[32] If not along administrative
lines, divisions and cracks of other kinds will inevitably appear in the
"unitary republic of mankind." It is still necessary to say how order
among the parts is to be organized and maintained. Although he shuns
the theme, even Wagar acknowledges that a world government would
be needed that, among other functions, would "guard against counter-
revolution and civil warfare."[33]

To enumerate the general design questions that should be
addressed by any world order model is in effect to provide a guide for
the critical analysis of such designs. This reasoning can be reversed
as well: A good way to arrive at general design questions is to undertake close critical analysis of specific world order models. In this
sort of critical review one is more concerned with the nature of the
questions that are taken up than with quality of the particular answers
that are given.

Political design, and world order design in particular, should
never be reduced to a scholarly game of scoring points in critical
analysis and academic arguments. The work should be constructive
and cumulative, not only producing elegant blueprints but building
toward the actual innovation of more desirable political worlds. There
is no division of labor that affords the political architect the luxury of
handing over his designs to some contractor who can assure implementation. The designer himself must follow through, pushing for the
adoption of his proposals. He will usually fail. But he succeeds if he
learns from those failures and, as a result, then produces better
designs.[34]

We should work to cultivate the art of political design to show
that it is possible, legitimate, and worthwhile. It needs to be developed in depth so that those who do it can do it better, and in breadth
so that more of us can do it. And it should be raised to fuller self-
consciousness so that we can appreciate that the political structure
of the future is in fact ours to decide.

NOTES

1. On the constrained imaginations of empiricists and futurists, see Henry Kariel, "Expanding the Political Present," American Political Science Review 63, no. 3 (September 1969): 768-76; Harry Targ, "Social Science and a New Social Order," Journal of Peace Research, no. 3-4 (1971): 207-20; Elise Boulding, "Futuristics and the Imaging Capacity of the West," in Human Futuristics, eds. Margoroh Maruyama and James A. Dator (Honolulu: Social Science Research Institute, 1971), pp. 29-53.

2. Charles Hampden-Turner, Radical Man: The Process of Psycho-Social Development (Garden City, N.Y.: Doubleday-Anchor, 1971), p. 364.

3. Oliver Benson, "The Policy Sciences and Problem-Solving," Social Science Quarterly 52, no. 1 (June 1971): 168.

4. Hampden-Turner, Radical Man, pp. 364-65.

5. Herbert A. Simon, The Sciences of the Artificial (Cambridge, Mass.: M.I.T. Press, 1969). In his account of the design process from the engineer's perspective, Krick quotes Theodore von Karman's observation that "Scientists explore what is and engineers create what has never been." See Edward V. Krick, An Introduction to Engineering and Engineering Design (New York: Wiley, 1969), p. 36. On the move to humanize the social sciences, see E. F. Schumacher, Small Is Beautiful: Economics As If People Mattered (New York: Harper and Row, 1973).

6. R. J. Rummel, "The Roots of Faith," mimeo., Department of Political Science, University of Hawaii, May 1973, pp. 52-53.

7. Cf. Gabriel A. Almond and G. Bingham Powell, Jr., Comparative Politics: A Developmental Approach (Boston: Little, Brown, 1966); Philip E. Jacob, Alexine L. Atherton, and Arthur M. Wallenstein, The Dynamics of International Organization, rev. ed. (Homewood, Ill.: Dorsey, 1972). It is sometimes argued, as in Richard S. Rudner's Philosophy of Science (Englewood Cliffs, N.J.: Prentice-Hall, 1966), that it is not necessary to analyze social systems in terms of values or preferences, that is, as teleological systems. Certainly it is not necessary, but it is still both possible and useful.

8. For a more thorough treatment, see George Kent, Prescribing Foreign Policy (University of Hawaii, Dimensionality of Nations Project, Research Report no. 59, January 1972).

9. There are many who prefer not to make this distinction. Some, like Davis Bobrow, speak of "designing" courses of action, using the term in the broader sense of prescriptive policy analysis. Similarly, to David Wilkinson, "'political design' would mean the creation—the conceiving and the realizing—of political initiatives (from policy proposals through organizational instruments) aimed at some

future good and based upon some explicit body of theory and data." David Wilkinson, "Political Design and International Studies," paper presented at the 1973 annual meeting of the International Studies Association. The design approach to international studies was vigorously supported at this meeting by the incoming president of the association in his presidential address. See Alexander L. George, "Some Thoughts on an Agenda for International Studies," ISA Newsletter, no. 3 (June 1973): 8-13.

10. Robert Boguslaw, The New Utopians: A Study of System Design and Social Change (Englewood Cliffs, N.J.: Prentice-Hall, 1965), pp. 7-8.

11. W. Warren Wagar, Building the City of Man: Outlines of a World Civilization (New York: Grossman, 1971), p. vii.

12. Yehezkel Dror, "The Planning Process: A Facet Design," in Planning Programming Budgeting: A Systems Approach to Management, eds. Fremont J. Lyden and Ernest G. Miller (Chicago: Markham, 1967), pp. 93-116. An interesting typology of planning may be found in Warren L. Ziegler, "The Future of Education: Who Speaks for Mankind," presented at the Congress on the Future: Education, December 1970.

13. George A. Morgan, "Planning in Foreign Affairs: The State of the Art," Foreign Affairs 39, no. 2 (January 1961): 271-78.

14. Arthur I. Waskow, "Looking Forward: 1999," in Mankind 2000, eds. Robert Jungk and Johan Galtung (Oslo: Universitetsforlaget, 1969), p. 83.

15. Charles W. Williams, Jr., "Inventing a Future Civilization," The Futurist 4, no. 4 (August 1972): 139. In a similar vein, Maldonado characterizes most planning as being without hope, in contrast to most designing. See Tomas Maldonado, Design, Nature, and Revolution: Toward a Critical Ecology (New York: Harper and Row, 1972).

16. Christopher Alexander, Notes on the Synthesis of Form (Cambridge, Mass.: Harvard University Press, 1964), pp. 15-16, 18-19.

17. Ibid., p. 196. For C. West Churchman, in contrast, "The environment of the system is what lies 'outside' of the system." C. West Churchman, The Systems Approach (New York: Delta, 1968), p. 34.

18. Alexander, Notes, pp. 17-18.

19. Waskow, "Looking Forward: 1999," pp. 80-81.

20. This theme is discussed more extensively in Kent, Prescribing Foreign Policy, Section 4.4.

21. The political emasculation likely to result from bad design is illustrated by the Military Staff Committee of the United Nations, which regularly conducts purely ritual meetings without even the pretense of fulfilling any substantive function. See Hanna Newcombe,

"Alternative Approaches to World Government," Peace Research Reviews 1, no. 1 (February 1967): 30.

22. Elisabeth Mann Borgese, The Ocean Regime (Santa Barbara, Calif.: Center for the Study of Democratic Institutions, 1968), Art. V.

23. Ibid., p. 3.

24. This and other phases of the design process also are discussed in George Kent, "Plan for Designing the Future," Bulletin of Peace Proposals 3, no. 3 (1972): 280-85.

25. Alexander, Notes, p. 65.

26. See Sylvester J. Hemleben, Plans for World Peace Through Six Centuries (Chicago: University of Chicago Press, 1943); W. Warren Wagar, The City of Man (Baltimore: Penguin, 1963); Edith Wynner and Georgia Lloyd, Searchlight on Peace Plans (New York: E. P. Dutton, 1944).

27. Quincy Wright, On Predicting International Relations: The Year 2000 (Denver: University of Denver Monograph Series in World Affairs, 1969).

28. Of course this point is debatable. George Modelski, for example, equates hierarchical systems with empires (power monopolies), and views the present nation-state system, in contrast, as an autonomy system consisting of independent states. See George Modelski, Principles of World Politics (New York: Free Press, 1972).

29. Johan Galtung, "On the Future of the International System," Journal of Peace Research, 1967, pp. 303-33, republished in Mankind 2000, eds. Jungk and Galtung; Philip E. Jacob and James V. Toscano, eds., The Integration of Political Communities (Philadelphia: Lippincott, 1964); Joseph S. Nye, Jr., Peace in Parts (Boston: Little, Brown, 1971).

30. Andrei D. Sakharov, Progress, Coexistence, and Intellectual Freedom (New York: W. W. Norton, 1968).

31. Wagar, Building the City of Man, p. 31.

32. Ibid., p. 143.

33. Ibid., p. 140.

34. Some of the problems of implementation are discussed in George Kent, "The Application of Peace Studies," Journal of Conflict Resolution 15, no. 1 (March 1971): 47-53.

3

**REORDERING THE
PLANET: THE FOUR
PHASES OF WORLD
ORDER DESIGN**
Louis René Beres

This son of good family,
A wearer of glasses,
Pale, studious, trusting,
But trusting no longer
In power of goodness,
Will do anything now, for
Ends justify means.
(So he hopes.)
Ah, honest-dishonest!
Now wiping his glasses
To see things more clearly,
He sees no barrels—
No gasoline barrels!
It's an idea he sees—
An abstract conception—
Until it explodes!

> Chorus describing The Ph. D. in
> Max Frisch, The Firebugs

RATIONALE

The people of earth are faced with a planetary crisis of terrible urgency. War, population pressure, diminishing resources, environmental pollution—these are only the most dramatic manifestations of an endangered world. There are also a great many other reasons for believing that, unless an improved world future is self-consciously and systematically sought, there will be no world future at all.

This search must become the immediate work of growing numbers of scholars. It must culminate in the conceptualization and investigation of diverse world order models—analytic descriptions of alternative global patterns that are presumed better than what we have today or what we are heading for tomorrow. These models can become the working blueprints for a new and more harmonious organization of planetary life.

Many will think this is an awfully pretentious task. Nothing could be farther from the mark. Recognizing the presently precarious condition of all human life support systems, it is infinitely more pretentious not to become involved in the search for a better world. Today, idealists and realists have changed places. It is the idealist who urges "business as usual" while the realist clamors for a fundamental change in direction. As scholars, we can no longer be content with knowing that our present planetary course is a hopelessly ill-fated one. We must also accept a primary role in designing and urging a better course. (This essay deals only with the first part of this role, designing alternative world futures.)

If we do not accept this role, we are apt to find ourselves in the strangely pathetic part of The Ph.D. in Max Frisch's play, The Fire-bugs. At the conclusion of the performance, this unenviable character reveals that he has known all along about the activity of arsonists in the house of Biedermann (the protagonist) but has remained silent nonetheless. Only when it is already too late and the house is ablaze, does he offer the following statement:

> I can no longer be silent. [He takes out a paper and reads.]
> "Cognizant of the events now transpiring, whose iniquitous
> nature must be readily apparent, the undersigned submits
> to the authorities the subsequent statement . . . ." [Amid
> the shrieking of sirens he reads an involved statement, of
> which no one understands a word. Dogs howl, bells ring,
> there is the scream of departing sirens and the crackling
> of flames. The Ph.D. hands Biedermann the paper.] I
> disassociate myself . . . .

Sadly, we cannot disassociate ourselves. Unlike Frisch's Ph.D., we live in the "house" that is about to burn. This house is coextensive with the dimensions of our earth.

What is to be done?

This brings us to the primary task: to direct our attention to the satisfactory conceptualization of alternative world futures. To accomplish this task, it is important to remember certain guidelines for inquiry. The precise character of these guidelines is revealed in the following discussion. It is not unreasonable to suggest that the fruitfulness of our prospective scholarship depends not only upon how closely these guidelines are followed but also upon how creatively they are applied.

THE GUIDELINES

The study of world order can be divided into four basic phases: values, hypotheses, models, and recommendations. With the exception of the last, each phase is a prerequisite for its successor. It follows that the student of world order must concern himself with the character and content of all four parts, as well as their particular patterns of interdependence.

Values

Studying about world order means studying about alternative world futures. Recognizing the extant world system as merely one case in an extraordinary variety of possible world systems, such study concerns the systematic and imaginative conceptualization of "preferred worlds." The preferred quality of these worlds is necessarily a personal kind of judgment. It is always tied to one's own individual system of values. Given the heterogeneity of values and preference orderings that guide human behavior, there can be no universally agreed upon image of an optimum condition. One man's preferred world need not be another's. Indeed, it may even resemble his vision of dystopia.

There can be no "objectively" appropriate vision of an improved world order. Any suggested alternative is desirable if it tends to maximize the particular personal values at hand. Desirability is always evaluated from the standpoint of these values and no others.

This brings us to the very first thing that must be done in studying about world order: specifying the values. After experiencing the realization that this is not "the best of all possible worlds," scholars must begin to probe underneath their judgment. This brings them to specific values. Self-consciously or otherwise, these values spark the initial feeling of dissatisfaction. Without them, there can be no criteria by which to assess the adequacy of the extant system.

Where do these values come from? Clearly, they are not simply gathered episodically. Nor are they self-consciously sought. They are the ongoing and inadvertent product of many components and impressions of each person's unique biography. At the same time, there is an infinite variety of experiences that may give these values form and substance or even help to define them.

One of these is the visual experience of art. A walk through the Museum of Modern Art in New York City, for example, is certainly apt to leave a world order imprint on the imagination. Henri Rousseau's "The Dream" provides a rich tapestry of the flora and fauna of a newly verdant life. Salvador Dali's "The Persistence of Memory" suggests some remarkable connections between time and world order. Clock time is surely alien to what has been learned about the inner stream of duration or inner time, and Dali's portrayal of melting clocks points to the preservation of the lived experience of pure flow from quantification and spatialization. Peter Blume's allegory "The Eternal City" offers a synthesis of images inspired by fascist dictatorship in Italy while Francis Bacon's "Painting" portrays a dictator whose anonymity makes him all the more menacing (a good visual representation, perhaps, of Kafka's nightmare in The Castle). All these paintings are merely the tip of the iceberg, not only of art generally but even of what is available in one particular collection or museum. From the standpoint of world order studies, Picasso's dictum is remarkably appropriate: Art is a lie that makes us realize the truth. (For each of us, of course, our own particular values are the truth.)

There are, of course, innumerable other sources of values. Art, or what we have called the visual experience, is merely an exceptional and idiosyncratic one. Literature is another. For the most part, however, it is the homogenized and intricately woven pattern of each individual's complex biography that ultimately determines his guiding preferences.

Once the scholar has been able to isolate a fairly specific set of values, he must undertake a somewhat unpleasant task. This task involves rank ordering the values. Why must he do such a thing? Why can't he simply attempt to create a system that is favorable to all his values?

The answer centers on the simple fact that, once he is into the process of designing an alternative world future, he may be faced with a condition of competing values. A configuration that tends to maximize one particular value may do so at the expense of another. For example, the system that seems most peaceful may also be unjust. To handle this problem, he will have to accept certain tradeoffs. And if these compromises are to be rational in the technical sense of that word, they will have to be accomplished according to some predetermined ordering of preferences. What all of this really boils down to is that, since one can't have everthing in world order study, it becomes necessary to decide upon the relative desirability of particular values. This decision will at least permit the scholar to piece together a perfectly rational (if not perfect) world order design.

One last word about values. It was mentioned earlier that the overwhelmingly heterogeneous character of personal value systems implies that there can be no "objective" notion of desirability. Whether or not a system is judged desirable depends entirely upon the values and orderings of values of individual scholars.

But this says nothing about the difficulties of implementation. Even if the heterogeneity of values means that desirability is always personally defined, we must still come to grips with the problem of reconciling large numbers of different world order visions. The fact that each of these visions may satisfy the criterion of desirability (because they may all be consistent with individual preferences and preference orderings) does not make the problem any easier. As long as there are differences over just what is desirable, we must ultimately still deal with competing images of a preferred world order.

To get around this problem, certain scholars have thought it appropriate to tackle the heterogeneity of values at the outset. By securing agreement on certain specific values at the beginning of inquiry, it is believed, all notions of what is desirable must necessarily be the same. After all, if desirability is always defined in terms of specific individual preferences, and all individuals share the same preferences, there can be no competing images of preferred world futures.

This has been the prevailing reasoning behind the Institute for World Order's World Order Models Project. By stipulating a general commitment to the three basic values of nonviolence, economic welfare, and social justice, project participants have sought to create a single common vision of what is desirable. Regrettably, they have done nothing of the kind. There mere fact that different world order "teams" can agree upon nomenclature for basic value guidelines signifies nothing about the actual meanings of those guidelines. Even where it is generally agreed that primary attention must be paid to nonviolence, economic welfare, and social justice, the precise meanings attached to these values may be profoundly diverse. Indeed, there are likely to be as many different interpretations of each of these values as there are teams (let alone individuals) speculating about them.

It follows that, in order to secure genuine agreement on basic values at the beginning of inquiry (thereby averting competing images of desirability later on), much more must be done than creating a common set of overarching value categories. What is needed is a common understanding of the specific contents and character of each of these categories. Ironically, this may require some sacrifice of diversity. In fact, it may not be unreasonable to suggest that overcoming the problem of competing images of preferred world orders and preserving the world's diversity are irreconcilable objectives.

Hypotheses

Armed with an explicit set of ranked values, the student is now ready for another crucial phase of world order design. This is the phase in which values are linked up to a variety of factors that are tentatively expected to maximize or sustain them. These presumed linkages or connections are known as hypotheses. In these hypotheses, values serve as dependent variables or subjects to be explained.

Let us consider an appropriate illustration or example. Suppose that one begins world order studies by affirming a primary commitment to the peace value. The next step involves speculation about the factors that might be most important to supporting this value. If it is supposed that some more centralized distribution of power and sovereign authority (that is, collective security or world government) is needed, one is likely to specify an explicit kind of relationship between peace on the one hand and the configuration of power and sovereignty on the other. This statement represents an hypothesis in which peace is the dependent variable (the subject to be explained) and power and sovereignty are independent variables or explanatory factors.

It follows from this that phases 1 and 2 are closely intertwined and that there can be no hypotheses in planetary design without prior statement of values. Even where it is not self-consciously understood, these values provide the material from which the dependent variable is created. They are the basic building blocks of an alternative world future.

Why is this the case? After all, what is it about hypotheses that is so important to the task at hand? The answer is remarkably simple. Just as in any other inquiry, world order studies must begin with suggested explanations of particular problems. Known as hypotheses, these "happy guesses" are needed to guide the search for order among facts. Without these hypotheses, there exists no way of determining which facts are relevant and which irrelevant. Every inquiry must begin with hypotheses. World order studies are no exception.

As to the sources of these hypotheses, there are a great many different kinds. Hypotheses, of course, are not constructed in conformity with any given set of rules. Rather, they represent the product of various forms of creative speculation. Some of these forms may be tutored by such unorthodox materials as poems, paintings, and fiction literature as well as by advertisements in the popular press, the movies, or television.

For example, the March 1973 issue of Harper's magazine contains a special wraparound section on utopias. This material suggests a number of exciting ideas about an improved world future. Similarly, one can get a potpourri of world order visions by scrutinizing the advertisements for planned recreational opportunities in magazines or even by leafing through the Whole Earth Catalogue. This is not even to mention the host of publications devoted specially to problems of the future, such as Futures, Futurist, Extrapolation, and Technological Forecasting.

As to more specific realms of hypotheses, ideas about world government are not confined to world politics textbooks or esoteric journal articles. One may be moved to argue for "structural" reform by coming across the printed policy statements of groups like the World Federalists or the International Movement for Atlantic Union. Ideas about human oneness can be discovered apart from the writings of well-known cosmopolitan thinkers like Marcus Aurelius (Meditations), Dante (De Monarchia), Herder (Reflections on the History of the Human Race), Pierre Teilhard de Chardin (The Phenomenon of Man), or Sri Aurobindo (The Mind of Light). Indeed, the conviction that any improved system of world order must draw its animating vision from the idea of human unity can be sparked by current action movements like the Planetary Citizen Registration Campaign (which has even printed up a planetary passport application to dramatize its commitment to the "family of man") or by Auroville, an experimental "world city" in India. In its charter, Auroville is described as "a site of material and spiritual researches for a living embodiment of an actual Human Unity."

Literary materials and films also are apt to yield hypotheses linking individual human transformation to alternative world futures. A reading of Bach's Jonathan Livingston Seagull or a viewing of the latest movie version of Lost Horizon (from the novel by James Hilton) can lead to creative speculation about the behavioral underpinnings of world order. In much the same way, Herman Hesse's Siddartha, Franz Kafka's Metamorphosis, Jean-Francois Steiner's Treblinka, and the movie version of Anthony Burgess's A Clockwork Orange suggest many things about what an improved world order might entail and how to get there.

Those who read very little and avoid the cinema may find their hypotheses elsewhere. One may stress the importance of individual human transformation by way of programs in "consciousness evolution" such as the Arica Institute in America or the Phenomenon of Man Project. This latter activity takes it name from the masterwork of Teilhard de Chardin and spreads the message of human "totalization."

As with our earlier discussion of values, these sources of world order ideas are certainly not exhaustive. They are merely among the most exciting and the least appreciated. By and large, however, it is not from a variety of readily identifiable discrete materials that

scholars draw their hypotheses about world order but from the continuous flux of their own stream of conscious states. This flux consists
of the awareness of what is unfolded by consciousness, the instantan-
eous awareness of temporality and memory.

Models

Models of world order are determined by particular hypotheses.
The models are created for the purpose of examining these hypotheses.
Different kinds of hypotheses lead to the creation and investigation of
different kinds of models.

For example, if one hypothesizes that the effectiveness of power
management or war avoidance will be enhanced to the extent that the
system becomes more centralized, the most appropriate models
would be the balance of power, collective security, and world government configurations. This is the case as long as these patterns are
paralleled by increasingly centralized distributions of power and sovereign authority. These models would provide the context within
which the strength of the hypothesized connection could be evaluated.
And this is their only raison d'etre: to examine a previously suggested
relationship. The spark of creation in world order modeling must
involve more than an imaginative intuition. It must derive from a
tentative explanation in the form of a hypothesis.

If one hypothesizes that the effectiveness of power management
improves as the system shifts from a bipolar to a multipolar state,
the two basic models that must be created are, of course, bipolar and
multipolar ones. As in the case of the balance of power, collective
security, and world government models, these two structural descriptions are provided for the purpose of hypothesis investigation. They
must not be examined without the benefit of a particular hypothesis.
To do so would be to commit the fallacy of backward explanation.
After all, without a hypothesis to order inquiry, there is no sound
reason for favoring one set of conclusions over another.

If a hypothesis is advanced suggesting that the effectiveness
of power management improves as the number of "nuclearly
capable" national actors increases, one would have to create still
other models. These models would be characterized by a successively
increased number of actors in possession of nuclear weapons and supporting infrastructure. The subsequent investigation of these models
would be carried out for the purpose of evaluating the hypothesis.
Just as in the previous cases mentioned, the models follow the hypothesis. Exactly which models of world order are to be considered depends upon the particular hypotheses one wishes to examine. These

hypotheses, in turn, depend upon the particular values held by the individual analyst.

Recommendations

Once the models have been carefully investigated, it is up to the scholars to decide whether or not to recommend them. This decision must be informed by the twin criteria of desirability and feasibility. For a new system of world order to warrant serious attention, it must appear both highly attractive (in terms of the initial values that prompted inquiry in the first place) and reasonably capable of implementation.

With respect to the first of these criteria, the world order scholar must confront some disturbing dilemmas. As noted earlier, however desirable a system may appear, it must ultimately come up against vastly different value hierarchies. Because world order design is a uniquely personal kind of activity, a tension is created between intent and outcome, between a deliberate attempt to improve the world and the private character of any recommended alternative. Even where it is self-consciously created for planetary adoption, one scholar's preferred world is apt to be countered with a multiplicity of competing images.

Perhaps this can be averted by securing general agreement among scholars on the precise contents of specific values, but this entails many new difficulties. In the first place, it undermines the diverse character of global life. In the second place, it does nothing about the continuing heterogeneity of preferences and preference orderings among the world's peoples. After all, not much is accomplished if agreements among scholars are not paralleled by their respective populations, or at least by their respective leaders. And finally, even if all these problems could be eliminated, we would still be left with vast differences over matters of strategy. Even if general agreement were secured on exactly what values were to define a desirable world future, and even if such agreement were universal, major disagreements would still prevail over how to bring this common vision to fruition.

This brings us to the second criterion of world order scholarship. As can be seen from the foregoing discussion, feasibility is closely tied to desirability. They are interdependent criteria. Depending upon the extent of agreement on what constitutes a desirable alternative world system, the feasibility of a particular recommendation will vary considerably. This is not to suggest, however, that widespread agreement automatically signifies feasibility. Continuing differences over strategies of implementation may still render any recommendation thoroughly unattainable. Moreover, a number of technological factors may inhibit feasibility. And this may be the case even where general agreement exists on definitions of desirability and on matters of strategy.

CONCLUSION

If there is any single feature of world order design that stands out above all others, it is its incredible difficulty. The fact that we now face a planetary crisis of terrible urgency only magnifies the consequences of this difficulty. Unless we succeed in reordering the planet, we must surely perish prematurely. Unless we are able to construct alternative world futures, we must surely capitulate to forces that signal the onset of unbearable global conditions.

This essay has not offered an assured way out of this difficulty. It has not even offered a set of guidelines that can assuredly produce such a way. Taken by themselves, the four phases of world order design merely outline a course. They point to a way. Whether or not this way will bring us where we want to go depends upon more than a willing acceptance of certain progressive and interdependent stages of inquiry. It depends upon more than a coherent and successive movement from values to hypotheses to models to recommendations. It depends upon creative interpretation.

Creative interpretation—what does this mean? Perhaps we cannot know until we see it taking place more often. Perhaps we can see it taking place more often now that the guidelines have at least been articulated.

4

OUTLINE FOR A
NORMATIVE
FORECASTING/PLANNING
PROCESS
Michael Washburn

Devoid of imagination, as the Philistine
always is, he lives in a certain trivial
province of experience as to how things go,
what is possible, what usually occurs. . . .
For philistinism thinks it is in control of
possibility . . . it carries possibility
around like a prisoner in the cage of the
probable, [and] shows it off.

—Kierkegaard, The Sickness Unto Death

INTRODUCTION

Accepted practice in the field of social forecasting is to make a
distinction between exploratory or descriptive forecasts and normative
forecasts.[1] A further distinction is often drawn between forecasting
and planning.[2] Instead, we have chosen to start from a somewhat
broader and hopefully sharper definitional base.

Note: This essay is closely related to work I have been doing
with Thomas E. Jones on a chapter entitled "Anchoring Futures in
Preferences" for inclusion in Forecasting and International Relations
(forthcoming, W. H. Freeman and Company) edited by Nazli Choucri
and Thomas Robinson. I am particularly indebted to Thomas Jones
for allowing me to include in this paper a summary of his contribution
to that book on the "good reasons approach" to moral reasoning.

All forecasting is normative. All forecasting is neither value-free nor assumption-free, and properly speaking, one should not make a distinction between exploratory and normative forecasting. Furthermore, the distinction between a forecast and the uses to which it is put (the planning it makes possible) is not as clear and absolute as is usually assumed. Certain kinds of forecasts lead most easily to certain kinds of planning by certain actors. In other words, the normative uses and implications of a particular forecasting process may be implicit in that process and in the methods or techniques used, whether or not the forecaster has an explicit intention of using his forecast to elucidate a preferred alternative future or to develop a program of policy and action. It is quite possible, for example, for ostensibly non-normative forecasting to be done in one setting, say an academic institution, while it is used by a separate group in another setting, say government, as one basis for policy planning and implementation. The forecast is compatible with the needs of and acceptable to the policy planner at least as much because there is a shared set of assumptions about beliefs, values, and methods as because the forecast meets some general standards of scientific rigor.

Our intention is not to blur the useful distinction between normative steps, tasks, and procedures and those that are essentially descriptive. Neither is it our intention to undermine, ignore, or throw out the criteria or standards used to guide and evaluate descriptive social science research. These standards remain appropriate and important elements in any forecasting/planning process. But they cannot reign absolute nor operate as a shield protecting such research from evaluation according to other procedures and criteria.

More specifically, forecasting is a multistep process in which essentially descriptive methods are matched with essentially normative methods to produce statements about the future that have as principal components estimations of probability or feasibility and desirability. One can separate and evaluate independently the constituent parts of such a process, but in the final analysis each part must be judged as well within the context and characteristics of the process taken as a whole. That process is inherently and unavoidably normative and should be analyzed and evaluated as such.

Historically, there is much justification for the descriptive/normative distinction. Normative futures work has generally meant genius forecasting, utopian thinking, and armchair speculation. In the world affairs field, this strand is associated with work on world government reaching back to Dante and the Duc du Sully[3] and up to the recent past with the sophisticated writings of Grenville Clark and Louis Sohn and a few others.[4] This approach suffered from several critical deficiencies, aptly summarized by Richard Falk:

1. No conception of transition linking the present
to the future;

2. A failure to envision world order solutions other
than by the replication on a global level of the concentrations of power and authority of the sort now manifest in
the governance of large sovereign states;

3. [A presupposition] . . . completely contrary
to observed fact, that the existing structure of world
order is administered by reasonable men of goodwill who
are susceptible to persuasive techniques of influence.[5]

The strength of these attempts lay in their presentation of a
clear vision of a preferred future, their functional/institutional specificity, their specification of value goals and their translation of these
into institutional arrangements and principles of operation.

As we will mention, several advances in the last twenty years
in such diverse areas as public international law, general systems
theory, and policy science offer ways to strengthen explicitly normative work on world politics. In particular, world order studies are
an effort to combine these several strands into a coherent intellectual
strategy of normative forecasting, design, and planning. Some of the
problems encountered in the first world order design effort, the
World Order Models Project of the Institute for World Order, are
discussed in this essay, and it is our intention that this essay will be
a contribution to making world order design efforts even more systematic, useful, and persuasive.[6]

In the last few years, it has become equally clear that the
descriptive end of forecasting is far less scientific—that is, distortion-
free—than originally hoped and claimed. It is generally recognized
that the outcomes of a particular forecasting exercise can be affected
by one or more of several extra or nonscientific factors such as the
value preferences of the forecaster, forecasters' assumptions about
time and cause and effect, the selection of method, the selection of
problem focus, and the interpretation of results.[7] This development
has been fueled in the international relations field by the breakdown
in the postwar foreign policy consensus, as analysts and commentors
have been forced to articulate basic assumptions and goals in order to
explain or justify their differences. In short, what is traditionally
described as exploratory or descriptive forecasting is often vulnerable to criticisms similar to those leveled at old-style normative
forecasting.

A close look at the two approaches as practiced today (with
normative futurists seeking to be more systematic and descriptive
futurists increasingly recognizing the importance of values and
assumptions) suggests very strongly that the two are not incompatible.

Rather, they have been unnecessarily polarized through historically separate development and practice and through the growth of semantic confusion. Emphasizing the overall forecasting process and viewing its constituent parts in that context should help to identify the compatibilities and possible linkages between descriptive and normative procedures.

This essay outlines a basic, five-step forecasting/planning process and attempts to focus on some of the key choices and problems that arise when seeking to make every step in the process as explicit and as considered as possible. In addition, we will try to show that there are a variety of techniques available or inventible that could be used to strengthen both the normative and the descriptive elements in the forecasting/planning process and their linkage.

This approach has at least three important implications:

First, by placing in their proper place and weight in the forecasting/planning process the evaluative criteria of science, world order scholars are encouraged to give equally serious and precise consideration to other evaluative standards, where they are called for.

Next, various forecasting techniques can be liberated from the implicit value context they are normally associated with and used in new sequences or for new purposes in any forecasting/planning process.

Finally, some bases can be established for comparing the results (and the procedures) of very different forecasting/planning efforts. For example, a useful distinction might be drawn between those forecasts whose purpose is to map the realization of alternative preferred futures, that is, discontinuous value sets, and those whose purpose is to reduce uncertainties about the probability and feasibility of a future much like the present, that is, of continuity. But the moment will inevitably come when two such different forecasts will be placed side by side and debated publicly or bureaucratically. Only one will emerge as the basis for policy. By making normative and assumptive loadings explicit and by requiring explicit attention to the implications of each choice of method and procedure throughout the forecasting process, the approach outlined below makes possible relatively straightforward and thorough comparison on normative and scientific grounds of seemingly disparate forecasts.

STEPS IN THE FORECASTING/PLANNING PROCESS: AN OVERVIEW

Hasan Ozbekhan distinguishes three stages or phases of what he calls "normative planning."[8] We will start from and build upon his formulation since it captures the essence of what is usually thought of as the normative forecasting process while at the same time it is easily amended to become a general formulation for all forecasting/planning efforts.

The first stage in Ozbekhan's formulation involves the selection of goals. Decisions are made concerning what ought to be done. The second stage consists of devising strategies that can achieve the selected goals. A feasible route from the present state of affairs to a preferred future state is worked out. In the third stage, decision makers determine how, when, and in what sequence the chosen strategies will be implemented. The first stage formulates the normative plan; the second, the strategic plan; the third, the operational plan. These three interrelated stages are interactive. They function as parts of a single integrative, iterative planning process.

As Ozbekhan remarks, "Decisions made in the light of . . . future 'images' initiate that backward chain of calculable events which when they reach the present can be translated into it in the form of calculated change."[9] In this way, anticipating a future may become causative of future-oriented action in the present. Hence, normative planning can overcome the tendency of policy making to be mainly responsible to current events rather than "futures-creative." When goal evaluation is explicitly integrated into the forecasting process, decision makers' options are increased. "A multiplicity of goals based on a multiplicity of norms enlarges the traditional boundaries of the practical and thereby lengthens the spectrum of alternative policies among which we could choose."[10]

For purposes of this discussion, the key point in Ozbekhan's argument is not so much that can implies ought. Rather, it is that the universe of oughts tends to be limited or circumscribed by the universe of cans so long as the forecaster seeks to emulate the ideal of value-free science. However, the universe of cans can be made to expand through the application of the discipline of searching for ways to achieve a variety of oughts. This in turn leads to the notion that no amount of improvement in descriptive forecasting techniques can alter the limiting quality of nonexplicitly normative approaches. The way out is by letting normative considerations play an active role in the forecasting process. The result should be, as Ozbekhan suggests, a broader range of alternative futures and probably a higher estimation of probability for many of the more desirable ones.

In accepting the basic Ozbekhan argument for explicit treatment of goals, one need not totally adopt his three-stage approach to the forecasting/planning process. We take exception to his approach in two important and related respects; the amendments we will suggest result in a five-stage instead of a three-stage iterative process that will become the basis for the remainder of this essay.

The first difficulty with the Ozbekhan approach is that it does not accord a sufficiently central role to estimations of probability, that is, to the results of a variety of descriptive forecasting procedures. As a method, it could suffer from a tendency inherent in all efforts with explicit goals to overestimate the probability of achieving the desired outcome. The need is both for a separate stage of descriptive forecasting to serve as an evaluative base for the overall process and for the use of descriptive techniques to test the feasibility of strategies devised to breach the envelope of "cans."

If the first problem is one of possible utopianism, the second is the opposite: The Ozbekhan approach may be essentially conservative, a procedure for better enabling present elites to hold onto or enhance their positions of power. The notion of planning strongly suggests operating from a position of status and strength. Indeed, it may be that only groups already having both can afford to undertake systematic forecasting and planning efforts. It is essential, therefore, that the process include a clear statement of the assumptions, special interests, and affiliations, as well as the goals of the forecasters. With this information, the reader can begin to separate the probability of a given outcome from the predispositions and self-interests of the forecaster. In addition, a special effort must be made in the feasibility testing and implementation planning stages to see if manipulables that are not solely in the hands of or dominated by elites of various kinds have been adequately identified and utilized. There must be room as well for nongovernmental, noncorporate, and nonbusiness arenas for action and levers of change.

The forecasting/planning process we are suggesting is outlined below. While it is straightforward, even obvious, in the abstract, it does have the advantage of minimizing the possible distorting effects of hidden assumptions and procedures. Each step therefore requires conscious deliberation and choice on the part of the forecaster and is in turn open to systematic evaluation by others.

TASKS TO BE COMPLETED IN A NORMATIVE FORECASTING/PLANNING PROCESS

1. Clarification of assumptions:
   a. Definition of problem focus: area of activity, scope, time, horizon, and delineation of relevant context or environment.
   b. Definition of the purpose of the forecasting exercise: What is the goal of the study, who commissioned it, for what purpose, who is it intended to aid or influence, and why? What goal or

societal end state, generally described, is the subject of the
investigation?
c. Other assumptions about time, causality, human nature and so
on (see below for one possible detailed listing).

2. Explicating and incorporating value preferences and goals to be
realized.

3. Selection of forecasting methods and strategies:
a. Define key processes, structural properties, and manipulables
for the relevant social system.
b. Model, if possible, this social system.
c. Select the optimal descriptive forecasting technique or procedure
given the forecasters' goals and assumptions and the available
data and theory.
d. Project the existing social system into the future, making whatever choices about time scale and the probability of major shifts
in policies etc. seem warranted. Produce a range of alternative
futures having different probability estimates, being sure to
include middle-range futures as well as those that are highly
probable.

4. Discovering and designing alternative preferred futures:
a. Identify from stage 3 above several promising alternative
futures:
● Estimate their ability to realize the goals outlined in stage 2
and their workability in social process terms.
● Select and model the more interesting alternatives.
● Roughly assess the feasibility of each alternative in the appropriate terms: political, cultural, economic, etc.
● Design and conduct sensitivity analyses and experiments to
increase reliability of estimates of the costs and benefits of
the alternatives that still appear promising.
● Select the alternatives that continue to meet minimum standards for further investigation.
b. Invent (several, if possible) alternative images or designs if
none of the projected alternatives appears to meet the minimum
standards and repeat step 4a.
c. Assess as precisely as possible the feasibility of the surviving
alternatives:
● Pay special attention to issues of incentives, belief systems,
latitude and power of decision, consensus formation, structural rigidities and constraints, lead time factors, countervailing trends and forces.
● Develop and experiment with detailed transition strategies.

- Select the optimal alternative.

5. Developing an operational plan:
   a. Determine specific programs and policies needed to operationalize the preferred future alternative.
   b. Set priorities, determine allocation of required resources, and work out a sequence of action programs.
   c. If appropriate, prepare necessary documents (legislation, proposal, manifesto, news release) and plans for administration.
   d. Design procedures for periodic review and repeat of steps 1 through 4 if experience suggests the necessity of reworking the desirability/feasibility calculations.
   e. Begin implementation.

Three general points about this five-stage approach seem relevant before we discuss each stage in some detail:

1. The whole forecasting/planning sequence is not meant to be terminal or rigidly sequential. The sequence should be ongoing, being repeated as new experience, new data, and new ideas become available. Within the whole sequence, various steps may require a repetition of preceding steps if relevant standards are not met.

2. Each step involves first a series of decisions about the appropriate techniques and the standards they must meet, and then their sequential application. Normative or descriptive considerations may predominate in any given step but each step usually includes each of these elements. This interaction serves to maintain the overall thrust of the forecasting/planning exercise by compensating when necessary for the weaknesses of each of the approaches, by taming down the excesses of each, and by maintaining a focused tension between considerations of probability, feasibility, and desirability.

3. Each step in the overall sequence establishes the basis for the next step; each flows into the others and influences the outcome. The choices made at each step are therefore terribly important. Evaluation of the output must include an evaluation of the choices made and methods used at each step along the way.

STEP 1: CLARIFICATION OF ASSUMPTIONS

A forecaster's beliefs and basic nonmethodological assumptions can, in conjunction with his goal or value preferences, whether explicitly stated or not, condition his purpose in forecasting, his selection of overall method and of particular techniques, and his resulting forecast.

Especially important are a forecaster's beliefs about causality. Although such beliefs condition his selection of forecasting methods, they typically extend beyond what is embodied in the formal requirements of such methods. Such beliefs frequently influence forecasters' judgments concerning the directions in which trends are likely to proceed and concerning the human ability to shape the future.

Many of us come to the task of forecasting with a Western, scientific world view, a liberal, democratic political philosophy, a generally optimistic, evolutionary sense of history, and a belief in the efficacy of human action. At the same time, we may hold some strong doubts about the inherent goodness or perfectability of humans or, conversely, of social institutions. Most of us belong to an elite in terms of professional training and associations and in terms of access to the centers of power in government, business, education, the media, and the foundations.

Some ways in which this profile can affect our forecasts include:

1. Central importance given to technology while little weight is given to the role of belief systems, images, value trends, and ideas in social change.

2. Stress on past and present facts over future values in assessment of forces that shape the future, a deterministic bias that asserts the power of current structures and patterns and severely limits the range of human choice and influence.

3. Choice of methods and procedures that reinforce the stress on the past and present.

4. Problem selection that tends to conform to needs and concerns of topdog actors and their policy makers, that is, national governments, large corporations and foundations; national security over human rights, growth over distribution, ecology over development, and stability over changes (continuity and predictability over discontinuity).

5. A focus on, and perhaps an overvaluing of, the manipulables and choice points within the control of these same major actors. Certainly an undervaluing of the capabilities and opportunities available to other actors, particularly transnational, nongovernmental actors in the global arena and individuals and action groups in domestic arenas.

Because of the above kinds of conscious and unconscious assumptions and predispositions and many others like them, a forecaster's calculations of probability could be distorted in an establishment, more or less deterministic direction. Continuous futures that conform to established values may be given an excessively high probability rating, while discontinuous futures that involve marked shifts in values may be excessively discounted. This distortion can in turn

affect calculations of desirability. The seeming improbability of discontinuous futures may promote the upgrading in value terms of continuous futures, because they appear much more tolerable when
perceived as inevitable. Such futures then become the basis for policy
as the only preferable futures we can realistically hope for.

The distortions described above are not too troubling if we
accept by and large the prevailing social order and are concerned
with more of the same while seeking to better manage certain current
and potential problems. The only apparent problem in relation to
values and assumptions is one of internal consistency. Are our values
consistent with our views of human nature and the nature of polity and
economy? Do they conform to our concepts of cause and effect? And
so on.

If we are not comfortable with a method that rests so heavily on
our own perceptual predispositions or if we do not in the end really
prefer the kinds of alternative futures we project, there are a few
corrective measures that might be tried. One approach would be to
vary the different assumptions and compare the resulting alternative
futures and estimates of probability. There is a limit to this approach,
one imposed by the limited extent to which you can vary the assumptions without drastically altering or entirely switching the forecasting
methods. Another approach would be to give the same assignments
to forecasters representing different cultural, political, socioeconomic,
and even psychological groups. But here again the overlap between
Western social science and descriptive forecasting is so great that
the inherent limitations of the methods should prove too much for
these forecasters—depending, of course, on how much they themselves
aspire to the Western ideal.

An even more thorough approach stressing justification and analysis of the implications of value and other assumptions is the kind of
approach that we prefer. Systematic explication and analysis of starting biases makes outside understanding and evaluation of one's forecasts far easier. Even more important, a critical treatment of
assumptions enables us to use them consciously and selectively
throughout the forecasting sequence in ways that can strengthen the
reliability and usefulness of forecasts.

One approach to making nonmethodological assumptions explicit
involves the use of comprehensive checklists. In "A Paradigm for the
Analysis of Time Perspectives and Images of the Future," Wendell
Bell, James A. Mau, Bettina J. Huber, and Menno Boldt categorize
some kinds of assumptions that forecasters make—either explicitly
or, more often, implicitly.[11] Likewise, in Futures Studies and Research Curriculum Guide, David C. Miller and Ronald L. Hunt have
compiled lists of similar assumptions.[12] Our own summary list,
which is derived from these and other sources, is presented below.

CLARIFICATION OF ASSUMPTIONS

1. Class and cultural frames of reference
    a. How sensitive to and explicit about the influences of one's own culture and class background in defining and setting one's values?
    b. How conscious of the paradigmatic blinders placed by culture and class?
    c. To what extent attempt to correct for or include other class and culture frames of reference?

2. Assumptions about human nature
    a. Basically good, neutral, or evil: What is meant?
    b. Basically rigid or changeable?
    c. Kinds and strengths of limits on rate and direction of change?
    d. Can humans "make" themselves or are they fundamentally the products of impersonal forces?
    e. Basic direction of human nature through history: stayed the same, is improving, is deteriorating?
    f. Same or different for races, cultures, groups, sexes?

3. Assumptions about the nature of society, polity, and economy
    a. Basically good, bad, or neutral: What is meant?
    b. Basically rigid or dynamic?
    c. What kinds and strengths of limits are there on change? Stable systems versus dynamic systems (essentially slow evolutionary, rapid evolutionary, revolutionary, cataclysmic)
    d. To what extent can humans shape their social, political, and economic environments; to what extent are there inherent limits and factors beyond human control?
    e. How much potential for change is there in the material realm; how much in institutions; how much in attitudes, norms, and values?
    f. What patterns and cycles of social change are there?
    g. What is the population or subpopulations basis for evaluating the performance of societies?

4. Assumptions about cause and effect
    a. Basically supernatural causative forces or causes in humans, societal structures, and their interaction with the environment?
    b. Basically deterministic or uncertain and problematic? Degree of human choice and control? Which agents are potent for what reasons?
    c. Single factor or multiple factor explanation of social events?

d. Are there or are there not limits to what can be known about cause and effect and about which factors in what proportions?

e. What weights are given to relative importance of social, psychological, technological, political, economic, physical environmental factors?

f. Basic orientation toward past, present, and future in the cause of each: that is, does history propel present into future; or is the past drawn into the future by present images, needs, desires; or do past continuities tend to persist and cycles tend to recur?

g. Do ideas have independent causal power or are they interdependent with social action, or do they function just as "ideology" to justify actions?

5. Orientation to the dimension of time

a. Is basic notion of time one of clock and calendar; one of historical/structural eras, cycles; one of shifts in moods, consciousness, and other psychological or subjective factors; or a mixture of these?

b. Are past, present, and future seen as largely independent of each other or as connected and interpenetrating?

c. What are the weightings given to past, present, and future in relation to relevant factors, trends, actors, data, and actions/policies?

There are a few pointed methods for clarifying assumptions, purposes, and problem focus. Much more work needs to be done since it is not easy to identify fully one's own biases or to tease out biases in the work of others. Decision-theoretic techniques currently being developed and tested by Ward Edwards now of the University of Southern California and Marcia Guttentag of Harvard indicate that a good deal can be done to make explicit forecasters' generally implicit frames of reference and belief systems.[13] Impressive research also has been done in the last ten years to relate world views and philosophical outlook to personality structures[14] and to the societal processes of political socialization.[15]

We know of no detailed study of assumptions and perceptual distortions associated with international relations forecasting and are not in a position to present such an analysis ourselves at this time. However, Bell and his colleagues do offer such a study of another social science field, namely psychology, which illustrates the profound impact these kinds of assumptions can have on the therapeutic process (which is, of course, a kind of forecasting, planning, acting process).[16]

STEP 2: EXPLICATING AND INCORPORATING
VALUE PREFERENCES

Value preferences and systematic normative reasoning are fundamental components in reliable, effective forecasting and planning. Normative thinking is central to the entire forecasting/planning process in several ways. For example:

1. Definition of preferred alternative futures, that is, of value goals (or clarification of value assumptions if value goals are not easily identified or disentangled).
2. Identification of linkages, tradeoffs, and possible conflicts among relevant values.
3. Clarification through normative reasoning, such as the good reasons approach described below, of appropriate value hierarchies and of decision rules. [17]
4. Evaluation of the range of alternative futures forecast.
5. Treatment of likely and possible changes in public value priorities and the effect of these on social policy and structures. [18]
6. Management of the shuffling back and forth between goal specification and feasibility determination.
7. Operationalization of goal values, that is, linkages between formal models and normative constructs. [19]

We cannot explore in this section each of these in detail. We have chosen to deal with points 1, 2, and 3 in a presentation of the good reasons approach to normative thinking. Further references on each are provided in the notes. Points 4 and 6 will then be discussed as part of the next sections on the selection of forecasting techniques and methods and the selection and design of alternative preferred futures. As important as points 5 and 7 are, we deal with them in this chapter only in the notes.

Normative Reasoning: The Good Reasons Approach

Answers to questions about which goals are better than others or about which actions ought (or ought not) to be performed are evaluations and imperatives that cannot be logically deduced from statements that describe empirical facts. [20] To function as nonarbitrary guides to wise choices, evaluations and imperatives must be rationally justifiable. Is it possible to reach rational decisions about which goals are better than others and about which actions ought to be performed? Or are value judgments and moral judgments merely used to express arbitrary attitudes and to influence the attitudes of other people?

A nonarbitrary method for resolving normative disagreements (or a group of similar, overlapping methods) has been formulated in philosophical ethics. Whether we speak of a method or methods is largely a semantic matter. Careful analysis of the approaches advocated by several moral philosophers discloses that their methods are refinements of our best procedures for answering ethical questions in everyday life and diverge relatively little from each other. This method can nonarbitrarily resolve many, although not all, moral disputes.

The good reasons approach, which sets forth this method, is best understood in the light of its origin in twentieth century moral philosophy. The outcome of the debate between intuitionists (G. E. Moore, Ross), ethical naturalists (John Dewey, R. B. Perry), and emotivists (A. J. Ayer, C. L. Stevenson)[21] was the good reasons approach (J. Rawls, W. Frankena, R. Brandt, K. Baier, S. Toulman, and others).[22] According to this approach, moral judgments are not primarily "property-referring" (descriptive of natural properties like pleasure) as the ethical naturalists had held, and therefore are not reducible to statements that can be tested by the scientific method. Nor do moral judgments refer to the intuitionists' mysterious intuited "non-natural properties." Yet we cannot properly conclude, as the emotivists did, that people use moral judgments merely to express their own arbitrary attitudes and influence the attitudes of others. Rather, we can formulate a rational, nonarbitrary method for guiding choices and impartially resolving cases of conflicting claims.

A standard method that reflective people commonly utilize is dubbed the qualified attitude method by Richard Brandt.[23] Ordinary moral reasoning consists of a complex interplay of attitudes, principles, formal requirements for principles, and rules for discounting. Brandt elicits the crucial elements and steps from such reasoning and systematizes them:

1. To resolve particular ethical problems, we appeal to principles that we have more or less explicitly in mind and to our attitudes (our feelings of obligation, our preferences).

2. We correct our principles if they are incompatible with our criticized attitudes, which we also use to weigh and fill out our principles.

3. Our judgments must be consistent and, if particular, capable of generalization.

4. We discount our attitudes if they are uninformed, partial, the product of an abnormal state of mind, or incompatible with having a consistent set of general principles not excessively complex.

Brandt argues that an ethical statement should be asserted if and only if it satisfies the conditions of this qualified attitude method. He successfully employs this method to combat the claim that all conflicting moral judgments are permissible. Admittedly, different people might apply the method properly and derive conflicting answers to some ethical questions, but this limited relativism in no way vitiates the worth of rational argumentation on many fundamental issues. [24]

Upon analysis, the moral-point-of-view method expounded by William K. Frankena turns out to be remarkably similar to Brandt's qualified attitude method. Frankena states that normative discourse is:

> a language in which we may express our sentiments—approvals, disapprovals, evaluations, recommendations, advice, instructions, prescriptions—and put them out into the public arena for rational scrutiny and discussion, claiming that they will hold up under such scrutiny and discussion and that our audience will concur with us if they will also choose the same common point of view. [25]

Against meta-ethical relativism, which claims there is no objectively valid way of justifying any basic moral (or value) judgments in cases where such judgments conflict, Frankena observes that it is "extremely difficult to show that people's basic ethical and value judgments would still be different even if they were fully enlightened, conceptually clear, shared the same factual beliefs, and were taking the same point of view." [26]

Frankena also argues "that one is taking the moral point of view if one is not being egoistic, one is doing things on principle, one is willing to universalize one's principles, and in doing so considers the good of everyone alike." [27]

Similarly, Rawls defined a class of competent judges and a class of considered judgments as part of his search for correct principles that all agents in a situation may apply to justly adjudicate cases of conflicting interest claims. When different people meet the conditions of the moral point of view as best they can and moral disagreement remains, they can ascribe the disagreement to imperfect fulfillment of the conditions but must be tolerant and open-minded if they are to refrain from going outside the moral institutions of life and utilizing nonmoral techniques of coercion.

The good reasons approach can provide an impartial, systematic procedure for goal selection and moral assessment of strategic and operational plans. Use of this method of evaluation for normative forecasting would import explicit theory into the largely unformalized normative stage. Besides being used to reach particular normative decisions, the good reasons approach could be utilized to formulate a normative system that would be appropriate to the present historically unprecedented global situation. Forecasters of international relations also could use the good reasons approach to formalize evaluations both in normative forecasting and at the end of exploratory forecasting. Moreover, once concealed normative biases that distort forecasts have been uncovered, this approach could be used to evaluate them as well.

Much effort still needs to be focused on developing a detailed approach to the normative components of the forecasting/planning process. As Ozbekhan has perceived, one condition for societal adoption of normative planning is a worked-out theory and methodology.

Who Decides on Goals?

Unfortunately, normative forecasting and planning can be instrumental in the attainment of goals that, either in themselves or in their consequences, are contrary to the best interests of most people. Besides, the means employed may be productive of undesirable consequences that more than cancel out benefits derived from achievement of the goal. An extreme example would be provided by the creation of a totalitarian world government to solve global ecological problems. Furthermore, sharp disagreements exist concerning which goals and paths are preferable. And so, as part of this brief exploration of normative thinking in the forecasting/planning process, we must pose the following question: Who should decide the goals and who should decide the paths for whose best interests?

In the absence of institutionalized public participation in the choice of goals and appropriate means, normative forecasting might be dictatorially monopolized by elites that would control the communications media. Being concerned with their own interests, such elites might not engage in the types of normative forecasting that are intended to be instrumental in increasing the general well-being. That is, their goals might not focus on satisfying the individual needs of as many people as possible. On the other hand, lack of expert advice on complicated issues (such as interrelated ecological problems) could lead to kinds of public normative planning—or the failure to engage in such planning—that would be to the detriment of all. What seems required is a blend of expertise and popular participation in the formulation of goals that, if actualized by effective normative planning, would shape the destinies of all involved.

Gerald Feinberg has proposed the creation of institutions that would promote maximum participation of all human beings in choosing fundamental goals.[28] Seeking to transcend ideological differences, these institutions would emphasize those aspects of the future that are of common interest to all people. Alvin Toffler has offered two similar proposals in somewhat less mystical terms; Toffler has made a broad appeal for a major reorientation of schools around the future and for broad individual and community involvement in technology assessment and policy.[29] Unfortunately, most forecasting and planning in international relations in the near future is likely to issue largely from experts, governmental bureaucracies, and political figures. It is likely, too, that most of these will reside in the developed world and see the world and future goals from that perspective. If we are correct about the influences that all these factors have on actual forecasts, we can expect a continuing flow of reports that are entrenched in the way the world is and in ways of keeping it that way, more or less.

Even if wide public participation in goal setting were achieved, what about future generations that will be affected by the planned changes implemented by the present generation? Certain policies (such as increased R & D expenditures for controlled fusion) might open up new options for our descendants, whereas consequences of others (such as depletion of nonrenewable natural resources) would foreclose options. Granted that we should take the preferences of our descendants into account, how can this be done? The value priorities that are currently judged to be proper for policy formation may not be the same as those of our descendants, who will be affected by the policies. To what extent can we anticipate our descendants' priorities? To what extent should those priorities condition our policies? If we could not anticipate likely changes in public value priorities, even normative forecasting would have a built-in conservative bias. Without proposing answers to these knotty questions, we suggest that the use of both the good reasons approach and historical sociology would be conducive to anticipating changes in value priorities.

STEP 3: SELECTION OF FORECASTING METHODS
AND STRATEGIES

Some forecasts picture the most likely future as one of relatively continuous, progressive evolution of the scientific-technological, economic, informational, and rational genre; others, as one of discontinuous change (abrupt quantitative and qualitative change) resulting in a far worse future unless basic intentionally induced changes create a preferable discontinuous future. After inferring the likelihood of discontinuous, disastrous futures from a continuation of interrelated trends and unresolved problems, the forecasters tend to use normative planning to show that radically different, desirable futures could be "invented" by appropriate changes in value priorities, institutions, policies, and/or technologies.

What explains this disagreement concerning the kind of a future that is most likely? A good part of the explanation is to be found in the methods chosen. Forecasts of relatively continuous futures are formulated primarily by trend extrapolation; of discontinuous futures, by modeling. Examples of images of relatively continuous futures are those presented by Herman Kahn and Anthony J. Wiener in their "surprise-free" projection for the year 2000 (The Year 2000), by Kahn and B. Bruce-Briggs in a similar projection for the 1970s and 1980s (Things to Come), and by Zbigniew Brzezinski ("America in the Technetronic Age"). Images of discontinuous futures emerge in forecasts formulated by Willis Harman (Alternative Futures for Education), Richard Falk (This Endangered Planet), Dennis Meadows's team (The Limits to Growth), and Jay Forrester (World Dynamics). [30] Both Forrester and the Meadows team forecast the probable collapse of the world population and the industrial system unless exponential growth of both population and industrialization is soon stabilized.

Continuous futures may appear more likely because they are easier to conceptualize and because trend projections may seem value-free. However, trend extrapolation is rather simplistic and produces little that is not intuitively obvious. By directing forecasters to imagine the future in the images of the past and present, trend extrapolation can induce a conservative bias. Such a bias is indeed agreeable to typical bureaucratic users of forecasts who do not encourage deviation from expectations. But excessive reliance on trend extrapolation hinders insight into discontinuous opportunities and perils. For instance, is it not misleading to assume that all crucial trend-altering innovations in international relations have already occurred?

Modeling, which takes into account the effects of feedback from causally interrelated factors, is more aligned to anticipating system breaks. Nevertheless, diametrically opposed forecasts have been formulated by changing the assumptions of a model. For instance, Robert Boyd revised the assumptions of Forrester's computer model to coincide with those of technological optimists. [31] The resulting computer runs showed that these assumptions imply worldwide industrial growth that is both extensive and sustainable.

One purpose of this essay is to carry this argument one step further and to add two other key distinctions. The general point is that the method one chooses will in some ways condition the kinds of futures one forecasts and the estimations of probabilities one is able to arrive at. It follows that the choice of method should in turn be conditioned by a dual awareness of the nature of the particular forecast task and purpose and of the particular characteristics and capacities of a range of alternative methods and combinations of methods.

The traditional sharp distinction between trend extrapolation approaches and modeling approaches must then be supplemented by two other distinctions of crucial importance if normative forecasting/ planning is to become a powerful and sensitive strategy for shaping the future: First is the distinction between methods based on a relatively high level of available theory and data and those utilizing verbal models and a greater degree of speculation; second is the distinction between methods based on logical structure and regularity, and those designed to draw out the intuitive insight and the transcendent creativity of the forecaster/planner.

It generally is assumed that high theory/high data approaches are better than those that are less precise and rooted, and that rational methods are better or at least generally more reliable than intuitive ones. However, the overall approach to forecasting/planning developed here suggests a somewhat qualified appraisal of this assessment. There are likely to be important circumstances where the opposite is really true, that is, where verbal models may serve the purpose better than mathematical ones or intuitive approaches may get one much further than logical ones (although, of course, the logic of the intuition may become apparent later). For example, a particular forecasting/planning problem may involve critical values or goals that are inherently not quantifiable or subjectable to mathematical manipulation.[32] Or the methods available may lead to no acceptable solution necessitating a creative effort at transcendence. Even more likely is the situation where close observation and analysis of the workings of rational, sophisticated methods triggers an intuitive insight that results in a new formulation of the whole exercise.

In other words, the forecaster/planner should be as aware as possible of his options and of the consequences, the costs and benefits, of making selections of particular methods or strategies (that is, meta-method). One very useful step in this direction would be the creation of a catalogue of forecasting/planning techniques, methods, and strategies. Each entry should include such information as the following:

Area of primary application: normative, descriptive, speculative, or intuitive
  For what purpose(s): justification, projection, evaluation, probability estimation

Area(s) of secondary application:
  For what purpose(s)

Theory requirements

Data requirements

Underlying assumptions

Distorting effects

Implicit value biases

Best employed:
    For what kinds of problems
    In what time frame(s)
    At what level of analysis
    In conjunction with what other methods

Incompatible or inconsistent with what other methods

Unsuitable for which kinds of problems

Can be used in place of what method(s)
    Under these conditions
    If these limits are recognized

Can be evaluated according to these criteria
    By these methods

The notion of a repertoire of forecasting/planning methods, each with its own strengths, weaknesses, and appropriate applications, suggests three further points about method selection:

1. A single method can be used for different purposes and at different stages in the same or separate forecasting/planning sequences. Thus scenario writing or systems dynamics can be used for both forecasting (descriptive) and planning purposes. Each could be used as a generative procedure or as an evaluative procedure.

2. Sequences or combinations of methods may yield results that exceed the normal capacity of each one operating alone. For example, one might use a scenario-writing technique to create unobvious paths to a preferred alternative future and then use a computer simulation method to test the feasibility (or level of probability) of such a path. That in turn might suggest other ideas to be spun out imaginatively and again tested and so forth.

3. All of the above suggests that there can be no single set of procedures and standards for evaluating the results of forecasting/

planning efforts. Strictly speaking, each step or choice made in the process should be subject to evaluation according to criteria appropriate first to the nature of the particular choice and then to the method chosen. In addition, of course, there should be standards for evaluating a research exercise taken as a whole, the particular standards to be applied depending on the purposes of the exercise, and the overall structure or intellectual character of the effort.

Furthermore, it is at least as important that the forecaster/planner employ sound evaluative procedures at each step in the process as it is that all research reports be independently evaluated. Each evaluative procedure produces the information one needs in order to decide whether to go on to the next step in the forecasting/planning process; whether to repeat the previous step, with which changes in assumptions or method, utilizing which method. In other words, evaluative steps are the keying device for the entire forecasting/planning process.

STEP 4: DISCOVERING AND DESIGNING ALTERNATIVE PREFERRED FUTURES

Here is the heart of the matter. It is here that the tension between feasibility and desirability, so fundamental to the entire forecasting/planning process, is brought to fine-point focus. Tools for selecting, designing, and evaluating alternative preferred futures are underdeveloped and untested.[33] They need to be fashioned from many sources (organizational theory, systems theory, historical sociology, program planning, social psychology, political organizing and mobilization, and so on), applied to a variety of world political issues, and shaped to fit together as a supple methodology.

In short, this phase in the forecasting/planning process is the one most in need of creative conceptualization and experimentation. We are encouraged to find that a few efforts with a world order focus are now under way: the work of Hayward Alker and Nazli Choucri on alternative global energy regimes; Louis Rene Beres and Harry Targ's initiative in drawing together this series of essays on the epistemological and methodological underpinnings of world order design; and, of course, the World Order Models Project of the Institute for World Order, which became available for critical analysis in 1975.[34]

Three issues will receive brief comment here. All arose in the work of the World Order Models Project groups and caused significant difficulties.

First, assuming that one's preferred future is not one of the more likely alternatives forecast, where does one start? The Models Project methodology called first for a relatively detailed model of the preferred future, followed by the construction of a transition strategy for getting from here to there. Typically, such a strategy was thought to involve working back in time from the preferred future through the identification of a sequence of necessary preconditions. Although some also sought to identify contemporary trends supportive of or embodying the preferred future and work them forward, the World Order Models Project approach emphasized rooting transition in the preferred future. In fact, it was often argued that the discipline of searching for ways to realize the preferred model would bring to light opportunities and positive factors that might never be seen if one started from present reality.

Not surprisingly, it now seems that this approach suffers some important deficiencies. An approach that involves systematic working both toward the preferred future and back from it appears difficult to devise, but necessary. The principal problem is that we have no systematic methods for working backward and must therefore rely on essentially speculative and intuitive modes of thinking. Interesting ideas can be produced, but they are sometimes difficult to link into a complete transition picture and they are not easy to evaluate, without employing a more analytical mode of thinking and a systematic method. There is in this approach as well the inherent tendency to overestimate the feasibility and effectiveness of each of the suggested steps. The opposite tendency (to underestimate the likelihood and strength of preferred trends) is the problem with starting from the present. The complex gestalt of the present supports marginal thinking and inhibits creative thinking outside of it.

Robert North and others have suggested to us the technical feasibility and considerable advantages of starting with a dynamic model. [35] Through the systematic manipulation of assumptions and variables, a series of generations of alternative futures can be produced. Once a sequence leading to one's preferred future is identified, it should then be possible to determine what would have to happen and how for each manipulation of a variable or assumption. The result would then be a coherent long-term plan for social change.

Our sense is that there is still some value in starting from the preferred future as well. It could function as a kind of brainstorming session out of which would emerge unusual ideas for the manipulation of variables or the introduction of new factors in the dynamic model. It also would be interesting and potentially useful to run such models backwar, manipulating things until one has a sequence that leads to a model something like the present.

Closely related to the above problem are the questions of how much and what kind of specificity are needed for one's preferred future model. The World Order Models Project assumption in the beginning was that a high degree of specificity, preferably in the form of a constitutional/institutional model, was required. Clearly such a model is needed if one is going to work backward to find a transition path. However, Richard Falk, in his World Order Models Project book, A Study of Future Worlds, now argues forcefully against "premature specificity" and suggests that only a broad normative and structural image is sensible.[36] This would fit very nicely with the evolutionary modeling approach to transition and is more likely to be conducive to creative speculation as well, since one would not be inhibited or misled by an overly concrete and structured model of the future.

Here again, however, an approach that combines the virtues of two opposite methods might prove optimal. We have accordingly suggested in our outline of the forecasting/planning process (on pp. 66-67) an approach that starts with several alternative preferred futures, roughly sketched, and proceeds through a rough assessment of feasibility to the selection of a few alternatives. These are then more carefully analyzed (which involves adding specificity to the model), winnowed, and finally the remaining two or three are subjected to detailed testing of feasibility.

There is a different, often overlooked, dimension to the specificity question. In addition to the test of feasibility, alternative preferred futures should also be subjected to tests of workability. Will they work in social process terms? Would they realize the values attributed to them? Answering these questions obviously does require the degree of specificity needed to simulate the operation of the system in question or otherwise evaluate how it would operate. But what kind of specificity: constitutional/institutional, political process, structural, cybernetic, cultural, or what? We will leave that as a question except to say that constitutional/institutional models would seem to be the least suited to systematic evaluation of workability.

Speculation, intuition, and brainstorming were all mentioned above. Much fuller investigation of their potential role in the forecasting/planning process is now required, for we run the substantial risk that for all our sophisticated methods we will not have solved the fundamental problem, namely, that in the world order area even modestly preferable alternative futures to not appear feasible. Discontinuous futures are by definition, although in varying degrees, breaks from what we know. Genuine insight or creative synthesis is required to see them, to comprehend them, and to communicate them. This is the imaging capacity defined and explored in Fred Polak's Image of the Future. Elise Boulding explains Polak's concept of imaging capacity:

> Social planning, blueprinting, and the technological fix
> are not what Polak had in mind. Social prediction based
> on extrapolation of existing trends or predicted break-
> throughs are not what he meant either . . . The "ideal
> type" of the image of the future has both eschatological
> and utopian elements. The eschatological, or transcend-
> ent, is the element which enables the visionary to break
> the bonds of the cultural present and mentally encompass
> the possibility of a totally other type of society. [37]

Exhorting futures researchers to become more creative is obviously a hollow, if not a futile, crusade. We do what we can do as best we can. Or so we assume. But do we in fact usually do only what we think we can do as best as we think we can? We really do not know very well how to think the unthinkable or how to allow ourselves to think the unthinkable. Are there ways we can learn to enhance our capacity for problem-specific creativity? Are there methods for fostering group and individual creativity?

Recent brain research and explorations in the psychology of consciousness provide a suggestive and encouraging basis for answering these questions, [38] as do research and practice in methods of enhancing individual and group creativity. For instance, the method of brainstorming can be used for group creativity, as can "synectics." [39] Fritz Zwicky sets forth a morphological approach to creativity, a way of seeing parts in terms of wholes. An attempt is made to visualize all interrelations in structural relationships, thus exploring all possible solutions to a problem. [40]

Of course, being more imaginative does not necessarily imply being less realistic. Science fiction writers, who have their imaginations unfettered by institutional constraints, have sometimes painted more accurate portraits of the future than have professional forecasters. [41] More to the point, however, is the fact that the results of any creative or speculative process should be subjected to scrupulous evaluation and testing before being incorporated as significant features of an evolving strategic plan.

STEP 5: DEVELOPING AN OPERATIONAL PLAN

At this stage we move from the general question of feasibility to the detailed concerns of effective implementation or action in the present and short-term future. The problems at this stage are to embody the goals in concrete programs, policies, and patterns of behavior; to assess the physical, political, economic, and social resources required; and to set priorities and sequences for the implementation. This task involves specification of a temporal continuity of actions capable of overcoming the disruptive effects of systemic consequences of any of the actions.[42] In view of the possibility of unanticipated consequences and of disruptions caused by exogenous factors, contingency plans may be formulated insofar as present knowledge allows.

Relevance tree techniques are helpful for formulating operational plans since they are systematic approaches to priority setting, program sequencing, and resource allocation. Relevance tree techniques, which include the Honeywell Corporation's PATTERN and the U.S. Department of Defense's PPBS, have been used extensively by industry and government.[43] Such techniques seek to ascertain which current decisions or other actions are relevant to fairly distant objectives. The first step is to construct a scenario assessing the objectives, activities, missions, and tasks of the system to be forecasted. In the second step, this scenario and other exploratory forecasting methods are utilized to identify and relate relevant primary, secondary, and functional systems and subsystems that are ordered according to level of generality. In the third step, normative criteria are assigned to each level. Criteria are matched with levels by means of a matrix. The fourth step weights each criterion in accord with the degree of emphasis one chooses to place on it, and assigns significance numbers to each item of each level. Thus, "one has a measure, however crude, for deciding how to apportion one's energy, decision-time, budget, material, etc., among the relevant items at each level"[44] (for example, for deciding how much effort should be put into promoting which set of objectives).

Relevance tree techniques have not been used extensively to develop plans of action for the realization of discontinuous futures. They have been used primarily within an establishment context and tend to rely on group assessment and expert opinion techniques for defining appropriate normative criteria and the weightings assigned to each. Expert intuitive judgment is a questionable method of moral evaluation, and we would urge that work be done with these techniques along the lines we suggested in the section of step 2 above. Also, as mentioned earlier, we would like to see an effort made to build into the operational plan greater participation for affected publics and greater openness to nonestablishment procedures and institutions.

CONCLUSION

The function of futures research is not just to reduce uncertainty (with certainty) about what is likely to happen. Its function is also to extend the range of public and elite vision to encompass new alternative futures. Forecasting is pragmatically justified when it becomes reliable enough to improve the quality of societal guidance. Relative to the norm of scientific prediction, forecasting can thus be useful at quite a low level. But pursuit of the goal of scientific prediction typically means that forecasters must restrict themselves to methods that meet the highest standards of science and topics for which an extensive theory and data base have been developed. This set of restrictions severely limits the range and usefulness of world politics forecasting.

While significant advances have been made in the field of international politics and theory-building issues have been the subject of extensive discussion,[45] a rough extrapolation does not indicate to us that a suitable general theory of world politics will be available to forecasters in the next twenty years. It is not clear whether this goal can ever be approximated, and it does not seem sensible to postpone the implementation of research strategies like the one outlined in this essay for the great and urgent problems of the globe in order to put most of the available research resources into the development of high theory. A period in which pragmatic experimentation under perhaps suboptimal conditions receives some support would seem a more balanced and productive approach, especially in light of the increasing urgency and massiveness of certain global problems.

At the same time, it would certainly be desirable to continue to improve the theory and data base that world politics forecasting must utilize. The question is: Which problems do you stress, which developments do you push? It all depends on your goals. Which brings us back to where we started and suggests what we should have known all along. Namely, that each piece of research we do is part of a larger normative forecast and plan related to the societies we live in as well as the fields we work in. So let's begin at the beginning: What are your goals, what are your purposes in engaging in international politics forecasting?

NOTES

1. See Thomas E. Jones and Michael Washburn, "Anchoring Futures in Preferences," in <u>Forecasting and International Relations,</u>

eds. Nazli Choucri and Thomas Robinson (San Francisco: W. H. Freeman, forthcoming), for a detailed discussion of the descriptive-normative distinction. Several other contributions to that book also are worth consulting to see how essentially descriptive techniques can be used in international relations forecasting.

2. See Hasan Ozbekhan, "The Triumph of Technology: 'Can' Implies 'Ought,'" in Planning for Diversity and Choice, ed. Sanford Anderson (Cambridge, Mass.: M.I.T. Press, 1968), for one clear presentation of the linkages between forecasting and planning. Also, Raymond Studer, "Human Systems Design and the Management of Change," General Systems 16 (1971): 131-43; W. G. Bennis, K. D. Benne, and R. Chin, eds., The Planning of Change (New York: Holt, Rinehart & Winston, 1969).

3. F. H. Hinsley, Power and the Pursuit of Peace (Cambridge: Cambridge University Press, 1967); Hanna Newcombe, "Alternative Approaches to World Government," Peace Research Reviews, February 1967; Edith Wyner and Georgia Lloyd, Searchlight on Peace Plans (New York: E. P. Dutton, 1946); Sylvester John Hemleben, Plans for World Peace Through Six Centuries (Chicago: University of Chicago Press, 1943); W. Warren Wagar, The City of Man (Boston: Houghton-Mifflin, 1963).

4. Grenville Clark and Louis Sohn, World Peace Through World Law, 3rd ed. (Cambridge, Mass.: Harvard University Press, 1966); A Constitution for the World, Papers on Peace no. 6 (Santa Barbara, Calif.: Center for the Study of Democratic Institutions, 1965); Elizabeth Mann Borghese, The Ocean Regime (Santa Barbara, Calif.: Center for the Study of Democratic Institutions, 1968).

5. Richard A. Falk, "Reforming World Order: Zones of Consciousness and Domains of Action," in The World System, ed. Ervin Laszlo (New York: George Braziller, 1973), pp. 78, 81, reprinted in this volume as Chapter 9.

6. Rajni Kothari, Footsteps Into the Future (New York: The Free Press, 1975); Saul H. Mendlovitz, On the Creation of a Just World Order (New York: The Free Press, 1975); Ali A. Mazrui, A World Federation of Cultures (New York: The Free Press, 1975); Richard A. Falk, A Study of Future Worlds (New York: The Free Press, 1975); Johan Galtung, The True Worlds: A Transnational Perspective (New York: The Free Press, forthcoming); Ali A. Mazrui and Hasu H. Patel, eds., Africa in World Affairs (New York: The Third Press, 1973); Jagdish N. Bhagwati, ed., Economics and World Order (New York: Macmillan, 1972).

7. See Jones and Washburn, "Anchoring Futures in Preferences," pp. 7-11 for an outline of this argument and citation of several examples from the international relations literature.

8. Ozbekhan, "The Triumph of Technology," pp. 212-13.

9. Ibid., p. 213.

10. Ibid., p. 214.

11. Wendell Bell, James Mau, Bettina Huber, and Menno Boldt, "A Paradigm for the Analysis of Time Perspectives and Images of the Future," in The Sociology of the Future, eds. Wendell Bell and James Mau (New York: Russell Sage Foundation, 1971), pp. 44-55.

12. David C. Miller and Ronald L. Hunt, Futures Studies and Research Curriculum Guide, an ADVENT publication (San Francisco: DCM Associates, 1973).

13. See, for example, Marcia Guttentag and Yutaka Sayeki, "A Decision Theoretic Technique for the Illumination of Cultural Differences," mimeo.

14. See, for example, William Eckhardt, Compassion (Oakville, Ontario: Canadian Peace Research Institute, 1972), and "Research and Education As Approaches to Peace and Justice," Peace Research Reviews 4, no. 4 (February 1972).

15. Louis Kohlberg, "Education for Justice: A Modern Statement of the Platonic View," Ernest Burton Lecture on Moral Education, Harvard University, April 1968.

16. Pauline B. Bart, "The Myth of Value-Free Psychotherapy," in The Sociology of the Future, eds. Bell and Mau.

17. See Davis Bobrow, "Transitions to Preferred World Futures: Some Design Considerations," Chapter 5 in this volume, for an excellent discussion of decision rules.

18. Nicholas Rescher, "What Is Value Change?" in Values and the Future, eds. Kurt Baier and Nicholas Rescher (New York: The Free Press, 1969); Irene Taviss, "Futurology and the Problem of Values," International Social Science Journal (UNESCO) 21, no. 4 (1969); Milton Rokeach, The Study of Human Values (New York: The Free Press, 1973); Benjamin Nelson, "Scholastic Rationales of 'Conscience,' Early Modern Crises of Credibility, and the Scientific-Technocultural Revolutions of the 17th and 20th Centuries," Journal of the Scientific Study of Religion, 1968, pp. 157-77.

19. Raymond A. Bauer, ed., Social Indicators (Cambridge, Mass.: M.I.T. Press, 1966); Galtung, "Appendix on Social Indicators"; Peter Henriot, "Political Implications of Social Indicators," paper presented at 1971 annual meeting of the American Political Science Association; Peter Henriot, "Political Questions About Social Indicators," Western Political Quarterly 23 (June 1970): 235-55; J. David Singer, "Individual Values, National Interests, and Political Development in the International System," Studies in Comparative Social Development 4, no. 9 (1970-71); O. W. Markley, Alternative Futures: Contexts in Which Social Indicators Must Work (Menlo Park, Calif.: Educational Policy Research Center, Stanford Research Institute, 1970).

20. In the parlance of moral philosophy, to deduce prescriptive conclusions from purely descriptive premises is to commit the "naturalistic fallacy." To make the deduction valid, a prescriptive premise must be supplied, but such an assumption of what is to be proved amounts to begging the question. Although the relation between purely descriptive premises and a prescriptive conclusion is not one of logical deduction, empirical facts are by no means irrelevant to prescriptive conclusions. The "good reasons approach" can be used to make justifiable inferences.

21. See Mary Warnock, Ethics Since 1900 (London: Oxford University Press, 1960).

22. Among other moral philosophers who advocate the good reasons approach are Englishmen S. E. Toulmin, P. H. Nowell-Smith, and J. O. Urmson, and Americans Morton White and H. D. Aiken. Of special interest are the following works: William K. Frankena, Ethics (Englewood Cliffs, N.J.: Prentice-Hall, 1963); Richard C. Brandt, Ethical Theory (Englewood Cliffs, N.J.: Prentice-Hall, 1959); John Rawls, A Theory of Justice (Cambridge, Mass.: Harvard University Press, 1971); John Rawls, "Outline of a Decision Procedure for Ethics," Philosophical Review 60 (1951): 177-97; Kurt Baier, The Moral Point of View (Ithaca, N.Y.: Cornell University Press, 1958); S. E. Toulmin, An Examination of the Place of Reason in Ethics (London: Cambridge University Press, 1960); P. H. Nowell-Smith, Ethics (Baltimore: Penguin Books, 1954); Morton White, Toward Reunion in Philosophy (Cambridge, Mass.: Harvard University Press, 1950).

23. Brandt, Ethical Theory, Chapter 10, especially pp. 249-51.

24. Ibid., pp. 251-64. For a critique of ethical relativism, see Chapter 11, pp. 271-94.

25. Frankena, Ethics, p. 19.

26. Ibid., p. 92.

27. Ibid., p. 96.

28. Gerald Feinberg, The Prometheus Project (Garden City, N.Y.: Doubleday, 1969), pp. 222 ff.

29. Alvin Toffler, Future Shock (New York: Random House, 1971), Chapter 18, "Education in the Future Tense"; "Value Impact Forecaster: A Profession of the Future," in Values and the Future, eds. Baier and Rescher.

30. Herman Kahn and Anthony J. Wiener, The Year 2000 (New York: Macmillan, 1967); Herman Kahn and B. Bruce-Briggs Things to Come (New York: Macmillan, 1972); Zbigniew Brzezinski, "America in the Technetronic Age," Commentary, 1968, and Between Two Ages (New York: Viking Press, 1970); Willis Harmon, Alternative Futures for Educational Policy (Menlo Park, Calif.: Educational Policy Research Center, Stanford Research Institute, 1970); Richard A.

Falk, This Endangered Planet (New York: Random House, 1971); Donella Meadows et al., The Limits of Growth (New York: Universe Books, 1972); Jay W. Forrester, World Dynamics (Cambridge, Mass.: Wright-Allen Press, 1971).

31. Robert Boyd, "World Dynamics: A Note," Science, August 1972, pp. 516-19.

32. Lawrence Tribe, "Policy Science: Analysis or Ideology?" Philosophy and Public Affairs 2, no. 1 (Fall 1972).

33. In addition to the selections in this book, the following are some available sources of interesting thoughts on social design: Bell and Mau, eds., The Sociology of the Future; Anderson, ed., Planning for Diversity and Choice; Bennis, Benne, and Chin, eds., The Planning of Change; Hayward Alker, "Methodological Implications of Interdependence Controversies," paper for delivery before International Studies Association, March 21, 1974; Dennis Pirages and Paul Ehrlich, Arc II (New York and San Francisco: Viking Press and W. H. Freeman, 1974).

34. See note 6 above. On this point, see especially the general introduction to the series by Saul H. Mendlovitz, contained in the Kothari, Mendlovitz, Mazrui, Falk and Galtung volumes.

35. In private conversations, October 1974, at M.I.T./Institute for World Order Conference on Forecasting and International Relations.

36. Richard A. Falk, The Study of Future Worlds (New York: Free Press, 1975), Chapter 3, Section 1.2.

37. Elise Boulding, "Futurology and the Imaging Capacity of the West," preconference volume, 1970 American Anthropological Association, Cultural Futurology Symposium. Also see Fred Polak, The Image of the Future (Amsterdam: Elsevier, 1973); Robert Jungk, "Imagination and Future," International Social Science Journal 21, no. 4 (1969): 557; Robert Jungk, "The Role of Imagination in Future Research," in Challenges from the Future (Tokyo: Kodansha, 1970).

38. See Robert Ornstein, The Psychology of Consciousness (New York and San Francisco: Viking Press and W. H. Freeman, 1972).

39. For example, William J. J. Gordon, Synectics (New York: Collier Books, 1961); George M. Prince, The Practice of Creativity (New York: Harper and Row, 1970).

40. Fritz Zwicky, Discovery, Invention, Research (New York: Macmillan, 1969).

41. Charles Hampden-Turner, Radical Man (Cambridge: Schenkman, 1970), p. 340; Dennis Livingston, "Science Fiction Models of Future World Systems," International Organization, spring 1971; Lyman Tower Sargent, "Images of the Future in Science Fiction," paper for delivery at 1974 annual meeting of the American Political Science Association.

42. Ozbekhan, The Triumph of Technology, p. 216.

43. See discussion in Thomas W. Robinson, "On Using Several Methods of Technological Forecasting in International Relations," in Choucri and Robinson, Forecasting and International Relations, Chapter 16.

44. Ibid.

45. See, for example, Raymond Tanter and Richard Ullman, eds., Theory and Policy in International Relations, a special issue of World Politics (Princeton, N.J.: Princeton University Press) 24 (1972), especially the articles by Oran Young and Davis Bobrow; Klauss Knorr and James Rosenau, Contending Approaches to International Politics (Princeton, N.J.: Princeton University Press, 1969); Karl Deutsch, "Experiments and Political Theory" in Experimentation and Simulation in Political Science, eds. J. A. Laponce and Paul Smoker (Toronto: Toronto University Press, 1972).

5

TRANSITIONS TO PREFERRED WORLD FUTURES: SOME DESIGN CONSIDERATIONS
Davis B. Bobrow

The modest intent of this essay is to suggest some considerations and a direction of work to lessen our embarrassment as international relations analysts when someone asks us, "Well, if you don't like the way the world seems to be headed, what do you recommend to change its direction to one you like?" The work recommended consists of developing a strategy of design to help us devise "courses of action aimed at changing existing situations into preferred ones."[1]

Our exploration is in four parts: (1) what a design perspective involves and why it is needed; (2) general lessons suggested by the World Order Models Project; (3) pertinent ideas and findings from other areas of work; (4) a summary and some suggested next steps.

───────────

Earlier versions of parts of this paper were presented at a World Order Studies Workshop, East-West Center, Honolulu, July 1972; at the meetings of the International Political Science Association, Montreal, August 1973; and at those of the American Political Science Association, New York, September 1969. Financial support at various stages was provided by the National Science Foundation (Grant GI-3944), the Institute for World Order, and the World Order Studies program of the University of Minnesota. Mitchell Joelson provided helpful research assistance and especially helpful suggestions and encouragement have been provided by Robert Kudrle, Robert North, and Michael Washburn. Substantial portions of this paper appear in "An R & D Strategy to Produce Desirable and Feasible Public Policy for Technology-Related International Problems," Occasional Paper no. 4 (Pittsburgh: International Studies Association, 1974). The author and editors are grateful to ISA for offering its permission to use these portions for this piece.

PERSPECTIVE AND ASSESSMENT

Familiar Approaches

Common responses to requests for recommended transition strategies tend to be of three kinds. The first, descriptive utopianism, consists of statements of the form "The desired world will have properties $X_1 \ldots X_n$." The statements may deal with states of affairs (such as economic distributions), decision structures (such as a world parliament), and decision rules (such as taxing the rich to aid the poor). Descriptive utopian responses lack a transition strategy and do not face the issue of empirical support for the feasibility of the utopia working as asserted. Just as the Sears Roebuck catalogue used to be, they are "wish-books." (Parenthetically, one may accept the statements just made and still attribute consciousness-raising usefulness to descriptive utopianism.)

A second common response, negative prescription, offers statements of the form, "To attain the desired world, we must eliminate attributes $X_1 \ldots X_n$ of the world as it is and appears to be developing." The attributes earmarked for elimination may once again involve states of affairs (such as resource consumption), decision structures (such as the nation-state), and decision rules (such as assured destruction). Negative prescriptions provide at best only the middle stage of transition strategy. They do not stipulate appropriate antecedent and consequent developments. More baldly, they do not tell us how to act to eliminate the unwanted attributes or, if successful, how to go on to secure those properties we want the world to have. Again, one may accept this view of negative prescriptions and still grant them some value as warnings and partial agendas for design, but not as designs of transition.

Before we discuss a third type of response, we can usefully note that one cannot adequately compensate for the weakness of the negative prescription or descriptive utopian approaches simply by combining them. Antecedent requirements are still relatively ignored, as are causal process connections between the attributes to be eliminated and those to take their place.

The third customary response tries to provide such causal connections through macromodeling. It typically begins with a formal model that links the values of highly aggregated attributes of the international system (and its component elements) to outcome variables represented in the criteria used to judge alternative world futures. The attributes used may vary from economic to attitudinal. Using historical or simulation data, the analysts establish a particular relationship between the values of the aggregated attributes and those that result on the criteria variables. One then can calculate the sensitivity of future world outcomes to different attributes' values. And, once one specifies the desired criteria variable positions, the analyst can prescribe the needed aggregate attribute value.

As a strategy of design, macromodeling seems more satisfactory than the two types discussed previously. Yet it has two major inherent weaknesses, and often a third. First, it does not deal with the design of a transition strategy that tells us how to achieve the desired aggregate attributes. It simply tells us that we need one and provides an incentive for its creation and implementation. Second, it usually assumes a stable relationship between the aggregate attributes and the criteria variables. Yet the aggregate attributes desired may differ sufficiently from those found historically to make a stability assumption unwarranted. And when a simulation to explore unexperienced futures freezes the relationships in its computer program or rules of play, instability is suppressed. Even if these problems are avoided, the stability assumption only holds when the transition steps necessary to achieve the desired aggregate attribute value do not have massive direct or indirect effects that fracture previous relationships. One must believe that feasible and probable transition strategies operate in ways that insulate or buffer the relationships one wishes to preserve. We should note a contingent shortcoming: indeterminacy. Analysis may show that numerous alternative combinations of aggregate attribute values yield a similar set of outcomes on the criteria variables. Alternatively, we may find only weak, if statistically significant, relationships between aggregate attribute values and criteria variables. We conclude that macromodeling approaches are desirable but insufficient in themselves.

One makes less of the inadequacies we have attributed to descriptive utopianism, negative prescription, and macromodeling if one believes that factors external to the design will provide the missing pieces. That assumption seems to be unwarranted. Most political leaders do not know how to achieve their goals for their own polity. Most public policies do not realize their stated objectives. Most public executives do not know the de facto decision rules that they and their organizations follow. Most public institutions do not maintain their devotion to their initial raison d'etre. Most political operatives primarily secure information found to be important, positively or negatively, in the past. Changes in information demand, and thus supply, tend to come after rather than before substantial environmental changes.

A Design Approach

The design approach seeks to produce a blueprint that, if followed, results in an outcome selected in advance. It involves three types of statements: performance goals; operational requirements for their realization; and action instructions to meet the requirements. Statements of each type carry time subscripts.

For world futures, performance goal statements stipulate that the world will have attributes $A_1 \ldots A_n$ during the period $t + x$ through $t + y$. A more complex design will stipulate intermediate performance goals in time, such as $0.5 A_1$ by $t + 3$. The designer sets the aspiration level by means of an explicit matrix of performance goals (i) by time points (j). Success occurs when the implemented blueprint produces results identical with those in the performance goal matrix. A formal rule of success may attach equal or different weights to each cell in the goal matrix. These weights should be derived with due recognition of germane discontinuities and nonlinearities.

As this statement implies, consensus on performance goals exists only when there is agreement on the attribute and time structure of the matrix; the values in each cell; and the formal success rule. Obviously, prespecification of the success rule provides the designer with policy guidance as to time phasing and goal tradeoffs. A bit less obviously, the designer also benefits when he has a specification of nonconsensual performance goals in the comparative terms that the matrix and alternative formal success rules can provide. Alternative designs can be relevant to the different decision makers involved.

Operational requirement statements state the necessary and sufficient conditions to achieve the goals identified by the time points stipulated. They also state the conditions necessary and sufficient for those goals to be met throughout the time range previously chosen. For any given cell in the performance goal matrix, the designer wishes to specify a function of the form $A_{i,j} = f(R_1 \ldots R_n)$. Since goals are specified in time, requirements also must be, with due consideration for the leads and lags between diverse requirements and their impact on the goal attributes. For complex problems of collective action, requirement sets usually will involve states of affairs, decision structures, and decision rules. A formal rule of success for requirement statements is that they deterministically produce $A_{i,j}$. A more helpful rule is that they are successful as the probability of $A_{i,j}$ approaches 1.

The discussion of requirement statements to this point has dealt with the simplest case, that in which the causal process for any particular $A_{i,j}$ is independent from that for any other. In this case the problem of compatible requirements does not arise. More probably, some of the requirements for several cells in the goal matrix are incompatible; for example, a requirement for centralization and one for decentralization. The prospect that the results from attempts to work out requirement specifications for each cell in the goal matrix will at least surface incompatibilities gives them value for the serious designer. If the designer has a weighted success rule for performance goals, he has a criterion for what must give in cases of incompatibility.

Interdependence among the cells in the goal matrix need not take the form of incompatibility. It may take that of precedence; that is, a necessary condition for a particular $A_{i,j}$ may be prior attainment of some other $A_{i,j}$. The success of a particular set of requirement statements depends on the success of the set of statements for the prior $A_{i,j}$. Failure to recognize the importance of such contingent probabilities can lead to false estimates of the success of a requirements exercise. If it is recognized, the designer's priorities for the development of requirement statements are clarified. Also, he is more likely to work in a way that will indicate promptly whether the initial goal matrix and success rule require modification.

One may find the necessary and sufficient causal process embodied in requirement statements sufficiently unattainable to turn away from the design of world futures altogether. The future is too hazy, the interdependencies too complex, the frequency and importance of untrended change too great. This reaction seems warranted if requirement statements must embody completely preprogrammed decisions, that is, eliminate decision making. However, we do not have to commit ourselves to that extent. Instead, we may include in our requirement statements decision structures that apply their decision rules to updated information.

We accept the wisdom of multiple-step transition strategies. We admit that we are much clearer about initial steps and performance goals than about intervening situations and specific actions appropriate to them. The more certain we are about the nature of future uncertainties, the more attractive and important it clearly becomes to require decision competence that can adapt to those uncertainties. Accordingly, an important consideration in evaluating how well a designer deals with the requirements for attaining goals involves the statements he makes about needed decision competence.

Action instruction statements, the third major element of the design approach, stipulate what to do in order to realize the requirements. Since the requirement statements carry time terms, action instructions must do so. Just as requirement statements provide the necessary and sufficient conditions to realize performance goals, action instructions provide the necessary and sufficient conditions to realize requirements. Requirement statements tell us what states of affairs, decision structures, and decision rules our preferred futures call for. Action instructions tell us how to achieve those states of affairs, decision structures, and decision rules. Accordingly, they treat factors that relevant actors can manipulate as directed. And that is a far more stringent condition than if action instructions could deal with factors that were manipulable in principle but not in practice by existing actors in existing situations. Action instructions tell existing institutions and groups (which can be dissident or minority actors) what to do out of the set of things that they can do in the specified time period.

This stricture does not condemn world future designs to marginal degrees of change. When the design calls for a chain of transition steps, some of the early steps can seek to change the set of factors that are manipulable by existing actors or the distribution of leverage. The latter strategy can include creating new actors.

A third important aspect of action instructions involves willingness or at least compliance. The action instructions in a world future design remain interesting collector's items unless people implement them. The instructions must give guidance that actors have sufficient incentives to carry out. Of course, the early steps in a transition strategy can involve creating appropriate incentives as well as appropriate capabilities.

Let us review the action instruction component of a world future design. First, the designer must provide a process that will cause requirements to be met by the times specified. Second, that process must be specified to the point of identifiable actions assigned to specific actors. Third, those actions must be within the capability of the designated actor—accordingly, the designer needs to have in hand a capability profile of the relevant actor(s). Fourth, those actions must be sufficiently compatible with the interests of the actor(s) to be followed—accordingly, the designer needs to have in hand a description of each actor's utility structure.

Obviously, the designer must engage in an iterative process to arrive at a set of action instructions that provide the needed causal impetus and still lie within capability and utility constraints. If no set of necessary and sufficient actions falls within existing constraints, the designer must formulate action instructions that will relax the constraints in appropriate ways. When the designer cannot do so, his overall design lacks feasibility. When he can do so, he must take into account the time needed to alter capability and utility constraints and modify requirement statements and the performance goal matrix. Accordingly, the designer cannot tolerate the luxury of assuming that desired capabilities and utilities are present. Design starts with whatever ones characterize the period and context within which the first steps of the transition strategy are to be acted on.

The problems of compatibility and precedence discussed with reference to requirements also are germane to action instructions, and much of that earlier discussion applies here. Feasibility concerns make it particularly important to face compatibility and precedence problems for the capabilities and utilities of the set of relevant actors. Accordingly, the designer must not stop with a set of designs arrived at by treating problems serially. He needs to consider the suitability of his design elements when they are operating simultaneously. Confronted by substantial uncertainty, the designer may find it wise and necessary to adopt the strategy called for in our discussion of requirements. That is, he may resort to designing decision structures and rules that will lead to the choice and implementation of the most appropriate action for the environment that prevails at the point of choice. In doing so, he acts in the spirit of the design approach when several concerns prevail. The first is to provide the decision structure not only with certain capabilities but also with a certain utility matrix. The second is to deal with the transition between existing decision structures and ones with appropriate capabilities and utilities.

LESSONS FROM THE WORLD ORDER MODELS PROJECT

A particularly impressive and creative recent attempt to state and formulate ways to achieve preferred world futures has been the World Order Models Project (WOMP), involving teams drawn from Japan, India, West Germany, the Soviet Union, Africa, Latin America, the United States, and, to provide a nonterritorial perspective, Norway. I do not intend to provide a detailed critique or comprehensive assessment of their work.* My limited concern with WOMP in this context centers on how well it follows the design approach suggested in the preceding section and the implications of the aspects in which it does not for the design of preferred world futures. All of the teams agreed to take the matrix shown in Figure 5.1 as an orienting framework.

---

*Not all of the products are available; others are available in other than final form. The manuscripts are extremely varied in many senses. However, given the importance of the effort and the attention its results have and will receive, some general comments are in order. No doubt any particular comment is not adequate for some part of some team's report. I do believe that, as a general characterization, what follows is accurate and fair.

FIGURE 5.1

Matrix for the Study of World Order:

World Values with Minimal-Maximum Range

Inter-actor violence: Minimization of violence to prevention of violence.

Economic welfare: Creation of tolerable conditions to maintenance of prosperity.

Social justice: Creation of tolerable conditions to maintenance of human dignity.

World ecological balance: Restoration of balance to preservation of balance.

Participation: Positive self-identity to active involvement in achievement of a preferred world system.

Achievement scale: 1 (low) – 5 (high)

Substantive Dimensions → (processes)	Arms Policy	Peace-keeping	Conflict Resolution	Economic Welfare	Technological and Scientific Revolution	Environment	Social Justice
Dimension Elements →							
World Actors (Structures)* Year							
World 1970 1980 1990 2000							
International 1970 1980 1990 2000							
Regional 1970 1980 1990 2000							
Transnational 1970 1980 1990 2000							
Nation-state 1970 1980 1990 2000							
Infranational 1970 1980 1990 2000							
Individual 1970 1980 1990 2000							

*Social movements, institutions, organizations.

100

Each team was supposed to accept the basic values, although they could weight them differently. They were to complete the matrix by doing the following. First, they were to envision and describe a relevant utopia, that is, a world system capable of achieving at least minimum levels of satisfaction on the basic values should it exist in 1990-2000. Utopias were relevant if developed in sufficient detail for a reader to make a reasonable judgment about the probability of the model coming to pass and yielding the desired benefits. The matrix seems to provide many of the same features of attributes to be achieved by time points that we called for with regard to performance goals. It does not indicate through what time period the goals are to be sustained, or establish consensus on cell values or on a success rule. Indeed, it may not specify the performance matrix for each of the world value attributes sufficiently to insure compatibility of goal structure across teams.

The teams' second task was to determine the requirements for a relevant utopia based on an analysis of current world problems and their trends. What are supporting trends to build on and negative trends and situations to overcome? Also, the teams were to pay special attention to the authoritative institutions required for the utopias to work as intended. Again, we find a general similarity with the design approach in this emphasis on requirement statements. The concern with authoritative institutions seems to pick up the elements of decision structures and decision rules, and that with trends to involve states of affairs. We can anticipate that the requirements task will be particularly difficult given the underspecification of the performance goal matrix. Also, the diversity and number of goals and the levels of analysis that make up the rows in the world order matrix imply that the designer must be especially alert for problems of compatibility and precedence among requirements. In no area does this seem more called for than in the temporal and causal interdependence between environmental states of affairs ("trends" in the language of the charge to the teams) and decision structures ("institutions").

Third, the teams were to devise a transition process to reach at least one of the relevant utopias that seemed desirable to them, and to formulate a transition strategy that could actually make the posited transition process take place. Again, we see a similarity between our discussion and the guidance to the WOMP teams, that is, action instructions. Obviously, the ability of the teams to succeed in this third task depends on results from the first two—in particular, the attribute clarity, time-specific compatibility, and precedence established.

To introduce a discussion of lessons from the WOMP experience, we note some specific attributes of the world of 2000 that the organizers expected (and dreaded) would occur unless prevented by purposeful action. With 1950 as a base year, carbon monoxide in the atmosphere will be 15 percent higher in 2000. From a level of 3.3 billion in 1973, population will rise to about 5.8 billion in 2000. From the 1963 level of $100 billion, armament expenditures will reach over $300 billion by 2000. The economic disparity between the 20 to 25 richest nations in the world and the others will shift from the per capita income ratio of 12-14:1 in the early 1970s to a ratio of 20:1 in 2000. Accordingly, from a technical perspective the WOMP teams could have had a formal success rule at least for the end year (2000), which would be the disparity between the cell values and those initially expected. Also, from a technical point of view, they could have had a rather specified set of performance attributes to deal with through the time columns of a performance goal matrix.

In practice, WOMP did not operate from a specified set of performance attributes, consensus on the cell values in a performance-goals-by-time matrix, or consensus on an operational success rule. The WOMP authors then came to face very substantial difficulties with requirements and action instructions.

In the WOMP papers, the treatment of trends and suggestion of institutions seek to fill the role in design that we assign to requirements. However, two major elements are absent. The first involves timing. When must trends be affected or new institutions made operational to have the desired effects by 1990? The numerous requirements posed by leads and lags in cause and effect processes are slighted partly because temporal leads and lags are unspecified.

The second missing element is that of decision rules to operate in institutions. Voting and representation schemes are not equivalent to decision rules as we use the phrase. A decision rule is a contingent instruction to pursue one or another policy line. Without decision rules of some directive sort, there is no very good reason to think that institutions will operate on trends in a desired and timely fashion. Voting rules indicate the coalition needed to make a choice but not what the rationale for choice should be; representation schemes determine who gets involved in the making of a choice but not what rationale they should use to arrive at a preference. Preferences as to decision rules—for example, on economic distribution or conflict resolution—should drive the selection of voting or representation schemes. If one is concerned with global outcomes, then factional representation and mass participation in the selection of representatives are not sufficient requirements. Several others quickly come to mind. One is that factional priorities, that is, the analogue of local or special group interests, become transformed at least in the vote aggregation process into collective welfare priorities. And with mass electoral systems, this means that the masses support representatives with such priorities. Shortfalls from this requirement clearly lengthen the time required for the new institutions to take nonincremental global actions.

The democratic/populist perspective that many of the WOMP participants share imposes on them the responsibility to address the decision
rules of mass populations as well as of the new global institutions.
Yet they barely address what those decision rules should be.

Timing and decision rules matter crucially even if the WOMP
designers are concerned with the requirements for only one world
order value. Since they are concerned with the requirements for all
five values, the relative omission of these considerations raises
doubts about the quality of their designs in general. Lack of attention
to timing implies lack of attention to the precedence of some requirements for some goals over others. The need to resolve precedence
issues is not met by the expedient of establishing one condition as a
precedent for all others with the timing of the others undifferentiated.
The timing issue becomes critical if one agrees with the authors that
trends are moving adversely with great force and speed and that very
different institutions must be devised to cope with these evils. Obviously, the capacity such institutions need to cope is a function of when
they get to work on the undesirable trends.

The absence of decision rules is particularly serious because
the requirements for different world order goals may well be incompatible. The failure to confront incompatibilities tends to make the
discussion of trends and institutions less one of requirements for
goals than one of utopian description. At only a modest risk of undue
caricature, it is as if many of the authors believe that "right-thinking
people" will not confront value dilemmas. What experience supports
the view that massive redirection of social systems—which is what
they want—can simultaneously optimize on peace, social justice,
political participation, economic welfare, and environmental quality?

In discussing the treatment of requirements in WOMP, we have
concentrated on the problems of timing, decision rules, and compatibility. Three more general points seem important to note before we
turn to action instruction or, in WOMP terminology, transition strategies. First, relatively little attention is paid to matters of the supply
of relevant commodities (such as wheat, oil, or missiles) other than
to point to inequitable distribution. Yet it is clear that absolute shortages of life-sustaining commodities pose one set of requirements for
attaining the world order goals, while maldistribution-based shortages
pose another. Clearly, world goals require some demand-supply
relationship, and under different conditions of damped demand or
increased supply the requirements call for different measures. And
supply is dependent on technology and economic incentives. Yet considerations of technology and economic incentives receive little
attention.

Second, relatively little attention is paid to administration and
program implementation. The new institutions are discussed mainly

in legislative, judicial, and high-level policy-setting terms. Yet we all know that even the most well-conceived policies depend for impact on how they are carried out. What are the required delivery systems for the achievement of world order goals? Perhaps the relative lack of discussion of administrative infrastructure reflects more general habits in the academic discussion of public policy. However, it may also result from the relative inattention to the maintainability of world order goals and institutions. There is little discussion about how to insure that the goals will not be lost if attained and that the institutions will continue to work as envisioned.

Third, the WOMP participants apparently did not agree to reassess performance goals after exploring requirements. Obviously, the vaguer the requirement statements (especially in terms of timing), decision rules, and compatibility, the less pressure exists to do so and the more difficult it becomes. However, to the extent that requirements are deemed unlikely to be achieved, goals should be modified as design ends.

Modification is only one reason for reassessment. Another is to determine the grasp one has on the requirements for a given goal. How much confidence does one have that, by meeting the stipulated requirements, the probability of the performance goals approaches one? If the answer is not very much, the designer sees the need to do more work on stipulating requirements. Even if the designer believes that no more can be said at present to improve the determinacy yielded by the requirements, a benefit still results if there is more confidence with respect to some goals than to others. The payoff from work on transition strategies or action instructions seems more assured when the requirement statements are compelling in terms of the goal than when they are inconclusive. Obviously, if the requirements are apparently out of the question there is little point in working on transition strategies. In instances where WOMP participants did not reassess performance goals in the light of requirement statements, they in effect deprived themselves of help in wisely allocating their remaining energies to transition strategies.

We can now turn to the treatment of transition strategies. What are the general lessons suggested by the work on this aspect of world futures design by the WOMP participants? As implied earlier, the hierarchical nature of design as we conceive of it calls on the designer to become increasingly detailed as he or she moves from goals to requirements to action instructions, and to become increasingly constrained by the existing situation.

First, because of weaknesses in the earlier elements in the world order designs, a clear framework was not provided for guiding work on transition strategies. There was insufficient clarity about what must be accomplished by when, what second-order effects should be accepted or avoided, and what resources must be developed.

Second, a curious anomaly tended to pervade the treatment of current establishment actors. On the one hand, they were perceived as extremely powerful, often actively malevolent, and at best passively hostile to world order goals. Yet the transition strategies suggested rarely were drafted to show how the deliberate opposition of the entrenched "haves" to efforts at change would be dealt with. One sees more rhetorical than pragmatic attention to the problems of opposition. Yet a transition strategy prescription really is a set of statements of the form: If certain actors take the steps specified and if the consequences of those actions are not nullified by others, then a requirement for a world order goal will be realized.

Third, many of the WOMP papers do not relate their transition strategy instructions to particular implementing actors. At best, they tend to relate them to broad demographic groups. Until actions or transition steps are tied to particular actors, designers cannot assess the extent to which they fit with the capacities or utilities of those actors. The WOMP manuscripts as a whole are characterized by very slight treatment of the capacity or utility profiles of relevant actors as they exist or may be extrapolated to exist. Associated with this weakness is the omission of the whole matter of incentives for actions different from those now taken. To be more precise, the problems of incentives for transition are simply not handled adequately by positing an alternative world future in which those incentives exist. The problem is how to locate incentives in the current world to produce the actions necessary to move toward the preferred world.

Fourth, the transition strategies suggested often do not show tactical sensitivity to multiplier effects. To illustrate with an outstanding exception, if the point of population control is to lessen demand for and consumption of scarce resources, priority should go to limiting the sections of the global population that are disproportionately heavy consumers. This sort of discriminating transition step also differs from general recommendations (such as: limit population) in that it is associated with certain actors more than others. Suggested multipliers provide focus for an examination of capacities and utilities. In contrast to transition strategies that have as their first step semi-universal value changes, some multiplier suggestions can in principle be implemented by existing institutions and persons without their accepting world order values.

Finally, just as we see little general agreement on a strategy to review goals in the light of work on requirements, we see no common policy on reassessing requirements in the light of work on transition strategies. From a design point of view, we may be left with an unrealistic residue of requirements and thus of goals. Also, the paucity of reassessment obscures the extent to which the transition strategy will suffice to attain the requirements in timely fashion.

The comments on WOMP from a design point of view may seem unduly harsh and negative. That is not their intent. The most appropriate acknowledgment of the commitment and creativity of the WOMP participants is to build on their experience in order to advance beyond their accomplishments.

SOME RULES OF THUMB FOR WORLD FUTURES DESIGN

Up to this point we have concerned ourselves with some general criteria for a design activity and an appraisal of the WOMP effort in that light. This section deals with some considerations or rules of thumb to help us meet the criteria and to design world futures and transitions to them. The diagram of the design problem in Figure 5.2 provides a useful orientation.

The design problem is to achieve a particular international outcome or set of outcomes by a particular time(s). The outcome achieved depends on the previous state(s) of the international environment element as operated on by stimuli from the implementation element. These stimuli or actions are the product of program specification and resource consumption and release decisions made within the implementation element. Such decisions are in turn a function of the previous state(s) of the implementation element as operated on by program guidance and resource allocations from the policy element. These policy element inputs are the product of the treatment goals, issues, and alternatives within the policy element. To continue working backward, such treatments are a function of the previous state(s) of the policy element as operated on by estimates from the assessment element. These estimates result from the previous state(s) of the assessment element as operated on by additional information about the implementation and international environment elements. All the elements are analytic rather than concrete entities. That is, in the real world they may not be distinct, identifiable organizations.

The utopian designer's problem is to devise a complex of assessment, policy system, and implementation elements that, given some international structures and processes, will produce the desired international outcome(s). The pragmatic designer's problem includes the need for such invention but adds other tasks. Most important, he also must devise a strategy that will induce the existing actors in policy, implementation, and assessment elements to accept the changes

FIGURE 5.2

The Design Problem

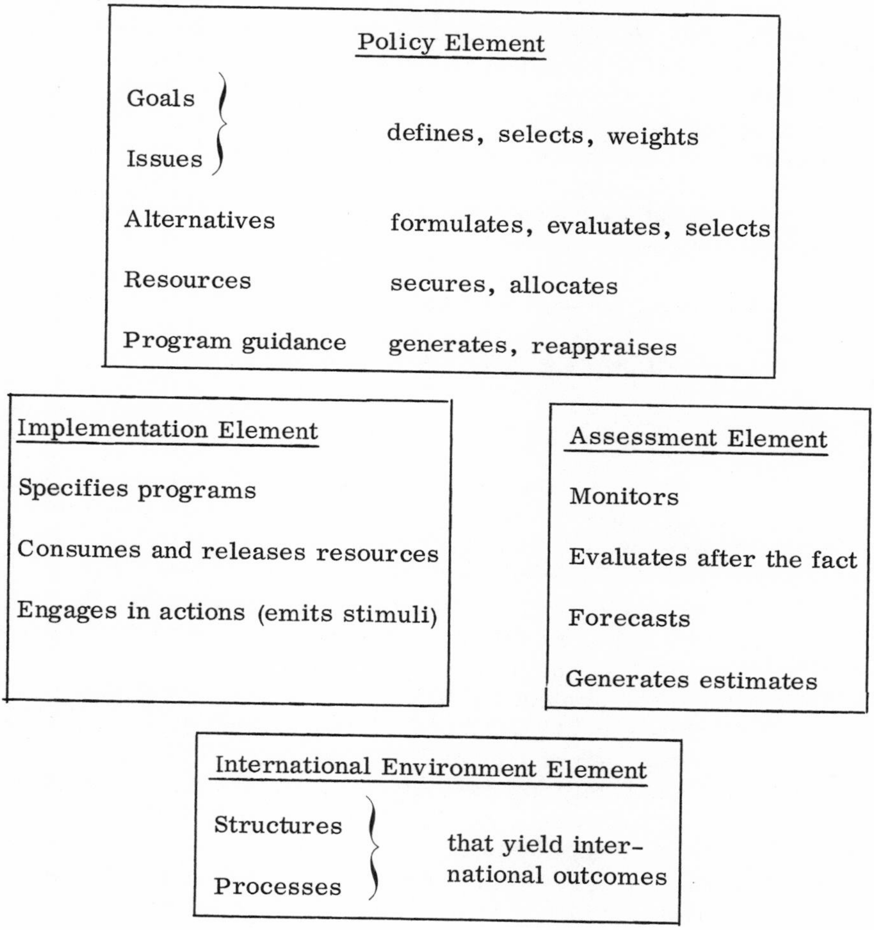

Policy Element

Goals $\left.\right\}$ defines, selects, weights
Issues $\left.\right\}$

Alternatives   formulates, evaluates, selects

Resources   secures, allocates

Program guidance   generates, reappraises

Implementation Element

Specifies programs

Consumes and releases resources

Engages in actions (emits stimuli)

Assessment Element

Monitors

Evaluates after the fact

Forecasts

Generates estimates

International Environment Element

Structures $\left.\right\}$ that yield inter-
Processes $\left.\right\}$ national outcomes

called for. We will refer to this need as the requirement for a transition strategy. We are assuming that the designer does not have the authority to force compliance with his design but must provide a transition program acceptable to those actors relevant to particular steps.

International Environment—Stimuli to Outcomes

We turn first to what the designer would like to know about international outcomes and how they follow from the existing characteristics of the international environment and stimuli from the implementation element. We treat this aspect of design first because what we learn about it, including what we learn about uncertainty with regard to it, should drive the definition of the design problem with respect to assessment, policy, and implementation elements.

Ideally, what the designer would like to have is a valid perspective model of the general form:

$$\psi(t + 1) = F[\psi(t), \alpha(t), \beta(t), \gamma(t)]$$

$$\pi(t) = G[\psi(t), \alpha(t), \beta(t), \gamma(t)]$$

where:

$\psi(t)$ = a set of variables defining the state of system at any given time, such as production capacities, prices, weapons inventories, natural resource reserves.

$\pi(t)$ = a set of output variables that operate as performance, that is, international outcome achievement measures such as income, growth rates, calories per capita, infant mortality, pollution levels.

$\alpha(t)$ = a set of parameters defining the structure of the system (often rate of change of variables between levels and input-output coefficients) such as migration rates, price elasticities, military expenditures as related to war deaths.

$\beta(t)$ = a set of environmental variables, such as natural disasters, assassinations.

$\gamma(t)$ = a set of policy instruments such as investment alternatives, tariffs, supplier price fixing, overseas basing of military forces, suppression of political dissidents.[2]

The designer wishes to use the model to ascertain what will happen relative to π given different implementation element actions (γ) and environmental characteristics (ψ, α, β). If he begins with a set of normative constraints on what are acceptable programs, he will limit his attention to those lying within the constraints. He will be reluctant to bet on any particular program no matter how well it meets his preferred values for π if he discovers that the π values are more sensitive to the environmental characteristics than to the action stimuli. Note that in exercising the model he deals with aggregate relationships and discrete, nonprogrammed events. Note also his concern at this point with programs as implemented stimuli and not with the determinants of the gap between policy intentions and actions really taken.

If he has a valid model of the above type, he will then have five particularly helpful kinds of information. The first is when the system is approaching lock-in in terms of π, that is, when the future value of π can be predicted regardless of intervening stimuli or environmental occurrences. We can conceive of this information as a transition probability matrix. It tells us when actions may still affect outcomes, when it becomes urgent to take action lest undesirable outcomes become overwhelmingly probable, and when a desirable outcome is relatively assured and one can relax about it.

The second deals with the decomposability of the system and of program stimuli relationships with the system. If we know about the decomposability of the processes that produce different variables in the performance measure set π, we know when aspects of the system state (the future world) can be treated in isolation from others. If we know which program stimuli are in significant input-output relations to one or several elements in π, we know when they must be weighed in terms of one or several outcome implications.

The third involves the specification of lead times, that is, the time that elapses between the application of a stimulus and change in π as mediated by α and by β.

The fourth deals with the impact of different volumes or strengths of a particular stimulus on π. In other words, the model can help us determine how much is enough and which policy instruments have particularly great leverage. For any given set of aspirations with regard to π, knowledge of lead times and volume differentials is important for evaluating alternative stimuli.

The fifth and final benefit we wish to note from such a model is one of updating. As new information comes in on ψ, α, and β components, it is fairly easy to reassess the consequences attributed to different implementation element actions.

Obviously, a model may have the desired properties, yield information of the kinds mentioned, and still be irrelevant to the design problem. The relevance of such causal models depends in principle on the extent to which they have embodied three elements in the definition of the problem (the production of π) with which they deal. We may refer to these as appropriate operationalizations of states of affairs central to the goal structure of the design problem, an appropriate time focus, and appropriate disaggregations of the distribution of π.

The first is the classic problem of construct validity and has obvious importance when we try to move from loose normative

language to scientific statement. The second, time horizon, with regard to international outcomes obviously involves the set of generations
of concern. Is one primarily oriented toward the fate of people alive
in the period after 2000? The lives of those around for the next ten
years? Clearly decisions not only set the outer time limit for the
values of π but also the extent to which it becomes important to know
what the values of π will be at which intermediate points in time.
Finally, a choice about necessary disaggregation tasks the model with
reporting different distributional aspects of the goal or performances
that make up π. Persons or groups concerned with the impact of
program stimuli on international outcomes need not limit themselves
to one operationalization, time horizon, or disaggregation level. Indeed, they should include the set of those relevant to the ultimate
users of the model and especially to actors whose use of the model
is central to the transition strategy. Unfortunately, the effort required
to attain the causal analysis capacity desired increases rapidly as the
list of appropriate operationalizations, time point, and disaggregations
increases.

    If we would like to have a model of the form sketched, we would
like to have even some of the benefits it can yield. One may be justi-
fiably skeptical about the current feasibility of such modeling for international outcomes. However, even pinpointing the ignorance that
prevents us from building a useful model clarifies the nature of the
uncertainty with which we want the assessment, policy, and implementation elements to cope.

    Also, feasible techniques exist to give us some benefits of the
full model. Transition probabilities can be calculated from historical
time series; decomposability in the gross can be determined by a
variety of statistical techniques such as factor analysis and cluster
analysis; regression analysis can clarify the impacts of particular
policy stimuli; systems dynamics can inform us about multiple-step
feedbacks and interaction effects. And emerging sets of techniques
for working with human judgments can blackbox the infrastructure of
the international environment. This last point merits brief discussion.

    The argument for techniques that aggregate human judgments
about consequences is not that judgments beat data on "observables."
It is one of augmentation and complementarity. A variety of elicitation
techniques are available, such as the cross-impact matrix and Bayes-
ian procedures. They can illuminate what are for relevant actors the
performance measures of interest and their relative weight, the
importance attributed to particular parameters for outcomes on these
measures, the impact expectations for particular program stimuli,
the importance of particular information items for outcome estimates.
Uncertainty need not be masked. Sampling methods and pretests of
elicitation protocols can minimize distortion in estimates of utilities

and probabilities as a result of who is asked and what is asked. One may question whether a scientist should rely on such judgments to draw conclusions, and we do not wish to get into that general issue. The designer has to define somehow the problem that the assessment, policy, and implementation elements must be able and inclined to cope with. The more clarity he can get about that problem, and the more certain he can make the existence of uncertainty, the better off he is.

Policy, Implementation, and Assessment Elements

Work on the causal relationships between program stimuli and international outcomes yields a set of requirements for the three other components of an international outcome design: the policy, implementation, and assessment elements. It also clarifies the adequacy of the existing elements that deal with those functions. We only face a design problem when we conclude that the existing elements are inadequate.

Without clearly stated requirements, we cannot specify optimal or even satisfactory designs for these elements. Since there is no single generally valid way to organize for everything, valid theory of organization suggests contingent actions, contingent on what one wishes to accomplish and on the context in which the accomplishment is to take place. It does seem useful to note some considerations pertinent to choice between alternative designs for policy, implementation, and assessment elements.

Policy Elements

In designing policy elements, the following questions are central across situations: What institutions will pursue the goals formalized in π as weighted by an appropriate set of normative choices (the success rule mentioned in an earlier section)? What institutions will have the wisdom to identify issues germane to goals in a timely fashion, to formulate and judge and select appropriate and efficient alternative programs? What institutions will have the power to decree what programs are needed with sufficient authority? How will institutions that are wise and powerful about collective goals and means also manage to achieve and maintain the needed flow of resources?

As a design problem, much depends on the extent to which we are certain from our previous analysis of what stimuli we want emitted from the implementation element. The more we know what we want to program the implementation element to do, the more focused becomes the task of designing the policy element. It is highly unlikely that we can be very certain for global, diffuse, and long-run international outcomes. Accordingly, we want to design policy element institutions so that they will evolve appropriate power and wisdom within a general goal commitment. We want to maximize flexibility and innovativeness but, given the possibilities of imperfect design, we want to hedge our bets by also maximizing responsiveness to emerging popular wishes and limiting the power of institutions to go their own way. Thus it seems rather inappropriate to concentrate on detailing formal organizations. This would lead us into a wealth of specificity about work processes, authority, influence and decision making, evaluation and appraisal, rewards and penalties to members, communication and exchange of ideas within the organization, identification (part to whole), affective relationships within the organization, and perpetuation through staffing and training. Instead, we want to concentrate on general institutional properties.

We may think of institutions as translatable into five sorts of matrixes. The first if an interest matrix in which we want to have cell values consistent with our preferred international outcomes. The second is an internal control matrix that indicates which institutions have what leverage over the actions of the policy element as a whole. The third is an external control matrix that indicates which institutions in the policy element have what control over the actions of the implementation element. The fourth is an internal information matrix that indicates which institutions in the policy element have importance in that they hold the information needed for wise decisions. And the final matrix deals with external information and indicates which institutions have importance in determining what information the assessment element supplies.

A design ultimately must deal with all of these. A transition strategy inevitably rests on decisions about which are most vulnerable to desired change and will exert the most leverage toward achieving the set of alterations desired.

Obviously, if we stop with the set of matrixes we have only as much reflection of an institution as a set of cell cross-sections provides of an organism. We also need to deal with the terms of interaction between entities important within each matrix and between those important across matrixes. The policy element can be thought of as an economy of supply and demand and the relationships tell us much about what such an economy will produce in terms of wise and authoritative actions with proper intent. As in an economy, information is crucial to the behavior of producers and consumers, resource allocators and constituents, and we need to know to what extent clear information circulates about producer and consumer expectations and preferences. We need to know how, in the absence of information, demand and supply relationships deviate from rationality.

In sum, the design of a policy element involves commitments to particular matrixes of interests, internal control, external control, internal information, and external information. It also involves generating a set of institutions with a chosen pattern of supply and demand relationships. And furthermore, it involves stipulating processes that will insure that signals are transmitted and received with some chosen level of fidelity and timeliness.

It seems useful to note some examples from theory and experience of helpful generalizations to illustrate the kinds of choices involved. I will group these under (1) flexibility and innovation and (2) responsiveness and limited power. I am more concerned here with the sort of generalization helpful in the design of policy elements than with the correctness of the example.

On flexibility and innovation:

- Policy elements are more flexible as they have less formal structure; the members with influence are also those with information; and they engage in internal confrontation as contrasted with smoothing over differences.
- Policy elements are more likely to generate innovations when they have a diverse membership; the converse is true for the probability that innovations will be adopted. If diversity makes it easier to find some encouragement for offering an innovation, it makes it harder to put together sufficient support to get it accepted.
- A policy element's capacity to generate new proposals benefits from growth, which elaborates missions and increases the heterogeneity of the membership.
- Decentralization can increase the chances that innovations will be ratified if it limits the scope of their effects to the subunit involved.
- The more diverse the incentives for entities in a policy element and the more even the distribution of internal control, the longer it takes to get any innovation adopted and the less the likelihood of boldly unequal allocations of new resources or nonincremental reallocation of old resources.
- Crises perceived to threaten the survival of the whole policy element are conducive to innovations being adopted because failure to change can hurt every institution in it.
- Institutions are less flexible and innovative the older they are and the longer the length of service of their members.
- Institutions that specialize in internal and external information roles are less flexible and innovative to the extent that they are in a monopolistic role and/or believe the demand for information to be invariant.

On responsiveness and limited power:

● Producing and regulating institutions will be responsive to resource suppliers to the extent that suppliers appear to have alternative recipients. For example, a health department will be more responsive if budgetary committees can give funds to the department or to some other entity than they will be if the committee has the department as the only producer of health care.

● Producers will be more responsive to consumers to the extent that the latter have alternative producers to choose between with little or no cost penalty.

● Within these conditions, responsiveness increases as clear behavioral signals are possible. And signals are clear to the extent that they are specific to some item of supply or demand, rather than an aggregate of some broad and diverse package.

● Any institution in the policy element has less power to the extent that it is in competition with other institutions with similar goals and functions.

● Any institution has less autonomous power to the extent that its membership overlaps with that of other institutions not completely subordinate to it.

● Any institution declines in autonomous power as its members belong to other normative reference groups.

Implementation Elements

Implementation elements receive program guidance and resources from the policy element and generate stimuli that operate on the international environment. The key design requirements concern compliance, response speed, response capacity, resource absorption, and goal commitments. Many of the points raised about the policy element also apply to these complex mediating institutions. The nature of the interests of their members, internal control and information distributions, terms of interactions, all affect whether they will do what they are told to do, how they will construe general program guidance, how long it will take them to implement an instruction, what instructions they are capable of carrying out, and how much of the program resources they will consume rather than pass on into the international environment. Implementation elements stand between policy as declaration and policy as action. And the historical record leaves little doubt that implementation elements take on a life of their own.

Avoiding Monopoly Power

The designer should take great pains to insure that individual implementation element institutions cannot present policy element resource and mandate suppliers, or international environment recipients, with a de facto "play it our way or else" situation. Having more than one implementation element institution that purveys a given commodity does not provide sufficient safeguards against de facto monopoly behavior through collusion. The purveyors should have different incentive systems to which they are responsive as well as being kept in check by the surveillance discussed immediately below.

Minimizing Deception Incentives

Both compliance with and the adaptiveness of policy elements suffer when members of implementation elements have incentives to mask what they are really doing. From a design viewpoint, an effort to lessen deception involves establishing perceptions about behaviors that will invoke rewards and sanctions. Some possibilities are: (1) to attach rewards to compliance with policy element directives as distinct from compliance with implementation elements; (2) to provide implementation institutions with the capacity to engage in reward-producing behavior; (3) to create the perception among members of implementation institutions that their behavior is under independent audit for the stimuli generated rather than the level of activity reached within the implementation element; (4) to devise systems for differentially rewarding and punishing implementation institution members with reference to their role in generating appropriate program stimuli.

Attaching Negative Consequences to Resource Absorption

Members of implementation institutions have little incentive to stress efficiency if they are rewarded primarily as the total budget or size of their institution grows. Rewards should be tied instead to the rate of growth in the proportion of resources received passed on to the international environment. And rewards for efficiency gains must be available to the members of implementation institutions who are made redundant as well as to those who are not. Those whose services are no longer necessary need to be assured of viable alternative ways of satisfying their interests.

A particularly moot issue is the extent to which the designer wishes to use the implementation element as a hedge against the consequences of inappropriate behavior by the policy element. To the extent to which one wishes to do so, straightforward compliance no longer is a dominant design goal. Instead, one seeks to establish contingent compliance, contingent on the directives from the policy element being consistent with preferred international outcomes. Appropriate goal commitments must be designed into implementation institutions and their members must be buffered against unacceptable punishment should the goals dictate disobedience to policy element directives. These are difficult challenges, and attempts to meet them may only result in hindering all attempts at generating more than incrementally different program stimuli.

In many contexts the injunctions presented about the implementation element all carry a substantial time cost in terms of the lag between general program guidance and the emission of stimuli to the international environment. If some of the other analysis in the design activity indicates that rapid action must be taken in order to attain a preferred international outcome, one may have to sacrifice some of the desiderata involved in designing the implementation element to provide a "check and balance" on the policy element. There is no general priority rule. It does seem wise to confront the tradeoff question in the context of the whole set of transition steps necessary to attain the preferred international outcome and maintain it for a stipulated period.

Assessment Elements

We can now turn to the last of the four elements: assessment. We wish to design this element in ways that will insure that it generates and transmits estimates needed for the proper functioning of the policy element. Accordingly, the design must provide the assessment element with the capability to secure needed information from the implementation element and the international environment. Also, it must establish those internal characteristics of the assessment element conducive to the transformation of the information received into the estimates supplied. Many of the points made in regard to policy and implementation elements also apply here.

We can usefully think of the information that should be available to the assessment element as an indicator system. The assessment element cannot tolerate and need not be informed about every little bit of the implementation element and the international environment. Rather, it needs to receive only information pertinent to the estimates needed by the policy element. Design should be sensitive to the problems of information overload and information cost and provide for exclusion as well as securing of information. In deciding what should be in an indicator system that will allow the assessment element to generate estimates for policy, several criteria seem helpful. These hold whether the estimates are of current situations (monitoring), changes since last stimulus from the implementation element (evaluation), or future realization of international outcomes (forecasting):

● Relevance to policy element goals. An indicator system is useful insofar as it gives sufficient information (completeness of state description) to estimate accurately the position of the international environment relative to a designated outcome now and in the future. Knowledge of what are preferred international outcomes plays a critical role in the design of an indicator system.

• Variability. An indicator system has policy value if its elements are open to variation in value along a policy-relevant timespan. If the time constants of the elements are too long (variability is low), monitoring the elements provides little information upon which to base decisions. Of course, indicator systems also may be valuable if they demonstrate that elements previously thought to vary in a useful manner do not in fact do so.

• Manipulability. An indicator system has value insofar as it: (1) clarifies which elements of the international environment and implementation element are and are not manipulable; (2) contains some indicators that trace manipulable elements; and (3) makes visible the amount and rate of impact that changes in the manipulable variables exert on the international environment position relative to the preselected international outcome. Of course, whether or not an element is manipulable depends on the timespan under consideration and the actors whose influence is under examination. In any event, without the three properties noted, the system can only support warning estimates. With these properties, the indicator system can support sensitivity estimates.

• Stability. An indicator system has value in excess of its cost if its components retain their relevance and validity for a minimal period of time. How long that is depends on the nature of the end states and the processes that produce them, as well as on the relevant manipulable variables that interact with other parts of the indicator system. We can define the minimum time period required to meet our stability criterion as equal to or greater than the time required: (1) to measure the initial state of the international environment relative to the chosen end state(s); (2) to select and implement a deliberate alteration in one or more of the manipulable elements and allow enough time for those manipulations to have an impact on the position relative to the end state(s); (3) to measure the subsequent position of the international environment; and (4) to select, implement, and receive information about the impact of a second manipulation. Anything less implies that we must construct a fresh indicator system for every decision-making cycle in an issue area. Such a high degree of instability makes the cost of collection and analysis prohibitive.

• Need. Indicator systems are needed only to the extent that international outcomes cannot be predicted robustly by the immediately preceding states of the international environment. If the predictions are strong, then the labor required to construct and test indicator systems does not provide a substantial information dividend.

● Efficiency. An indicator system is efficient insofar as each of its elements reduces uncertainty about current and future positions relative to some international outcome. Accordingly, a diminishing returns principle operates beyond some point with regard to the value of additional indicators. When additional measures contribute little information to the indicator system, they are of little use, regardless of their ease to collect or their familiarity.

The extent to which these considerations can be met in practice depends to a great extent on the success of the preceding parts of the analysis. The designer of assessment elements needs to have a good grasp of the policy element in terms of probable goals, issues, alternatives, and program guidance. The designer needs to understand what program stimuli the indicator system should pick up and what international environment state variables, output variables, system structure parameters, and environmental variables must be traced. And a good understanding of the implementation element underlies the ability to designate indicators of compliance, response speed, response capacity, resource absorption, and goal commitment. This is why we have put design of the assessment element last.

With an indicator system identified, the information needs of the assessment element can be specified. The forms of access required to secure that information will of course depend on the incentives actors in the other elements have to forward or withhold germane items. Obviously, access requirements also depend on the extent to which institutions in the policy and implementation elements are designed to alter as circumstances unfold and on the degree of continuity in international environment structures and processes. To the extent that any or all of these are fluid, the assessment element will have to have some anticipatory capability to modify its indicator system. Even if the policy and implementation elements and international environment are fluid, the designer will wish whenever possible to build in incentives to forward germane information to the assessment unit. A transition strategy problem is how to gain the information pending the time when reporting incentives become sufficient.

We have had enough experience with the behavior of assessment of "intelligence" elements in large private and public institutions to suggest some recurrent problems and possible solutions pertinent to their internal characteristics and placement relative to the policy and implementation elements.

With regard to individuals:

1. Problem: Tendencies to modify information in order to protect from and ingratiate with superiors and peers.

Remedy: Assign assessment responsibility to persons who are (1) professionally not dependent on superiors; (2) characterized by low needs for group approval; (3) attached to reference groups that esteem nondistorting use of the indicator system; (4) members of organizations that are in fact and principle charged with reporting bad as well as good news; (5) in contact with and under the partial protection of alternative authority figures.

2. Problem: Tendencies to modify information to protect favored programs.

Remedy: Assign assessment mission to persons and organizations that have no direct responsibility for developing or managing particular programs.

3. Problem: Tendencies to fit indicator system and estimates to previous cognitions and affects.

Remedy: Assign assessment to persons and organizations that are: (1) diverse in the previous cognitions and affects represented; (2) aware of the conservative biasing tendencies of all persons; (3) in frank and frequent communication with persons and groups with diverse memories and world views.

4. Problem: Tendencies to ignore information and long-range effects beyond tenure in role.

Remedy: Assign assessment responsibility to persons with career commitment to assessment as distinct from particular organization, program, or policy.

With regard to organizations:

1. Problem: Tendencies to act parochially toward estimating and to deal only with questions relevant to subset of preferred future purposes.

Remedy: Assign assessment to an organization: (1) whose members do not view organizational survival as dependent on any particular partial goal or alternative means; (2) whose mission is aggregative analysis of the world rather than of some subset of programs; (3) that does not have a clientele whose interests are better served by some international goals and means than by others.

2. Problem: Tendencies to reduce information to fit with growth, style, and reputation of assessment institutions before it reaches decision centers.

Remedy: Assign assessment to organization that: (1) has little hierarchy and reports directly to the highest relevant part of the policy element; (2) has not aged to the point of evolving a uniform, constraining set of internal norms; (3) prefers adversary proceedings and dissents to an appearance of consensus.

3. Problem: Tendencies for policy evaluation and forecasting to be pushed aside by immediate operational tasks and monitoring.

Remedy: Assign assessment to organization that has no operational responsibility and deny it the resources to acquire any. Separate burdensome detail functions of constructing and updating indicator system and of monitoring from evaluation and forecasting institutions.

4. Problem: Tendencies to monopolize design and use of indicator system.

Remedy: Assign indicator system to organization that is kept honest by: (1) independent, professionally competitive peers who have full knowledge of the logic and contents of the system; and (2) influential, autonomous institutions in the assessment and policy elements that stand to benefit from different outputs from the indicator system and have access to it.

The role of assessment elements in designs for preferred international outcomes and of transition strategies is important but limited. Indicator systems and estimates will never completely resolve uncertainty, and the resources and time consumed in improving them lessen the amounts available for other activities. Strategically, those who want to change the direction of the movement of the world or even keep it under close scrutiny need to devise an information strategy that at any step provides the minimal clarification needed at minimal cost. Three helpful ingredients merit special notice. We can call these information exploitation, information feasibility, and information priority.

Information exploitation refers to the ability to secure and make use of inputs currently received the the existing assessment element. Matters of freedom of information and independent analysis groups are relevant here.

Information feasibility refers to the design of instruments that make it feasible to provide indications of phenomena hitherto regarded as elusive or prohibitively expensive to observe. These instruments range from sociological measures of basic aspirations to satellites such as the Earth Resources Technology Satellite (ERTS).

Information priority refers to the ability to generate demand on existing assessment elements to supply previously underemphasized estimates. One way to do so involves generating issues that call for some reply from existing institutions. When combined with an information exploitation strategy, such attempts may provide some of the basic observations needed to develop international outcome designs and to monitor transition paths.

Suggestions for Evaluation

Whatever designs are evolved for the elements discussed up to this point will have to be evaluated at least with regard for the feasibility and acceptability of the transition strategy involved. We suggest that the necessary evaluation should involve a number of assessments analogous to those in engineering design. The weight attached to the results of each assessment need not be equal or always held constant. The extent to which a less than perfect score across a set of appraisals results in rejecting the proposed design depends on considerations external to the proposal.

We suggest that the following questions be asked of suggested policy, implementation, and assessment elements:

- Stability and reliability. To what extent will the proposed elements handle expected and unexpected but possibly critical developments in the international environment? What risks of institutional breakdown are we running, and what are the costs if we underestimate those risks? For example, is there enough redundancy? Would we be worse off than if we had not turned to the new institutions in place of their predecessors?

- Compatibility. To what extent are the institutions that make up the elements designed in ways that make them capable of working together to produce the international outcomes we want?

- Operability. To what extent are the institutions and their relationships sufficiently simple for people really to make them work?

- Efficiency. To what extent will the elements themselves consume resources (skill, money, trust, time) that should go into their outputs?

- Lead time. How long will it take us to achieve the proposed elements? Can we wait that long without incurring unacceptable costs? Will they be effective in the context of the period during which they will be operational?

- Duration of adequate service. Even if the institutions will be of service when they first come into being, will they serve our purposes for a sufficiently long period to make all the effort of creating them worthwhile? In part, the consequences of this assessment depend on the next dimension.

- Retirement and salvage. Can we insure that we can get rid of the institutions when they are no longer of service? If they have several levels of usefulness, can we insure that when their usefulness at the highest levels is exhausted they will shift to making a contribution at a lower level? (Obviously, the more one calls for transitional institutions, the more important this dimension becomes.)

If we have substantially new elements, transition strategies amount to evolving a complex system. Several generalizations provide helpful guidance with that task:

- The time required for a complex system to evolve depends on the number and distribution of stable intermediate forms. These forms may be stable only locally as distinct from globally in the system under analysis.
- Complex systems are easier to build if they lend themselves to being treated as a hierarchy. Hierarchy here refers to the presence of nearly decomposable subsystems and not to dominance.

The above statements have relatively clear implications. Try to break down transition strategies into steps that, once achieved, do not "come unglued." Try to find some fairly independent pieces to attach. A third generalization will lead us into the complexities of framing transition strategies.

- Stable institutional structures will emerge more quickly if all information is filtered through a central point. However, that strategy provides less satisfaction for members than does a more decentralized information pattern.

Obviously, the ease or difficulty of maintaining sufficient satisfaction to preserve membership and avoid disintegration affects the pursuit of the benefit held out.

Even if we have only modest goals for change in the policy, implementation, and assessment elements, several considerations are crucial to the success of a transition strategy:

- Limit number. Any particular step is probable to the extent that it requires agreement among a small number of actors.
- Build momentum. A transition strategy is more likely to succeed when the initial steps are likely to succeed and to generate a sense of efficacy in realizing future changes. Early transition steps that are primarily fear-arousing may defeat a longer-run transition strategy by weakening rather than strengthening a sense of efficacy.
- Accommodate incentives. Transition steps are likely to be realized to the extent that they (1) are compatible with the incentive structures of actors who must cooperate and (2) seem to fit with or to be irrelevant to the incentive structures of actors in a position to block them. Accordingly, those whose transition strategies call for

building new institutions should link them to incentives or interests that exist but are not adequately met or perhaps even addressed by operating institutions. They should try to avoid unnecessary mobilization of resistance on the part of existing institutions and groups. In their early stages, transition strategies should emphasize not changing existing interests and incentives but redefining what pursuing them effectively involves.

• Anticipate opposition. Any substantial change either in who counts or of only a distributive kind will encounter purposeful opposition from skillful adversaries. Transition strategies are likely to be well drawn to the extent that they anticipate opponent strategy and tactics.

• Multiple time horizons. In addition to accommodating to different incentives, all of which may support particular steps, the strategy should accommodate to different discount rates. This requires that each particular step should be associated with payoffs according to the time horizon of participants whose support is vital to that step. To the extent that many of the transition strategy steps inherently involve distant payoffs, support must be secured from actors with an appropriately long time horizon and low discount rate. These are most likely to be the affluent rather than the poor, the elites rather than the masses.

As the reader has probably recognized, the sets of considerations discussed in the last few pages seem remarkably compatible with the Mitrany-Monnet design for European unity. Yet the obvious slowness and tenuousness of progress toward that particular international outcome suggest that the considerations noted above need to be supplemented. Two important supplements are those of transition rate and transition magnitude. If these are set too low, the transition strategy is as prone to failure as if they are set too high.

It would be unfortunate to conclude that nothing can be done about designs and transition strategies until all the points touched on in our discussion of rules of thumb have been addressed and resolved. A more appropriate conclusion is that the design and transition strategy process should be pursued with awareness of the points noted. And the results of that pursuit should inform our evolving courses of action. From this standpoint, one seeks commitment to certain processes and a few initial actions rather than acceptance or prematurely comprehensive and detailed blueprints.

SUMMARY AND SUGGESTED NEXT STEPS

It seems useful at this point to reintroduce in summary form some of the distinctions and suggestions made earlier.

Concepts Stressed in the Design of World Futures

Approaches

> Descriptive utopianism
> Negative prescription
> Macromodeling
> Design

Design Approach

> Performance goals:
>
>> attribute by time period matrix
>> weighting functions
>> success rules
>
> Requirement sets:
> states of affairs

decision structures	by time	as uncertain		compati-
decision rules	periods	decision	as inter-	bility, time
		competence	dependent	precedence

> Action instructions:
> manipulables assigned to actors
> actor capabilities
> actor utilities

Design guidance

> International environment:
> model (state, outcome,
> environmental variables,
> system structure param-
> eters, policy stimuli)
> Major choices (output oper-
> ationalization, time
> focus, disaggregation

evaluated
as yield of

transition
 probabilities,
decomposability,
time leads and lags,
sensitivity,
updating

Policy elements

matrix structures (interests,
    internal control, external
    control, internal infor-
    mation, external infor-
    mation
general tendencies (institu-
    tional flexibility and
    innovation, responsive-
    ness and power)

} as related in terms of → supply and demand, communication

Implementation elements

major attributes (compli-
    ance, response speed,
    response capability,
    resource absorption,
    goal commitment)
suggestions (avoid monop-
    oly power, minimize
    deception incentives,
    attach negative conse-
    quences to resource
    absorption)

} as constrained by → time, urgency

Assessment elements

indicator systems
internal processes (prob-
    lems and design
    solutions)
information strategy (exploi-
    tation, enhanced feasi-
    bility, changed priorities)

} evaluated in terms of → goal relevance, variability, manipulability, stability, need, efficiency

Design evaluation

stability and reliability
compatibility
operability
efficiency
lead time
duration of adequate service
retirement and salvage

Transition strategy suggestions

stable intermediate forms		
decomposable subsystems	within	transition rate,
minimize number of actors	constraints	transition mag-
build momentum	of	nitude
accommodate incentives	needed	
multiple time horizons		

To ask any particular small group to generate designs and transition strategies for the globe and to meet as encompassing a set of
goals as the WOMP participants set for themselves seems highly
unreasonable. There are some tasks that, while formidable, are
more limited and discrete. Pursuit of these tasks makes up the
agenda of next steps to increase our ability to design preferred world
futures and to devise transition strategies to realize them. The tasks
noted below are not in any order of priority. Each may be pursued in
a large number of specific ways:

• Project constraint envelopes. Any attempt to pursue particular international outcomes must take into account some fundamental
constraints, for example, of natural resources and population. Knowledge of these constraints sets the ground within which recommended
policy, implementation, and assessment elements should operate to
achieve the outcome sought. Knowledge of these constraints underlies
formulations of requirements and action instructions to attain goals
in realistic settings. If we have envelopes rather than point projections, we can take into account the different major possibilities that
may occur about basic attributes of national, regional, and global
systems. This sort of work can, in addition to helping us confront
hard choices, shift our discussions from arguments about point predictions to the more important questions of what are the reasonably
probable alternatives to which we must accommodate. Politics and
policy may not be the art of the possible, but they surely do involve
making the best one can out of the possible. The attributes in question
for such forecasting activities are relatively inelastic. This increases
our confidence in gross-envelope forecasts as frameworks for designing courses of action.

• Identify relevant actors and map their current and emerging
utilities and capabilities. Estimates of consequences if results are
introduced into the current world depend crucially on knowledge of
who matters, what they want, and what they can do. Recognition of
the need for new institutions for policy, implementation, or assessment also depends on such knowledge. And the initial steps in any
transition strategy to realize the new institutions must secure at least
someone's support in the current world. At present, we have

relatively little descriptive knowledge of many potentially key actors, among them bureaus and interest groups within nation-states and emerging transnational governmental and nongovernmental organizations. The proposed maps can help us search efficiently for intersections of utility and capability suited to desired forms of behavior. They can give us a more realistic basis for selecting and rejecting alternative policies and transition strategies than do images stressing that all relevant actors are essentially alike to entertain only a single dimension of value.

● Decompose the global system. High priority should go to analyses to locate aspects of the international future that are suitable for separate design treatment. The need to establish decomposability seems to be of the utmost importance if design problems are to be tractable and transition strategies are to be manageable. Since our concerns are with affecting the real world, we need systematic analysis to locate those pieces rather than assuming independence or interdependence on the basis of geographical habit and disciplinary orientation.

● Purposive gaming and simulation. We usually are unable to deduce in any very credible way what are the necessary and sufficient conditions to secure the behaviors we want either from the "world" or particular decision units. We usually have great difficulty in pinpointing how much particular changes in the world or in decision units will affect their other attributes or their behavior. It seems reasonable to try to use games and simulations in a purposeful way to establish what set of characteristics and relationships does produce the behaviors we want. What has to be present in and absent from a game, a man simulation, a computer simulation for its output to reach some previously established target? Because it is so difficult to stage international field experiments, the diagnostic use of games and simulations is a particularly attractive alternative even though the results must be approached with due caution. Obviously, such games and simulations are most relevant when they take advantage of the results from the three types of projects previously suggested. If with that knowledge of parametric constraints, incentives and capabilities, and discrete problems, we cannot devise a game or simulate a world or decision system that behaves as wished, we clearly are not ready to advocate strongly any set of institutions or policies for real world use. Games and simulations also allow us to pursue a rather large number of policy and institutional alternatives at reasonable cost and minimum jeopardy to the current operating system.

● Issue area prototypes. Probably the best way to learn how to design preferred future worlds and to devise transitions to them is by trying to do so. Obviously, progress with the steps mentioned above will help. Even so, there probably is no effective substitute

for actually attempting design and transition strategy analyses. Since
the primary benefit of at least the initial trials involves learning about
how to work on design and transition, the issue area picked should be
sufficiently compact and well-understood for us to critique our efforts
and their consequences, and to go through a full set of technical
steps. When we try to do such prototypes, we should try to insure
that our efforts deal with all of the following tasks through whatever
combination of methods seems most helpful:

1. Assess the problem in terms of international outcome goals.
It is necessary to be clear about what the design is to accomplish.
Some goals must be postulated in operational terms. And these must
be expressed not in terms of scientific but of social achievement.
The goal statement is particularly helpful when it includes time terms,
that is, when the desired accomplishments are sought by some specified points in time. Obviously, it is difficult to translate the general
language of collective performance goals—such as welfare, development, governmental legitimacy, environmental quality—into valid
operational terms. To complicate the problem further, unidimensional
goal statements are not very helpful. In the real world, a particular
goal seems worthwhile only up to a point where its pursuit conflicts
with other values. However, if these problems can be handled, the
following benefits result. First, we have a clear performance criterion
against which to evaluate alternatives before and after the fact. Second,
we are forced to confront instances where no alternative seems very
efficacious and either modify our initial goal notions or switch to other
goals that seem more attainable. Third, we avoid confusing means
with ends and substituting accomplishment of necessary steps for the
end that ostensibly motivated activity.

2. Model the relevant international environment and work through
the impact of alternative program stimuli. We need to capture analyt-
ically the structures and processes that determine what international
outcomes different policy treatments of a germane international environment will produce. Even if we do not choose to invest in substantial
data bases and formal modeling, we can still construct models that
force us to use judgment and experience systematically and to make
unknowns explicit. The need to be able to assess the relationships
between stimuli and international outcomes seems critical if we are
to have any basis for choosing programs. And if we cannot choose
programs, it is difficult to see how we can relate our outcome concerns to a choice of institutions.

3. Analyze existing institutions (policy, implementation, and
assessment) for the stimuli they will transmit to the international
environment. Project to the time in the future when the international
environment must receive certain stimuli as a necessary condition

for the preferred international outcome. In order to determine what changes are needed, we need to know what stimuli current institutions are likely to generate, the disparity between those and the stimuli needed for the outcome sought, and the reasons for the disparity if any. A minimal test of the merit of an innovation is the difference between the state of affairs it will secure after it has been completed versus that which will probably prevail in the future in the absence of the innovation. Such appraisals are particularly helpful when they rest on trends and recurrent fluctuations as well as on current behavior.

4. Formulate alternative institutions (policy, implementation, and assessment) and appraise them in a political framework). It is distressingly inefficient to postpone consideration of political incentives and disincentives until after designs have been worked out in detail. The introduction of political considerations need not assume that the political situation is static. Indeed, it should recognize probable change and developing client and constituency demands. A prescriptive analysis is not successful when it only prescribes what ought to be done apart from whether or not the prescription can be filled.

5. Draft enabling documents and participate in the process of review and approval. The enabling documents that emerge from bureaucratic review and approval processes can all too easily take forms that bend the design away from the international outcome goal that is its reason for existence. The design can become stalled because alternatives raised by participants in review and approval processes are not promptly evaluated and their consequences reported in an informative and credible manner. Experts must be able and willing to translate their design preferences into simple and reasoned explanations and into action specifications. They must be able to provide fast-response appraisals of the costs and benefits of alternatives raised during review and approval processes. This requirement implies the existence of models and data resources applicable to questions and possibilities that will come up.

6. Devise a regime for securing systematic observations on the success of transition strategy and the implemented elements of the design. Provide a mechanism for the use of this feedback to modify remaining elements of design. Any pretense to perfect foresight is best discarded at the beginning of a design effort. Our theories are so loose, our data so fragmentary, and the world so complex that we need to establish an observation, feedback, and design modification regime. Appropriate resources, incentives to use them, and communication and sanction arrangements must be built into the design if it is to be an ongoing process. This sort of de facto field testing and modification seems particularly important if we are proposing

institutional change as distinct from altering program stimuli in the existing institutional context. The reasons are relatively straight-forward and stand in marked contrast to the design of purely techno-logical systems. Many of the humans involved have discretion over whether or not to participate. Many of them will retain numerous other memberships even if they do participate. The new institutions will have to compete successfully and persistently for money, legit-imacy, and human capital. They will have to secure some modicum of acceptance from existing institutions.

NOTES

1. Herbert A. Simon, The Sciences of the Artificial (Cambridge, Mass.: M.I.T. Press, 1969), p. 55.
2. Adapted from Michael H. Abkin and Thomas J. Manetsch, "A Generalized System Simulation Approach to Agricultural Develop-ment Planning and Policy Making," in Systems Approaches to Devel-oping Countries, eds. M. A. Cuenod and S. Kahne (Pittsburgh: Instrument Society of America—distributor, 1973), p. 100.

6

CONSTRUCTING MODELS OF PRESENTS, FUTURES, AND TRANSITIONS: AN APPROACH TO ALTERNATIVE WORLD FUTURES

Harry R. Targ

INTRODUCTION

A multiplicity of global problems are haunting the international relations scholarly community. Along with their traditional concern for war avoidance, members of this community are viewing with growing alarm the interrelatedness of ecological spoilation, resource depletion, population explosion, alienation, poverty, and oppression. Because of their recognition of the great urgency of these dangers, these academics are moving from the value-neutral and prescription-avoiding posture of an earlier era to one that is essentially normative and change-oriented.

This new focus has led to the legitimization of a number of novel scholarly rubrics: alternative world futures, peace studies, peace research, and world order studies. Despite the variety of labels, these research and teaching efforts seem to have two features in common: (1) emphasis is increasingly placed upon normative theory that criticizes existing socioeconomic systems and prescribes new systems and (2) the substantive value concerns motivating research are transcending the narrow focus on war and its avoidance to include what Johan Galtung calls "structural violence" and conditions of "positive peace."[1]

The crises of our time, both domestic and international, and the concomitant groping for purpose currently evident among international relations scholars, lead directly to a special concern for the future. The construction of images of more desirable futures must precede any movement toward viable social change. International relationists can thus participate in and stimulate change by involving themselves in the study and construction of alternative world futures.

Such study should not replace public discourse and political action, nor should international relations scholars view themselves as new social engineers who can design the future for citizens to create. Rather, the academic task in this area is to broaden the conscious awareness of the full range of global possibilities among students and among the general population.

The material below seeks to provide a framework for research and teaching that relates to the construction of alternative world futures. It discusses the necessity of positing models of presents, futures, and transitions and examines some already existent models. More specifically, four overarching questions will be examined: (1) What values should a more desirable world future maximize? (2) What are desirable alternative world futures and how do we posit them? (3) What national and international processes inhibit the achievement of the values and the alternative world futures most commonly posited? (4) How can international relations scholars think about the movement from the present to a more desirable future?

VALUES FOR A MORE DESIRABLE FUTURE

The question of values is in many ways the most difficult. For some analysts, values are so personal and so subject to particular institutional and cultural forms that no broad consensus can be achieved. For others, some very specific values are ascribed universal applicability irrespective of culture, history, or personal psychology. Barrington Moore has briefly treated this problem in reference to the questions of human happiness and human suffering.[2] Moore argues that political philosophers have posited innumerable conceptions of happiness, often contradictory ones. Happiness can be viewed from the vantage points of the life of the mind, the full gratification of sensual desires, the participation in organic communities, or the freedom from social groupings and constraints of any kind. Happiness can even be defined in terms of doing evil to other people. Moore therefore concludes that "on the score of happiness, it is difficult to say anything more than that its sources seem infinitely various, and that disputes about tastes are notoriously hard to resolve."[3]

Although Moore dismisses the prospect of discovering a singular conception of human happiness, he does feel that the obverse or human misery can be clearly delineated. Far more agreement can be reached about the nature of human misery and its sources. Moore asserts that most people would not like to suffer torture, violent death, starvation, sickness, economic oppression, punishment for stating unpopular views, and other related conditions. The social causes of these miseries he suggests are pretty clearly "1) the ravages of war; 2) poverty, hunger, and disease; 3) injustice and oppression; and finally 4) persecution for dissident beliefs."[4]

Perhaps Moore is correct in asserting that human happiness is beyond universal conceptualization. It may be that alternative world futures ought not to be constructed with happiness as synonymous with the values to be maximized. However, he also seems correct in asserting that human suffering is more standardized across cultures and across time. This suggests that a desirable alternative world future ought to minimally create the conditions whereby human suffering is ameliorated or precluded from occurring. This means that any desirable alternative world future must end torture, violent death, starvation, sickness (as much as is technically possible), and economic and political oppression. These conditions or their abolition may be called social values. To Robert Paul Wolff, social values involve "any experience or state of affairs whose definition makes essential reference to reciprocal states of awareness among two or more persons."[5] Essentially, the dimensions of human misery seem to be a shared experience among millions of people, and the social values for which alternative world futures must be directed are the shared experiences that emerge from the obverse of human misery. The problem with the concepts of human happiness is that they are in fact illustrations of what Wolff calls private values, or objects of "interest whose definition makes essential reference to the occurrence of a state of consciousness in exactly one person."[6] In substance, the values to be maximized by any alternative world future are social values, which emerge from the shared experience of human misery and the shared experience that such misery ought to be alleviated or ended.

Some scholars of alternative world futures may choose to derive values from other sources. In earlier works, this author has adapted the need hierarchy of Abraham Maslow to serve as a checklist for assessing the "success" of any ongoing social system or any proposed alternative.[7] Maslow's food, sex, shelter, and security were called self-preservation needs; love, and a sense of belonging were called community needs; and self-esteem and self-actualization were called self-determination needs. Each of the needs posited by Maslow has its referents in the obverse of human miseries discussed by Moore. The Maslow need structure remains useful as a checklist, and it and other variants can appropriately be adapted at the outset by alternative futures researchers to assess newly postulated socioeconomic systems.

It seems, however, that Moore's discussion avoids some of the pitfalls imbedded in the Maslow scheme. For example, the researcher can avoid the problem of verifying the existence of needs. Further, the researcher can avoid the debate about hierarchical ordering of needs. Finally, the researcher can avoid the problem raised by Moore, that is, the implicit assumption in the need hierarchy argument that the fulfillment of needs will inevitably yield human happiness, which carries with it an implied unitary conception of human happiness. Again, what can be discerned through reflection, through the questioning of persons around the world, and through the gathering of data on human suffering, is a list of human miseries. It is to the elimination of these miseries that alternative futures scholars should be committed.

POSITING DESIRABLE ALTERNATIVE WORLD FUTURES

The positing of alternative world futures per se requires two distinct procedures: (1) the imaginative construction of new forms of political, economic, and social systems and (2) the assessment of the fit between prearticulated values (social values that end human misery) and the proposed alternative world future.[8] The first step, the construction of a model or various models, can be aided by a number of historic and literary sources. Alternative world futures scholars can utilize the speculations of social critics who present alternative social patterns as a byproduct of their ongoing critiques of society. The writings of utopians, anarchists, and world order theorists provide useful schemes for system change and reform. Science fiction writers present readers with the starkest alternative visions of humane as well as dehumanized social orders. Finally, researchers can draw upon historic and contemporary examples of different forms of social organization. Some creative insights can be gathered from the study of the Greek city-state, medieval monastic life, nineteenth and twentieth century communes around the world, and such current experiments as the Kibbutz movement in Israel and variants of political decentralization in Cuba, Tanzania, and Yugoslavia. The sources for speculation are numerous and they may singly or synthetically lead to a vision of political and economic forms, norms and lifestyles, work and leisure patterns, and other structures and processes that may be integral to a new world society.

Once a model is constructed, the researcher must then begin to examine systematically the capacity of the alternative world future to fulfill the social values or the human needs posited at the outset. This may lead to the generation of a number of specific hypotheses that can and must be empirically examined. If, for example, a central value is self-actualization, how can this be achieved in the given future vision? Do work rotation schemes or programs of equal reward for all work provide for self-actualization? Does smallness of size of a social organization coupled with communal decision making increase a sense of belonging among community members? Do decentralized political systems minimize human misery? Through historical and crosscultural analyses, the researcher can take tentative steps toward the confirmation or disconfirmation of propositions embedded in the particular model that relates to the ultimate values with which he is concerned. Essentially, this suggests that the researcher constructs models, then tests the validity of various propositions embedded in them as they relate to certain basic social values.

Although the potential kinds of alternative world futures seem endless, most researchers are constrained in their conceptualization of alternatives by their own experiences and by insights from history. This need not be counterproductive in that the study of alternative world futures may begin with the visions must often expressed through history. By constructing modern variants of classical visions, researchers can begin to construct, debate, and test existing alternatives and move from there to more ingenious, lesser-known alternatives.

Researchers can begin to examine the relative utility of the three dominant kinds of alternative world futures: community, international regionalism, and world order. The community tradition derives from the writings and experiments of utopians and anarchists who see the maximization of human potential as tied inextricably to the construction of small, face-to-face and self-sufficient communities of people. [9] These theorists, as well as the "practitioners" of community, construct models of social organization that give consideration to alternative forms of decision making, community interactions, work roles, sex roles, educational processes, and technological adaptation. Modern activists and theorists of this tradition call for a radical decentralization of form and function from the ever-centralizing and homogenizing nation-state and international society.

More recently, the regionalist tradition has emerged primarily as a result of the perennial problem of war between neighboring states. [10] The continual strife among contiguous national territories has led certain theorists to posit various forms of social, political, and economic organization that transcend the nation-states that participate. The most successful experiment of this kind is the European Economic Community. It is assumed that, by achieving economic and then political cooperation between nations, a new spirit of regional solidarity will emerge. Regionalism will lessen age-old national hostilities and increase the prospects for the emergence of new regional states that not only may reduce the likelihood of wars between regional members but also will provide more adequately for the welfare and consumption needs of regional "citizens."

Finally, the world order tradition has dominated normative theory for centuries.[11] Generally, this vision is of a unified global society consisting of shared social, cultural, economic, or political forms. There are three discernible conceptions of the world order tradition. The political-structural conceptions of world order recommend the creation of centralized political institutions that are worldwide in scope, power, and authority. Functionalist conceptions look to increasing worldwide networks of nonpolitical organizations that ultimately will lead to the creation of unified world bodies to deal with man's social welfare needs. The functionalists have emphasized cooperation among peoples on specific social welfare dimensions from health to travel to ecology. It is sometimes hoped that through increased crossnational functional cooperation, human interaction will be increasingly depoliticized and a new world order will emerge that circumvents politics altogether. The universal cultural conception of world order does not begin with political structures or with functional organization but underlines the need for the emergence of a unity of human consciousness, world view, philosophy, religion, and values. The emphasis here is upon cultural movement to homogeneity as a prerequisite for political and/or functional cooperation.

World futures research, then, might begin with a thorough examination of these alternative futures traditions. The researcher can examine the prescriptions of individual writers in each tradition to assess the link between vision and value maximization. He can work with composite models from each tradition. He can seek to construct a synthesis of all three models in various combinations to discover the potential of each combination. Finally, the researcher can construct models from various sets of validated hypotheses relating structures and processes to values. Fundamentally, it is argued that scholars of alternative futures can begin their research profitably by systematically utilizing the wealth of writing and experimentation relating to these three traditions.

PROCESSES INHIBITING THE ACHIEVEMENT OF
ALTERNATIVE WORLD FUTURES

Any holistic conception of alternative world futures research must consider the present conditions from which the future must come and the transition strategies that must lead from specific present conditions to desired world futures. Put differently, the researcher must first seek to understand the forces that create or maintain human misery or inhibit the achievement of what were defined as the social values to be maximized. He may then begin to conceive of linkages between the articulated present and the desired future.

A useful first step in this process entails an examination of the literature of social critical theory. This is a literature that began to emerge with the industrial revolution and has since grown with the number of social analysts who look with disfavor at the development of the modern state in general and its paradigmatic case, the United States, in particular. Social critical theory has been described as follows:

> Social-critical theory seeks to describe and explain particular relationships and often to predict future developments from current trends. Its findings are viewed as justification for criticisms of the present. As values inevitably tutor inquiry, the social critic's analysis recognizes the disparity between what he views as desirable and what actually exists.[12]

One can point to five principal kinds of social critical theory that describe structures and processes within modern states[13] and three principal kinds of theory that have social critical implications for the entire international system.[14] Each of these kinds of theory illuminates a model of present social organization that is believed to exacerbate human misery.

The five kinds of social critical theory suggested here include the organizational/technocratic perspective, the statist perspective, the political elitist perspective, the economic perspective, and the cultural perspective.

1. The organizational/technocratic perspective views the modern state as a centrally organized assemblage of science, an ethos of expertise, and a bureaucracy. The resultant synthesis yields a social order that resembles a well-oiled machine quite beyond human control. Bureaucracy seeks to expand its control over man and nature, and man becomes a shell of his former self. Representative theorists of this model include Theodore Roszak, Roderick Seidenberg, and Jacques Ellul.[15]

2. The statist perspective emerged from the anarchist critique of the modern state, an institution that increasingly acquired power and authority at the expense of the individual and the community. This particular institution, the modern state, took control of politics, work, education, and property away from man and gave it to elites distant from the locus of tangible human experience. Statist critics include Petr Kropotkin, Robert Nisbet, and Robert Paul Wolff.[16]

3. The political elitist perspective emphasizes the role of political institutions and political elites in the process of centralizing power. Elites, whether singular or plural, act to maximize their private values at the expense of those they dominate. [17]

4. The economic perspective views capitalism as the central source of domestic malaise, international violence, and the continuing gap between rich and poor. Revisionist historians and neo-Marxist sociologists like Norman Birnbaum reflect this model of the modern state. [18]

5. The cultural perspective assumes that behind economic, political, and institutional forces lie world views, lifestyles, and value patterns that maximize a competitive struggle for existence and an ethos that justifies poverty and war. The cultural contexts within which modern states find themselves mold the character of societal structures. [19]

Theorists of the international system have often portrayed state interaction in such a way as to show how and why the perpetuation of human misery is a continuing problem. Three international-systemic perspectives highlight the obstacles to the achievement of social values:

1. Political realist perspectives emphasize a world of independent nation-states in continuous struggle for power, prestige, and material gain. From Thucydides's account of the Peloponnesian War to Hans Morgenthau's Politics Among Nations, the unrelenting drives of man are said to undergird the perennial problem of war. [20]

2. Stratification perspectives go beyond the view that war and poverty are functions of a social universe bent on power and acquisitiveness to reflect an image of the present international system that is analogous to domestic systems of stratification. Johan Galtung, for example, views interpersonal, intergroup, and international relations as dominated by the ranking of actors on a number of salient dimensions. Nations can be either topdogs or underdogs in reference to a number of factors. [21] Nations that have mixed top and underdog rankings are most likely to aggress to reestablish rank equilibrium. A. F. K. Organski and Steven Speigel also paint a hierarchically organized system with great, middle, and weak powers. [22] Along with social position flows the relative achievement of social values.

3. The endangered planet perspective presents not a model in the strictest sense of the term but a series of interconnected structures and processes that promote violence, ecological spoilation, gaps between rich and poor, and alienation. Central forces behind human misery stem from the state system, the legitimation of violence, and the rapidity of unplanned change. [23]

FIGURE 6.1

A Framework for the Study of Presents and Alternative Futures

Social Values	Domestic Obstructions to Social Value Achievement	International Obstructions to Social Value Achievement	Alternative Futures
End to human miseries:			
Torture	organizational/technocratic	balance of power political realism	community
Violent death	statist		regionalism
Starvation		stratification	
Sickness	political elitist	rank-disequilibrium	
Economic oppression	economic		
Political oppression			
			world order
Or satisfying human needs:			political
Food, sex, shelter, security (self-preservation needs)	cultural	endangered planet	structural
Love, sense of belonging (community needs)			functional
Self-esteem, self-actualization (self-determination needs)			universal cultural

139

Consequently, social critical theorists seek to link these hypothesized structures and processes to various conceptions of human misery. The alternative futures researcher can profitably examine the relative utility of each theory as an accurate description and explanation of the present. The models found most descriptive of the "real world" can then be used to create linkages to desired world futures.

The models can be used in several ways. First, the researcher may be convinced that one model best describes the most significant structures in the world today. For example, organizational/technocratic theorists see the emergence of the technocracy as the central force of our time: Not only is the United States the fullest embodiment of technocratic premises but the Soviet Union, European nations, and even the third world nations are moving doggedly to the creation of technocracies. One can project a global society, then, that encompasses the worst features of existing national technocracies. Others see political elitism as the dominant feature of the globe's national societies and, hence, most basic to human misery. Essentially, any of the five domestic social critical theories or some variants may be discovered to be the most accurate description of the present. On the other hand, some may find more explanatory power linking one or another international theory to human misery.

Second, researchers may discover that some combination of domestic and/or international social critical theories best explains the perpetuation of human misery. Empirical research may yield findings endorsing the combined importance of domestic technocratic developments and political elitism within an international context of stratification. This mix of forces will affect the way researchers think about transitions to the future.

Finally, researchers may be convinced of the relative utility of each of the eight models for understanding human misery and may develop models of the present that synthesize weighted factors derived from the models. This development would necessitate the most complex description of the present and the most sophisticated conceptions of movement from the present to the future.

FROM THE PRESENT TO A MORE DESIRABLE FUTURE

The construction of models of the present and possible world futures in the light of prearticulated values leaves the alternative world futures scholar with one remaining primary concern: the problem of transition from present to future. This remains the most complex problem. It may be broken down into two primary questions:

(1) What structures and processes existent in present domestic and international systems must be changed to achieve the desired alternative world future? Structures involve agents of stability and change that affect national and/or international systems of interaction. Processes involve the interaction patterns of agents of change and stability. (2) What kinds of strategies for social change can maximize the prospect of achieving the desired alternative world future with the greatest regard for the dominant social values sought by change-oriented actors?

A number of typologies of currently relevant structures and processes can be constructed to facilitate a discussion of transition to alternative world futures. At an early stage of analysis of transitions, a typology of structures and processes should be sufficiently specific to provide some clear analytical distinctions and at the same time be sufficiently general to encompass a broad range of change agents. Perhaps the best categorization of structural and process variables at this time is an adaptation of that by James Rosenau.[24] He constructs a "pretheory" of comparative foreign policy decision making by looking at the relative salience of five kinds of variables: individual, role, governmental, societal, and systemic.

The individual variables include all the characteristics that are unique to individual decision makers or critical elites within a society. In terms of alternative world futures research, concern must be reflected in a consideration of the role and interaction patterns of individuals in institutionalized and noninstitutionalized settings. The individual variables, Rosenau suggests, include "values, talents, and prior experiences" manifest in individual behaviors. The role variables encompass "external behavior of officials that is generated by the roles they occupy and that would be likely to occur irrespective of the individual characteristics of the role occupants."[25] If the institutional positions occupied by key elites circumscribe the behavior of individuals, then those positions must be viewed as central to understanding the operations of an ongoing system and what needs to be changed to create a new system. Governmental variables include "those aspects of a government's structure that limit or enhance the foreign policy choices made by decision-makers."[26] Models of present systems can be assessed in terms of governmental structures as well as nongovernmental, institutional ones that are deemed vital to perpetuation of the present and change to new systems. Societal variables include aspects of a society external to specific institutions and roles. "The major value orientations of a society, its degree of national unity, and the extent of its industrialization are but a few of the societal variables which can contribute to the contents of a nation's external aspirations and policies"[27] as well as internal developments. Finally, Rosenau suggests that systemic variables involve

"any nonhuman aspects of a society's external environment or any
actions occurring abroad that condition or otherwise influence the
choices made by officials."[28] Different models of present domestic
systems may assume different levels of relevance for external forces.
Similarly, nonhuman aspects of the international system (ecology, for
example), can affect the present state of that system.

Rosenau presumes that decision making in different kinds of
polities may be most affected by these variables in different degrees.
From the standpoint of alternative world futures study, the researcher
can seek to assess the relative importance of each of these variables
(structures and interactions of structures, that is, processes) for
each of the eight kinds of social critical theory. After the relative
importance of these variables is noted, the researcher can then begin
to deduce the kinds of changes in structures and processes that are
required to move from any present to any future.

Figure 6.2 tentatively assesses the degree of salience of each
structural variable to the existence and perpetuation of each model of
the present national and international political system. For example,
if the world of national actors is best understood as a multiplicity of
organizational technocracies in being or becoming, then one would
expect the impact of idiosyncratic decision-maker behavior in maintaining the systems to be slight, the impact of the technocratic role
to be great, the impact of governmental and corporate institutions to
be high, the acceptance of the scientific ethos by the culture at large
to be moderately important, while external systemic criteria would
be of little import. Assessments of each of the other models can be
made in a similar way, thus providing the alternative world futures
scholar with a more precise estimate of critical elements in ongoing
political systems that require change in order to achieve prestated
social values.

The researcher also can examine the structural variables that
can be presumed relevant to the creation and maintenance of any
desired world future. Figure 6.3 speculates about the relative potency
of the five structural variables as they would relate to community,
regionalism, or world order. For example, the individual factors
seem of greater salience in community and universal visions; role
variables more salient in the regional and functional schemes;
governmental and institutional variables more relevant to regional,
functional, and political structural visions; societal factors more important to community and universal cultural visions; and systemic
variables most relevant to political structural conceptions of world
order.

Figures 6.2 and 6.3 therefore provide a framework for viewing
variables relevant to presents and futures. The researcher can then
assess the relative fit of each present (or the present that is discovered

FIGURE 6.2

Structures Salient to Present Models of Domestic and International Systems

	Salient Structures*				
	Individual	Role	Governmental and Nongovernmental Institutions	Societal	Systemic
Organizational/ technocratic	L	H	H	M	L
Statist	L	M	H	L	L
Political elitist	M	M	M	L	L
Economic	L	L	H	H	L
Cultural	H	M	M	H	L
Political realist	H	M	M	L	H
Stratification	L	H	H	H	H
Endangered planet	L	L	H	L	H

*Degree of salience for models of present:
  H = highly salient
  M = moderately salient
  L = low or peripheral salience

FIGURE 6.3

Structures Salient to Three Alternative Futures

	Salient Structures*				
	Individual	Role	Governmental and Nongovernmental Institutions	Societal	Systemic
Community	H	L	M	H	L
Regionalism	L	H	H	M	M
World order: political structural	L	M	H	M	H
functional	M	H	H	M	L
universal cultural	H	L	L	H	L

*Degree of salience for models of futures:
  H = highly salient
  M = moderately salient
  L = low or peripheral salience

to relate most directly to the "real world") to each desired future. From this, he can begin to assess the dimensions of change required to achieve his preferred world and hence the defined social values. Some futures may be relatively consistent with some presents. The regionalist alternative is estimated by Figures 6.2 and 6.3 to be similar in structure to the organizational/technocratic model of the present. Other futures are at variance with certain models of the present. Structures implied in the organizational/technocratic world view are in contrast with four of five components of the community alternative future. Such linkages between presents and futures may underscore differences between present-future combinations that require reformist changes and those that necessitate revolutionary changes.

What must be emphasized in this exercise is that the variables implied from models of the present and from models of the future are fundamentally the form of each model, not the content. Once critical variables for change are isolated, the researcher must begin to fill in in greater detail the ways in which each variable must change, to what degree, and by what procedures. The elucidation of elements critical to ongoing and future systems facilitates systematic inquiry into the later problem, the procedures or strategies of social change.

As an analytical category divorced from existing conditions and desired futures, strategies of social change may be examined in a number of different ways. One might begin by looking at two dimensions: the unit of action (from individual action to collective action of various kinds) for social change and the type of action (from nonviolent to violent action) for social change. Examining these dimensions together, four categories of social change strategies emerge, as shown in Figure 6.4.

Each of the four cells reflects a kind of action that has a historic referent. The researcher can examine a multitude of strategies fitting each cell or some combination of cells in the light of his assessment of the present and his preferred world. Debate concerning strategies for social change should be preceded by some conception of the present and some view toward the future.

Finally, strategies must be considered in reference to the values one desires to achieve and the impact various strategies can have upon the creation of those values. Essentially, the alternative world futures scholar must make an empirical and ethical evaluation of social change strategies. Researchers might posit strategies and construct transitions from presents to futures that are less efficacious in the short run but do less long-term violence to values sought.

Before concluding, it may be useful to illustrate the methodology proposed here in a brief and rather impressionistic way. A researcher may accept the basic outlines of the organizational/technocratic

FIGURE 6.4

Strategies of Social Change: Unit and Type of Action

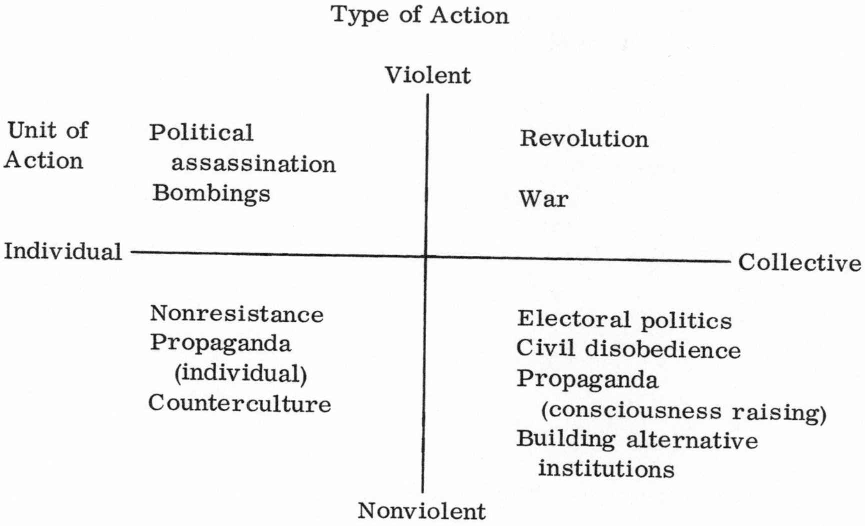

Type of Action

Violent

| Unit of Action | Political assassination Bombings | | Revolution War |

Individual ———————————————————————— Collective

| | Nonresistance Propaganda (individual) Counterculture | | Electoral politics Civil disobedience Propaganda (consciousness raising) Building alternative institutions |

Nonviolent

perspective. Roszak and others have defined the state as comprising a superstructure of organizational control coupled with the expertise of scientists who, through their particular skills, have converted knowledge into power. This is reinforced by a culture that gives particular legitimacy to science and rationalism. Figure 6.2 suggests that the critical elements of this domestic system include the role of expert and the institutions of government and corporation as well as a quiescent but supportive public and culture. The researcher who defines community as the alternative that can best maximize the social values discussed above seeks to create a social organization where the salience of individual and collectivity is high and the salience of specified roles and institutions is low. The problem then is to decrease the role and institutional variables and to increase the salience of individuals as citizen decision makers and the society in terms of major value orientations and organic unity. This task leads to an anlysis of strategies for change. A careful evaluation of strategies in the four cells might suggest that individual and collective violent strategies will not both destroy roles and institutions and increase individual participation in decision making and community spirit. Among the nonviolent strategies, electoral politics also may be ill-suited for the task. Perhaps optimal strategies will incorporate passive resistance to ongoing institutions and active propaganda campaigns against prevailing roles, institutions, and norms. This in turn must be coupled with the building of alternative community institutions that are subordinate to community values.

It must be emphasized further that the brief illustration above does not capture the depth of analysis required to link presents to futures. The linkages must be drawn fully from quantitative analyses, experimental methods, historical case studies, and careful deductive exercises. The researcher moves from (1) positing values to (2) constructing alternatives that maximize these values to (3) establishing presents to (4) comparing structures and processes in presents to desired futures to (5) providing strategies to move from the present to the future. Each step in the process of studying alternative world futures requires great care and the marshaling of the best products of substantive and methodological scholarly concerns.

NOTES

1. Johan Galtung, "Violence, Peace and Peace Research," Journal of Peace Research, 1969, pp. 167-91.

2. Barrington Moore, Reflections on the Causes of Human Misery (Boston: Beacon, 1973).

3. Ibid., p. 1.

4. Ibid., p. 2.

5. Robert Paul Wolff, The Poverty of Liberalism (Boston: Beacon, 1968), p. 181.

6. Ibid., p. 170.

7. Louis Rene Beres and Harry R. Targ, Reordering the Planet: Constructing Alternative World Futures (Boston: Allyn and Bacon, 1974); Abraham Maslow, Toward a Psychology of Being (New York: Van Nostrand, 1972).

8. For a more extended discussion of these ideas, see Harry R. Targ, "Social Science and a New Social Order," Journal of Peace Research, 1971, pp. 207-21; Beres and Targ, Reordering the Planet, pp. 9-23.

9. Beres and Targ, Reordering the Planet, pp. 63-91.

10. Ibid., pp. 92-109.

11. Ibid., pp. 110-43.

12. Ibid., p. 24.

13. Ibid., pp. 24-25.

14. Ibid., pp. 46-61.

15. Theodore Roszak, The Making of a Counter Culture (Garden City, N.Y.: Doubleday Anchor, 1969); Roderick Seidenberg, Post-Historic Man (Boston: Beacon, 1950); Jacques Ellul, The Technological Society (New York: Vintage, 1964).

16. Petr Kropotkin, Mutual Aid (Boston: Extending Horizon Books, 1902); Robert A. Nisbet, Tradition and Revolt (New York: Vintage, 1970); Robert Paul Wolff, In Defense of Anarchism (New York: Harper and Row, 1970).

17. C. Wright Mills, The Power Elite (New York: Oxford University Press, 1959); Theodore Lowi, The End of Liberalism (New York: Norton, 1969).

18. Norman Birnbaum, The Crisis of Industrial Society (London: Oxford University Press, 1969).

19. Jules Henry, Culture Against Man (New York: Vintage, 1963); C. B. MacPherson, The Political Theory of Possessive Individualism (London: Oxford University Press, 1962).

20. Thucydides, The Peloponnesian War (Baltimore: Penguin, 1954); Hans Morgenthau, Politics Among Nations (New York: Alfred Knopf, 1960).

21. Johan Galtung, "A Structural Theory of Aggression," Journal of Peace Research, 1964, pp. 95-120; "A Structural Theory of Imperialism," Journal of Peace Research, 1971, pp. 81-119.

22. A. F. K. Organski, "The Power Transition," in International Politics and Foreign Policy, ed. James N. Rosenau (Glencoe, Ill.: Free Press, 1961); Steven Sieigel, Dominance and Diversity (Boston: Little, Brown, 1972).

23. Richard A. Falk, This Endangered Planet (New York: Random House, 1971).

24. James N. Rosenau, The Scientific Study of Foreign Policy (New York: Free Press, 1971).

25. Ibid., p. 108.

26. Ibid.

27. Ibid., p. 109.

28. Ibid.

7

THE STUDY OF PEACE AND JUSTICE: TOWARD A FRAMEWORK FOR GLOBAL DISCUSSION

Saul H. Mendlovitz
Thomas G. Weiss

"I do not wish to seem overdramatic but I can only conclude from the information that is available to me as Secretary-General, that the members of the United Nations have perhaps ten years left in which to subordinate their ancient quarrels and launch a global partnership to curb the arms race, to improve the human environment, to defuse the population explosion, and to supply the required momentum to development efforts.

"If such a global partnership is not forged within the next decade, then I very much fear that the problems I have mentioned will have reached such staggering proportions that they will be beyond our capacity to control."

—U Thant, 1969

Many of the points in this essay can be found in expanded form in the authors' forthcoming book, Shaping the Future: A Primer on Constructing a More Humane World Order, in particular in Chapters 1 and 3. These ideas were first stimulated by participation in a German Conference on Peace Education, and this argument appeared in shorter form as "A Framework for the Policy Studies of Global Peace and Justice," in Kritische Friedenserziehung (Handbook on Peace Education), ed. Christoph Wulf (Frankfurt/Main: International Peace Research Association, 1973).

INTRODUCTION

The present volume is a series of essays about world order, and the main objective of the contributors is to provide a basis for reorienting the conventional methods of inquiry about international relations so that analysis may become more explicitly and simultaneously systemic, normative, and futuristic.* This essay focuses on four essential questions: what are (descriptions), are likely to be (prognoses), should be (preferences), and can be (feasibilities) world political and social processes. At the risk of oversimplification, we suggest that conventional approaches to the study of international politics are concerned primarily with the relationship among states. We are concerned with value solutions to five global problems: war, poverty, social injustice, ecological imbalance, and mass alienation. In taking issue with more conventional perspectives, we hope to make explicit an operational frame of reference for discussion of planetary dangers as a first step in their solution. The remainder of this essay is concerned with differentiating these two perspectives and with specifying the consequences of our preference for world order thinking.

We begin by reporting the development of a growing concern with global peace and justice, or what has gradually become known as world order.[1] During the past two decades an increasing number of responsible and thoughtful individuals and groups throughout the world have come to understand that the human race faces a set of interrelated problems threatening its survival. In addition, they have serious doubts as to whether this planet can provide a tolerable quality of life for all human beings. Furthermore, many of these people believe that many world problems must be dealt with rapidly and systematically.

For the purpose of a common discussion, it is sensible to present briefly some of the data that sustain this new global consciousness.[2] The armaments race, which accounted for $100 billion of the world economic system in 1973, now costs well over $230 billion and by the end of the 1970s is likely to consume over $300 billion.

---

*We are not implying that all our concerns have not been investigated or have been completely ignored by such scholars as Hans Morgenthau or Inis Claude and others in the traditional fields of international relations, organizations, or law. What we are suggesting—and what will become clear as we proceed—is that the perspective given by world order provides a new methodological tool for viewing world problems, one that is likely to elicit more relevant information and more humane policy actualization than the traditional modes of inquiry.

Furthermore, it is probable that a minimum of three and as many as six other nation-states will have joined the nuclear club by that time. One can select a single item among the many troublesome trends that threaten our environment: Using 1950 as a baseline, conservative estimates are that the carbon dioxide in our atmosphere will increase a minimum of 15 percent by the year 2000, with effects, while not yet clearly understood, likely to have very severe if not tragic consequences for human society. The human population increased from 1 billion to 2 billion in the period 1830-1930, to 3.3 billion by 1971, and will approach 7 billion by the year 2000. This suggests a host of problems with regard to welfare, development, social justice, authority processes, and the outbreak of violence. Again utilizing conservative estimates, the 20 to 25 most economically developed states presently have a per capita income that is 12 to 14 times as great at the other 120 states. This gap is likely to increase to 20 to one by the year 2000, with 50 percent of the projected population of 7 billion probably no better off than they are today, namely living on $100 to $125 per capita income. It is likely that the lowest 10 percent (700 million people) will be living on $50 per capita income. These figures are of course straight-line projections in constant dollar figures and do not reveal the dynamics of the social processes that propel them, but they do reflect the set of problems that concerns many responsible and thoughtful individuals.

While this set of problems is well known, many of the individuals and groups working on remedies are doing so separately. As we see it, there has been no consensus either on the world they wish to achieve or on a systemically formulated strategy of transition for achieving that world. We believe that the nature of the problems is sufficiently interrelated and the scope sufficiently global to warrant a common discussion framework and set of analytical tools. This essay attempts to provide them.

Therefore, within the context of what global cultural, economic, political, and social processes are, are likely to be, should be, and can be, world order thinking highlights five problems: war, poverty, social injustice, ecological instability, and mass alienation. For people concerned with these problems, "solutions" are the realization of human values. Thus one might say that those concerned with these global problems are trying to accomplish the realization of peace with tolerable conditions of economic well-being, social justice, ecological stability, and participation.*

---

*
Some confusion may result from use of the term "values" as the affirmative statement of solutions to problems. The values are intended to connote the general realization of conditions in which the

We shall provide a formal definition and matrix for this frame of reference, but now present briefly our overall intention to proceed in a straightforward fashion that could be labeled "naive realism." The urgent nature and scope of world order problems compels us to overlook for the moment the host of subtle, important, and relatively complicated questions that academicians and sophisticated political activists might prefer to have clarified.

We will not, for example, explore the relationship of ideas to action, the issue of whether "ideas are the switchmen" of history. The question of whether there is a uni- or multicausal frame of reference for understanding war also will be glossed over. Nor will there be a major discussion of the extent to which counterintuitive behavioral systems analyses are needed for an understanding of our present circumstances. And, finally, we will not explicate a philosophy of history and, at least consciously, we will avoid subscribing to any particular intellectual or ideological position on the nature of human society.

Having made these disclaimers, we nevertheless realize that all these matters are woven into our exposition. One cannot avoid taking positions on the issues raised by these questions, nor do we wish to. However, we hope to perform a service that recognizes the complexities of the above issues and yet bypasses them. Thus, naive realism allows one to move forward and develop a comprehensive

---

world order problems would not longer be problems or their dangers would at least be minimized. This use is relatively straightforward and unambiguous for four of the problems, which do represent tangible albeit very complex issues whose characteristics are relevant concerns for peoples across the globe. Violence, starvation, discrimination, and polluted water are all characteristics whose structural sources and links are basically equivalent in many parts of the world. The problem of "alienation," however, is actually two very separate problems. One connotes an exclusion from the authority and decision-making processes that are important to one's well-being. The other sense of alienation is the estrangement from processes in which one is included. The former sense essentially expresses the sensations of many of the world's "have nots" who do not possess even minimum control over their destinies. The latter meaning of alienation basically refers to sentiments of malaise, frustration, and social anomie of some of the world's "haves" who find that certain of life's tasks no longer have meaning. While in some sense the two problems overlap, the value of participation most clearly attempts to overcome the lack of control over decision making of many groups of people. It also has limited ability in ameliorating certain symptoms of identity crises, although this is not its primary purpose.

frame of reference for discussions among those interested in achieving
global peace and social justice. One can move ahead on this front without debating and becoming lost in the interesting, yet endless, debating
points of the above issues.

The first realization that results from this naive realism, world
order framework is that global problems are phenomena that the vast
bulk of humankind has participated in and accommodated throughout
recorded history. Humanity has, in other words, considered these
matters to be "in the nature of things."

Foremost among these is the institution of war. It is still a
conviction widely held throughout the world that war, springing from
innate aggressive impulses, is an inevitable and enduring institution
of human society. The pervasiveness of this conviction is not diminished by the fact that scientific data tend to undermine the belief that
large-scale organized violence is a necessary outgrowth of the
aggressive impulses experienced by the human species.[3] Present
understanding of the human mind and social psychology leads to the
conclusion that, while humans may be aggressive animals, their
aggressive impulses may take various forms, many of which are
actually constructive in ways probably indispensable to the future of
civilization.

Furthermore, the attempt to eliminate war as an institution—
rather than merely to diminish its horror and brutality—is of relatively
recent vintage. Since neither the United States nor a large number of
other states were participating members of the League of Nations, it
can be said that the first major attempt at the global level to outlaw
war was the Kellogg-Briand pact of 1928. For the first time in history,
leaders of nation-states that had the capacity to initiate international
war renounced it as an instrument of national policy. In 1945 the
creation of the United Nations, building on the League of Nations and
the Kellogg-Briand pact, represented an even more significant commitment to outlawing war. Nevertheless, the United Nations has had
only the most modest success over the first thirty years of its existence. The present world political system, dominated by individual
nation-states that refuse to surrender sovereignty on matters concerning their own security, now contains the threat of such large-scale
violence that the institution of war has emerged as one of the great
survival problems of humankind. It is our position that solutions to
poverty, social injustice, ecocide, and individual alienation are inseparable from the future of war. These five problems are becoming
generally recognized as worldwide problems, although each varies in
its relevance and history for different civilizations.

It is appropriate to consider the most significant social processes of the modern era. During the last few centuries three revolutions—the scientific-technological, economic-independence, and

egalitarian-ideological—have brought world order problems to an explosive global point. The growth and tempo of the technological revolution has made it possible for one or more nation-states, acting on their own authority, to destroy much of humanity in minutes. Industrial growth may accomplish this more gradually. Furthermore, it is increasingly clear that revolutions in energy, computers, and biochemistry will inaugurate problems, challenges, and opportunities for which the world is at the moment very much unprepared.

The recent food and energy crises have made abundantly clear the basic reality of interdependence. The prolonged inability of nations to control the burgeoning world population, to moderate the race between the depletion of resources and the long-term achievement of universal welfare and ecological stability, to control the eruption into violence of newborn and ancient rivalries and tensions, to achieve minimal standards of social justice, and to include the vast majority of humankind in decision-making processes is leading to the breakdown of authority structures and to pervasive suffering.

In addition, the explosion of egalitarian ideologies into mass consciousness has led to an unprecedented situation in which demands for justice and improved conditions of material well-being are occurring with increasing insistence. The realization that material, social, and political situations are neither always nor everywhere equivalent has increasingly led the world's "have nots" to demand their fair share.

Despite and because of these processes, it is within the human grasp to eliminate war as a social institution and to provide tolerable conditions of economic well-being, social justice, ecological stability, and participation. Human sacrifice, cannibalism, and slavery are human institutions that at one time or another existed in many societies. Yet it now seems clear that they are unlikely to reenter global society in the foreseeable future. Many world order problems are of no greater magnitude than several human institutions that already have been eliminated. With appropriate analysis and social action—political mobilization based on understanding of political process—it is also feasible to make significant progress on world order issues.

It is contended that the existing mainstream literature on international politics is inadequate for conceptualizing the nature of the survival problems that have been identified.[4] We apply the following rather stark and oversimplified characterization to traditional international relations theorizing for the purpose of description.

As we have previously indicated, the discipline of international relations consists principally of the study of interactions between individual governments. The focus is at times exclusively on the nation-state, to the comparative neglect of all other relevant actors. The time dimension is the recorded past (usually excluding the past

of Oriental, African, and New World civilizations), with an overriding
emphasis on the period since 1945. The central objective is to understand scientifically the reasons that nations behave the way they do.[5]
The goals of the discipline are primarily explanatory and empirical.[6]
The idea that one has a prior and primary commitment to certain
goals that would, if realized, require a drastic change in the international system, and that one conducts research in the hope of discovering clues about how this system might be transformed, is foreign
to most students of international relations.[7] The more traditional
balance-of-power notion of the international system was of a billiard
table on which the balls (nation-states) would knock against each other,
causing some isolated repercussions but not altering basic structures.
The balls were seen as impermeable units, permanent structures
resistant to fundamental change.[8]

Modern analysts feel that technology has transformed the
essentially nineteenth century image of the world into one of a system
of interconnected parts, each of which continuously acts upon, and to
varying degrees alters, the others.[9] The world as a holistic system
is now taken seriously as an analytical frame of reference. J. David
Singer has remarked that "the international system itself is the key
element in explaining why and how nations attempt to influence the
behavior of one another."[10]

Two schools of thought predominate among contemporary students of international relations who find the concept of systems analysis instrumental for studying the international system. One maintains
that it is more relevant to study the behavior of one subsystem, particularly the nation-state, as it manifests itself with reference to
other subsystems. Such analysts believe that each subsystem will
manifest different behavior patterns in particular situations and relationships, and these need to be thoroughly catalogued before meaningful generalizations or theories can be constructed. The other school
maintains that study of the whole system will reveal patterns of interaction among the actors that enable the student to make comprehensive
generalizations with some predictive power.[11]

World order is more aligned with this latter, holistic systems
approach to international relations. In his book Theory and the International System, Charles McClelland summarizes:

> The outermost boundaries of international relations are
> suggested if we imagine all of the exchanges, transactions,
> contacts, flows of information, and actions of every kind
> going on at this moment between and among the separately
> constituted societies of the world.[12]

However, world order inquiry is not motivated primarily toward
deriving an understanding of the dynamics of interstate relations, but

rather toward finding workable solutions to recognized global problems. These problems exist throughout the world system and are endemic to the present organization of the planet. Since they threaten survival at the same time that the technological capacity exists to solve them, it seems morally grotesque not to ask the question: Knowledge for what?[13] This does not deny the usefulness of new knowledge that reveals regularities of behavior among nation-states, or of the behavioral patterns of the system as a whole. However, we view such knowledge not only as a basis for understanding and predicting the probable world, but more importantly as a basis for formulating credible strategies of transition to preferable systems that maximize world order values.

We are explicitly seeking to develop a method of analysis that leads to drastic change and does not perpetuate the status quo or its values. Nonetheless, a word of explanation is in order about the term "world order," which may have misleading connotations for some readers. The expression itself may seem dull, static, unrelated to the pursuit of justice, and without any concern with the creation of a global community based on notions of solidarity and participation. Perhaps such phrases as "global community values" or "terrestrial unity" or "world ethical consensus" would more appropriately describe our concerns than "world order." However, it seems important to abide by accepted terminology. There is a developing awareness among students of international affairs of what generally has been identified as world order studies. Indeed, such an identification generally has been regarded as a progressive development within academic circles, particularly in North America, by initiating normative concerns. In brief, world order is a systematic inquiry into maximizing the values of peace, economic well-being, social justice, ecological stability, and participation. Its scope is global and extends into the future. It has no disciplinary boundaries. It is not propaganda but rather a synthetic educational tool for structuring comprehensive discussions among all the world's peoples about human problems and their resolution.

It is a basic premise for our remarks that it is necessary to consider seriously not only the rhetoric but also the reality of the term "the global village." It seems clear that an increasing percentage of humankind views the entire world as a global society. This phenomenon, it should be underscored, is a psychohistorical first and has had a drastic impact on our images and attitudes in regard to authority structures within domestic societies as well as the international community. If we are permitted a mixed metaphor, the recognition of the global village is an image change similar to the Copernican revolution. We refer not only to its significance but also to its general nature since individuals and nations must humbly realize that their self-interests are no longer capable of being placed at the center of the universe. However, at the same time that images are beginning to change, policy making has not. We, in trying to speak for world interests, seem to be in the same position, vis-a-vis decision-making elites, where Columbus stood in trying to get Queen Isabella's ear. The image of a global village offers new potentials as well as responsibilities, although elites are hesitant to act.

One implication of saying that there is a global village is that sometime within the next two decades many people throughout the globe are likely to begin to discuss seriously the governance of that global village in ways that had previously been eschewed. Our loose sense of the dynamics of social change for a world order social movement makes use of such a development. We view the next three decades as periods of consciousness, mobilization, and transformation. [14] In the first ten-year period, emphasis is on changing value priorities and images within existing centers of decision and control as well as among world citizens more generally. In this initial period, the most important payoffs are likely to involve consciousness-raising efforts at all levels. The framework presented in the latter half of this essay is intended to contribute to this initial process and thereby eventually facilitate the transition to latter periods in which large masses of people can be mobilized to reflect their concerns about drastically transforming the world political system.

It is worth noting that the process of global discussion has already begun and is being fueled by the growing number of responsible and thoughtful people and groups attempting to understand and cope with the major global problems. The complex crisscross of problems, historical processes-revolutions, and concerned individuals has been moving the globe steadily toward the point at which discussion of a new governance for the world community has become a definite possibility.

At this time, we express our judgment—more than a prejudice or idle speculation—that, based on a study of the matters just outlined, there is little doubt that there will be some form of planetary guidance by the year 2000. It is becoming apparent that the concentration of power taking place in the economic, technological, and scientific centers of the world is carrying us forward in that direction. However, we have concentrated thus far upon developments that represent positive potential contributions to solving world order problems, and it is necessary to briefly express contrary developments.

A more likely planetary guidance system is a Darwinian one in which the "haves" attempt to consolidate their position of dominance and wealth. It has recently become clear that conditions of energy scarcity stimulate regressive measures by the major powers. It is quite possible that global domination by one or a few large powers

might occur before the end of the century, and such a system may be
effective in managing certain global problems. Control over resource
depletion, supervision of technology, enforcement of regulations controlling the population, and some semblance of ecological balance
could perhaps be instituted in a top-down fashion by dominant powers.
A more difficult way to obtain physical and economic stability (not to
be confused with cultural and spiritual stagnation) would be to resist
domination and encourage cooperation in the establishment of a more
participatory, just, and equitable planetary guidance system. As is
usually the case, domination is more likely than the emergence of
equitable relationships. However, there is human choice and effort
involved, and manipulative and nonegalitarian alternatives are not
inevitable. Therefore, a critical question is in what manner a planetary guidance will come into being, and whether it will be benign or
totalitarian. It is time, therefore, that those who believe in democratic processes and just institutions begin to think of ways in which
the peoples of the world will be given an opportunity to participate in
the development of world institutions.

We turn now to a detailed exposition of our own framework for
discussing planetary dangers.

DEFINITION OF WORLD ORDER

World order designates the study of international relations and
world affairs that focuses on the manner in which humankind can significantly reduce the likelihood of international violence and create
minimally acceptable conditions of worldwide economic well-being,
social justice, ecological stability, and participation in decision-
making processes. In short, a student of world order seeks to
achieve and maintain a warless and more just world and to improve
the quality of human life.

So understood, it becomes important to understand the impact
and range of significant actors. The continuum of actors thus includes
world institutions, international organizations, regional arrangements,
transnational units, nation-states, intranational groups, and individuals. The student evaluates such actors as they relate to the following
dimensions of world community processes: peacekeeping, third party
resolution of disputes and other modes of pacific settlement, disarmament and arms control, economic development and welfare, the
technological and scientific revolutions, ecological stability, all
human and social rights, and individual participation.

A world order inquiry involves the use of relevant utopias culminating in the statement of the investigator's preferred world. A

relevant utopia is the projection of a system of world economic, political, and social processes capable of preventing organized international
violence and of providing adequate worldwide economic welfare, social
justice, ecological stability, and participation. The use of relevant
utopias also involves analysis of the present system as it relates to
these problems. In addition, relevant utopias describe, as rigorously
as possible, the trends and prognoses with respect to these problems
over a period of one to three decades. Within this context, relevance
means that there is a sufficient description of details in behavioral
terms so that the reader and formulator have a reasonable basis for
making a statement about the probabilities of the emergence of such
a model. It does not mean, however, that the model or utopia is
politically feasible.

Similarly, a concrete behavioral statement of transformation
from the present system and to the projected model is necessary. In
dealing with the concept of transition, special emphasis is given to
the possibility of drastic alteration in the system without recourse to
large-scale violence.

A preferred world is a blueprint of a recommended structure
and guidelines for achieving it in order to maximize world order
values. Testing alternative world order models and their transition
processes, structures, and strategies allows the investigator to
select or invent, from various facets of these relevant utopias, a
preferred world.

Throughout the inquiry, formalized and authoritative conditions
of world legal order are emphasized. They are related to economic,
political, and social processes and structures that facilitate achieving
and maintaining community in a warless, more just, and ecologically
stable world. In addition, the student of world order makes a continuous effort to state operational definition(s) of world interest in terms
of the central problems.

USE OF THE WORLD ORDER DEFINITION
AND MATRIX

We constantly refer to the world order theoretical framework
in the discussion of policy scenarios and global problems. It is the
lens through which we observe events in the world and give them
meaning. However, this lens is nothing permanent; it should be
altered in whatever ways are deemed useful by those investigating
world order problems. It may serve only as a model for other, more
creative lenses. As a theoretical construct, it is organic. Its shape
and composition may be changed; indeed, such a flexible evolution is
eagerly anticipated by the authors.

The previous definition provides the basis for the framework, and it is supplemented by the world order matrix consisting of categories arranged along horizontal and vertical axes (see Figure 7.1). The horizontal categories are the problems (and their components) we consider most relevant to the study of creating a more peaceful and just planet.* The vertical line includes the categories of actor-participants that may contribute to a social movement, an organization, or an institution affecting the outcomes of the problem areas. An investigator may decide to delete certain categories as irrelevant or of secondary priority, or alternatively may add others.

In effect, the matrix is a highly generalized shorthand for viewing the world system. It permits the student of world order to examine what systems analysts call the exchange relationships of the total system. The world system operates organically, according to the actions and interactions of its subsystems, a set of functions determined largely by the structural characteristics of subsystem parts and the total system. The matrix, in effect, permits one to observe, project, and evaluate the functioning of the whole system in relation to the achievement or negation of world order objectives. It also allows scrutiny of the most discrete unit of the system insofar as the individual can influence the global processes that militate for or against world order values. The relationships between the structures of value realization (reflected by the actors) and its processes (reflected in the problems) highlight the operation of the total system.[15] These relationships are organized according to different time intervals so that, by predicting outcomes, one is able to devise an appropriate strategy for social change.[16]

With regard to our techniques—the examination of the four procedural steps of diagnosis, prognosis, relevant utopias, and a transition to a preferred world—we use the matrix to help identify the most salient actors and processes for change and the interrelationships

---

*The reader should note that we have made explicit the generally accepted components of minimization of violence: arms policy, peacekeeping, conflict resolution. In an earlier version of the matrix, we elevated these components to the same level as the distinct problems of social injustice and poverty because of what we felt were the survival implications of war prevention. We now have no hierarchical distinctions among the values, asking that each participant define the components considered most important within each category. A particular investigator, however, still has the option to consider a particular problem such as ecological balance of such overwhelming importance for survival as to elevate its components, say population and pollution, to a par with the other values.

FIGURE 7.1

Matrix for the Study of World Order

Actor	Year	Minimization of Violence			Maximization of Economic Well-being			Maximization of Justice			Maximization of Ecological Balance		
		Arms Policy	Peace Keeping	Conflict Resolution	Per Capita Income	Life Expectancy	Education and Health Guarantees	Participation	Race Equality	Human Rights	Population Equilibrium	Pollution Control	Resource Balance and Growth
World (e.g., UN)	1970												
	1980												
	1990												
	2000												
International	1970												
	1980												
	1990												
	2000												
Regional	1970												
	1980												
	1990												
	2000												
Transnational	1970												
	1980												
	1990												
	2000												
National	1970												
	1980												
	1990												
	2000												
Infranational	1970												
	1980												
	1990												
	2000												
Individual	1970												
	1980												
	1990												
	2000												

Impact on Key Processes and Their Elements (can be ranked on a 10-point scale)

NOTES TO FIGURE 7.1

Achievement Scale for World Order Values with Minimal–Acceptable–Maximal Range (–5 to 0 to +5)

Peace:
    total war
    to
    minimization of violence
    to
    prevention of violence

Economic well-being:
    starvation
    to
    creation of tolerable conditions
    to
    maintenance of universal prosperity

Social justice:
    oppression
    to
    creation of tolerable conditions
    to
    maintenance of human dignity

Participation:
    totalitarianism
    to
    self-identity
    to
    active involvement in achievement of preferences

Ecological balance:
    collapse of ecosystems
    to
    restoration of balance
    to
    preservation of balance

FIGURE 7.2

World Order Methodology

World Order Value → Tasks ↓	Minimization of Violence	Maximization of Economic Well-Being	Maximization of Social Justice	Maximization of Ecological Balance
		(1) resources / food / energy (2) population (3) science and technology		
Diagnosis of present global situation				
Prognosis of existing trends: positive negative				
Prescription of "preferred worlds"				
Transition strategies				

162

among all problem areas (see Figure 7.2). These categories and their interrelationships are meaningful only insofar as the information they yield is relevant to the realization or negation of the basic value objectives. The order of magnitude (ranging from -5 to +5) one assigns to these relationships is called an achievement scale and refers to the investigator's estimate of the potential impact of the key processes over the next three decades.

In sum, the matrix and formal definition attempt to provide a concrete idea of the normative and empirical boundaries of world order. In other words, the investigator is asking: What is relevant to achievement of these goals? This set of analytical tools allows us to prove reality, discover new knowledge relevant to desired outcomes. They provide a cognitive map to perceive and order reality, to shape the future.

Three comments should be made concerning the relationship between the definition and the matrix before continuing the exposition. First, there may still be some confusion between the terms "problems" and "values." Although we are isolating problems, our response to them is not in terms of solutions but as human values to be realized. We prefer to use the term values, which has a dynamic and process-oriented connotation, rather than the term solutions, which seems too definitive and static and insufficiently open to continuing change.

Second, the matrix identifies participation as part of the value of social justice. However, a goodly number of individuals have concluded that participation is such an important ethical and pragmatic component in the construction of a viable, global political society that they isolate it and give it the significance accorded to the other values. We do not imply a secondary importance to participation in the matrix, but rather have judged its inclusion under social justice as more logical.

It also should be noted that, while the time periods shown in the matrix run from the decade 1970 to the year 2000, there is no theoretical reason why this particular frame of reference could not be utilized to review, analyze, and evaluate recorded history, the present, and future (although empirical data would not always be available for the various epochs). Much contemporary work in futurology has failed to deal with discontinuity, let alone the possibility that people may suddenly reshape their futures. We thus urge individuals concerned with global peace and justice to wrench themselves from history as much as possible. Humankind must formulate provocative scenarios of the future that can be actual guidelines for political behavior in the contemporary world.

SOME ADDITIONAL COMMENTS ON CONCEPTUALIZING
PEACE AND JUSTICE

It is important that international relations and world affairs have been linked in the first paragraph of the definition. This formulation recognizes that, in the images put forward by social scientists and decision makers, the nation-state system is still central to the dynamics of world politics. Nevertheless, that system is no longer a totally accurate empirical depiction of today's world, and it is even less likely to be so in the long run. Hence the term "world affairs."

We wish to reiterate the argument that this framework is problem-solving and value-realizing in its orientation. At this juncture, the authors do not seek to put forward a coherent ideological position. The important point is that many responsible and thoughtful people around the world have now recognized some world order problems as crucial to global survival with dignity, and it is imperative to begin holistic discussions of them.

One additional remark must be made here. Solutions to these problems do not necessarily imply global institutions. Problem-solving networks can be communal, local, national, transnational, regional, or global. Furthermore, it should be clearly understood that the distinctions between domestic, transnational, regional, and global interactions no longer have the heuristic value political scientists and activists gave to them earlier. There is now an interpenetration of these various arenas in which a fundamental realization is that responsibility for human problems and suffering is worldwide and the fate of all people is tied to finding appropriate global responses.

We turn to the operational standards for each problem area. A viable operational standard demands that one move beyond slogans and develop workable, action-oriented criteria. It is our contention that world order values are now capable of being defined in more precise terms than previously. One can begin with the problem of violence. As an initial matter, it is necessary to delineate the phenomena we shall investigate. Thus, the fact that some 150,000 people are killed and some 6 to 7 million injured on world highways annually is a matter of world concern. However, for reasons that at the moment remain commonsensical and intuitive, we argue that these figures are not now a part of the world order problem of violence, and here our naive realism comes to the fore. In other words, we begin to delineate the problem of violence with a recognized international rule: The threat of the use of force by one state against another is sufficient to invoke a response from the world community. A response could be forthcoming in the classic form of large-scale violence as one governmental bureaucracy calls for its military to cross a national boundary.

For the purposes of definition, it matters not whether one or one million casualties result, only that in such a situation the world community must respond.

While focusing initially on the existing rule and having excluded 150,000 automobile fatalities, naive realism might lead many people of good will and common sense to the view that the world community should intervene in a large number of instances of violence ordinarily considered within the domestic jurisdiction of states. The doctrine of noninterference raises several questions when such a doctrine leads to the carnage of 200,000 to 3,000,000 people in Indonesia, Somaliland, Bangladesh, Burundi, and Nigeria. Are existing definitions and methods of dealing with large-scale violence and war prevention sensible, let alone morally acceptable, for the world community? Are there some conceptions of humanitarian intervention or modified peacekeeping or some other doctrine that the world community might utilize to prevent such horrors? Another way of conceiving this standard would be to assign specific numeric alternatives to present statistics on death due to large-scale violence and military expenditures. Thus, for example, how does one organize a world in which by 1995 worldwide automobile deaths are down from the present annual figure of 150,000, and world military expenditures have fallen from $240 billion to $20 billion?

In formulating a standard for economic well-being, we should recall previous data indicating the gap between per capita incomes in the economically underdeveloped and overdeveloped areas of the world. Here we ask the question: Is it really possible to speak of solving global problems if the bottom 10 percent of the world population is not provided with some minimal standard, let us say $400 to $500 per capita? (Perhaps this would be better phrased in quality of life rather than dollars.) Does this not imply a maximal standard? Answers to these questions of per capita income are only part of the operational standards for economic well-being. One must not only consider a redistribution of income but also measures to insure access to work, education, housing, food, and medical care. Perhaps more fundamentally, is it not fitting to ask whether there is some notion of economic well-being related to the self-realization of each human being, and therefore some overlap with the notion of social justice?

Operationalizing social justice is a difficult task. Many seek a universal writ of habeas corpus, or equality for women, or liberalization of drug laws. While it seems extremely difficult to agree upon a globally meaningful definition of social justice, one area does seem to have emerged very clearly for world community action. With one notable exception in professed creed (South Africa), and despite a relatively large number of lamentable exceptions in practice, the world community has agreed that discrimination based on race is outrageous. Our hope is that this outrage could mobilize large numbers of people, and that action on such a clear criterion will help make other criteria of social justice generally acceptable over time.

Ecological balance connotes varying standards to various people, but there are some well-known and established data. Hence operational standards are more easily developed than for social justice. This does not mean that the ecological system does not involve a very complex set of interrelated problems; it does mean that more or less objective standards can be formulated.

Individual participation in decision-making processes is also a difficult standard to operationalize. Such a value demands sensitive consideration of cultural differences. However, since the sense of individual impotence has the potential to negate the realization of other world order values, new efforts at fostering participation are immediately necessary. Because individuals should be in control of their own lives, we must consider the tradeoffs that may be made—such as community control over medical and educational facilities—to compensate individuals for the fact that distant, large institutions regulate their lives in ways that previously went unregulated.

Next, an explicit recognition of the organic relationship among the problem areas is necessary. One approach to world order thinking contends that, in order to think of one problem area, one must immediately talk about all the others. This implies that at the United Nations Conference on the Human Environment in Stockholm during 1972, it was eminently sensible that talk about pollution and resource depletion was immediately related to discussions of disarmament and development. If one were to consider not crossing national boundaries as a method of delimiting violence, then the subject of white minorities also must be included. In other words, it is necessary to determine the kind of violence that can be sanctioned in order to reverse the structural violence within the racist system of South Africa. One standard might result from considering that black life expectancy there is 35 to 40 years while that of white counterparts is 70 years. How much legitimate violence by which groups and under what authority can be used to topple that white regime and narrow the gap shown in these statistics? While life expectancy is an available statistic and therefore relatively easy to consider, similar questions must be asked in relationship to other indicators of the general quality of black life in South Africa. Any viable analysis of peace and justice must come to grips with the linkages among values. Such a focus is more pertinent given our commitment to drastic systems change. As well as fairness dictating a comprehensive solution, interconnected political calculations also are necessary. In this fashion, the losses to any actor on a particular issue are offset by a sufficient net gain in the total system.

Our commentary now turns to two points concerning the actors participating in the potential solution of interrelated world order problems. First, it is necessary to emphasize the range of actors. Many discussions of peace and justice still exclusively employ the nation-state terminology appropriate to international law but, due to changes in underlying processes, increasingly irrelevant in political analyses. Second, by focusing on all actors between the individual and world institutions, we attempt to remain flexible and utilize the full range of actors with potential for initiating systems change. When a nation-state can accomplish a necessary portion of a strategy for peace and justice, why not utilize it? At other times, when transnational or world community inputs are more appropriate in problem solving, the nation-state system should be deemphasized. This is particularly important given our belief that various types of transnational groupings will become increasingly important and provide a solid basis for system-transforming processes. The business, communication, artistic, and church communities are likely to be the movers in transnational groupings demanding major change in the global political system.

Next, the meaning of relevant utopia leads to an important methodological point. Most simply, it is a concrete description of what a particular world would look like at some future time, and a trend analysis in similarly concrete terms of how that particular system could be realized. No utopia is irrelevant because it appears to be politically impossible at the moment. Any utopia is relevant if it describes in specific behavioral detail the process by which a more desirable world political system could be brought into being.

One reason for reviewing the range of relevant utopias stems from the fact that, despite a slowly growing consensus on global problems, there are no universal standards for the world we wish to achieve, or well-accepted methods for getting there. It is thus of crucial significance that as many individuals as possible throughout the world become involved in describing desired worlds and transition steps. These discussions have the potential to be learning mechanisms for transforming the system. Furthermore, unlike the behavioral scientist interested primarily in concretization and prediction, we want to be influenced by all possible views so that the standards ultimately will be more universally acceptable.

Reviewing the range of relevant utopias is not sufficient. Too many academic analysts have presented trends and facts without stating their own policy preferences and defending them. The component of a preferred world necessitates a value judgment and commitment by the investigator. One must select a vision from the total range of relevant utopias and then make a commitment to action so that this preferred world becomes more likely.

A few words about the role of law in facilitating peace and justice, and thus as a positive factor in social mobilization, seem appropriate. It is evident that radical politics, whether reactionary or progressive, will continue to be significant and attractive for many social and political movements at both the domestic and international levels. What has not yet been made sufficiently clear within this context is that the development of world institutions could be a radical notion. We are so accustomed to thinking of radicalism only in terms of revolution against authority that it requires a special effort to realize that the appeal of world law could be radically progressive, although law has traditionally been a method for controlling and restricting change to a minimum by the forces of order. Conservative speculations lead us to believe that the problems of the 1970s and 1980s—war, population, hunger, race relations, pollution of the environment, urban sprawl and the new set of problems arising from automation, interplanetary explorations, microbiology and eugenics, to mention but a few of the more salient possibilities—are fraught with the potential for large-scale social disorganization. Within such a context, it may very well be those individuals previously attracted to radicalism and revolution who will demand of their governments a more sane and just world system.

In other words, law is a universal experience. Whatever its limitations, law can be and should be appealed to as a rational method for achieving peace and justice. To be sure, law has operated oppressively and ineffectively, and these are good reasons for the suspicions of and hostility to solutions based on legal institutions. However, these are not objections to law itself but to its substantive content or a particular application. Aside from philosophical anarchists, most people (and this includes revolutionaries and victims of oppression) can envision a world in which proper law is used to control violence, resolve conflicts, redress harms, and promote social justice. In short, law as a method and goal for a world peace and justice movement can make sense to the peoples of the world.

Lastly, one must consider transition, admittedly the most difficult and therefore in some ways the weakest aspect of analyses of peace and justice. We are asking: Now that the problems have been identified as important, what specific kinds of drastic steps would lead to a global political system in which the world order values are important?

Soviet Academician Andrei Sakharov has described one transition strategy to his preferred world order:

> In the opinion of the author, it is necessary to have a tax on the developed countries equal to 20 per cent of the national income for the next fifteen years. The introduction of such a tax would automatically lead to a significant decrease in expenditures for weapons. Such joint aid would considerably help to stabilize and improve the

position of most underdeveloped countries; it would limit
the influence of extremists of all types . . . . Mankind
can develop painlessly only by viewing itself in the demographic sense as a unit, as one family without divisions
into nations, except from the point of view of history and
traditions. [17]

Whether Sakharov has articulated a desirable and feasible strategy is
debatable. What is important is that increasing numbers of people
have seriously begun to propose similar kinds of sweeping transition
steps. Our own transition strategy for the 1970s foresees the development of sufficient consensus about global problems so that a mobilization and societal transformation can occur in the final two decades
of this century. At this time, our own view is that the transition problem is most directly linked to education and global consciousness
raising.

CONCLUSION

This essay began with a quotation that we can now evaluate in
terms of our own values and methodology. We have argued that the
world order framework is a most appropriate frame of reference for
any person who wishes to analyze or work for global peace and justice.
The statement of former U.N. Secretary-General U Thant indicates a
basic agreement with our position. There is a set of global problems
and a decade within which to make some substantial progress in dealing
with them, or they "will have reached such staggering proportions that
they will be beyond our capacity to control." With this in mind, one
must carefully examine the prevailing drift of American foreign policy.
It is our belief that the world order discussion framework provides
an evaluative outline for the statement about the preferred world order
that many decision makers in the developed nations have articulated.
Two questions arise immediately: Do President Ford and Secretary
Kissinger conceive of problems globally, from the viewpoint of either
survival or the quality of life? Even if they do, would the image of the
world that they project furnish guidelines and solutions by which we
are willing to abide?

For the authors, the answer to both of these questions is an
emphatic no. Quite frankly, our view is that the elites of major powers
seem to be concerned with world order problems insofar as they may
cause unpleasantness, friction, or the threat of force among them.
Whatever their intellectual awareness of these problems, the elites
within this new pentagonal form of multipolarity have not truly

integrated their importance emotionally or ethically into a viable world view. For the moment at least, a five-unit balance-of-power world conceives Vietnam or mass human starvation as mere footnotes to history. This is so devoid of a visition of a global community with compassion that even if it were to work—and we have strong doubts that it would[18]—we would personally not want to become part of it. We know that there are hundreds of millions of people throughout the world who share our sentiment.

We urge all individuals, either as academicians or political activists, to see the question posed by U Thant and the solution suggested by the present administration as the underlying world order issue of the next decade. The basic motivation behind this essay is our conviction that it is essential for large numbers of individuals throughout the world to begin to produce more humane and compassionate visisions of a future global political system than that proposed by Messrs. Ford and Kissinger and implemented by the decision-making elites of many other nations.

NOTES

1. Two recent analyses of this theme are Dennis Pirages, Seeing Beyond: Personal, Social, and Political Alternatives (Reading, Mass.: Addison-Wesley, 1971), a collection of essays that suggest methods for overcoming dominant social paradigms and developing alternative lifestyles without violent revolution; George Lakey, Strategy for a Living Revolution (San Francisco: Freeman, 1973), which outlines a plan for a nonviolent revolution for industrial society. For a discussion of alternative jobs and careers with details about how to pursue positions in social change, see Charles R. Beitz and A. Michael Washburn, Creating the Future (New York: Bantam Books, 1974).

2. A summary discussion of these trends is John McHale, "World Facts and Trends," Futures 3, no. 3 (September 1971): 216-301, and "Comparative Indicators: World Facts and Trends," Futures 3, no. 4 (December 1971): 385-96.

3. We are not talking of a world without conflict within which there would be complete harmony, or the lion lying down with the lamb. The process of positing alternative world futures is not a question of choosing according to our temperaments or moods the brighter or darker side of human nature, but rather perceiving both together. Thus, we are referring to the possibility of achieving a world without large-scale organized violence but in which the processes of conflict, basic aggressiveness, and struggles for control are still present and therefore require an institutional means for their nonviolent resolution.

At the same time, however, we are not abandoning our original claim that war—as well as the other world order problems—is not inevitable. It is interesting to note, for example, that this opinion is shared by anthropologists like Margaret Mead, who feel that war is not a biological necessity or a sociological inevitability but just a bad invention. In terms of human "inventions," war may be analogous to marriage or cooking food instead of eating it raw. Mead states: "Whenever a way of doing things is found universally, such as the use of fire or the practice of marriage, we tend to think at once that it is not an invention at all but an attribute of humanity itself." "Warfare Is Only an Invention—Not a Biological Necessity," in Peace and War, Charles R. Beitz and Theodore Herman, eds. (San Francisco: Freeman, 1973), p. 113. It is sufficient to find peoples like the Eskimo or the Lepchas of Sikkim who do not understand war because they have never known it to demonstrate that war is not inevitable. What we are attempting to emphasize here is not the existence or nonexistence of aggression as a human drive, nor even its relative importance, but only that humankind acting collectively in war is characterized by institutionalized patterns of violence that have little or nothing to do with individual aggression or self-assertiveness.

4. This argument is developed rapidly in this essay because of the constraints of time and space. The interested reader is referred to a much longer discussion of conventional trends in teaching international politics, and some alternative themes and propositions for converting existing courses into world order ones. See Norman V. Walbek and Thomas G. Weiss, A World Order Framework for Teaching International Politics (New York: Institute for World Order Teaching Resource, 1974).

5. This applies not only to strict behavioralists but to nonbehavioral traditionalists like Hans Morgenthau, who use the concept of power to analyze nations' behavior in their international context and, less directly, to systems analysts like Morton A. Kaplan, who says: "The crux of the matter is whether regularities can be discovered which permit the organization of the materials of international politics within a simple framework of reasonable explanatory or predictive power." System and Process in International Politics (New York: John Wiley, 1967), p. 3.

6. Hans J. Morgenthau speaks disparagingly of the "idealist" school, which has little active following among students today, in Politics Among Nations (New York: Knopf, 1973).

7. In characterizing international relations, strategic studies, and peace research (which world order resembles in important respects), Michael Banks states:

> Exponents of all three fields would agree that their
> propositions ought to be established as a result of a

positive or value-free process of inquiry and theory-
testing, as the term "value free" is understood in social
science. But most international relations and strategic
scholars believe that their research can, at best, have
the ultimate effect of making only slight modifications to
the international system, by making it function rather
more smoothly. Peace researchers, in contrast, tend
to accept the proposition that ways can be found to transform the whole international system into something "less
costly economically and less outrageous morally."
(Boulding, 1969) In the minds of peace researchers, the
institutions of world politics function as they do at least
partly because of the fatalism of those who have studied
them, as well as because of the skepticism or even
cynicism of those who operate them. . . .

Peace research or conflict theory is concerned
with useful knowledge . . . it is concerned with constructing a set of theories which will facilitate not just
the smooth maintenance of existing relationships, but
the promotion of active peace and justice, and the planned
avoidance of cataclysms.

Michael Banks, "The Relationship Between the Study of International
Relations, Peace Research and Strategic Studies," paper presented
to UNESCO Advisory Meeting of Experts on UNESCO's Role in Devel-
oping Research on Peace Problems, Paris, July 21-25, 1969, pp. 5-6.
See also Irving Horowitz, ed., The Use and Abuse of Social Science
(New Brunswick, N.J.: Transaction Books, 1971).

8. See Arnold Wolfers, "The Actors in International Politics,"
in Theoretical Aspects of International Relations, ed. William T. R.
Fox (South Bend, Ind.: University of Notre Dame Press, 1959), pp. 83-
106. For collections of readings on this image and the others, see
Stanley Hoffman, ed., Contemporary Theory in International Relations
(Englewood Cliffs, N.J.: Prentice-Hall, 1960); James N. Rosenau,
ed., International Politics and Foreign Policy (New York: The Free
Press, 1969).

9. Karl Deutsch, The Nerves of Government (New York: The
Free Press, 1963); Ernest Haas, Beyond the Nation-State (Palo Alto,
Calif.: Stanford University Press, 1964), and Tangle of Hopes
(Englewood Cliffs, N.J.: Prentice-Hall, 1969).

10. J. David Singer, "International Influence: A Formal Model,"
American Political Science Review 57 (June 1963): 432.

11. See J. David Singer, "The Level-of-Analysis Problem in
International Relations," in The International System, eds. Klaus Knorr
and Sydney Verba (Princeton, N.J.: Princeton University Press, 1961),
pp. 77-92.

12. Charles A. McClelland, Theory and the International System (New York: Macmillan, 1966), p. 20. For a more detailed discussion of a whole or complex system, see pp. 22-23.

13. Harold D. Lasswell, in a discussion of the knowledge-for-what problem, maintained: "The point is that all the resources of expanding social science need to be directed toward the basic conflicts in our civilization." "The Policy Orientation," in The Policy Sciences, eds. Daniel Lerner and Harold D. Lasswell (Palo Alto, Calif.: Stanford University Press, 1951), p. 8.

14. We wish to acknowledge our debt to Richard Falk for his formulation of the transition strategy in these terms. See, for example, "Toward a New World Order: Modest Methods and Drastic Visions," in North American essay for the World Order Models Project, On the Creation of a Just World Order: Preferred Worlds for the 1990's (New York: The Free Press, 1974).

15. Charles A. McClelland's statement, "systems analysis is neutral with respect to the employment of any number of alternative approaches to inquiry," is applicable here. In using the matrix as an organizational frame of reference by which one searches for, organizes, and analyzes data, one may use both traditional or behavioral modes of research. "Historical, comparative, statistical, experimental and simulative approaches can be used in the work of system analysis one at a time or in combination." Charles A. McClelland, Theory and International System (New York: Macmillan, 1966), p. 192.

16. Although the matrix is amenable for use in a variety of research techniques, the futuristic time orientation of world order makes the techniques of forecasting particularly relevant: specifically "brainstorming," the Delphi technique, game theory, computer and mathematical modeling, decision-making analysis, relevance trees, operations research, and contextual mapping. For a good discussion of these, see Erich Jantsch, Technological Forecasting in Perspective (Paris: OECD Press, 1967). Moreover, since the empirical phenomena to be comprehended cover a huge variety of social processes, virtually all the social sciences as well as input from the humanities and natural sciences are relevant and necessary to world order research.

17. Quoted from a translation of the Russian original in Jagdish N. Bhagwati, Economics and World Order: From the 1970's to the 1990's (New York: The Free Press, 1972), p. 10. The complete document is available in English: Andrei D. Sakharov, Progress, Coexistence, and Intellectual Freedom (New York: Norton, 1968).

18. Charles Yost, formerly U.S. ambassador to the United Nations, supports this view: "We might begin by recalling that when Franklin Roosevelt and Cordell Hull helped set up the United Nations they did so in the firm conviction that the old-fashioned 'balance-of-

power' system had failed to prevent World Wars I and II and was bound to keep on failing simply because no strong nation is ever satisfied with a 'balance' unless it 'tilts' in its direction; unless each nation believes itself a little better armed, a little more potent than its rivals. So 'balance-of-power' is really a deceptive formula for competition, intrigue, and instability, rather than for international order, cooperation and peace." "Some Suggestions for the New Man at the U.N.," New York Times, January 25, 1973, p. 39.

8

A METHODOLOGY OF WORLD ORDER: JOINING HUMANISM AND SCIENCE

Francis A. Beer

METHODOLOGY AND WORLD ORDER

The essay attempts to delimit, in a very general way, an appropriate scope and method of world order. To undertake such a task, especially in such a small corner, may seem immodest or foolish. Yet it is justified by the concern of the volume in which it appears. Global design is a synonym for world order; planning for global design and the study of alternative world futures are methods for studying and perhaps changing it. [1]

Two Dimensions of World Order

The scope of world order is defined by two dimensions or sets of meanings for order and disorder. The first set of meanings shows a general humanistic concern. It is associated with the contemporary world order movement and comprehended in the terms: peace and violence. In this context, world order as a condition, desirable or actual, includes the attainment of certain core human values identifiable as peace. It also implies the absence of direct violence and the attainment of equity in the distribution of important social resources, justice, prosperity, liberty, fraternity. World disorder, in this definition, includes the opposites: direct and indirect violence, poverty, repression, and general hostility.

The idea of world order in this first humanistic sense is not new, nor are plans for reaching it a product solely of the twentieth century. A long list of illustrious historical figures including Dante,

Kant, Rousseau, and Bentham have developed architectonic plans for achieving a universal political system.[2] In recent years, interest in world order seems to have come to a new flowering. Even if one defines the domain quite narrowly, a number of groups have appeared with concrete world order interests. Important American publicists of the movement have included such academic figures as Falk, Mendlovitz, Boulding, and Fuller. If one construes world order more broadly, peace studies and peace research movements over the globe have contributed to the stream of interest and activity.

In spite of such growth, the world order movement has continued to be concerned with the problem of effectiveness. World order plans have yet to come to fruition. Although men have achieved partial empires, these have been based largely on military conquest. Both regional and universal international law and organization still have a considerable distance to travel before we can think of them as autonomous and authoritative, just and fulfilling in their own right. Given this continuing problem of effectiveness, it may be useful to continue to think about the methodology of world order. We must try to distinguish between what can be accomplished, what may not be achievable, and the appropriate way to deal with both.

A second set of meanings of world order and disorder is associated more closely with science. It centers around regularity and irregularity and assumes the existence of a coherent set of global relations, including war: a system discovered or discoverable through systematic study.[3] Conversely, world disorder represents a situation in which such regularities do not exist—a somewhat less popular view.

Such a conception of world order is one of the fundamental assumptions of logical empiricism, the dominant philosophy underlying contemporary social science, and is reflected in the generally accepted methodology of contemporary social science. At the same time, its assumption of a natural order is similar to an earlier belief in natural law. The covering laws of history are, in this conception, equivalent to general laws describing the functioning in societies in general and in particular.

Three Tasks of Methodology

The appropriate methodology for achieving world order in the humanistic sense of values to be maximized depends on one's assumptions about world order in the scientific sense of regularity. This essay analyzes the tasks implied by three such assumptions: natural world order, artificial world order, and world disorder. Depending on one's perspective, methods of science, engineering, and ethics may make important contributions.

THE METHODOLOGY OF NATURAL ORDER: WORLD SCIENCE

If we assume that order, in the sense of regularity, exists naturally in the world, we may undertake its discovery through orthodox scientific procedures. An elucidation of world order in this sense, moreover, can help us better understand world order in the other sense. The humanistic values and disvalues of world order, peace and violence, become the dependent variables that we must try to describe, explain, and predict. World science should reveal the extent and distribution of peace and violence as well as their causes.

A Morphology of Peace and Violence

One way to the systematic study of peace and violence is the development of a morphology, a taxonomy, to help us define what we mean by peace and violence.[4]

The broadest morphology in general use so far was developed by Johan Galtung.[5] It relies largely on a distinction between two types of violence—personal or direct, and structural or indirect—and two related types of peace—negative and positive (see Figure 8.1).

Direct violence involves consequences that are both manifest and intended. It includes easily identifiable objects being immediately and concretely harmed. It also implies observable subjects who are responsible for the damage.[*]

Indirect violence includes latent and perhaps even unintended effects. Indirect violence lacks the specifying characteristics of direct violence: the crass brutality of destruction or killing. Yet it can accomplish the same results more slowly through such instruments as poverty, disease, and hopelessness. It can comprehend

---

[*] The first condition is probably more important than the second. Thus accidental violence, for example, the legal category of manslaughter, probably ought to be included in the category of direct violence because it meets the first condition of direct harm, even though it fails to comply completely with the second.

FIGURE 8.1

Galtung's Morphology of Violence and Peace

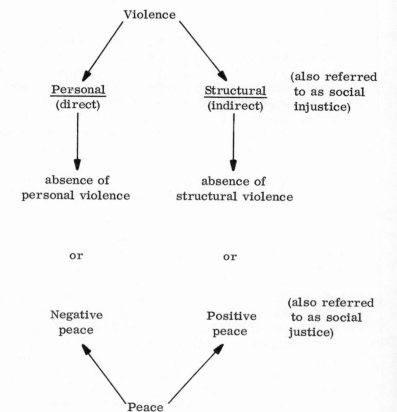

Source: Johan Galtung, "Violence, Peace and Peace Research,"
Journal of Peace Research, no. 3 (1969): 183.

political, economic, social, cultural, psychological, and technological dimensions. Indirect violence includes more abstract and circuitous relationships, where it is more difficult to pinpoint specific responsibility for the damage. Indirect violence is a form of violence that kills slowly and often anonymously. Where direct violence can be measured in immediate deaths or damage, a measure of indirect violence is "avoidable deprivation of life, measured in lost man-years."[6]

If we turn the coin, negative peace is essentially the absence of direct violence. Positive peace represents the elimination of indirect violence as well.

Galtung's morphology helps us begin to discriminate between different modes of violence and peace. We need not take it as the final word but may view it instead as an early prototype of an intellectual invention, which may be refined and developed.

We believe that it would probably be useful to add other properties to the morphology. A first aspect that has seemed important to contemporary scholars of international relations is the scope of communal activity or the level of analysis. We would distinguish between international, national, subnational, and individual violence and peace.[7]

The two dimensions are combined in Table 8.1, in which modes of violence and peace are arranged horizontally and levels of society vertically.

TABLE 8.1

An Expanded Morphology of Violence and Peace

	Modes of Violence		Modes of Peace	
	(1)	(2)	(3)	(4)
Level	Direct	Indirect	Indirect	Direct
1. International	war	injustice imperialism	justice	brotherhood of man
2. National	civil war revolution	oppression	due process	fraternity
3. Subnational	class war group war	domination	pluralism	solidarity synergism
4. Individual	homicide assault suicide	exploitation repression threat hate	equality liberty	self-realization love

Once such a matrix has been created, one should try to give appropriate names to each of the cells. (Better terms may be available than the ones we chose for particular cells; if so, the reader should add or substitute them.) This is relatively easy in column 1, which groups examples of direct, immediate physical harm with clearly defined subjects and objects. As one proceeds down the column, the scope of violence tends to diminish. International war is generally considered more extensive than civil or internal war, other things being equal. Revolution and class war may achieve a global scale; more often they occur relatively discretely within particular states. Group warfare includes race war, gang war, or range war, generally of subnational scope. Homicide, assault, and suicide may be components of larger social happenings, but they are also used to describe individual behavior.

The problem of nomenclature is more difficult in the remaining columns. The terms are harder to order and rank because they are quite general and no usually confined to a specific level. Most are widely used in a number of different contexts. Richness and resonance in our common-language vocabulary helps confuse attempts at analytic specificity.

I have arranged them subjectively, based on my own evaluation of the weight of common usage. Nevertheless, they can be applied to other levels simply by adding the name of the level involved, for example, international justice, national justice, class justice, individual justice, and so on. Although such phenomena at different levels are related, they are not the same thing.

In the second column are the elements of indirect violence. Injustice, following Galtung, is presumed to be generic, almost equivalent to the category of indirect violence itself. [8] Imperialism is an obvious international manifestation.

Most of the remaining terms are applicable to each level. Oppression, domination, exploitation, repression, threat, and hate suggest indirect violence whose scope may vary. We have arranged them in column 2 roughly in order of the scope they seem to us to usually suggest.

What Galtung calls negative peace implies the absence of direct violence at all levels, although indirect violence may still occur. Contrary to Galtung, we believe that our congruent term, indirect peace, also should include the general attainment of justice; order based upon law; the equal access of groups through the safeguards of due process and the workings of a healthy pluralism; and individual equality and liberty, defined to a considerable extent by guaranteed rights.

We would reserve the term direct peace for the characteristics described in column 4, when conflict itself has disappeared and is

replaced by a totally cooperative order, which includes the brotherhood of man, fraternity, solidarity, synergism, [9] and self-realization.
Direct peace places a greater weight on the collective and affective
aspects of man's nature. Even self-realization must come as part of
a larger social context. For example, at the individual level, such
self-realization involves the attainment of peace of mind and at least
some progress toward such currently metaphysical conditions as the
peace which passeth all understanding and eternal peace. [10] All this
implies a collective environment that we can not only admire but also
love.

An expanded morphology like the one we have presented can be
useful in a number of ways. First, it can help us to analyze and evaluate the implications of different political ideologies. In a sense, the
whole tableau orders the terms of Marxist belief. The violence of
columns 1 and 2 sketches phenomena found in advanced capitalist
society. The aspirations of column 3 are a sham, the superstructure
of capitalism which can never mean anything under present conditions.
The main hope for the future is the intensification of the malignant
dynamics of violence to such an extent that the whole system apocalyp-
tically lurches into fully developed socialism, the direct peace of
column 4.

Pragmatic liberalism is, at the same time, more optimistic
and more pessimistic. It is more optimistic because, while it recognizes the problems of columns 1 and 2, it does not really believe they
are as serious as Marxism suggests or that they will necessarily
bring on cataclysmic collapse. Liberals are more pessimistic because,
by and large, they share with conservatives a skepticism about the
possibility of ever reaching column 4, at least in this life. Most of
their money goes down on the solutions of column 3, indirect peace.
The dynamics of the free political economy, the normative ends posited by legalistic, rationalistic, individualistic theory, imply constraints and limits.

Western socialism, much of the New Left, and the contemporary
counterculture, however, do look toward the possibility of achieving
the direct peace of column 4, transcending both the revolutionary
dynamics of orthodox Marxism and the structures of democratic
liberalism.

A morphology such as the one we have sketched also helps us to
begin to define and arrange the scope of our scientific concern. It is
the first step in creating an analytic structure to link with empirical
data, the multiple objective indicators of global reality.

A World Field Theory

An ultimate aim of social science is a world field theory—an integrated model that would describe, explain, and predict the regularities of world order. Such a theory would be a world field theory in two senses. It would bring together, refocus, and expand what has hitherto been the rather amorphous disciplinary field of international relations. It also would elaborate a complex analytical network of global causal relations.

Our morphology of violence and peace is a step in the development of this field theory. We must, however, go beyond it in a number of important respects. To begin, considerable detail should be added to the infrastructure of the matrix. Table 8.2 suggests one possible way to proceed. As before, we may separate the scope of activity into international, national, subnational, and individual levels.

Now, however, we add another dimension—sector of activity; and we specify three aggregate areas—political-military, socioeconomic, and psychocultural.[11]

In this new field matrix we place plus and minus signs that differentiate between peace and violence, and forces tending to support them.

TABLE 8.2

The World Field: A Matrix

	Political-Military (1)	Socioeconomic (2)	Psychocultural (3)
1. International	+	+	+
	-	-	-
2. National	+	+	+
	-	-	-
3. Subnational	+	+	+
	-	-	-
4. Individual	+	+	+
	-	-	-

Viewed in this way, we see that even our expanded morphology represented only a small part of the picture. The world field is broader than the morphology. It not only contains everything we had previously believed important but goes well beyond it. Thus the negative political-military elements in the world field include what we had labeled direct violence, while positive political aspects comprehend indirect peace. Similarly, the elements of indirect violence are to a considerable extent negative socioeconomic valences; direct peace, positive psychocultural ones.

A full inventory of the world field obviously should include additional elements.[12] In this essay, however, we cannot provide and justify a complete catalogue.

We wish not only to be able to name all the relevant elements in the world field but also to know their relations to each other, how they interact in causal sequences. We already have partial attempts in the pioneering efforts of Quincy Wright and A. Andreski. These models do not allow for activity at different systemic levels, nor do they distinguish between sectors. Yet they do specify additional variables that might be included within our matrix, and they suggest some of the possible relations among them.[13]

We need to build upon such efforts, synthesizing and integrating current knowledge to provide a comprehensive path model for violence and peace. Beyond the simple drawing of causal arrows, it is also necessary to begin to add in numerical coefficients, based on the results of empirical research.

As the world field theory is elaborated, our models of the international system will increasingly look like contemporary econometric models of national economies. At the end of the line lies a set of field equations, analogous to the unified field theory so sought after by and elusive to post-Einsteinian theorists of natural physical order.

THE METHODOLOGY OF ARTIFICIAL ORDER: WORLD ENGINEERING

The world field theory will be useful not only in explaining the past and present but also in predicting the future.[14] Presumably, if there is a natural world order and we have a unified field theory delineating it, we will know about future states of peace and violence as well as past ones.

Conceivably, the ultimate conclusions of such an investigation might be that world order in both senses—humanistic value maximization and scientific regularity—already exists. Perhaps the existing world actually represents the best that man could hope for. Perhaps, in economic terms, we have already reached Pareto optimality. Human investigation and experimentation might reveal that the story of the Garden of Eden is not retrospective[15] and that alternative world orders are worse.

Those who self-consciously study world order suspect that such optimality does not presently exist. The degree of violence, material inequality, and repression is such that they not only hope but assume that there must be room for improvement. Beyond "pure" science lies applied world engineering. Areas of natural regularity that world science discovers can themselves be used as levers to create new areas of more "artificial" regularity and humanistic value enjoyment. World order in this sense is analogous to positive law, helping man self-consciously rearrange the elements of his society in such a way that positive values are achieved in better configurations.

A unified world field theory, like a blueprint, will help us to elaborate projections and policies for the future to provide the maximum chance for peace and the minimum for violence.

Alternative Future Projections

A first step in world engineering is the elaboration of alternative world projections, pictures of how the world field may look within different time periods extending into the future. A good deal of work already has been undertaken in this area.[16] Nevertheless, just as the field theory promises to bring together empirical knowledge of the past and present, it also can help to further consolidate our considerations of the future.

The world field concept will allow us to specify different directions of future development. For example, we may label two alternatives Opening and Closing World Order. Opening World Order is a scenario in which the numerical signs are positive, in which the dynamic of the system tends toward increasing realization of the values of world order studies, the vision of Chardin. Opening World Order thus implies a reduction of direct and indirect violence and movement toward the justice, equality, liberty, brotherhood, love, self-realization, and other characteristics of indirect and direct peace. Closing World Order, on the other hand, represents a situation in which the valences are negative and the system tends toward the realization of disvalues, for example, the anti-utopias of Orwell. Here armed conflict, injustice, repression, hate, and other elements of direct and indirect violence increase while peace seems an increasingly distant, unrealizable, hopeless prospect.

Complex computer simulations may help to elaborate variations of these alternatives, pretesting the interactions of the field's components under different conditions. The simulations in turn will be like a book of maps, a set of preexisting constructs against which to test the configuration of present empirical events.

Alternative Future Policies

As events unfold, we will be able to see more clearly in which direction we are heading. We will have a clearer idea of which parameters of the field are relatively determined, which are subject to variation—and the probabilities involved. We also may know which can be changed with the resources available to public policy makers and citizens. [17] We will then be able to assess in a more systematic fashion the relative utilities, the prospects and costs of alternative future policies.

The world field theory will assist us predictively in elaborating systematically alternative future states that may occur, and normatively by helping us to define details of conditions we may wish to avoid or achieve. Obviously, given a choice, we would wish to travel along the path of Opening World Order, or at least avoid Closing World Order.

The world field theory will be a radar for spaceship earth, providing important information on critical variables. With it we will have the machinery in place to provide continuous monitoring of key indicators in the international system. We will be able to detect undesirable shifts and danger points. And we will be able to undertake action with some assurance that it offers the best chance of achieving the optimal realization of desired values within a world of finite resources and boundaries.

It will give states, corporations, groups, and individuals common bases of information about their path vectors, indicating, among other things, whether they are on collision courses. Secretaries general, experts, and delegates in international organizations; national leaders, bureaucrats, and other foreign-policy elites; and private citizens are all called upon to act or not in different ways in the international arena. With an elaborated and accepted world field theory, they will know better which way to turn, when and where to speed up and slow down.

THE METHODOLOGY OF ACTION: WORLD ETHICS

A third task of world order methodology is the development of world ethics, providing a code of action. These ethics are appropriately based on the humanistic value of peace, but they vary according to the degree of regularity implied by world science and engineering. We present a simple typology of ethical modes in Figure 8.2.

FIGURE 8.2

World Ethics: A Matrix

Engineering	Science	
No	No	Yes
	deontology	determinism
Yes	teleology: experimentalism	teleology: rationality

Deontological Ethics

Deontological ethics are the ethics of action in that part of the world where choices are difficult, where regularities are either limited or obscure. Where the regularities of world science and engineering are absent, or only primitively developed, deontological ethics suggest that acts have meanings in themselves, regardless of their subsequent consequences: "A deontologist contends that it is possible for an action or rule of action to be the morally right or obligatory one even if it does not promote the greatest possible balance of good over evil for self, society, or universe. It may be right or obligatory simply because of some other fact about it or because of its own nature."[18] Deontological ethics imply that, rather than the ends justifying the means, the means justify the ends.

Such an absolute conception of morality is often associated with religion, for example the golden rule of Christianity, or philosophy, as in Kant's categorical imperative, or contemporary existentialism.[19] Nevertheless, it is also at the root of humanistic science; for example, the Hippocratic Oath taken by physicians to try to preserve life, an absolute value.

From this perspective, attempts to discover and build world order through the development of world science and engineering are in themselves deontological ethical acts, with primary value placed on peace in the broadest sense. We hope that they will succeed, yet our belief is intuitive, not something we can really adduce from firm knowledge or from an empirically based calculation of probabilities.

Even if it were unsuccessful, the work of world science and engineering still would be ethically legitimated. As we hopefully wait for its products to accumulate, our thought and study, research and teaching represent important forms of social creation by themselves— at the least a kind of affirmation or witness.

Teleology

Teleological ethics imply that acts be undertaken in such a way that the chances of achieving valued ends are maximized by the choice of antecedent means. Action is justified and legitimated on the basis of the "value that is brought into being."[20]

One form of teleological action is experimentalism. Its scientific foundation is limited, as in the case of deontological action. Yet experimental action opens the door to world engineering. Actions are guided by a teleological imperative. They are carefully and systematically chosen and monitored to measure their results and compare alternative actions under multiple sets of circumstances. Not only politics but even science itself is thus subject to the test of performance.

To the extent that world science and engineering help describe world systems and relate them to the core humanistic values of peace and violence, they make a contribution to ethical action in this sense. Even if they do not dot the last i or cross the t of world regularities, they increase our ability to achieve ends and means appropriate to man.

More rigorous teleological action, rational decision, is only possible when both science and engineering have established a relatively advanced state of regularization. Such rationality is only meaningful if there is some certainty—or at least knowledge of the distribution of probabilities—about the relationship between actions and their consequences. It is the ethics of structure, of an ordered system, in which there are clearly defined and predictable causal relations. It is the ethic of fully developed bureaucracy and administration.

Determinism

The progress of science and engineering are theoretically self-limiting. We could conceivably arrive at the point that we were aware of all the determinants and consequences of our actions; and this perfection implied the futility of any attempt to alter them.

Such progress would negate the very possibility of ethical action. Ethical action is only possible where the field is mixed, where some irregularity exists. In our accepted conceptions, abstract terms generally are defined by their opposites, by the possibility of their falsification. If the world were totally regular, unethical action would simply be impossible. The same would be true if it were totally irregular. In these cases, ethics would cease to be a meaningful concept for our lives.

We are, however, very far from such perfection. Both regularity and irregularity are important dimensions of our present world; they are likely to continue in the future as well. Even if new areas of regularity are found or created by world science and world engineering, there will still remain substantial sectors of irregularity. Even if world science and engineering help isolate and shrink these, they will probably not eliminate them. Even world radar will not be able to ascertain the wakefulness of its guardians. Indeed in some bizarre cases, like insurance fraud, captains may willingly sink their ships. Different decision makers may wish to adjust matters by adjusting different components of the equations, and such adjustments may still leave enough room for mutual error that violence at all levels will result.

One major focus of contemporary humanism is an absolute imperative of the preservation and improvement of life.[21] This seems an appropriate bias on which to found world science and world engineering, an ultimate end against which to measure teleologically justified means. It offers a counterpoint to the temptations of "realism," despair, or nihilism, to the call of the system one cannot beat to join it, to flow with the tide, the process. At the same time, it leaves an important place for a spontaneous, immediate, and intuitive humaneness, without which any future world, no matter how orderly or justified in other respects, represents a terrible irony.[22] It is important that those concerned with world order bear this in mind lest they work against the very goals that must legitimize their activities.

NOTES

1. A number of friends and colleagues were kind enough to provide encouragement, comments, and suggestions. I am particularly indebted to the careful and detailed remarks of Jack Jacobs and Karl Schmitt and to the stimulation of Michael Washburn and the World Order group at the University of Texas.

2. See E. Wynner and G. Lloyd, Searchlight on Peace Plans: Choose Your Road to World Government (New York: E. P. Dutton, 1946); F. H. Hinsley, Power and the Pursuit of Peace: Theory and Practice in the History of Relations Between States (Cambridge: Cambridge University Press, 1967).

3. If such natural regularity does not indeed exist, our attempts to discover it through systematic study would of course hinder rather than help us to understand the "real" situations. See E. Husserl, The Crisis of European Sciences and Transcendental Phenomenology, trans. D. Carr (Evanston, Ill.: Northwestern University Press, 1970).

4. There are significant and sometimes acrimonious definitional differences between those presently at work in the field. In spite of the common concerns of those who identify themselves with world order or peace research, there often seems to be a cleavage between those who are more positively inclined and focus on peace and others who concentrate more explicitly on the negative aspects of reality, or violence. This gap is not necessarily bridged by the substitution of the word "peacelessness" for violence. See C. Wulf, ed., Handbook on Peace Education (Frankfurt/Main and Oslo: International Peace Research Association, 1974). In some cases, differences are appropriate because the concerns and motivations of the researchers are actually opposed. In other cases—for example, when all feel themselves to be concerned with the achievement of peace and the elimination of violence—they are unfortunate. Moreover, similar differences exist between subgroups concerned with particular topics, each of which seems, to those involved with it, to be of primary importance.

See B. Carroll, "Peace Research: The Cult of Power," Journal of Conflict Resolution, December 1972, pp. 585-616. In such instances, the fact that different researchers are concerned with different aspects of the same general problem results in the irony of intra-peace research conflict.

It is difficult to join the parts without some explicit analytical scheme that shows the relationship of each of these to the others, and to the general problem of peace and violence. Unfortunately, the problem is made more difficult because there is no one determinate way in which the different elements may be synthesized and arranged. Moreover, the terms used by those with different concerns are

applicable in many different contexts and overlap across categories.
In spite of the difficulties involved, it is possible to work toward the
construction of a comprehensive and complex morphology of peace
and violence. A step in this direction is the combination of two dimensions that previously existed in relatively separate identity: the modes
and the levels of peace and violence.

5. See J. Galtung, "Violence, Peace and Peace Research,"
Journal of Peace Research, no. 3 (1969): 167-91.

6. See J. Galtung and T. Høivik, "Structure and Direct Violence:
A Note on Operationalization," Journal of Peace Research, no. 1
(1971): 73-76.

7. See K. N. Waltz, Man, the State and War (New York:
Columbia University Press, 1959); J. D. Singer, "The Level of Analysis Problem in International Relations," World Politics 14 (1961):
77-92; J. Rosenau, ed., Linkage Politics (New York: Free Press,
1969); and K. W. Deutsch and D. Senghaas, "The Steps to War: A
Survey of Systems Levels, Decision Stages, and Research Results,"
in Sage International Yearbook of Foreign Policy Studies, vol. 1,
ed. P. J. McGowan (Beverly Hills, Calif.: Sage, 1973).

Distinctions between these levels reflect the variation in human
social activities and concerns of different scope. We should, however,
bear in mind that they are not entirely faithful to the complex inter-
penetrations of social reality, and they continue to contribute to the
reification of abstractions that are dysfunctional in many respects.

To think in terms of "national" activities, for example, may
draw our attention away from regularities at the higher and lower
levels that occur without much relevance to national boundaries.
Further, to the extent that we believe in the identity of the nation, we
also may place a positive value upon it and may commit violence in
its name. See J. S. Nye and R. O. Keohane, eds., Transnational
Relations and World Politics (Cambridge, Mass.: Harvard University
Press, 1971). The perspective of the general system does help to
put the nation, and the other levels, in their place. At the same time,
it promotes a new abstraction that can have similar implications.

8. Justice and injustice are central concerns of the world order
movement. O. R. Young, "On International Order," mimeo. (Austin,
1971), for example, provides an extended discussion of their relationship.

9. I acknowledge with thanks William Galston's suggestion of
the opposition between pluralism and synergism.

10. See A. G. Newcombe and H. Newcombe, "Approaches to
Peace Research," Peace Research Reviews 4, no. 4 (February 1972):
1-23.

11. See E. B. Haas, Beyond the Nation State (Palo Alto, Calif.:
Stanford University Press, 1965); J. D. Singer, "Modern International

War: From Conjecture to Explanation," in A. Lepawsky et al., Essays in Honor of Quincy Wright (New York: Appleton-Century-Crofts, 1971), pp. 47-71.

12. For example, it is clear that the positive socioeconomic and negative psychocultural dimensions need elaboration. Presumably justice includes both the optimal production of socioeconomic goods and their allocation according to consensual principles of equity. Exclusivist group identification and egocentrism are only two elements of the psychocultural foundations of violence. See E. Boulding, "The Child and Non-Violent Social Change," in Handbook of Peace Education, ed. Wulf, for a fascinating overview of our knowledge about the socialization of children for violence. J. D. Singer, "Individual Values, National Interests, and Political Development in the International System," Studies in Comparative International Development 6, no. 9 (Beverly Hills, Calif.: Sage, 1970-71), discusses the development of appropriate indicators for the different dimensions.

13. For these models, see Quincy Wright, The Study of International Relations (New York: Appleton-Century-Crofts, 1955), p. 564; A. Andreski, Military Organization and Society (Berkeley: University of California Press, 1968). Each of these early field models specifies causal orderings of variables believed to be important at the time. Of course the variables differ to some extent from each other and from our own initial selection. Some of them seem difficult to operationalize. These anomalies should be reconciled in a later-generation comprehensive and integrated world field model.

14. Here we undertake an important shift in focus, moving from cognitive to projective attempts to understand our world. J. Monod, Change and Necessity (New York: Vintage, 1972), p. 149, distinguishes between the two as follows:

Cognitive understanding: "To register events which, by the yardstick of . . . specific performances, are significant; to group them into classes according to their analogies; to associate these classes according to the relationship [of coincidence or succession] of the events constituting them; and to enrich, refine, and diversify the innate programs by incorporating these experiences into them."

Projective understanding: "To imagine, that is to . . . simulate external events and programs of action for [oneself]."

15. See M. Eliade, Myth and Reality (New York: Harper and Row, 1963), Chapter 2.

16. We cannot even begin to sketch the state of futurology here. Useful reviews appear in A. Toffler, Future Shock (New York: Random House, 1970); D. Livingston, "Science Fiction Models of Future World Order Systems," International Organization 25, no. 2 (Spring 1971): 254-70. See also E. B. Haas, "Future Worlds and Present International Organizations: Some Dilemmas," Bulletin of the International

Institute for Labour Studies (Geneva), no. 6 (1968), for a discussion of the crucial role of international organization in linking present and future worlds; M. D. Hancock and G. Sjoberg, Politics and the Post-Welfare State (New York: Columbia University Press, 1972), for a consideration of existing Western domestic prototypes for the future; and D. V. Edwards, Creating a New World Politics (New York: McKay, 1973) on the importance of our own images of process and change.

17. See J. D. Singer, "The Peace Researcher and Foreign Policy Prediction," Papers of the Peace Science Society 21 (International 1973): 1-13. Of course, active policy making complicates the problem of constructing the field theory itself. The theory will rest on deterministic and probabilistic foundations, on a relatively continuous conception of change. Human intervention increases the element of contingency, the possibility of sudden discontinuous variation. Presumably a metatheory will ultimately emerge that makes provision for change that is both continuous and discontinuous, and allowance for the effects of multiple countervailing and reinforcing elites becoming influential, under specified sets of future circumstances. Among these might be certain macrostrata, not only politicians, scientists, and engineers but also artists of different kinds.

18. See W. K. Frankena, Ethics (Englewood Cliffs, N.J.: Prentice-Hall, 1963), p. 14.

19. In view of J. P. Sartre, Search for a Method, trans. H. E. Barnes (New York: Vintage, 1963), pp. 85, 126, 150-51, 178-79, man is a creator, defined not only as an object, "a passive product, a sum of conditioned reflexes," but also as a participating human subject, a "mediator" who defines himself by his own project or plan, who helps to produce himself and others "by work and praxis" within the nexus of particular concrete historical events.

Scientific man is thus a deontological actor, "a practical organism producing knowledge as a moment of its praxis." See also S. de Beauvoir, L'Existentialisme et la Sagesse des Nations (Paris: Nagel, 1968); and G. Radnitzky, Contemporary Schools of Metascience, 2nd ed. (New York: Humanities Press, 1970).

20. See Frankena, Ethics, p. 13.

21. See J. S. Ackerman, ed., The Future of the Humanities, special issue of Daedalus (Summer 1969).

22. See H. Marcuse, One-Dimensional Man: Studies in the Ideology of Advanced Industrial Society (Boston: Beacon Press, 1964); J. Habermas, Toward a Rational Society (Boston: Beacon Press, 1970).

CHAPTER

9

REFORMING
WORLD ORDER:
ZONES OF
CONSCIOUSNESS
AND DOMAINS OF
ACTION
Richard A. Falk

WORLD ORDER: A NEW CONSCIOUSNESS

In 1971 U Thant, while secretary-general of the United Nations, told the twenty-sixth session of the European Economic Commission, "If the great French philosopher Descartes were alive today he would probably revise his celebrated rules for good thinking and add two new principles: the principle of global thinking and the principle of thinking well ahead into the future."[1] Such prescriptions for relevant thought properly address themselves to matters of spatial and temporal orientation. Such explicit imperatives respond to a widespread appreciation that we live at a time of danger and opportunity, not just as Americans or Nigerians or Frenchmen, but as human beings concerned with the destiny of our species and the welfare of our planet. This aroused concern has generated an unprecedented effort to achieve a planetary perspective on human problems and prospects.

There is, as yet, no consensus about how to achieve such a planetary perspective beyond the very elementary need to detach oneself, to the extent possible, from too firm an anchorage in the particularities of time and space. One approach to universalization of thinking is to move from considerations of quality to considerations of quantity. Numbers are more objective than words, data more

George Braziller, Inc., from "Reforming World Order: Zones of Consciousness and Domains of Action," by Richard A. Falk, appearing in The World System: Models, Norms, Variations, edited by Ervin Laszlo, reprinted with the permission of the publisher and author. Copyright © 1973 by Ervin Laszlo.

persuasive than opinions, charts more convincing than speculations
or prophecy. The scientific temper of the times reinforces this effort
to evolve a valid planetary perspective by so-called objective methods,
and indeed a whole subdiscipline of sorts has grown up under the label
"futurology."[2]

But somehow such exercises in quantification and projection are
not nearly enough.[3] One comes away from reading Kahn and Wiener's
The Year 2000, a characteristic effort, with a sense of having tra-
versed an intellectual desert, which despite the methodological games-
manship is unable to develop any orientation to the world -- the future
that is either useful or inspiring.[4] In the end, Kahn and Wiener are
technocratic prisoners of the present, as insensitive to the future and
the planet as a whole as if they had been given a severe dose of brain-
washing tranquilizers by the power wielders in the advanced industrial
countries who were terrified by the prospect of genuine visionary
thinking. To be more specific in my indictment, the time-future of
the futurologist is so uninteresting because it is devoid of either vision
or empathy, it lacks both the force of human imagination or the moral
strength that derives from feelings of solidarity with and sympathy
for the human race as a whole.

These shortcomings also afflict, I believe, the much more significant work of the Meadows group carrying out the project on the
Predicament of Mankind in association with the Club of Rome,[5] which
was so successfully promoted that it engendered a mainstream backlash from those who felt threatened by the covert ideology locked in
the phrase "the limits to growth."[6] Jay Forrester's public impact
is almost directly attributable to the use of the computer as a basis
for presenting an argument about the perils to the planet deriving from
the dynamics of economic and demographic growth. Such an argument
is qualitatively compelling, and in this sense is to be sharply distinguished from the inconsequentiality of Kahn-Wiener, but to connect it
up with the objectivity of numbers and the authority of the computer
is to engage, however unintentionally on the level of motivation, in a
gigantic public-relations hoax. We do not have sufficient information
to feed the computer, and we have no reason to regard its printouts
as trustworthy, at least not for a long time.[7] To work toward computer credibility is an urgent task of highest priority for those of us
seeking to follow U Thant's updating of Cartesian imperatives, but to
hire a public-relations outfit to preach as gospel the present printouts
is to participate, I fear, in the worst sorts of neoastrological games
of mystification; religion is not the only opiate of the people.[8]

William Irwin Thompson has provided a brilliant critique of
these technocratic forays into the future from the perspective of cultural history.[9] Thompson regards Aurelio Peccei, the founder of the
Club of Rome, as an example of a "new postindustrial manager" who

has the "institutional corporate politics of a Catholic Cardinal."
Thompson indicts Peccei's vision and his method as imperial, as
tending toward a coercive reordering of economic and political relations under concentrated secular power, and because it is prosaic,
unable to transcend the forms of thought that gave birth to the problems.[10] As Thompson puts it, "If you are going to humanize technology, you're not going to be able to do it within the limited terms of
books and civilization and other older containers. You've got to go
very far out."[11] In order to go very far out, Thompson has seriously
proposed an effort to bring about a reunion of scientific and mystical
thinkin；in small-scale institutions that embody a vision of the future.[12]
In my view, such an orientation, although preliminary and tentative,
provides solid ground upon which to build up a relevant kind of consciousness about the future receptive to knowledge and wisdom, and
yet oriented toward change and decency. My only caveat is that such
an enterprise may be too aloof from the urgent demands for present
response. To choose residence in a monastic sanctuary entails a
rejection of direct participation. Adherents become well-fed spec-
tators in a world of hunger and bloodshed, even unwitting accomplices
of those Forest Hills homedwellers who, while Kitty Genovese was
killed, watched from their living room windows without even lifting a
phone to summon the police. So I would add that we cannot become
trustworthy about the future unless we show signs of being trustworthy
in the present. For Americans, at least, it is morally (and hence
intellectually) impossible to propose a new Jerusalem, and yet at the
same time be agnostic or indifferent about genocide and ecocide in
Indochina.[13]

These comments about a new consciousness are designed to set
the stage for an inquiry into the future of world order. I accept fully
the mandate for a planetary, future-oriented perspective, but seek to
avoid any dogmatic assumptions that its realization depends on objective or detached knowledge. In this sense, the unity of thought and
feeling are essential ingredients of a relevant approach to the future.
With these considerations in mind it still seems possible and desirable,
indeed necessary, to propose new ways of envisioning—really re-
visioning—the future so as to break the bonds of present constraints
on moral and political imagination. In this sense my purpose is primarily educational, awakening the reason of men to the idea of wholeness as the basis for individual or collective sanity. Just as the
biologist tends to focus on survival as a normative touchstone,[14] so
the social scientist should be concerned with conditions of collective
health and welfare. Seneca observed that "between public madness
and that treated by doctors the only difference is that the latter suffers
from disease, the former from wrong opinions,"[15] and it is this
analogy that I would stress as focal to our efforts to provide the

ingredients of a preferred future capable of rekindling hope, and hence, of remobilizing energies for action. Unlike Seneca, however, I believe that public madness is a result of far more complex forces than merely wrong opinions, or, put differently, that the wrong opinions rest upon cultural and philosophical underpinnings that cannot be removed merely by argument or evidence.

For instance, the American involvement in Indochina illustrates an extreme form of public madness, but there is something very functional about its persistence given the realities of American culture. Kurt Vonnegut, Jr., correctly I think, places emphasis on Americans as winners in a world of scarcity and misery: "The single religion of the Winners is a harsh interpretation of Darwinism, which argues that it is the will of the universe that only the fittest should survive."[16] Inuring itself to the fighting in Vietnam all these years provides American society with the moral hardening needed in a world of growing inequity and desperation. To quote Vonnegut once more: "The Vietnamese are impoverished farmers, far, far away. The Winners in America have had them bombed and shot day in and day out, for years on end. This is not madness or foolishness as some people have suggested. It is a way for the Winners to learn how to be pitiless." And why is this necessary given America's prowess and prosperity? Because the Winners understand "that the material resources of the planet are almost exhausted, and that pity will soon be a form of suicide."[17]

Vonnegut's perception of the psychology of the ruling group is very important because it suggests that what is public madness on one level (the waste of resources, the dissent at home, the loss of international prestige—in other words the whole gamut of arguments that have turned liberals against the Vietnam war over the years) is the essence of rulership on another.[18] And this brings us to the essence of the world order context that exists at the present historical moment: Are the prescriptions of the Winners necessary or desirable? Are there alternatives?

Posing these questions somewhat differently: Is the Darwinian ethos adaptable to our contemporary situation? Does the notion of the survival of the fittest provide sound counsel for action on the part of power centers within the present system of world order? There is no doubt that profound challenges are being posed by the crowding of the planet and the depletion of its resources. These challenges are intensified by the destructive technology of warfare that is being spread throughout the world, as well as by the vulnerability of the postindustrial world to well-conceived disruption. We have a world order crisis of unprecedented magnitude, involving issues of irreversible ecological decay by accumulating pollution, phenomena of potential mass famine

and pandemics, and the possibility—never more than an hour away—
of catastrophic war.

In such circumstances, we are, recalling Seneca's precept,
confronted by a prime necessity to identify "wrong opinions" as quickly
as possible. This necessity can be approached from many angles. We
will here consider it from the viewpoint of world order reform: What
changes are desirable and possible within the next several decades?
How can we most effectively think about world order change so as to
conceive of real alternatives in a manner that is the captive neither
of present cliches nor prospective fantasies? We ask these questions
as a social scientist respectful of evidence and discipline, yet sensitive
to the criticism that "scientific method" as it has been understood by
Western social scientists has excluded many realities that will inform
the politics of transformation. William Irwin Thompson, Doris Lessing,
or Kurt Vonnegut are world order thinkers of relevance precisely because they are "open" to these nonrational sources of insight into the
present and future.

THE ORIENTING IMPERATIVES

Our approach to the study of world order reform is based on two
orienting imperatives: the methodological imperative and the normative imperative. Each of these imperatives requires some explanation.

The Methodological Imperative

We accept here the need for disciplined inquiry, for systemic
comprehensiveness, and for continuous revision of our designs for the
future. To be concerned with world order is to be concerned with basic
relations of power and authority that operate throughout the planet.
Such relations are not exhausted by an analysis of state sovereignty in
the modern world, although such an analysis is of great significance.
There are many actors on the world scene other than national governments that need, increasingly, to be taken into account. The activities
of the multinational corporations, international institutions, transnational associations (whether of airline pilots or Red Cross officials),
and of change-oriented social movements operating at all scales of
organization, are important aspects of the world order system, and
condition its potentiality for change.

Of basic significance is the hypothesis that authority is related to power, and that in the world order system of today power is concentrated in a relatively small number of large national governments and closely affiliated corporate entities. Such a hypothesis has tactical implications. It implies, for one thing, that changing the world order system depends on altering the perceptions, values, and personality features of ruling groups in these key actors or in replacing these ruling groups with new elites having different perceptions, values, and personality features. As far as method is concerned, there is a corresponding need to concentrate on what is happening with domestic social movements, especially in the largest states, and in depicting the shape of struggle, if any, between territorially based political power and market-based economic power, or put differently, between government leaders and multinational managers. [19]

Such an emphasis reverses a traditional concern of world order reformers with external relations between governing elites that are presumed responsive to the common interests of world society. These reformers have posited designs for new arrangements of power based on an idealistic image of peace on earth and goodwill. [20] These designs have never seemed relevant because they lacked a theory of change and were based on an ethos antithetical to the conflict-oriented ethos that follows from state sovereignty in a laissez-faire framework of centralized restraint and regulation. [21] Often these designs involved "world government" based on "law," an outlook embodied in the most influential modern variant of traditional world order thinking. [22] World order reform consists of convincing influential individuals that a particular set of proposals is desirable, and this persuasive strategy presupposes, completely contrary to observed fact, that the existing structure of world order is administered by reasonable men of good will who are susceptible to persuasive techniques of influence.

After World War I, but even more after the atomic explosions at Hiroshima and Nagasaki in World War II, the plea of world order reformers has rested on a claim of alleged necessity. In other words, the argument for reform is backed up by an assertion that the existing system is heading for destruction given the possibilities for catastrophic war that exist at the present time. [23] Such a warning has been recently bolstered by a declaration of ecological emergency on many fronts. [24] Here again, however, it is clear that such a plea has no capacity to induce fundamental world order reform. Indeed, the main impact of ecological pressure may be to drive the Darwinian tendencies of the present world order system to a further extreme, namely encouraging an even more explicitly imperial arrangement with a reduction in the number of relevant political and economic centers of decision and a widening gap between winners and losers. There are various ways to respond to an objective situation of world order danger, and it is not in any sense methodologically accurate to assume that "reform" is in a progressive direction given an idealistic outlook on man and the world. We insist, then that the idea of future patterns of world order take account of an array of alternatives to convey a sense of choice and of process.

At the present time there is a consensus among the powerful that adjustments in the world order system are needed to maximize the short- and middle-term interests of the strongest and richest governmental actors. The shape of this design has been spelled out by Richard Nixon, Gerald Ford, and Henry Kissinger, and must be understood for what it is, world order reform engineered by and for the sake of the winners. We do not have enough evidence at the present time to demonstrate that it won't work, if specified in relation to goals associated with the maximization of the security, wealth, and influence of these dominant actors and those aligned with them for the next few decades.

The Normative Imperative

Our method of inquiry leads us to realize that there are a number of plausible models of world order reform. Each model is capable of realization within the next several decades and each has its own immediate implications for policy, action, tactics, and belief systems. We believe that there is no objective way to demonstrate which model is preferable outside the realm of moral choice.

Given background conditions of war dangers, resource scarcity, and widespread misery, the fundamental normative choice is between an actor orientation and a community orientation with respect to world order reform. An actor orientation means that each national center of power and wealth orients its policy toward maintaining its position of preeminence in relation to others in the system (potential rivals) by reliance on threats, force, and cunning.[25] Beyond engaging in a pietistic rhetoric—that distracts attention from the real or operational code of behavior—there is no concern for the suffering of the victims or those who are denied the fruits of participation; indeed, there is constant vigilance against challenges from the dispossessed and a ruthless willingness to repudiate their claims and repress or persecute their spokesmen. This is the world order significance of the American role in Indochina and the Soviet willingness to accommodate foreign policy to such outrages despite adversary positioning in the conflict from a geopolitical perspective.

A community orientation means that the basic relationships of power and authority must become increasingly contractual and voluntary in character. Such goals mean that the problems of human

existence on the planet must be approached without deference to artificial boundaries, whether of states, races, classes, or castes. This
kind of problem solving means that issues of poverty, pollution, and
repression are essential concerns of world order reformers who are
guided by a vision of human community in which men live in harmony
with each other and in relation to their natural habitat. This outlook
can be implemented by a number of different models of world order,
the choice reflecting issues of feasibility and of time horizon. There
is no federalist scheme buried in the normative imperative that is
built up on a community orientation. Again, as with the basic concern
with reform prospects, it is helpful to explicate some alternatives and
to choose from these alternatives on the basis of principled judgment.
As we indicated in the introductory section, the sequel to thought is
action, the relationship being well comprehended by cybernetic terminology with its emphasis on feedback loops. Every assertion of
preference, whether in relation to the goals or tactics of transition,
needs to be continuously reconsidered in light of developments and
adapted to experiences and to changing forms of consciousness.

The permanent elements in the normative imperative are the
insistence on thinking of welfare in terms of wholes, the human
species, the earth, the overall pattern of linkage between man and
earth, as well as between the present and the future. It is the insistence on the coherence of the whole that makes the normative imperative
compatible with the methodological imperative and creates the basis
for substantive investigations of the present prospects for world order
reform.

A NEW APPROACH TO WORLD ORDER DESIGN

The failures of the present system of world order suggest the
need for alternatives. An important contribution by specialists would
involve the design of credible alternative systems of world order that
have some prospect of realization within the relatively near future,
say by the first decade of the twenty-first century. Such design concepts have in the past—within the wider tradition of utopography—been
harmed by two basic defects:

1. No conception of transition linking the present to the future.
2. A failure to envision world order solutions other than by the
replication on a global level of the concentrations of power and authority of the sort now manifest in the governance of large sovereign
states.

We propose a new social science approach to the design of future systems of world order that seeks to overcome these defects; this approach can be depicted in terms of its own set of orienting conditions.

1. The future system will itself be a step in a transitional process of political development on a global scale; in other words, processes of aspiration and projects for change are essential attributes of healthy behavior and parallel biological processes of evolution; there is no final solution of the world order problem but only a series of transitional solutions; each achieved utopia generates its own new horizon of aspiration.

2. The search for a new system of world order depends upon mobilizing support for a series of explicit values; world order change—solving the transition problem—depends on achieving and implementing a normative consensus.

3. This normative consensus is animated by an overriding concern with initiating a humane process of adjustment to dangers associated with problems of ecological imbalance arising from crowding, depletion of resources, and poisoning of the biosphere; as Jay Forrester has correctly suggested, "Civilization is in a transition zone between past exponential growth and some future form of equilibrium."[26] The focus of inquiry, then, should be directed toward dynamic equilibrium models of world order that can be achieved without undue trauma and that can be sustained without recourse to repression; these ethical dimensions of world order relate to attitudes toward violence, satisfaction of basic human needs, and social and political conditions that are compatible with a sense of human equality and with an affirmation of the worth of the individual human being.

In this essay we can give only a sense of direction.[27] Figures 9.1 and 9.2 attempt to set forth the basic framework of thought that has been developed in response to the five conditions laid down and discussed in the preceding paragraphs.

Figure 9.1 depicts the basic set of concepts that seem useful in developing a systematic method of thinking about future systems of world order (S_1, S_2. . . S_n) and of conceiving the transition path from $S_0 \rightarrow S_1$ (i.e., either in analytic terms of t_1, t_2, t_3 or in temporal terms of t_{1970s}, t_{1980s}, t_{1990s}). Figure 9.2 suggests one line of transition in relation to value priorities of peacefulness, social and economic welfare, environmental quality, and human dignity. This transition path emphasizes several sequences of development that appear to be preconditions to the emergence of S_1 (i.e., on the level of action the correlation between consciousness and t_1 or t_{1970s}, between mobilization and t_2 or t_{1980s}, and between transformation

FIGURE 9.1

System (S) 　　Level (S_0 = 　　S at origin)	$S_{-1} \longleftarrow S_0 \longrightarrow S_1 \longrightarrow S_2$
System level 　　(chronological 　　subscripts)	$S_{1914} \longleftarrow S_{1973} \longrightarrow S_{2000} \longrightarrow S_{2050}$
Transitional stages 　for the interval 　$S_0 \rightarrow S_1 \rightarrow S_2$	$S_0 \xrightarrow{} S_1 \xrightarrow{} S_2$ 　　$(t_1)(t_2)(t_3)\quad(t_4)(t_5)(t_6)$
Transitional stages 　for the interval 　$S_{1973} \rightarrow S_{2000}$ with chronological subscripts	$S_{1973} \xrightarrow{} S_{2000}$ 　　$(t_{1973})(t_{1980})(t_{1990})$

and t_3 or t_{1990s}; on the level of primary institutional arenas a similar sequence of correlations with t intervals is depicted). The basis purpose of Figure 9.2 is to embody a conception of global change that will have to accompany any serious process of designing and achieving a new system of world order. The number of stars in each box signifies additional emphasis that builds upon the achievements of the prior interval. Thus, by the end of t_2 both war and social and economic welfare considerations have six units of cumulative change. The distribution of stars is meant only to be a rough approximation of relative degrees of effort and achievement at the various stages of the transition process. It should be understood that this is a conception, or at most a prescription, rather than a prediction. In terms of our conception, it is possible, even likely, that t_1 will never come to an end; we are merely proposing that a way to move from $S_0 \rightarrow S_1$ is to proceed along this path of sequenced transition. The transition process proposed is but one of an infinite series; alternative transition paths $S_0 \rightarrow S_1$ can and should be studied as part of a broader inquiry into comparative systems of world order.

　　To make the point clearer that S_1 is itself a transitional solution to the challenge of world order, we depict in Figure 9.3 the subsequent process or transition from $S_1 \rightarrow S_2$ with a similar suggestive profile of sequenced transition.

　　Figure 9.3 merely suggests the more personalist follow-on to a successful effort to save the planet from misery and extreme danger. In a sense $S_0 \rightarrow S_1$ is concerned with a world-order rescue mission,

FIGURE 9.2

Transition Path S → S$_1$

Problem Focus— Change Orientation, Institutional Focus	War Consciousness: Domestic Arena	Poverty Mobilization: Transnational and Regional Arenas	Pollution Transformation: Global Arena	Human Rights Transformation: Global Arena
Analytic Stages / Temporal Subscripts				
t$_1$ — t$_{1970s}$	****	**	*	*
t$_2$ — t$_{1980s}$	**	****	***	***
t$_3$ — t$_{1990s}$	*	***	****	

Note: The number of stars in each box is roughly proportional to the degree of incremental emphasis in each t interval.

203

FIGURE 9.3

Temporal Interval \ Positive Goal	Creativity	Self-Realization	Joy
t_4 t_{2010s} 2020s	***	**	*
t_5 t_{2030s}	**	***	**
t_6 t_{2040s}	*	*	***

whereas $S_1 \rightarrow S_2$ is concerned with the positive task of building a system of world order that fulfills human potentialities for growth and satisfaction.

The only element that has not yet been portrayed in our approach is some conception of the structural character of the outcome of transition. Our focus is upon the basic arrangement of power and authority as an organizing energy in planetary affairs. Again, the objective here is to suggest a mode of thinking rather than to argue on behalf of a particular configuration of power and authority. At the same time, we would like to set forth models of world order that correspond with various relevant lines of real-world preference and prediction. In particular, we would like to offer four kinds of models of world order based on an acceptance of dynamic equilibrium as the fundamental requisite: Nixon-Kissinger (Figure 9.4); Doomsday (Figures 9.5 and 9.6); World Government (Figure 9.7); $S_0 \rightarrow S_1$ (Figure 9.8).

The basic attribute of the Nixon-Kissinger model of world order reform is the notion that existing centers of industrial capability, and hence military potential, are capable of providing a stable and acceptable system of world order for the indefinite future. This system rests on moderation of means and ends among the five dominant actors who work out patterns for efficient cooperation and limited competition, based on a general acceptance of the geopolitical and geoeconomic status quo. The Nixon-Kissinger model accords little emphasis to social and economic justice and it is preecological to the extent that it assumes the capacity of competing national units to behave in a manner compatible with the maintence of ecological balance. A concert of dominant actors may avert short-term breakdown in S_0, but it hardly provides a satisfactory response to the negative threats posed by the present crisis, nor does such a world order design offer any prospect of fulfilling the positive potential for human social and individual development.

Figure 9.5 depicts the breakdown of the present world order system (S_0) into a series of gravely weakened and uncoordinated units. These units may or may not possess a statelike formal identity, but there will be a loss of internal cohesion and a virtual collapse of any capacity to enter into stable external relationships. The state system will have disintegrated into a condition of world anarchy or chaos, and political organization of any comprehensive kind will not exist. Poverty, violence, disease will be rampant, and there will not be any prospects for recreating conditions of order and justice that are even comparable to S_0.

Figure 9.6 illustrates the other main line of response to the collapse of S_0. Here remaining power is concentrated at a single focal point. Planetary resources are exceedingly scarce relative to human needs, and privation is widespread. A small elite runs the

FIGURE 9.4

Kissinger Equilibrium Model

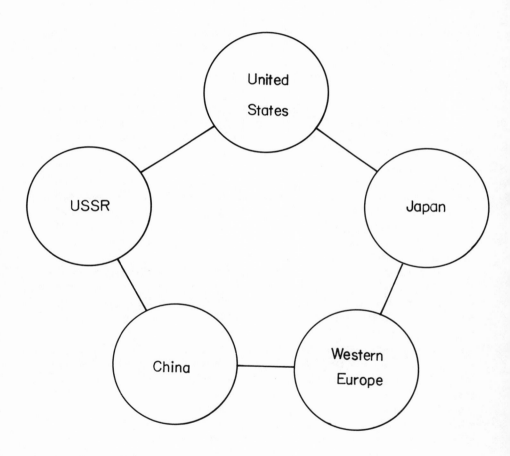

FIGURE 9.5

Doomsday Equilibrium Model: Breakdown

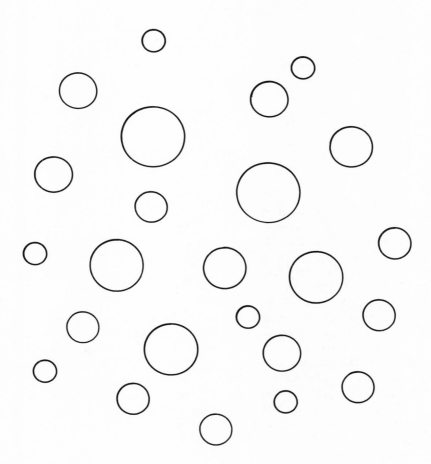

FIGURE 9.6

Doomsday Equilibrium Model:
Concentration

world in a highly dictatorial, repressive fashion. No opposition is
tolerated. The system of world order resembles a police state of the
sort now associated with the worst national tyrannies.

In effect, the collapse of S_0 is likely either to accentuate centrifugal tendencies (in which case Figure 9.5) or centripetal tendencies
(in which case Figure 9.6). In either eventuality, the present world
order system with all its deficiencies would itself look like a utopia
by comparison. It is important to understand that regression, as well
as positive change, is possible in relation to the future of world order.

Figure 9.7 depicts in very crude terms a world federalist
response to the inadequacies of S_0. Some constitutional conception of
this sort has dominated the visionary literature of world order for
centuries. The notion of world government seems to satisfy the basic
human craving for unity and order. As such, it captures something
very fundamental about the basic direction of world order reform. At
the present stage of international relations, however, a world government solution does not seem attainable except as a response to a
doomsday situation, in which case it is likely to be a dysutopia of the
sort projected in Figure 9.6. That is, there is no credible transition
path that can be followed over the next several decades that could lead
reliably toward world government of a benevolent character.

In addition, governmental solutions to human problems have not
often worked with success at a national level. The prospect of a huge

FIGURE 9.7

World Government Equilibrium

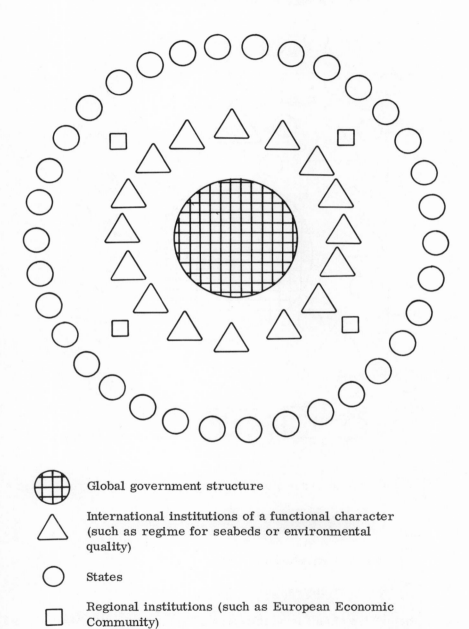

Global government structure

International institutions of a functional character (such as regime for seabeds or environmental quality)

States

Regional institutions (such as European Economic Community)

FIGURE 9.8

S₀ → S₁: Central Guidance and Local Autonomy—
A New Planetary Community

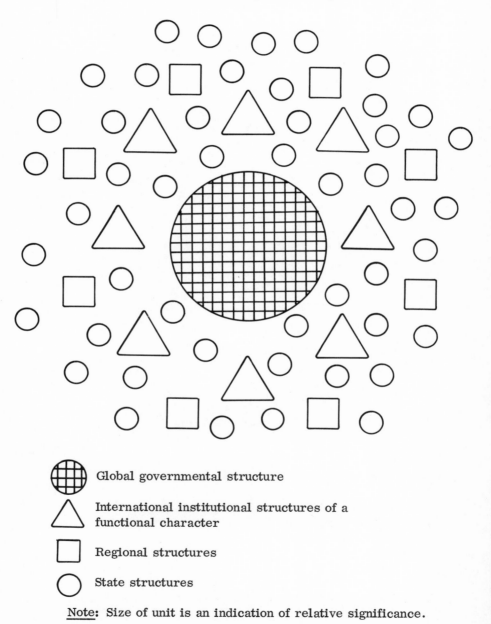

Global governmental structure

International institutional structures of a
functional character

Regional structures

State structures

Note: Size of unit is an indication of relative significance.

global bureaucratic presence, especially if combined with the sort of technological apparatus that will be available, does create inherent reasons to be wary of a world government sequel to S_0 even if it were attainable. These reasons include problems associated with domination, conformism, and excessive administration, as well as concern about such a concentration of military capabilities and political powers at this stage in the growth of human consciousness.

Figure 9.8 represents a compromise between the state system and the sort of world government solution projected in Figure 9.7. $S_0 \rightarrow S_1$ has to be conceived in relation to a systematic study of transition prospects, tactics, and sequences as suggested in Figures 9.1 and 9.2.[28] The basic constitutional principles embodied in the profile of S_1 are to achieve maximum coordination and guidance on the basis of minimum coercion and bureaucratic intrusion. Great emphasis is placed on diminishing the existing power apparatus in the superstates (rather than in transferring power upward) and in designing into the structure numerous checks and balances, as well as upward avenues of influence and participation.[29] Figure 9.8 does not indicate the presence of transnational groupings, which we believe will be very important in S_1, given especially the altered nature of political consciousness, which is a precondition for $t_1 \rightarrow t_2$. We believe that transnational economic, cultural, and political groupings will enjoy great importance in S_1, and indeed may provide an emerging focus for human loyalty displacing gradually the symbolism of national patriotism.

TOWARD A NEW DISCIPLINE: COMPARATIVE SYSTEMS OF WORLD ORDER

In the section above we set forth the skeletal elements of a way of thinking about the future of world order. This way of thinking is shaped by a normative orientation toward what is desirable in human relations and political arrangements. Such an approach amounts to a plea for restructuring inquiry into international relations in the direction of a newly conceived academic discipline of comparative systems of world order:

• Comparative in relation to past, present, and possible future arrangements of power and authority in human affairs.

• Systemic in the sense of being as rigorous as possible with respect to the totality of behavior embraced by the subject matter.

• World order in the sense of a normative orientation toward the appraisal of the performance or desirability of a particular global authority; normative both in relation to tasks performed (human needs,

peace, conservation of resources) and in relation to responsible aspi-
rational projects (conditioning goals by feasibility studies of transition
prospects).

On such an intellectual basis a new conception of world order can
begin to emerge that is sensitive to the role of thought and reason in
accomplishing an essential reunion between feeling and action. The
splits between thought and feeling on one side and between thought and
action on the other have often rendered analysis of world order sterile,
and conveyed either an impression of intellectual aridity or one of
political futility.

NOTES

1. April 28, 1971 (Release of United Nations Information Office).

2. Of the word, Herman Kahn has, with I suppose unwitting
irony, aptly written, "This is an ugly word, smacking of pseudoscience,
but we seem to be stuck with it." Kahn and B. Bruce-Briggs, Things
to Come: Thinking about the 70's and 80's (New York: Macmillan,
1972), p. 1.

3. Cf., for example, Thomas Stritch, "The Banality of
Utopia," Review of Politics 34 (January 1972): 103-6; Margaret Mead,
"Towards More Vivid Utopias," Science 126 (November 1957): 957-61.

4. Herman Kahn and Anthony J. Wiener, The Year 2000: A
Framework for Speculation on the Next Thirty-three Years (New York:
Macmillan, 1967); for critical assessments, see Marion J. Levy, Jr.,
"Our Ever and Future Jungle," World Politics 22 (January 1970):
301-27; William Irwin Thompson, At the Edge of History (New York:
Harper and Row, 1971), pp. 113-23.

5. The most celebrated, but by no means the only, product of
this project has been its report to the Club of Rome: Donella H.
Meadows et al., The Limits to Growth (Washington, D.C.: Potomac
Associates, 1972). Underlying this work has been the approach to the
analysis of social system developed in the work of Jay Forrester; see
especially Jay W. Forrester, World Dynamics (Cambridge, Mass.:
Wright-Allen, 1961). The Project Director, Dennis L. Meadows, has
provided important intellectual leadership as the prime interpreter of
Forrester's work and as the leader of an effort to evolve an adequate
computer model for the study of world dynamics. In my view, the
Forrester-Meadows undertaking, unlike that of Herman Kahn, is of
genuine and enduring importance. It undertakes to evolve and test by
the best data available a program for the most accurate possible computer model of world dynamics, and in that sense is a cumulative
enterprise whose eventual contribution to human understanding cannot

yet be assessed. My criticisms are directed mainly at the effort to gain authority in public thinking for its analysis of the world situation on the basis of numbers and the use of a computer modeling technique. This effort, although laudable, is not able to produce anything more than a qualitative argument at present of the sort available from many other authors who adopt an ecological view of the planet's drift into a position of irreversible jeopardy. See Paul R. Ehrlich and Ann H. Ehrlich, Population, Resources, and Environment, 2nd rev. ed. (San Francisco: W. H. Freeman, 1972); Barry Commoner, The Closing Circle: Nature, Man, and Technology (New York: Knopf, 1971); Harold and Margaret Sprout, Toward a Politics of the Planet Earth (New York: Van Nostrand-Reinhold, 1971); G. Tyler Miller, Jr., Replenish the Earth: A Primer on Human Ecology (Belmont, Calif.: Wadsworth, 1972).

6. Among the backlash literature, see Carl Kaysen, "The Computer that Printed Out W*O*L*F*," Foreign Affairs 50 (July 1972): 660-68; Rudolf Klein, "Growth and Its Enemies," Commentary, June 1972, pp. 37-44; and see the front-page review of the Meadows-Forrester books by Peter Passell, Marc Roberts, and Leonard Ross, New York Times Book Review, April 2, 1972.

7. These criticisms are particularly well-formulated in the essay by Kaysen, cited in note 6.

8. However, there is something to be said for sounding an ecological alarm, by whatever means, at this time. It is partly a matter of shouting "Fire!" in a theater attended by deaf-mutes. And in this sense the Club of Rome, Jay Forrester, and Dennis Meadows must be regarded as lifeguards of prime importance. It should also be noted that Jay Forrester and Dennis Meadows are sensitive to possible charges of pseudoscience and are careful in their statements about the present limits of their model.

9. See Thompson, At the Edge of History. Cf. also Thompson, "Planetary Vistas," Harpers, December 1971, pp. 71-78; Thompson, "The Individual as Institution: The Example of Paolo Soleri," Harpers, September 1972, pp. 48-62.

10. The most coherent formulation of Peccei's outlook is contained in his book The Chasm Ahead (New York: Macmillan, 1969).

11. Interview with Thompson, Time, August 21, 1972, p. 51.

12. In this spirit, Thompson has praised the intellectual dialogue between the Indian mystical philosopher Gopi Krishna and the German physicist-philosopher Carl Friedrich von Weizsacher. This dialogue is described in von Weizsacher's long introduction to Gopi Krishna, The Biological Basis of Religion and Genius (New York: Harper and Row, 1972). Cf. also Thompson's assessment of the architect Paolo Soleri (Harpers, September 1972) and Thompson's own conception of a learning/living

center based on the ideas of the medieval Irish monastery at Lindisfarne and outlined in his prospectus for a Lindisfarne Association.

13. That is, the dichotomy between future goals and present
responses suggests a form of distancing that is disturbing in its human
consequences in the same way as the more concrete circumstances of
nonresponse disclosed in relation to Kitty Genovese's murder before
the eyes of her passive neighbors. At issue also is the matter of
personal responsibility, its extent and character. In this sense, I
believe that responsibility to act to stop crimes of war of the sort
embodied in the Indochina war extends to all human beings. It is the
affirmation of this universal bond of involvement and accountability
that is the most significant outcome of the Nuremberg Judgment, and
of what has more recently come to be called the Nuremberg obligation
by American citizens who have been acting in opposition to the continuing American involvement in the Indochina war in an organization
called Redress.

14. See, for example, V. R. Potter, Bioethics: Bridge to the
Future (Englewood Cliffs, N.J.: Prentice-Hall, 1971).

15. The Seneca quotation is borrowed from Bradbury K. Thur-
low in a monthly newsletter distributed by a Wall Street brokerage
firm, Laidlaw & Co., Commentary (investment newsletter), November
1972, p. 1.

16. "In a Manner that Must Shame God Himself," Harpers,
November 1972, pp. 60-68.

17. Ibid. In a different vein, a similar kind of assessment of
the future is presented in Michael T. Klare, War Without End:
American Planning for the Next Vietnams (New York: Knopf, 1972).

18. Such as Chester L. Cooper, The Lost Crusade: America
in Vietnam (New York: Dodd, Mead, 1970); Roger Hilsman, To Move
a Nation (Garden City, N.Y.: Doubleday, 1967); Townsend Hoopes,
The Limits of Intervention: An Inside Account of How the Johnson
Policy of Escalation Was Reversed (New York: David McKay, 1969);
Arthur M. Schlesinger, Jr., The Bitter Heritage: Vietnam and
American Democracy, 1941-1966 (Boston: Houghton Mifflin, 1966).

19. See Stephen Hymer, "The Multinational Corporation and
the Law of Uneven Development," in Economics and World Order:
From the 1970's to the 1990's, ed. Jagdish N. Bhagwati (New York:
Macmillan, 1972), pp. 113-40.

20. See F. H. Hinsley, Power and the Pursuit of Peace (Cambridge: Cambridge University Press, 1963); Walter Schiffer, The
Legal Community of Mankind (New York: Columbia University Press,
1954).

21. Within national societies, laissez-faire has been a policy
where it has prevailed, but within international society it is an
inherent condition.

22. Grenville Clark and Louis B. Sohn, World Peace Through World Law, 3rd rev. ed. (Cambridge, Mass.: Harvard University Press, 1966).

23. On this point, compare Kenneth Boulding, "The Prevention of World War III," in The Strategy of World Order: Toward a Theory of War Prevention, eds. Falk and Saul H. Mendlovitz (New York: World Law Fund, 1966), vol. 1, pp. 3-13, with Robert Osgood and Robert W. Tucker, Force, Order, and Justice (Baltimore: Johns Hopkins Press, 1967).

24. See in addition to works cited in note 5, the manifesto of the editors of the British magazine The Ecologist published under the title Blueprint for Survival (Boston: Houghton Mifflin, 1972).

25. This reliance is exhibited in international policy by placing stress upon alliances, by intervening in foreign societies to assist the efforts of sympathetic elites to retain or acquire power in struggles against potentially hostile elites, and by ideological rationalizations that convey to one's own population a higher motive than the maintenance of position in the structure of international power, wealth, and prestige. These ideological mystifications often function in such a potent way as to entrap the power wielders in their claims, thereby inducing some poor calculations based on "principles" rather than "interests." Henry Kissinger's critique of pre-Nixon foreign policy making during the Kennedy/Johnson presidencies rests on this kind of assertion. See Henry A. Kissinger, "Central Issues of American Foreign Policy," in Agenda for the Nation, ed. Kermit Gordon (Washington, D.C.: Brookings Institution, 1968), pp. 585-614.

26. Jay W. Forrester, "Churches at the Transition Between Growth and World Equilibrium," Zygon 7 (Summer 1972): 145-67.

27. The approach in the remainder of this chapter is much more fully developed in Chapters III and IV of the final document of the North American Section of the World Order Models Project (available in mimeo. form from the World Law Fund).

28. Ibid. S_1 is depicted more fully in Chapter III, the transition process in Chapter IV.

29. The detailed character of these upward avenues of influence is depicted in Chapter III of the WOMP study.

PART

III

**APPLICATIONS
AND CONSEQUENCES**

10

**GROWTH, STAGNATION,
AND ALTERNATIVE
WORLD FUTURES**
Charles F. Doran

An axiom of much international relations theory in the 1960s was that, although the international situation might change, the nation-state was here to stay.[1] Another current of political thought has sought to challenge this position by emphasizing supranationalism and functional integration,[2] transnational organizations,[3] political ideal-ism,[4] and world government.[5] Not until the 1970s, however, did the cleavage between the former and the latter viewpoints narrow in the face of evidence that, regardless of political system or regime type, global political structures and societies might crumble under the weight of their own prosperity and growth.

In studying the epistemology of alternative world futures, one must establish both the limits and the validity of the world order perspective. Over the last ten years the field of valid world order speculation has expanded and grown more complex. War in the con-text of gross social and economic inequity is no longer a sufficient preoccupation of structural analysts who seek to modify the inter-national system so as to raise material standards of living while minimizing the use of violence. An epistemology of world order must now also contend with the potential inadequacy of the present system to sustain current rates of growth for some or all member polities. Governments may no longer be able to count on the general aura of progress and optimism that has held out promise even to poor coun-tries and dampened the propensity for violence. If absolute increases in well-being become impossible for the system to sustain, massive political frustration is likely to follow. Hence the boundaries of world order thought must expand to include these potential new sources of aggression as well as to ameliorate the economic and social conse-quences of pollution, crowding, and food and resource scarcity per se.

Establishing the validity of world order thought is perhaps even more difficult than defining the correct limits. If it is the task of epistemology to determine validity, then an appropriate standard and mode of evaluation for validity must be chosen. The concept of world order is so encompassing, however, that even when the purpose of the field is well established, the method of sorting out and judging alternative world order systems may remain unsatisfactory and ambiguous. Whatever the method for judging the appropriateness of world order systems, the chosen method must possess the capacity to treat hypothetical conditions. The method must allow a test of the model under differing political circumstances. In particular, the method must allow us first to propose solutions to problems facing any future system regardless of structure and then to evaluate how justly and efficiently each system seems to implement those solutions.

This essay can be seen as an attempt both to expand the more traditional concerns of world order thought in the context of post-growth equilibrium and to employ a revised simulation model to test several alternative strategies to achieve a more viable world order. The essay thus becomes both a statement of epistemology and an application of that epistemology to a preferred world society. Following a brief examination of the debate concerning postgrowth equilib-rium, the analysis turns toward the issue of how readily we can achieve a more egalitarian world society, namely, one in which rewards are distributed more fairly accompanied by less political stress.

NEW PROBLEMS, NEW PERSPECTIVES

Collapse of entire civilizations accompanied by devastating declines in population and eroded agricultural economies are historical antecedents to the modern prospect of postindustrial stagnation. But whereas the Persian Empire in the Fertile Crescent and the dying Roman Empire in North Africa were revived and transformed with the spread of Islamic fervor, a lasting depression encompassing most of the world could destroy the very basis of technocratic civilization. The paradox of future societal stagnation is that it is posited to emerge not in response to military defeat and the supremacy of competing social units but inwardly from the same forces that have spawned the high standards of living, cultural achievement, and education of current civilization, sparing no one. Complexly interwoven, these forces together effect a catastrophe that in past political systems would have created insignificant stress.

The primary societal forces are four in number: (1) unrestrained population growth that creates demand for more food, goods, services, and living space, (2) escalating inputs of capital to meet these demands, which in turn cause (3) pollution of air and water and (4) irreversible reduction of natural resource deposits. All these forces are connected by feedback loops carrying changes throughout the system very quickly but also ensuring that the course of movement for the society as a whole is inexorable. Evidence for the stagnation hypothesis comes from a simulation of social, economic, and political relationships using both real and hypothetical data projected dynamically over long time periods.

The impact of the new evidence on traditional theories of economic development and political modernization may be striking. For one thing, the whole modus operandi of traditional economic thought—namely, that growth is a primary goal and that the maximization, or at least the optimization, of profits is a legitimate instrument to this end—stands on its head. More than simple internalization of the social costs of growth, costs previously left out of the market equation, is at stake. Despite resource substitution and technological innovation, the Malthusian reality of a static resource base questions once again whether the true social costs of unrestrained population growth can ever be properly estimated in advance and internalized. [6] On the contrary, were society to so estimate the true costs of pollution, resource loss, crowding, increased potential for violence, and food scarcity, the logical response would be to cut back on further population expansion. But insofar as pairs of individuals, not Rousseau's General Will, must ultimately make each decision to procreate, and because of numerous lags in awareness and response time often amounting to a generation or more, the normal correctives of the market mechanism are not likely to work, especially on the grand scale of world economic and social relations.

However, assuming that, whether by individual decision or collective fiat, the members of society acknowledge the need to brake unrestrained population growth and the concomitant inputs of scarce economic resources, how would such a monumental act affect future world politics? What alternative patterns of constraint are feasible? Is a solution possible that is both equitable and efficient? If positive peace minus the condition that Johan Galtung calls structural violence fails to emerge, is negative peace with its accompanying injustices still a possibility? Or are the alternative world futures embodying the growth constraint all likely to lead to violent conflict of an intensity and magnitude that would preclude serious adoption?

Debate over these questions led Galtung to criticize the policy implications, if not the empirical conclusions, of the Club of Rome's well-known study, <u>The Limits to Growth</u>.[7] He found unacceptable the prescription that all societies, regardless of wealth or political circumstance, should submit to constraint. This would disadvantage the impoverished peoples who require more growth just to stay even with the development pace of the advanced industrial states that threaten to overwhelm and absorb them. Hence his unwillingness to consider the imperatives of population restrictions and resource shortages on the same level of political importance as global poverty, structural disequilibrium, and war.

Echoing part of this thesis, Nazli Chouchri and Robert North stress the association between the increasing scarcity of resources and war.[8] According to their findings, lateral pressure (the tendency for governments to expand territorially) is associated with the need to obtain resources. Highly industrial countries are obviously more subject to such pressure. In fact, as Edward L. Morse argues, only the highly industrialized countries are capable of distinguishing effectively between foreign and domestic policies.[9] As governments become more dependent upon external sources of petroleum, metals, and fiber, they also have a tendency to become more aggressive, thus wasting more of these scarce supplies in combat and hastening the process of resource exhaustion. Whereas Galtung appears to urge Meadows and Forrester to focus first upon problems of disease, poverty, and social inequity before attempting to stave off systemic decline, Chouchri and North seem to advocate an extension of the world dynamics model to include the vagaries of political conflict, which inevitably must affect decision making.[10]

If, on the other hand, some types of conflict are associated with resource scarcity and together they account for a large and increasing share of the total conflict behavior of the system, then one could plausibly demand limits to economic growth and population expansion as a means to international peace. But, as argued earlier, if one were dubious of the current system's ability to establish such constraints, then one also could obtain a very good brief for a radically different kind of world order that might encompass both the requisite constraints and the desired peace. Growth limits and peace are thus not seen as divergent (perhaps incompatible) goals, as was Galtung's apparent view; on the contrary, limits to growth are seen as a precondition of long-term stability. This is the essential perspective of Richard Falk, who builds his model of world order largely on the urgency of environmental reform.[11]

According to Falk, a political system at the global level incorporating a decentralized guidance mechanism instead of centralized bureaucratic authority could occur somewhere in the last decade of the twentieth century, emerging as the last in a three-phase transformation. The first phase, political consciousness and the domestic imperative, is devoted to expanding public consciousness of world order studies. The second phase, political mobilization and the transnational imperative, involves translation of changed public values into action across national boundaries. The third phase, political transformation and the global imperative, evokes the participation of national governments as well as other actors in an effort to move toward a self-sustained amalgamation of the world's governing centers and processes. The strongest institutions, Falk asserts, are committed to moderating the strains of growth without transforming the growth ethos. This he sees as a principal obstacle to the peaceful emergence of world order values and structures.

A number of possible outcomes of growth equilibrium thus lie at the heart of a study of alternative world futures. Galtung appears to assume that the only outcome of constrained growth is one harmful to the interests of the developing countries, while Meadows and Forrester tend to emphasize that the likely outcome of current planning is systemwide stagnation. North and Chouchri stress the possibility of war emerging from a lack of growth limits, yet they do not discuss that possibility as a consequence of such limits. Falk designs his model of world order in terms of the positive outcomes of growth equilibrium, but he does not explore possible negative outcomes. A systematic presentation of the variety of paths to growth equilibrium with analysis of the implications of each for alternative world futures might aid the search for a more viable world order.

Figure 10.1 outlines four possible outcomes of the movement toward equilibrium in population and economic growth. [12] This representation assumes that, regardless of the ultimate framework of world order, an initial cleavage exists between the rich and the poor sectors of the system. It also assumes that each sector can adopt either of two policies, continued growth or movement toward equilibrium. In actual practice there may be short-term and medium-term changes of policy. Or these policy differences may be manifested largely with respect to different rates of change, one sector approaching equilibrium more quickly or slowly than the other. The general categorization of policies and sectors is not, however, vitiated by these caveats.

Quadrant 1 depicts the situation that Meadows and Forrester have projected (using a single-actor model) as the likely outcome of current decision making when the pressures of population growth and pollution become so great as to exhaust the natural resource base and destroy the quality of life. Resulting from continued growth in both the advanced and developing sectors, global stagnation is essentially a nonsolution to the world's problems, leading to stagnation and probable conflict once the tensions of commercial competition are aggravated by actual starvation and material shortages in regions where stockpiles of arms exist.

FIGURE 10.1

Varieties of Postgrowth International Systems

Developing Countries (LDCs)	Advanced Industrial Countries (AICs)	
	Growth	Equilibrium
Growth	(1) Stagnating (nonsolution)	(2) Egalitarian (distributive solution)
Equilibrium	(4) Imperial (exploitative solution)	(3) Stratified, polycentric (elitist solution)

Quadrant 2 corresponds to the outcome envisioned by Falk in which equity is greater after rather than before the creation of the new world order. Indeed it is precisely the inequalities of income, power, and justice that drive the system toward the distributive solution in pursuit of a community free of collective violence. Environmental reform is necessary to sustain the productive capacity of the economy at a constant level while reducing its conflict potential through the limits on excessive growth and through enhanced social equality. The distributive solution invites a greater risk of conflict prior to achieving the good society. Powerful elites will resist losing the privileges built upon inequality, but once the distributive solution has been achieved, other social forces will tend to reinforce it.

The crucial problem for Falk is whether force is a legitimate means of effecting the new order, which itself is to have peace as its primary value. Regardless of practical exigencies, from a theoretical perspective force cannot be used to invoke a political order whose raison d'etre is the absence of forceful relations. To condone revolution in the first instance is to legitimize its possible use subsequently. This is a dilemma that every architect of alternative world futures encounters and must resolve.

Quadrant 3 seems to escape this dilemma because administrative brakes are applied everywhere with equal pressure. No sector is asked to curb population growth or environmental degradation any faster or any more severely than another. But for this same reason the solution is elitist. It leaves the stratification of the system exactly as it is today. Class politics is the way that Galtung has characterized this paradigm of limits-to-growth thought. More than just a confrontation between the rich and poor (which suggests the possibility of an uprising of the underdogs against the topdogs), is is rather a confrontation of the polycentric rich states against the fragmented and disorganized poor. But this does not lessen the conflict propensity of such a model. Nor does it reduce the injustice of perpetuating vast income discrepancies into a static future.

Quadrant 4 is the bleakest of all outcomes from the perspectives of world order. The imperial outcome taxes the poor, underdeveloped zones to pay for the continued prosperity of the advanced industrial regions. It is an exploitative solution because it allows the powerful regions or governments to continue to grow while placing the bulk of constraints on the poor and powerless. One technique is to extract raw materials and primary products from the developing sectors at unrealistically low prices while not encouraging industrialization there for fear of future commercial rivalry.[13] Another technique is to initiate large-scale population control programs in the poorer countries while the more economically advanced countries abstain from such centrally directed efforts. A further imperial method is to facilitate the migration of the dirty semimanufactures, such as the paper processors and oil refineries, while banning them at home.[14] When orchestrated collectively for the purpose of forcing the developing countries into premature equilibrium, this activity is imperial and highly destabilizing.

The work of North and Chouchri addresses the problems of imperialism, stressing the rivalry among the imperial actors, the potential for military intervention, and the aggressive responses of the target countries. What we must emphasize is that creation of a world government in no way eliminates the dangers of such exploitation. Indeed, centralized government with totalitarian methods is in a much better position to exploit its citizens because its techniques are more direct and its control much more encompassing. Tax procedures on the Latifundia in Peru, for example, or absolute control by the Soviet secret police in Estonia or the Ukraine are far more effective sources of revenue and compliance than externally imposed colonialism ever was or perhaps can be. Alternative world futures must therefore ensure that the limits-to-growth concept does not become the ideology of global repression.

Having discussed some of the literature of peace studies and world order in the context of the Malthusian dilemmas facing mankind, and having established a matrix of possible growth equilibrium outcomes, we now turn to an empirical examination of some of these hypotheses. Specifically, what relationship is likely to emerge between the advanced and the less-developed countries as the system as a whole faces growth constraints of various kinds? What are the possible systemic outcomes of continuing economic growth in one sector of the system for time t (although slowing population growth there, with greater resultant per capita increases in wealth) while approaching equilibrium in the other sector? Can an equitable strategy of resource allocation be developed? Is the resulting international system likely to be more or less stable than the current one? In exploring these questions, our model is a two-actor disaggregated version of Forrester's world dynamics model. [15] The assumptions, parameter values, and new functions are listed in the Appendix for both the advanced industrial and the less-developed actors.

The next section compares the results of Forrester's own projections with those of our disaggregated version of the model, which includes as well a trade loop between actors. We test two versions of the distributive solution, first by substantially reallocating wealth over a 25-year period, second by lowering the barriers to migration so that the poor but populous actor loses people and the rich but sparsely populated actor gains people. Policy implications and suggestions for future research follow these discussions. The results seriously question whether the nation-state in its present form, with its current set of economic and environmental values, is any longer the optimum territorial unit, whether in fact it can provide on a global scale the coordinated decision making required.

RICH STATES AND POOR IN THE CONTEST
FOR GROWTH AND TRADE

Our first task is to simulate world futures in terms of regional differences in income, population size, and development patterns. The technique used is the rather simple expedient of disaggregating the Forrester world dynamics model into two components or actors. By progressively adding constraints, we hope to explore the differential effect on the advanced industrial and less-developed worlds of the movement toward growth equilibrium via the distributive solution, the solution that in our view is likely in the long run to generate the least instability. [16] For the purposes of this analysis, political integration can be thought of as having progressed to the stage where only two actors remain, or the actors can be viewed as randomly selected countries drawn from each of two very different socioeconomic regions. The important consideration, however, is the fact of disaggregation along north-south lines.

Assuming that some attempt is made in each region to cope with population problems, a growth rate of 1.5 percent is selected as the

global norm. A number of Western nations display growth rates of
1.2 percent or less, but the 1.5 percent rate is perhaps not far above
the average.[17] The global norm would, however, be very difficult for
most developing countries to approach, as some of their growth rates
currently exceed twice this figure. But arguing from the standpoint
of equity, we consider the global norm to be an initial parameter
value from which the actors may in actuality diverge as the simulation
proceeds.

Second, we assume that trade occurs between the actors much
as in the current system. The advanced industrial regions exchange
capital (goods and services) for natural resources (primary commodities) from the developing regions. As the supply of natural resources
declines, the price of these imports (the ratio of the units of exchange)
increases. The less-developed region invests capital from abroad to
raise its per capita income. The industrial sector processes the raw
materials it imports to sustain its standard of living. Both benefit
from trade, although perhaps not equally.

One of our concerns is to ascertain who benefits most from this
trade. The richer actor also has the smaller population to support,
and on this count might be less dependent upon foreign trade. Exports
of capital to the poorer actor, when invested in agriculture for example,
might indeed supply the vast amounts of carbohydrates and protein
necessary to feed the larger population. On the other hand, the higher
standard of living and the larger economy of the former country certainly increase its dependence on foreign raw materials.

Another concern is to determine the nature of the equilibrium
once the system reaches the maximum growth that it is capable of
tolerating. A central issue here is whether an actor can achieve an
equilibrium at all and, if so, at what population level, material
standard of living, and quality of life. Related is the question of how
much oscillation accompanies such an equilibrium, thus affecting the
ultimate political stability of the society.

In model A, which traces the evolution of industrial society between 1900 and 2200, the point of maximum population growth is
reached in 2020. Capital investment continues to increase for a few
more years but plummets by the end of the twenty-first century.
Natural resource use is determined essentially by the large raw material imports from the developing region until about 1980, when stock-
piling ceases and both foreign and domestic supplies dwindle. Pollution
rises very rapidly at the turn of the twenty-first century (caused by
the strains on economic output, both manufacturing and agricultural)
and contributes to the conditions of disease, housing shortage, and
transportation collapse marking the population decline.

In attempting to offset the depressing effect of pollution and
other factors on food production, capital investment in agriculture—

which remains below 25 percent of total investment for most of the twentieth century—suddenly reaches a peak of nearly 75 percent of total investment. Lagging by a decade, the material standard of living follows the same pattern. The quality of life drops abruptly with the crisis conditions of the 2020s and then miraculously improves over the next two decades, only to plummet thereafter. Shifts in pollution levels are largely responsible for these gyrations. Food ratios remain quite high but only at excessive cost in terms of capital investment in agriculture.

The overall picture is of an affluent society suddenly gone awry, a society wrenched from pleasant expansion to collapse in a few brief decades. One might characterize the result as the combined effect of the Great Depression and the Black Plague, two events that we have been conditioned to believe are nightmares of an immature science and an inexperienced economy.

Model B, depicting the emergence of a developing country, yields a somewhat different picture. Population does peak around the year 2000, earlier than for advanced industrial society. Capital investment and pollution drop off a decade later. But the material standard of living and the quality of life are much lower, especially in the later periods, than in industrialized society. Nonetheless, in part because this is largely an agricultural country, the capital investment in agriculture remains high and no one starves. Crowding occurs, comforts are few, housing and sanitary facilities are insufficient, but the food ratio is sustained and the large population is adequately nourished.

Trade necessitates export of natural resources, which continue to fall throughout the twenty-first century. But the imports of capital probably contribute to the improvement in the material standard of living, which reverses in the mid-twentieth century. The general conclusion is that, even assuming the constraints on population growth rate that we make, the less-developed country is forced to accept equilibrium sooner than its richer counterpart. It does manage to sustain a well-fed and much larger population, but life is still quite nasty and brutish, if not short.

Which type of society, the less-developed or more-developed industrially, benefits most from trade? Computer runs not reported here to conserve space indicated that without trade, population growth peaks out in the year 1980 for the advanced industrial society, while for the agricultural society curbs on population growth occur at approximately the same time as with trade. Thus, if trade benefit means capacity to support a growing population, then trade, at least in raw materials, was far more important for the advanced industrial country than for the developing country.

If sustained by subsequent analyses incorporating more complex interactions between the two sectors, this discovery has important policy implications. Foreign aid perhaps should be looked at as further compensation for the sale of primary commodities that for various reasons are undervalued. While it may be true that the developing nation cannot alone extract and process mineral resources, for example, without the help of foreign capital, it appears even more true that without the import of raw materials the advanced industrial country is likely to be forced into growth equilibrium at a much earlier date. Moreover, for the industrialized country trade appears to facilitate a higher material standard of living at no apparent loss in the quality of life.

Concerning the question of alternative population growth rates, some experimentation was carried out with a higher overall rate of population expansion. As one would expect, a higher population growth rate of 2.25 instead of 1.5 percent yielded a population apex at an earlier time point while at the same threshold. The other variables peaked earlier also, but the pattern of their fluctuations remained essentially unchanged.

The question of variable fluctuation introduces the last issue dealt with in this section, the nature of the postgrowth equilibrium. Decided differences separate the developing and the advanced industrial societies in this regard. The industrialized societies appear to enter a phase of violent oscillation ending in stagnation. Their agricultural counterparts, on the other hand, seem to approach rather stable equilibrium. In search of a viable equilibrium, the industrial countries pass through transient prosperity and shocking depressions. The agricultural countries suffer a small population loss over a period of two centuries and increasing poverty, but the food ratio remains high. The violent shifts of capital investment, the material standard of living, and population size of the advanced industrial polities is by contrast certainly a more stressful environment, prone to the coercive use of force. How can the analyst explain such differences in political or economic terms?

One explanation is that the per capita wealth of the two types of actors is dissimilar. The task of maintaining an equilibrium around the higher income line of the rich society is much more difficult than around the lower equilibrium line of the poor state. Life in the poor state may be dismal, it surely is simple and plain, but the economic base of the society is not severely strained. Bluntly said, the poor have learned to live with poverty. What was a vice in an expanding society becomes a virtue in a contracting one. In the case of the affluent society, conversely, the problems of maintaining both a high material standard of living and a satisfactory food ratio are antagonistic and are never effectively resolved.

Another explanation is that oscillations of the kind experienced by the rich actor may be less the exception than the norm in population ecology. It is apparently rare to find a population in equilibrium that demonstrates little variance around the equilibrium line.[18] The opposite is the case. Variance is small during the upward sweep of an expanding economy when the vectors of momentum are unidirectional; variance is great when momentum slows down and begins to reverse itself. It is not surprising that oscillations around the trend line at equilibrium would occur in human as well as insect, animal, and bacterial populations.

Finally, the difference in equilibrium trend lines may arise from the difference in bureaucratic sophistication of the societies.[19] In the poor agricultural polity, the bulk of social and economic processes are completely deterministic; because deterministic, such changes occur quite slowly, a phenomenon only too familiar in attempts to help developing societies approach the takeoff stage of Rostow's self-sustained growth. Such inertia, however, may be advantageous to a society facing possible long-term stagnation. In contrast, in the advanced industrial state the government often intervenes directly in the economy through monetary and fiscal policy or in the social system through welfare or educational legislation. When facing crises of the dimensions described by the simulation, the tendency of the decision maker is to overreact, especially in very complex social systems that require fine-tuning to remain in equilibrium.[20] The equilibrium trend line is approached through a series of damped overreactions best exhibited by population change, capital investment in agriculture, and food ratio, where each successive shift narrows the variance around the trend line. Even more destabilizing is the attempt by policy makers to find single solutions to multiple social ills, exemplified by the increase in capital investment, which in turn accelerates the output of pollution, a process more damaging than a meager food supply to the country's inhabitants. The more complex the social system, the less informed the direct intervention into that system by bureaucracies, and the greater the lag in response times, then the more likely are oscillations of the type experienced by this simulated industrial society in the crisis of postgrowth adjustment.

The current anxiety of the rich industrial states over the future is more understandable in the light of these simulation results. Similarly, the relative complacence of the developing countries is more plausible given the apparent flow of trade benefits and the nature of postgrowth equilibrium.[21] This complacence may be rather empty, however, considering the level of poverty at which apparent equilibrium is bought. Our next task is to probe the futures of these two actors to see whether a fairer distribution of wealth and burdens might ease the problems that each faces in the equilibrium phase.

EFFECTING THE DISTRIBUTIVE SOLUTION

Of the four postgrowth outcomes discussed in the first section, only one—the distributive solution—appeared to be politically stable and workable as a long-term alternative world future. Each of the others invites political confrontation, especially in the face of economic depression and environmental chaos. One aspect of the distributive solution was implemented at the beginning of the simulation, namely, insistence that both halves of the international system adopt an upper boundary of 1.5 percent as a lid on population growth. Of course, the two populations greatly differed in size, in productive capacity, in resource abundance and in other ways (see the Appendix). After a series of modifications of this constraint, we recognized that it alone could not achieve equality and peaceful change.

Thus a second constraint was added in order that, beginning in the year 1975, in the midst of the dynamic growth phase, the disparity in wealth between the two regions would be reduced. By calculating the difference in per capita wealth in 1975 and transferring a fraction of this difference each year, the goal was to approach equality by the year 2000. This would surely meet the demands of the less-developed countries for fair play and compensatory treatment. The action could occur between two autonomous regions or within the sectors of a single global federation. One can conceive of the plan as a massive program of foreign assistance modeled after the efforts of the Marshall Plan for European reconstruction following World War II. Instead of gluing together shattered pieces at war's end, however, this plan would hopefully bind the system together so as to preclude the incidence of war in the first place.

A final constraint was added in a subsequent run, further reducing the burdens of inequality: elimination of all barriers to the migration of peoples. Indeed, an assumption was made that large-scale migration from the population-abundant to the population-scarce region would take place as a function of government policy. Studies of worker migration from Southern Italy and France to Norther Europe under the aegis of the Common Market show the reluctance of families to move to unfamiliar areas, despite the availability of jobs and improved living conditions.[22] Nonetheless, large-scale migrations have occurred, usually encouraged by religious or political flight or government incentive, to many countries—the United States, South Africa, and Australia, to name only a few. Although such migrations may be feasible, their possible impact on donor and recipient nations has too long been ignored by the literature on world futures.

According to classical trade theory, equalization of prices on goods and services can take place in either or both of two ways:

(1) through specialized production and trade or (2) through transfer of the factors of production, which are themselves responsible in part for specialization and differing factor costs.[23] However, since international trade does not necessarily equalize incomes and certainly does not equalize short-term market prices (indeed such equalization would mean the end of specialized production, of the rewards to trade, and hence of trade itself), the result is, as our initial simulation runs indicate, continued inequality although perhaps with differing degrees and types of specialization and at a different level of production and consumption.

In pursuing the distributive solution, we therefore encouraged direct transfers of capital and deliberate migration of people. Land, the third of the classical factors of production, remains immobile and is thus an unaltered source of difference in community structure. Our objective was not so much to erase all differences in societies, for homogeneity in itself is no guarantee of political prudence, but rather to remove the elements of privilege and inequity that create hostility and aggression. Balanced against the need to find a stable growth equilibrium is the need to build a stable political order. The distributive outcome, more than the others, could provide the latter criterion of a good society.

From the perspective of world order, foreign assistance and freedom of migration have several advantages in a two-actor model with severe initial inequality. First, elimination of tariffs on migration is sanguine for the political temperament of the two societies. A safety valve for frustrated, ambitious, and determined young men and women through opportunities abroad is a good thing for both donor and recipient nations. At the same time, motives of nationalism and blind parochialism are diluted by the influx of foreigners, not so much because they fail to transfer their allegiance with their lunch pails and their passports but because the native population will be obliged to interact and learn from them. Admittedly, moreover, for the bulk of the newcomers the thought of war with a country so recently called home surely reduces its possibility for a generation or so.

Second, the bane of the advanced industrial economy—too low a ratio of unskilled to skilled and highly educated manpower—would be alleviated by an influx of labor from the country where the inverse ratio prevails. Labor deficits could be eliminated by the very technique that solves the problem of labor surplus abroad. Third, the dilemma of lagging response time and overreaction that troubled the advanced industrial economy in the previous section could be avoided in the egalitarian outcome through the orderly shift of capital investment and manpower. The inverse movement of capital and labor is bound to have an immediate effect on both economies in the direction posited,

while the continuous movement is likely to supply confidence needed
to make the vast social adjustments.

Fourth, the distributive solution matches growth equilibrium
with political balance.[24] As the two actors become more similar in
wealth and population size, the relative discrepancy in their power
disappears. Wars bred of imperial exploitation could not occur without power disequilibrium. Inasmuch as wars escalating from miscal-
culated military interventions are thought to be currently most
dangerous, the balance achieved in the distributive solution is thought
to have structural advantages.

Fifth, although denigrated in many international politics texts,
a "reservoir of good feeling" much like that emerging between the
United States and Western Europe in the reconstruction era surely
might smooth the period of difficult adjustments facing such a political
system as the one currently simulated. The emotional health of the
system is as important as the legal and structural provisions and
alterations.[25] The distributive solution might satisfy some of these
psychological needs.

Let us now review the empirical findings in terms of the theoretical considerations outlined above.

Model C tests the implications for the advanced industrial
society of capital transfer beginning in 1975. The first observation
is that population peaks some 40 years earlier than without capital
transfer and at a population threshold some 12 percent lower. The
strain on the resources of the country is great enough to keep population growth down. The second observation is that maximum capital
investment is 60 percent higher without than with capital transfer.
The real cost to society, however, is paradoxically not so severe.
In fact, when we look at the material standard of living in the year
2200, admittedly very low, it is the same in both situations. Furthermore, the level of pollution throughout the period is far lower with
capital transfer and the quality of life in general is much better. It
is difficult to argue that capital transfer has hurt the lifestyle or
prosperity of advanced industrial society, although the power of the
state has been somewhat diminished.

The really striking feature of these results, however, is that
the violent oscillations of postgrowth equilibrium have disappeared.
Eliminated are the economic stresses resulting from abrupt booms
and busts. Missing also are the sharp fluctuations in capital expend-
iture, pollution, and the quality of life that are so dependent upon
economic variation. The society behaves as though it were less determined to retain its affluence. While population size is more than
halved in a 220-year period, the decline is steady and without significant crisis. Such a society by our standards might not be a very

attractive place to live or visit, but in contrast to the situation without capital transfer it is certainly the preferable place to exist.

Model D examines the impact of capital transfer on the developing sector, the actor for whose benefit the transfer was implemented. At first glance, the pattern of variation seems very similar. On closer scrutiny, however, we observe that population peaks slightly later and at a higher threshold. In general, with capital transfer the quality of life and the material standard of living are better. But what is surprising is the much sharper decline in population size, such that in 2200 the less-developed country receiving the capital transfer has one-quarter less population than if it had received none. How can such a drastic reversal of intuitive speculation be justified?

The answer appears to be that the transfer of capital is not very helpful to the less-developed country in the long run for two reasons. First, it uses the capital to facilitate greater population growth. Second, it eats up and uses up the proceeds of the investment in greater consumption. Five years after the transfer of capital is completed in the year 2005, capital investment begins a long downward slide that ends only with the termination of the simulation. Part of the difficulty may be that the less-developed country simply is unable to absorb such large transfers of capital profitably. A more critical message is that foreign assistance is of no value if it is used primarily to feed a larger population. Constraints on population growth appear essential if foreign aid is to have lasting benefit.

A cynical response to the experiment with capital transfer might be that money indeed seems to be at the root of evil: The advanced industrial country was better off without it; the developing country appeared to do poorly with it. A more tolerant view would be that money is no substitute for wise constraints on growth and that philandering may in fact make the application of such constraints impossible.

The decision to open the gates to large-scale migration late in a nation's maturity is a radical plan for restructuring the equilibrium setting. If people are maldistributed with regard to resources and wealth, a logical policy is to bring people to capital rather than to rely on capital coming to people. Such an idea is made explicit in this simulation in that a two-way flow is created: Goods and services flow from the advanced to the developing society; people flow from the developing society where they are relatively more numerous to the advanced society where conditions are less crowded. The novelty of the experiment is that, whereas most mass migrations have been tolerated only early in a nation's industrial phase, this program is initiated in 1975, well into the system's maturity.

Clearly the dual effect of inward migration and outward capital transfer is to depress the evolution of advanced industrial society (model E). The population peaks in 1985 despite a continued influx of foreigners for 15 more years. Both the quality of life and the material standard of living are distressingly low for most of the period. Sufficient food exists in spite of declining investments in agriculture, either a cause or an effect of the loss of people. With the termination of the interactor transactions in 2000, capital investment increases for a time under the severe pressure of a declining material standard of living, but this trend collapses by 2050 after failing to improve the material standard and worsening the quality of life. Thus, although the stress of violent social oscillations is missing from this outcome, one could hardly say that such massive population and capital transfers can be sustained by the industrialized actor.

How favorable have the shifts of factor endowments been for the poorer region (model F)? A rather familiar configuration emerged, with population growth continuing unabated for a longer time than was the case before transfer and migration but dropping sharply after reaching a maximum. On the whole, the quality of life in this society is higher than in previous instances. Again, however, the large population consumes the advantages accruing to capital influx. Population size does not benefit from emigration. It appears to increase in apparent compensation for the loss of population abroad, in a perverse application of Malthusianism; in fact, the population base is so great that this level of emigration can have no noticeable effect on overall growth.

These results hardly encourage one to believe that the egalitarian outcome is easily achieved. Both the advanced and the developing societies are richer in per capita terms (indeed about twice as prosperous) early in their development where population nears a maximum. This suggests that the overall population size of the world exceeds the capacity of the societies to properly clothe, feed, and employ its inhabitants. But the really sad discovery is that, in spite of intensive efforts to make the wealth of rich and poor converge through population and assistance programs, once these programs are terminated and the societies enter the stagnation phase, wealth again begins to diverge. The two societies are more alike at the end of the twentieth century than they are at the end of the twenty-first. Amid global misery, there remain gradations of poverty, and the poor get poorer.

A general conclusion must be that, attractive though the distributive outcome is from a political perspective, it cannot succeed unless resources and capital are replenished and unless population growth is sharply and opportunely constrained. Population migration cannot ameliorate the strains on the global community unless effective restrictions are placed on birth rates early in a country's development. Moreover, there really seem to be no economic advantages to the use of population migration rather than capital transfer as an equilibrium tool. Capital transfers are flexible and they appear to be potentially less disruptive. The political benefits of the distributive solution cannot, after all, be enjoyed by the system if the economic consequence is stagnation. In summation, it would appear that the best solution would involve immediate curbs on population growth throughout the system, together with capital transfers to continue for a minimum of 25 years. But for large-scale capital transfers to work, two reforms are essential. In advanced industrial society, a much more dynamic, pollution-free, technological base is needed to generate additional capital and to supplant disappearing resources. In developing society, reforms are needed to permit greater absorption of capital without accompanying temporary spurts of consumption and population growth. Such reforms could make capital transfers the fulcrum of the distribution solution.

POLITICS, GROWTH, AND PEACE

The object of this essay was to examine, both theoretically and empirically, some of the outcomes of postgrowth society. If the world is to have a future, then it is worthwhile or perhaps necessary to think about the contours of that future. What is the interrelationship between political order and the imperatives of structural change? By successively adding constraints to a two-actor model of the system for the period 1900-2200, we have begun to explore some of the differential effects that growth and equilibrium may have on the advanced industrial and less-developed regions of the system.

Further work with this model will attempt two things: first, to make the model more completely interactive by rewriting the algorithm so as to incorporate both actors simultaneously; second, to introduce probabilistic conflict statements based on the relationship between instability, resource scarcity, and perceived power. The analysis is not considered complete, nor has the simulation model been exhaustively tested. A number of preliminary conclusions, however, are possible:

1. The advanced industrial countries appear to be more dependent upon trade than their less-developed counterparts. This may be largely because of the needs of the industrialized countries for raw materials.

2. Higher effective population growth rates lead to earlier population peaks but do not seem to change whatever pattern of equilibrium the society would otherwise evolve.

3. When faced with monumental ecological crisis and economic depression, industrialized society is prone to overreaction and

unilateral corrective measures often accompanied by lags in response times. A consequence is a series of violent, but increasingly damped, oscillations in the postgrowth phase. Agricultural society does not display these characteristics.

4. Large-scale capital transfers depress population growth and capital investment somewhat in the donor country, but paradoxically do not worsen the material standard of living or the quality of life and in fact eliminate the violent swings in postgrowth adjustment that otherwise seem to plague the capital-rich actor.

5. Contrary to expectation, major capital transfers did not provide substantial benefits to the developing regions. Limited ability to absorb such volumes of capital, accelerated population growth, and a propensity to raise consumption immediately, all may explain this finding.

6. Population migration is not an effective means of redistributing the world's economic burdens and benefits. On the contrary, according to these results, once migration terminates and the population of the developing country peaks, per capita differences in the wealth of the two societies actually begin to worsen.

The simulation accentuates how difficult it is to effect policy changes as correctives to fundamental structural problems within the economy and society. [26] Social inertia is immense, as indicated by our attempt to erase differences in per capita wealth over a 25-year period, an attempt that led to a threefold reduction in this discrepancy but still had not achieved equality by the year 2000. Looking at the equation from the inverse perspective, it may be difficult to compel the advanced societies to continue capital transfers until equality is attained.

On the other hand, if the distributive solution can be justified on political grounds, namely, because it establishes the setting for diplomacy free from exploitative ventures and coercion, then nothing should stand in the way of such a policy from the perspective of growth equilibrium. Ironically, capital transfers seemed to benefit advanced industrial society in the long run rather than disadvantage it. There may be better and worse ways of effecting the egalitarian outcome but, whether within the context of a single polity or within a system of loosely affiliated regions or actors, egalitarianism cannot be dismissed as too costly or too socially disruptive. Yet the elimination of privilege does not guarantee the founding of achievement, although it may be the prerequisite of more than accidental achievement. Nor have we discovered the key to a stable growth equilibrium at a threshold that also promises inevitable political balance.

Yet our results do address the concerns of Galtung, who viewed the limits-to-growth thesis as drifting toward the self-serving purposes

of elitist alarmism. If it can be shown, as we have elsewhere maintained, that conflict follows the path of an actor's relative power and
fortunes, [27] then Falk is certainly correct in advocating a future
world order erected on an egalitarian footing as well as upon environmental reform, particularly insofar as the distribution of capital participation is to be altered. [28] We have tried to show that growth
equilibrium and political equilibrium are both essential to a viable
world system. More than this, growth equilibrium need not get in the
way of peace or order maintenance; rather, the two objectives are
complementary and inseparable. Growth is probably not essential to
peace and in the long run may be destructive of it. Thus we must
learn to synthesize a postgrowth equilibrium that will effectively
sustain the peace ethos.

NOTES

1. Stanley Hoffman, "Obstinate or Obsolete? The Fate of the
Nation State and the Case of Western Europe," in International
Regionalism: Readings, ed. Joseph S. Nye, Jr. (Boston: Little,
Brown, 1968), pp. 177-230; Hedley Bull, "The Grotian Conception of
International Society," in Diplomatic Investigations, eds. Herbert
Butterfield and Martin Wight (Cambridge, Mass.: Harvard University
Press, 1968), pp. 51-73; Hans J. Morgenthau, In Defense of the
National Interest (New York: Knopf, 1951); Kenneth N. Waltz, Man,
the State, and War (New York: Columbia University Press, 1959).
2. Karl Deutsch et al., Political Community in the North
Atlantic (Princeton, N.J.: Princeton University Press, 1957); David
Mitrany, A Working Peace System (London: Royal Institute of Inter-
national Affairs, 1943); Ernest B. Haas, Beyond the Nation-State
(Palo Alto, Calif.: Stanford University Press, 1964); Joseph S. Nye,
Jr., Peace in Parts: Integration and Conflict in Regional Organization
(Boston: Little, Brown, 1971); Leon Lindberg, The Political Dynamics
of European Economic Integration (Palo Alto, Calif.: Stanford Uni-
versity Press, 1963).
3. Samuel P. Huntington, "Transnational Organizations in World
Politics," World Politics, April 1973; Chadwick Alger, "The Multinational Corporation and the Future International System," The Annals,
September 1972; the entire issue of International Organization, summer
1971.
4. Inis Claude, Power and International Relations (New York:
Random House, 1962).
5. Grenville Clark and Louis B. Sohn, World Peace Through
World Law, 2nd ed. (Cambridge, Mass.: Harvard University Press,

1960); Hugh Gaitskell, "An Eight-point Programme for World Government," in Peace Is Possible, ed. Elizabeth Jay Hollins (New York: Grossman, 1966); Jan Baldwin, "Thinking About a New World Order for the Decade 1990," War/Peace Report, January 1970.

6. The single most troublesome issue both substantively and methodologically is the issue of resource substitution and technological innovation. Is our ability to substitute other materials for current scarce resources virtually infinite? How fast does technological innovation occur and how can it be measured? Answers to these questions could improve our ability to project outcomes by a large factor. See the technological optimists for one side of this story: Daniel Bell, "The End of Scarcity?" Saturday Review of the Society, May 1973; Herman Kahn and B. Bruce-Briggs, Things to Come (New York: Macmillan, 1972). Recycling is only a minor solution increasing our use of some metals, for example, by 20 percent but at considerable cost in energy and effort.

7. Johan Galtung, "'Limits to Growth' and Class Politics," Journal of Peace Research, nos. 1-2 (1973): 101-14. For more sympathetic views, see Garrett Hardin, "We Live on a Spaceship," Bulletin of Atomic Scientists, November 1972; Robert Heilbroner, "Growth and Survival," Foreign Affairs, October 1972. For more critical evaluation of the models, and perhaps of simulation itself, consider Karl Kaysen, "The Computer That Printed Out W*O*L*F*," Foreign Affairs, July 1972; Leo P. Kadanoff, "From Simulation Model to Public Policy: An Examination of Forrester's 'Urban Dynamics,'" Simulation, June 1971, pp. 261-68.

8. Nazli Chouchri and Robert North, "Dynamics of International Conflict: Some Policy Implications of Population, Resources, and Technology," World Politics Supplement, Spring 1972; Robert North and Nazli Chouchri, "Population, Technology, and Resources in the Future," Journal of International Affairs, no. 2 (1971): 224-37.

9. Edward L. Morse, "The Transformation of Foreign Policies: Modernization, Interdependence, and Externalization," World Politics 22 (April 1970): 371-92.

10. Donella H. Meadows et al., The Limits to Growth (Washington, D.C.: Potomac Associates, 1972); Dennis L. Meadows, ed., Toward Global Equilibrium: Collected Papers (Cambridge, Mass.: Wright-Allen, 1973); Jay W. Forrester, World Dynamics (Cambridge, Mass.: Wright-Allen, 1971).

11. See Chapter 4 of Falk's major contribution to the World Order Models Project, Institute for World Order: Richard A. Falk, This Endangered Planet (New York: Random House, 1971).

12. Further discussion of equilibrium is found in Herman Daly, "The Steady-State Economy: Toward a Political Economy of Biophysical Equilibrium and Moral Growth," in Toward a Steady-State

Economy, ed. Daly (San Francisco: W. H. Freeman, 1973), pp. 170-73; J. Mayonne Stycos, "Politics and Population Control in Latin America," World Politics, October 1967, pp. 66-82; Richard L. Clinton, "Opposition to Population Limitation in Latin America," in Research in the Politics of Population, eds. Richard L. Clinton and R. Kenneth Godwin (Lexington, Mass.: D. C. Heath, 1972), pp. 95-112.

13. H. W. Singer, "The Distribution of Gains between Investing and Borrowing Countries," American Economic Review 40 (May 1950): 473-85; R. Narkse, Problems of Capital Formation in Underdeveloped Countries (Oxford: Basil Blackwell, 1953).

14. Earl V. Anderson, "Pollution Control: A World Trade Problem," Chemical and Engineering News, November 8, 1971, pp. 13-18; Oil and Gas Journal, April 3, 1972; Charles F. Doran, Manfred Hinz, and D. C. Mayer-Tasch, Umweltschutz—Politik des peripheren Eingriffs: Eine Einfuhrung in die politische Okologie (Neuwied am Rhein/Berlin: Luchterhand-Verlag, 1973).

15. Forrester, World Dynamics.

16. Harold and Margaret Sprout, "The Dilemma of Rising Demands and Insufficient Resources," World Politics, July 1968, pp. 660-93; Bruce Russett, "Rich and Poor in 2000 A.D.: The Great Gulf," Virginia Quarterly Review, Spring 1968; Edward J. Woodhouse, "Re-Visioning the Future of the Third World," World Politics, October 1972, pp. 1-33; Charles F. Doran, "Conflict: The Missing Variable in 'Limits to Growth' Models," in Exploring the Limits to Growth, ed. David Orr (tentative title, forthcoming, University of Kentucky Press).

17. In 1800 Sweden, for example, the birth rate was approximately 0.03, the death rate 0.025. But in Canada today the birth rate is about 0.02 and the death rate 0.01, while these rates in Honduras are 0.04 and 0.01, respectively. Nathan Keyfitz and Wilhelm Flieger, Population: Facts and Methods of Demography (San Francisco: W. H. Freeman, 1971), pp. 9-11; Phillip M. Hauser, ed., The Population Dilemma, 2nd ed. (Englewood Cliffs, N.J.: Prentice-Hall, 1969).

18. See Charles J. Krebs, Ecology: The Experimental Analysis of Distribution and Abundance (New York: Harper and Row, 1972), p. 194.

19. Francis E. Rourke, ed., Bureaucratic Power in National Politics, 2nd ed. (Boston: Little, Brown, 1972); Graham T. Allison, "Conceptual Models and the Cuban Missile Crisis," The American Political Science Review 63 (September 1969): 689-718; Robert L. Rothstein, Planning, Prediction, and Policymaking in Foreign Affairs: Theory and Practice (Boston: Little, Brown, 1972).

20. Charles F. Hermann, ed., International Crises: Insights from Behavioral Research (New York: Free Press, 1972). The structure of the system may affect actor behavior where subsystems

dominance is less prevalent. For the interesting thesis that alliance reliability is greater in bipolar rather than multipolar settings, see Louis Rene Beres, "Bi-polarity, Multi-polarity and the Reliability of Alliance Commitments," Western Political Quarterly, December 1972, pp. 702-10.

21. Michael Wallace, "Status, Formal Organization, and Arms Levels as Factors Leading to the Onset of War, 1820-1964," in Peace, War and Numbers, ed. Bruce Russett (Beverly Hills, Calif.: Sage Publications, 1972), pp. 49-69; Marshall R. Singer, Weak States in a World of Powers (New York: Free Press, 1972).

22. S. Barzanti, The Underdeveloped Area Within the Common Market (Princeton, N.J.: Princeton University Press, 1965).

23. C. P. Kindleberger, International Economics, rev. ed. (Homewood, Ill.: Richard D. Irwin, 1958); G. A. Haberler, A Survey of International Trade Theory, Special Papers in International Economics, no. 1 (Princeton, N.J.: International Finance Section, Princeton University, 1955); Richard E. Caves, Trade and Economic Structure: Models and Methods (Cambridge, Mass.: Harvard University Press, 1963).

24. George Liska, International Equilibrium (Cambridge, Mass.: Harvard University Press, 1957); Steven J. Brams, "Measuring the Concentration of Power in Political Systems," American Political Science Review 62 (1968): 461-75; Kenneth N. Waltz, "International Structure, National Force, and the Balance of World Power," Journal of International Affairs 21 (1967): 215-31.

25. K. J. Holsti, "National Role Conceptions in the Study of Foreign Policy," International Studies Quarterly 14 (September 1970): 233-309; John R. Raser, "Learning and Affect in International Politics," in International Politics and Foreign Policy, ed. James N. Rosenau, rev. ed. (New York: Free Press, 1969), pp. 432-41; Herbert C. Kelman, "Societal, Attitudinal and Structural Factors in International Relations," Journal of Social Issues 11, no. 1 (1955): 42-56.

26. Aaron Wildavsky, The Politics of the Budgetary Process (Boston: Little, Brown, 1964); Randall Hindshaw, ed., Inflation as a Global Problem (Baltimore: Johns Hopkins University Press, 1972).

27. Charles F. Doran, The Politics of Assimilation: Hegemony and Its Aftermath (Baltimore: Johns Hopkins University Press, 1971), pp. 191-97; Charles F. Doran, "A Simulation Model of War and National Power," paper presented before the Southern Political Science Association, November 1974.

28. For a discussion of the relationship between the amount and distribution of conflict in hierarchic terms, see Charles F. Doran, "A Conceptual and Operational Comparison of Frustration-Aggression, Rank Disequilibrium and Achievement Discrepancy Models," paper

presented before the International Studies Association, March 1974; and the fuller discussion in Doran, "A Conceptual and Operational Comparison of Power-Based Theories of Conflict: Toward Synthesis via a General Theory of Conflict Dynamics," mimeo., February 1975.

APPENDIX

The simulation model used as a basis for this analysis is the world dynamics model developed by Jay Forrester of MIT. A complete listing of parameters and functions appears in his book World Dynamics (Cambridge, Mass.: Wright-Allen, 1971). Unless noted below, these same functions and parameters were used in constructing the advanced industrial and developing societies. In disaggregating the world dynamics model, we made the following assumptions:

1. The world is composed of only two actors, one largely industrial, the other largely agricultural.
2. The actors can choose policies that emphasize either growth or equilibrium, and that in turn will be reflected in the parameter values selected for each simulation run (see Table 10.1).
3. The choice will have both structural effects recorded by the computer and political side effects that can be discussed independently by the analyst.
4. Constraints will be added corresponding to differing policy decisions of the actors. The principal constraints were the introduction of interactor trade; the transfer of capital investment; and the elimination of barriers to migration (see Table 10.2).

For example, the trade loop channels natural resources toward the advanced industrial country and capital investment toward the less-developed country. The volume of trade is calculated on the basis of natural resource use in the advanced industrial country and the available supply in the less-developed country. As trade proceeds over the period 1900-2000, the ratio of natural resources exchanged for capital investment declines, in effect increasing the price of natural resources to the advanced industrial country as the world's total supply gets smaller.

One of the difficulties with all simulations of this type is knowing how "dynamic" to make the model. World dynamics, for example, holds constant certain standards or norms of behavior, such as an optimum crowding ratio, throughout the simulation. But who is to say that the standards are not themselves a function of technological

TABLE 10.1

Parameters and Initial Values

Symbol	Definition	Import–Export Loop $T_0 = 1900$		Distributive Solution $T_0 = 1975$	
		Advanced	Developing	Advanced	Developing
P	population	4.1250E + 08	1.2375E + 09	1.6717E + 09	5.4969E + 09
CI	capital investment	3.0000E + 08	1.0000E + 08	3.5566E + 09	1.1109E + 09
NR	natural resources	2.9970E + 11	6.0030E + 11	1.9997E + 11	5.4477E + 11
POL	pollution	1.7500E + 08	2.5000E + 07	1.2223E + 10	2.2899E + 08
CIAF	CI-in-agriculture fraction	2.5000E – 01	7.5000E – 01	3.1451E – 01	6.6165E – 01
BRN	birth rate normal	4.0000E – 02	4.0000E – 02	4.0000E – 02	4.0000E – 02
DRN	death rate normal	2.5000E – 02	2.5000E – 02	2.5000E – 02	2.5000E – 02
NRI	NR, initial	2.9970E + 11	6.0030E + 11	2.9970E + 11	6.0030E + 11
NRUN	NR, usage normal	1.5000E + 00	5.0000E – 01	1.5000E + 00	5.0000E – 01
LA	land area	5.4000E + 07	8.1000E + 07	5.4000E + 07	8.1000E + 07
PDN	P density normal	2.6500E + 01	4.0000E + 01	2.6500E + 01	4.0000E + 01
FC	food coefficient	1.0000E + 00	1.0000E + 00	1.0000E + 00	1.0000E + 00
FN	food normal	1.5000E + 00	5.0000E – 01	1.5000E + 00	5.0000E – 01
CIGN	CI, generation normal	1.0000E – 01	1.5000E – 02	1.0000E – 01	1.5000E – 02
CIDN	CI, discard normal	3.0000E – 02	2.5000E – 02	3.0000E – 02	2.5000E – 02
POLS	pollution standard	3.1500E + 09	4.5000E + 08	3.1500E + 09	4.5000E + 08
POLN	pollution normal	1.7500E + 00	2.5000E – 01	1.7500E + 00	2.5000E – 01
CIAFN	CIAF normal	2.5000E – 01	7.5000E – 01	2.5000E – 01	7.5000E – 01
QLS	quality of life standard	1.0000E + 00	1.0000E + 00	1.0000E + 00	1.0000E + 00
ECIRN	effective CI ratio normal	1.5000E + 00	5.0000E – 01	1.5000E + 00	5.0000E – 01

TABLE 10.2

Altered Functions

Developing world
 BRCMT = 1/1/1/1/1/1
 CFIFRT = 1/.875/.75/.625/.5
Developing world with import-export loop
 39 → ((1(USE[TIME - 1899] x IMR)) > (EXPORTS x NRFR))/L1
 40 NR ← (NR - DT x NRUR) + (IMR x USE [TIME - 1899])
 41 ZZ[TIME - 1899] ← 1(USE[TIME - 1899] x IMR)
 42 L2: POL ← POL + DT x (POLG - POLA)
 43 CI ← (CI + DT x (CIG - CID)) + IMPORTS
 47 LI: NR (NR + DT x NRUR) - (EXPORTS x NRFR)
 48 ZZ TIME - 1899 EXPORTS x NRFR
 49 → L2
 IMR = .8
 IMPORTS = 10000000
 EXPORTS = 5966792802
 USE = (E +8) (-3.00, -3.15, -3.30, -3.46, -3.62, -3.79, -3.97,
                             -4.15, -4.33, -4.52)

Advanced world with import-export loop
 39 NR ← (NR - DT x NRUR) + EXPORTS [TIME - 1899]
 41 CI ← (CI + DT x CIG - CID)) - IMPORTS
 44 USE [TIME - 1899] ← NR - NR1
 45 NR1 ← NR
 IMPORTS = 10000000
 EXPORTS = (E - 7)(4.36/4.31/4.26/4.22/4.17/4.13/4.08/4.04/
                             3.99/3.95)

 USE = 2.298585477 E 11

Developing world—distributive solution
With capital exchange only:
 41 CI ← (CI + DT x (CIG - CID)) + IMPORTS [+/TIME ≥ SW IMPORTS]
 IMPORTS = 98725022.9/yr from 1975-2001, = 0 thereafter
With population migration added:
 44 → (TIME > 2000)/0
 45 P ← P - 38250000

Advanced world—distributive solution
With capital exchange only:
 41 CI ← (CI + DT x (CIG - CID)) - IMPORTS [+/TIME ≥ SW IMPORTS]
 IMPORTS = 9.8725-22.9/yr from 1975-2001, = 0 thereafter
With population migration added:
 44 → (TIME > 2000)/0
 45 P ← P + 38250000

and cultural change? If that change is itself hard to predict, the effect of that change on standards of behavior will be doubly ambiguous. Ambiguous or not, these relationships can be explored if the assumptions underlying them are made explicit. Figures displaying the actual empirical results of the simulation at each stage are available from the author upon request.

11

**IMAGES IN THE
CONSTRUCTION AND
EVALUATION OF
ALTERNATIVE
WORLD FUTURES**
Michael S. Stohl

INTRODUCTION: THE IMAGE

We not only know, but we know what we know. This
reflective character of the human image is unique, and
is what leads to philosophy. Because of the extended
time image and the extended relationship images, man
is capable of "rational behavior," that is to say, his
response is not to an immediate stimulus, but to an
image of the future filtered through an elaborate
value system. His image contains not only what is,
but what might be. It is full of potentialities as yet
unrealized. [1]

In view of its extraordinary implications, this statement by
Kenneth Boulding warrants broad acceptance. Recognizing this need,
this essay proposes to confront the dominant image of alternative
world futures research—the world order orientation—with an equally
promising image: anarchism. Hence, after discussing the essentials
of an anarchist image of extant and possible societies, the principles
associated with this image will be utilized to evaluate alternatives

This is a revised and expanded version of "Images, Anarchism
and Alternative Futures," a paper presented to the annual meeting of
the Midwest Section of the International Studies Association, St. Louis,
April 19-21, 1973. The author thankfully acknowledges the criticisms
and suggestions of the editors and Norman Walbeck on that earlier
version.

in systems design and change that share the espoused goals of anarchist thought.

To the theoretician concerned about world futures, the impact of the image that one has of the world as it presently exists, or as one would like it to be, cannot be overstated. Regardless of the particular techniques or approaches favored and utilized by researchers (formal or informal models, structural or behavioral strategies, quantitative or qualitative evaluative methodologies), a priori notions about what variables are relevant and about a frame of reference from which these variables are derived are omnipresent. Boulding suggests that such notions or the image "acts as a field, the behavior [of men] consists in gravitating toward the most highly valued part of the field."[2]

Unfortunately, much social scientific study of alternative world futures has remained an "after the physical fact" brand of theory building. That is, it begins with acknowledgment of the status quo as its starting point and proceeds to explain how one can improve system performance or bring it into line with current "social realities." In other words, we usually attempt to assess how man can or does adapt to the world in which he finds himself. We thereby limit our potentialities by binding ourselves to strategies that involve changing present images into desired images on the basis of what is currently feasible. For example, Herbert Marcuse, not normally thought of as conservative, suggests that "as long as there is any gap between real and potential, the former must be acted upon and changed until it is brought into line with reason."[3] Reason is unfortunately often merely confined to what we currently know, or think we know.

Boulding therefore argues that, as in the natural sciences, this approach for success is bought at a high price:

> The price is a severe limitation of its field of inquiry
> and a value system which is as ruthless in its own way
> in the censoring of messages as the value system of
> primitive man. Messages which will not conform to the
> subculture are condemned as illusion. Furthermore,
> the world of the scientist is the world of the repeatable,
> the world of the probable. The rare occurrence, the
> non-repeatable event, the unanswerable question eludes
> him. [4]

If we were to be entirely true to this methodology of scientific research in the analysis of man's social potentialities, we would transform the reflective character and advantage of human thought into a branch of Reichenbach's scientific philosophy. [5] What types of futures research progress could we then achieve? For example, social change and its study has been placed within an evolutionary-adaptive paradigm. [6]

This paradigm may be a reasonable scientific explanation of how we have come to be where we are. This image of blind variation and selective intention is proposed to explain human development. Shall we therefore yield to the temptation to wait for variations to occur with the knowledge that in the end we will evolve to a higher stage of development? Or shall we explore alternatives that we find pleasing and then attempt to explore the problem of how to get there? Why should we wait until we run into an evolutionary dead end before beginning our new explorations?

There is, therefore, a need to create many images of possible world futures. Possible images are in principle unlimited, while in practice they are limited only by the ability of futurists to free themselves from the bonds of the past and present. We must begin to design alternative world systems not on the basis of extant or past social realities (whatever these are), but rather as we would like them. Once designed, we can (1) evaluate these world systems comparatively on the basis of their fulfillment of explicitly stated value criteria and (2) begin to solve the engineering problems of how to get from here to there.

FEASIBILITY AND THE DESIGNER'S RESPONSIBILITY

It often has been suggested that the study of alternative world futures should avoid utopianism and limit itself to the plans that appear to have maximum feasibility. There appear to be two major reasons for such a preoccupation with feasibility. First, by many estimates mankind has only between 30 and 50 years to solve the problems it has taken so long to create. Therefore, we must, if we are to be responsible futurists, think in "practical" terms and devote our thinking about alternatives to "realistic" solutions of current problems. Second, if we are to be relevant and responsible scientists we must also reflect these alleged virtues and not waste intellectual effort, time, and/or money on utopian schemes. As indicated above, this aspect of feasibility—conformity to the valued world of the scientist—is bought at the cost of limiting visions of the future.

As a necessary limit to the discussion of world futures, feasibility is just that—limiting. It may and often has prevented the exploration of more desirable world futures because they appear to be impossible given present knowledge. However, with the increase in technological advances at current exponential rates, who is to say what will be feasible or infeasible in even the near future? How many social scientists of 50 years ago would have thought it feasible that today we would have the capacity not only to send astronauts to the

moon but also to destroy every person, machine, and knowledge source
that cumulatively made it possible for them to get there? All this we
would be able to "accomplish" in less than the time of their roundtrip.
If man can "advance" so quickly in these two fields of research (transport and weaponry), is it not possible, given adequate resources and
commitment, to do likewise in the social and political spheres?
Following the advice of the French students of May 1968, we can be
realistic and demand the impossible.

The designer of an alternative world future or futures and the
critic of such futures have a responsibility to think beyond the feasible
to the desirable. It is only by doing so that we can hope to break out
of the structures that have brought about the inequitable distribution,
deprivation, the absence of justice, and the prevalence of violence as
the major mechanism of conflict management and social control. This
responsibility flows directly from the task the alternative world
futurist has taken upon himself: the design of a new social order that
is not merely a reflection of the immediate past.

DESIGN STRATEGIES

How, then, do we go about building models of alternative futures?
In The New Utopians, Robert Boguslaw suggests four approaches to
systems design that are employed by both the classical and the new
utopians: the formalist, the heuristic, the operating units, and the
ad hoc approaches. The formalist approach is characterized by the
use, implicit or explicit, of models. It has been employed by
classicists such as Fourier and by modern operations researchers.
These designs are, as the name suggests, highly formal and detailed.
This, Boguslaw asserts, is "the approach of preference when the
situations to be confronted are clearly established."[7] The formalist
design is thus one in which the designer constructs a model of the
system he wants to study and then begins testing its implications.
The design thus ties the designer to rules of logic that restrict his
ability to spin off variations. It thereby becomes a rigid methodology,
one that has severe problems in dealing with emergent situations that
may quite possibly be outside the realm of the model.

The heuristic approach to systems design uses principles as
guidelines for actions. The principles are employed to guide actions
even in totally unanticipated situations and thus in situations where
no formal model is available. As such, the principles are simply the
values that one proposes for the good society. Design consists in
searching for devices, associations, or actions that produce these
desired outputs.

The anarchist image of society is guided by this approach to futures. Proudhon and Kropotkin both employed this approach, setting forth general principles and value outcomes and insisting that the ideal society (an anarchist one) must act according to and produce these principles. The general solver of Newell, Shaw, and Simon is the most sophisticated example of the computer-programmed heuristic approach, using particular principles as guides to the search for a solution to any problem. [8] Since we will return to the anarchists shortly, a detailed discussion of the shortcomings of this approach will be held in abeyance. I should, however, at this time, point out one major objection usually addressed to this approach to systems design: that there is no clear picture of what the future would look like, only guidelines for its construction. Thus, critics consider this a "negative" approach because as a strategy it has been concerned with a detailed critique of existing situations and how they violate the principles of this image of systems design. Furthermore, it posits as a positive quality of its strategy no model of the future other than a continual application of the guiding principles. It thus offers nothing positively concrete for the critic to consider—there is no end state to evaluate.

The third method, the operating units approach, "begins neither with models of the system, nor with selected principles. It begins with people or machines carefully selected or tooled to possess certain performance characteristics."[9] B. F. Skinner's approach in Walden Two and Beyond Freedom and Dignity is of this nature and illustrates the concern with behavioral modification to create individuals with certain performance characteristics. The present stated concerns of the Institute for World Order with building institutions that will be tooled to improve man's capacity to deal with the problem of war and structural violence are illustrative of the operating units approach in the sense of machines that will possess the performance characteristics best suited to solving these problems. The institute seeks not to change current attitudes or individual lifestyles but rather to create institutions that would operate properly even in the absence of such changes. [10] This strategy does provide the ability to deal with emergent situations; however, the cost is the loss of freedom (both for the actors and the model) with each increase in the reliability of system performance.

The operating units approach would stagnate in its reliability. The reliable unit would be that of the repeatable, the nonchanging. Unless one feels that he in fact has all the answers and only needs to put them into operation, this strategy appears self-defeating as a tool in the search for alternative world futures and has very dangerous implications for those of us who might be selected as its operating units.

Boguslaw's fourth approach is the ad hoc. This is essentially a means of rising from the current state to some future state that may or may not be clear to the designer. This is not really an approach to design as much as it is an apology for pragmatists or realists and those who are tied to present images of reality. It does, however, provide a "model" for muddling through and intellectual closure for the author. But it should be stressed that, although ad hoc models of system design are capable of producing many alternative futures, they are by design incapable of producing alternatives that are not simply incremental changes tied to current conditions. As such, they are not very useful to the search for valued futures unless one is happy with the present state of affairs.

Which of these approaches to systems design is most useful to those interested in constructing alternative world futures? Given the limitations in our current knowledge, I would argue that the heuristics approach should be our choice. The formalist designer has difficulty in dealing with emergent situations and in creating many variations of his model. We hardly know what the present is; can we chance a design that is rigid for the future? The operating principles approach, on the other hand, can deal with emergent situations but since it has reliability as its goal it would stagnate when operating efficiently. The ad hoc approach has probably been responsible for getting us where we are today. In any case, in a design strategy the ad hoc approach begins with present conditions and trends but must be limited in its breadth and time frame, and thus limited in its usefulness for actually designing alternative world futures rather than falling into them.

It appears that we are left with the heuristics approach by default. But there also are positive reasons to prefer this approach. While we may not know what the future will look like in detail, we can at the least maximize the chances of its maximizing the values we prefer most. And if we are positing alternative world futures because we are dissatisfied with the principles of current systems and their value hierarchies and not merely their operation or formal design structure, is this not a desirable feature? We turn next to the question of value hierarchies in world order studies.

THE PROBLEM OF VALUE HIERARCHY

In an earlier draft, this essay was entitled "World Order Studies: The Negative Side of Peace Research." The debate concerning the negative aspects of peace research has been well developed in Europe and has recently made its appearance on this side of the Atlantic.

Herman Schmid and Lars Dencik argued that peace research, as it was originally focused, asked the question: How may we prevent violence and war?[11] It could therefore be seen as a technique of pacification. The proper question for peace researchers ought to be, as they and Galtung later argued: How do we create conditions of peace and for peace? The distinction here concerns the difference between preventing or managing physical violence on the one hand and preventing the problem of structural violence on the other.[12]

Yet until quite recently world order studies continued to concentrate on the negative approach to peace research:

> The central problem of world order is assumed to be the avoidance of thermonuclear warfare. All other issues of world order stem from the effort to grapple with this overriding problem of our times . . . . However, the danger of nuclear war impends the overall achievement of the prosperous and fully developed countries in such a singular fashion that it must inevitably dominate their political imagination.[13]

While one obviously would not wish to dismiss the importance of preventing nuclear war, it is important to note Richard Falk and Saul Mendlovitz's conclusion. The researcher's concern for preventing war dominates his imagination and he must then value order above creating the conditions of positive peace (equality, justice, welfare). This view of world order promotes research on institutions that produce stability, order, and reliability rather than on the creation of peaceful environments. It is also indicative that world order studies are most highly developed in the most developed nations. The less developed nations are more concerned with creating the conditions of positive peace than in preventing war between the superpowers.

Presently world order studies appear to be shifting their focus:

> World order is used here to designate that study of international relations and world affairs that focuses primarily on the questions: how can the likelihood of international violence be reduced significantly? And how can tolerable conditions of worldwide economic welfare, social justice and ecological stability be created?[14]

The strategy proposed in the latest Falk and Mendlovitz reader is contrary to the statement of the Institute for World Order in that Falk and Mendlovitz do not suggest that building institutions is the distinctive aspect of world order studies. Rather they propose only the evaluation of relevant utopias that will culminate in projections of preferred worlds consisting of an "image of a system of world political and social processes capable of dealing with the set of global problems at some tolerable level of human satisfaction." This is an important shift in principle as it rejects the position that it is necessary to impose some type of order and/or control structures to attain or maintain peace. Rather, it allows for the investigation of the position that nonmanipulative social systems that maximize individual differences and values are necessary to attain peace.

To illustrate the importance of the image, we will next introduce two rather complementary images (anarchism and functionalism), discuss their strengths and weaknesses, and finally evaluate functionalism through the perception of the anarchist image.

THE ANARCHIST IMAGE

Rousseau's oft-quoted statement, "Man is born free and is everywhere in chains," is indicative of the climate of ideas in which modern anarchist thought emerged.[15] Anarchism is a doctrine that developed out of the tensions provided by the conflicts between totalitarian and liberal democracy, and by capitalism and communism in the last 200 years. In its positive form, anarchism had four principal proponents during the nineteenth and early twentieth centuries: Godwin (1756-1836), Proudhon (1809-65), Bakunin (1814-76), and Kropotkin (1842-1921).

What is anarchism? What binds the thought of these men into one school of thought? George Woodcock asserts that "the common element uniting all its forms" is the "replacement of the authoritarian state by some form of non-governmental cooperation between free individuals."[16]

The links common to the philosophical anarchists are: (1) their criticism of existing society, (2) their view of a desirable future society, and (3) their means of passing to the future. The ultimate aim is always social change, and their method is always that of social rebellion, violent if necessary.

Here anarchist thought will be represented primarily by Kropotkin. There are a number of reasons for this. First, Kropotkin is the last of the major anarchist writers. He benefits from the works of the other three and from the further developments of the other trends of modern thought. Second, he is the most consistent of the anarchist writers, and the one who is most self-conscious in presenting a coherent doctrine of thought.[17] Third, there is an attempt to provide evidence for that which is assumed in both earlier and later anarchist thought.

The fundamental idea in Kropotkin's thought is that man is naturally a social animal. This is presented not as an ideal based on dialectical reasoning nor on the metaphysics of faith, but as a scientifically proven fundamental fact of nature. Kropotkin's view was a reaction to Herbert Spencer's doctrine of the survival of the fittest. He asserted that the element of struggle is indeed common to all species. However, it is not directed against members of that species but to the natural conditions, in the environment, that threaten the species. It is from this struggle that all species find that mutual protection and aid, rather than violence within species, is critical for survival:

> In the animal world we have seen that the vast majority of species live in societies, and that they find in association the best arms for the struggle for life, understood, of course, in its wide Darwinian sense—not as a struggle for the sheer means of existence, but as a struggle against all natural conditions unfavorable to the species . . . the unsociable species, on the contrary, are doomed to decay. [18]

A corollary to this fundamental idea was that native customs and morals are superior to and provide more liberty than the legislated legal systems. This is a reaction to both Spencer and the Hobbesian legacy of viewing primitive men as wild beasts who lived in small isolated families and fought one another for their food until a general authority was created and established social peace:

> In this manner, all our religious, historical, juridical, and social education is imbued with the idea that human beings, if left to themselves, would revert to savagery; that without authority men would eat one another; for nothing they say can be expected of the "multitude" but brutishness and the warring of each against all. [19]

Once again, Kropotkin draws upon the results of his scientific study of the development of societies and institutions and is, not surprisingly, brought to a different conclusion:

> It proves that usages and customs created by mankind for the sake of mutual aid, mutual defense, and peace in general were precisely elaborated by the "nameless multitude."[20]

This leads to a discussion of the nature of the state. He attempts to prove that the state was unnecessary for the accomplishment of the most vital functions needed for survival and defense and that, in fact, the very existence of the state is the cause of most societal evils:

> The State is, for us, a society of mutual insurance
> between the landlord, the judge, the priest, and later
> the capitalist, in order to support each other's
> authority over the people, and for exploiting the
> poverty of the masses and getting rich themselves.
>   Such was the origin of the State; such was its
> history, and such is its present essence.[21]

This description of the state also applies to the Marxian state which Kropotkin agreed with Marx is the highest form of state. For Kropotkin the Marxian state was, therefore, the most abhorrent. From his conception of state and authority is derived his view of the nature of law. Laws have a double origin; they are composed of two very different elements. In this manner all laws have one of two purposes. They are either intended to protect property and/or to protect the machinery of the government: "One of them strengthened (and fixed) certain habits and customs; while the other element of all laws was an addition to these customs."[22]

These premises form the basis for the condemnation of present society. What, then, would be the nature of the desirable future society, and how does man get there? The image of a desirable future society is not presented as a blueprint but rather as a set of operating principles designed to prevent the recurrence of current social structures:

> The Anarchist conceives a society in which all the mutual
> relations of its members are regulated, not by laws,
> not by authorities, whether self-imposed or elected, but
> by mutual agreements between the members of that
> society, and by a sum of social customs and habits—
> not petrified by law, routine, or superstition, but con-
> tinually developing and continually readjusted, in
> accordance with the ever-growing requirements of a
> free life, stimulated by the progress of science, inven-
> tion, and the steady growth of "higher ideals."[23]

The social revolution that would bring this about was conceived in terms of destruction of legal authority and the transition to autonomous

free federations of communes coordinating themselves without the
state and without capitalism. This social revolution did not necessarily
have to happen, however, through violence and terror.[24]

Although he himself never advocated violence, Kropotkin accepted
its use by men responding to conditions that the state had made unbearable. But while he did not advocate violence, he also dismissed the
idea of obtaining the social revolution through the use of a revolutionary
governmental authority or a vanguard party. As he saw it, revolution
and government, or institutionalized authority, were incompatible.
The revolution could only be accomplished through the initiative of the
people themselves. The revolution

> must take the form of a widely spread popular movement,
> during which movement, in every town and village invaded
> by the insurrectionary spirit, the masses set themselves
> to the work of reconstructing society on new lines. The
> people—both the peasants and the town-workers—must
> themselves begin with the constructive work, on more or
> less communist principles, without waiting for schemes
> and orders from above. From the very beginning of the
> movement they must continue to house and to feed every-
> one, and then set to work to produce what is necessary
> to feed, house, and clothe all of them.[25]

Compare this to the statement of Warren Wagar:

> The formation of revolutionary elites is therefore
> imperative. We cannot wait for the several popular
> masses to become so disenchanted with the status quo
> that the old orders collapse without a struggle. We
> must create a climate of expectation in which revolu-
> tionary heroes and messiahs will feel welcome, and
> in which elites can organize and seize initiatives
> without delay.[26]

These, then, are the major premises of Kropotkin's thought:
(1) man is by nature a social animal, (2) social relations worked out
by men among themselves are superior to the laws, authority, and
state imposed upon them, and (3) the social revolution must develop
in communal groups without the aid of a vanguard party or revolutionary
authority.[27]

If we accept the operating principles upon which Kropotkin's
image of a future society would be based, how are we to attain his
society? One way would be to sit and wait until we evolved into the
social state in which the people were able to rise up and create the

society in a swift and violent revolutionary overthrow of existing institutions. Another approach would be to attempt to subvert the existing system slowly and, as if through the back door, to get rid of the state by making it superfluous to the tasks that define its very reason for being. Essentially this is the thrust of the functionalist approach. Employing the principles of anarchism to assess the ability of this approach to attain the anarchist image will be the task of the remainder of this essay.

THE FUNCTIONALIST IMAGE

There are a number of sound reasons for choosing to analyze the functional approach to international organization in terms of anarchist thought.[28] First, the following fundamental premise concerning the nature of man is shared by functionalist and anarchist thought:

> Man by nature is good, rational and devoted to the
> common weal; when society is organized as to bring
> out man's tendency to mobilize his energies for the
> general welfare, the forces of peace and harmony
> rule.[29]

Second, the development of the state is seen as the principal object to the possibilities of human fulfillment:

> Pre-industrial and pre-national primary occupational
> groups were the true focuses for human happiness. . . .
> The rise of the territorially bounded, omnicompetent,
> national state has changed all that. . . . The unnatural
> state took the place of natural society.[30]

Third, while David Mitrany is not an anarchist, it is interesting to note that government and law come last in the sequence of functions to be performed.[31]

Fourth, the functionalist approach to international organization would proceed by means of the functionalist selection and organization of international relations. If one accepts Mitrany's notion of community as the sum of the functions performed by its members, then the next step, that of "binding together those interests which are common, where they are common, and to the extent . . . they are common,"[32] may be seen as the equivalent to Kropotkin's discussion of the growth of voluntary associations in the nineteenth century and the grouping together of communes for their mutual benefit. [33]

Fifth, it is at this point that many critics of functionalism and anarchism converge. James Sewell states, "the functionalist argument appears to rely on an inadequate appreciation of obligation—a crucial element in the practice and study of politics."[34] To this argument Kropotkin demands a study of the evidence. He contends that it is not obligation but need that is the issue, that man recognizes the advantages of mutual aid. Similarly, Mitrany would argue that the organization would develop because of the need of fulfilling this task. The functions that are deemed by a community as necessary, if they are not being fulfilled, will give impetus to the formation of the links between groups to solve problems. These competing contentions are amenable to empirical tests in any case.

FUNCTIONALISM AND ANARCHISM

Here it becomes important to differentiate between anarchist thought as exemplified by Kropotkin and functionalist thought. The first obvious difference is that the functionalists are willing to work around government to achieve their ends. They take the following as their strategy: "The most effective attack on sovereignty is not a frontal one—it is one which slowly but clearly deprives sovereignty of its substance and consequently of its prestige."[35] It is believed, then, that by solving, through the use of voluntary organizations, the economic and social problems that the state has not been able to meet, the myth of the state will be exposed. A corollary to this approach is advocated by Johan Galtung. Briefly, he identifies three types of loyalty: subnational, transnational, and supranational. The notion here is that, if organizational structures existed at all levels to which the individual directs his loyalty, this would create maximum disorder or messiness in the total system (entropy) and problem solving would be at its maximum. [36]

If one follows Kropotkin, the major objection to be raised here is that the functionalist strategy may, in fact, be the most efficient means of strengthening government. That is, if governments are themselves responsible for the problems one is trying to solve, why aid government to grow stronger by appearing to solve problems through governmental cooperation? Intergovernmental organizations (IGOs) would then be seen as a threat—as a still higher form of the state. Increasing the scope merely increases the possibilities of tyranny. (Is a united Europe a positive or a negative force?) The international nongovernmental organization (INGO) is really more akin to what is advocated by Kropotkin: the free association of individuals and groups for their mutual benefit. One must recognize that in following this path there are dangers of increasing the power of the state, not reducing it. Mitrany also fears the creation of a federal rather than a functionally integrated region. The danger as he sees it is that the regional scheme would become the nation-state writ large. [37]

Galtung suggests that a combination of different types of organization would be the most likely to result in the resolution of conflict:

> Rather the idea would be to go in for the co-existence of all types—to have maximum disorder, maximum messiness in the total system. According to this kind of thinking there would be very many ways of arriving at decisions and information, and in general, the more the better. All channels would be open and represent possibilities of communication and conflict resolution. [38]

If one is consistent with the proposed ends of anarchism, however, this is more a suggestion for an inappropriate transitional stage.

A second major criticism of functionalist thought concerns the nature of the state in this future world. Even if one does not increase the power of the state by aiding its problem-solving capacity, what will the role of the state be? Can we expect, for instance, that because functionalist organizations are solving problems, that the state will "wither away" when they take over all of the "important functions"?

A third criticism arises from the very nature of the functional organization. As envisioned by Mitrany, "one might hope that gradually the functional agencies would acquire a precisely technical form of management based no more even on contributions, but on the capacity of the managers for their jobs—it would be, one might say, equality in non-representation. "[39]

Thus Mitrany falls into the same trap that Kropotkin did 50 years earlier: the belief in the objectivity of science, the rationality of technology. It is at this level that it becomes appropriate to ask once again about obligation. Will the new society be able to control its managers, or will the managers become the new state? Neither Kropotkin nor Mitrany satisfactorily addresses himself to preventing this occurrence. There is justification for using the power of expertise to "advance" the community, but how does the community protect itself from advancement?

This concern over control of the expertise is probably more of a threat in the functionalist than in the anarchist society. While in the commune the community would, through its normal structure, provide the necessities of life and even many luxuries, [40] the function-alist society would be superimposed upon existing social relations. It would be necessary to coordinate across existing social structures and hence on a much larger scale simply to provide basic necessities. Therefore, the coordinators would have a greater capability to control the population.

Looking through the anarchist image, functionalism in its earli-est form suffered from a number of possible dangers. The neofunc-tionalists later argued that, in fact, there was little danger because a functionalist strategy would not produce European political integration by stressing technical cooperation. [41] Mitrany felt that cooperation in technical areas would spill over into cooperation in other areas. Haas and the neofunctionalists stressed that spillover contributing to political integration would occur more readily in the economic and political sector than in technical areas where encapsulation was the more likely result. They stressed first choosing sectors that were politically important and second creating institutions that would spill over and lead to further integration. In an important sense, then, the neofunctionalists began to advocate federal ends, and it was for this reason that Mitrany was unhappy with their strategy. Political inte-gration had not resulted from Mitrany's strategy; it was thus suscep-tible to criticism on empirical grounds. The data did not fit with the theory. The neofunctionalists turned their attention to producing a theory that would explain the development of the European community and directed their efforts to producing the proper institutional struc-tures of integration. The strategy of the neofunctionalist became more important than the image of the future Mitrany had advocated. Peace and welfare, and not a united Europe, was the issue for Mitrany. A rejection of functionalism as an adequate theory of the process of European integration should not have entailed the neofunctionalist rejection of the end state it posited. Strategies should not displace images if we are satisfied with the images we have posited.

CONCLUSIONS: IMAGES AND WORLD FUTURES

What can we learn from this exercise in image construction and in the evaluation of transition strategies and end states? First and foremost is the importance of recognizing the impact that alternative world images have on world futures scholarship. The image not only focuses our research but acts as a base upon which we evaluate other approaches. It is only by a continuing reexamination of our images that we can prevent the creation of futures that are not what we intended.

Second, the heuristic strategy of principles as guidelines for construction of alternative world futures provides a number of advantages. It encourages the greatest possible scope in our construction efforts while at the same time providing a clear and consistent basis for evaluating these efforts. Therefore, we are likely to continually confront the advantages and limitations of our models and thereby produce better designs.

Finally, this effort suggests that transnational stages also must be subjected to a continuing analysis. If it appears that the desired image of the future can only be implemented by violating the values that one points for the future, the preceding analysis suggests that both the transitional strategy and the image itself be reevaluated. We may thereby prevent our transitional strategies and momentary concerns from determining the world futures we have struggled to create.

NOTES

1. Kenneth Boulding, The Image (New York: Harper and Row, 1956), p. 25.

2. Ibid., p. 115.

3. Herbert Marcuse, Reason and Revolution (Boston: Beacon Press, 1965), p. 11.

4. Boulding, The Image, p. 71.

5. Hans Reichenbach, The Rise of Scientific Philosophy (Berkeley: University of California Press, 1951).

6. Donald Campbell, "Variation and Selective Retention in Socio-cultural Evolution," in Social Change in Developing Areas, eds. Herbert Barringer, George Blanksten, and Raymond Mack (Cambridge, Mass.: Schenkman, 1965).

7. Robert Boguslaw, The New Utopians (Englewood Cliffs, N.J.: Prentice-Hall, 1965), p. 70.

8. Ibid., p. 72.

9. Ibid., p. 17.

10. Statement of the Institute for World Order, 1973.

11. See Lars Dencik, "Peace Research: Pacification or Revolution," and Herman Schmid, "Peace Research as a Technology for Pacification," both in Proceedings of the International Peace Research Association Third Conference 1970, I; Johan Galtung, "Violence, Peace and Peace Research," Journal of Peace Research 3 (1969); "Peace Research in Transition: A Symposium," Journal of Conflict Resolution 16, no. 4 (December 1972).

12. See Galtung, "Violence, Peace and Peace Research."

13. Richard Falk and Saul Mendlovitz, The Strategy of World Order (New York: World Law Fund, 1966), vol. 1, p. 1.

14. Richard Falk and Saul Mendlovitz, Regional Politics and World Order (San Francisco: W. H. Freeman, 1973), p. 6.

15. J. L. Talmon, The Origins of Totalitarian Democracy (New York: Norton, 1970), p. 1, suggests that the two main currents that emerged from this eighteenth century climate were liberal democracy and totalitarian democracy. However, Talmon of course recognizes that there were other intellectual currents, such as anarchism.

16. George Woodcock, Anarchism (Cleveland: Meridian Books, 1962), p. 10: "Anarchos, the original Greek word, means merely 'without a ruler' and thus anarchy itself can clearly be used in a general context to mean either the negative condition of unruliness or the positive condition of being unruled because rule is unnecessary for the preservation of order." For a general introduction to anarchist thought in its various forms, see: Woodcock, Anarchism; James Joll, The Anarchists (London: Grosset Universal Library, 1966); Irving L. Horowitz, ed., The Anarchists (New York: Dell, 1964).

17. The only major contradiction in his thought occurs in 1914 re his stand on World War I. Prior to 1914 he is, like most socialists and anarchists, opposed to war. However, his great hate of German authoritarianism and militarism led him to support the allies openly. For a more complete discussion of this point, see Martin Miller, ed., Selected Writings on Anarchism and Revolution (Cambridge, Mass.: M. I. T. Press, 1970), Introduction; George Woodcock and Ivan Avakumovic, The Anarchist Prince (London: T. V. Boardman, 1950), pp. 342-87.

18. Peter Kropotkin, Mutual Aid: A Factor of Evolution (London: William Heinemann, 1908), p. 293.

19. Peter Kropotkin, Modern Science and Anarchism (London: Freedom Press, 1928), pp. 33-34.

20. Ibid., pp. 34-35.

21. Ibid., p. 81.

22. Ibid., p. 37.

23. Ibid., p. 45.

24. "Very sad would be the future of the revolution if it could only triumph by terror." Peter Kropotkin, "Revolutionary Studies," Commonweal (London) 7, no. 296 (January 9, 1892), cited in Miller, Selected Writings on Anarchism and Revolution, p. 23.

25. Ibid., p. 23.

26. W. Warren Wagar, Building the City of Man (New York: World Law Fund, 1971), p. 56.

27. I have not discussed the particulars of the desirable anarchist society; that is, the nature of production, distribution, etc. The

main principle is, of course, communist (from each according to his abilities, to each according to his needs); this is "scientifically" approached in Kropotkin, The Conquest of Bread (New York: G. P. Putnam, 1907), and Fields, Factories and Workshops (London: Thomas Nelson and Sons, 1912).

28. For a discussion of the differences between the functional analysis of international organizational scholars and sociologists, see Ernst Haas, Beyond the Nation State (Palo Alto, Calif.: Stanford University Press, 1964), pp. 1-6. "What matters is the notion of function: it is according to the explicit intent of the Functionalist writers, equivalent in meaning to 'organizational task,'" p. 6.

29. Ibid., p. 8.

30. Ibid., p. 9.

31. James P. Sewell, Functionalism and World Politics (Princeton, N.J.: Princeton University Press, 1966), p. 18.

32. David Mitrany as quoted in ibid., p. 17.

33. Peter Kropotkin, Mutual Aid, pp. 274-92; The Conquest of Bread, pp. 156-75.

34. Sewell, Functionalism and World Politics, p. 45.

35. Stanley Hoffman, "The Role of International Organization: Limits and Possibilities," International Organization 10 (August 1956): 365-66.

36. Johan Galtung, "Entropy and the General Theory of Peace," paper presented at the Second International Peace Research Association Conference, Sweden, Summer 1967.

37. David Mitrany, "The Prospect of Integration: Federal or Functional," Journal of Common Market Studies 4 (December 1965): 119-49.

38. Galtung, "Entropy."

39. Mitrany as quoted in Sewell, Functionalism and World Politics, p. 17.

40. Kropotkin, The Conquest of Bread, Chapter IX, "The Need for Luxury."

41. See particularly, Ernst Haas, Beyond the Nation State, and "The Study of Regional Integration: Reflections on the Joy and Anguish of Pre-theorizing," in Regional Integration: Theory and Research, eds. Leon Lindberg and Stuart Scheingold (Cambridge, Mass.: Harvard University Press, 1971), pp. 3-44.

12

**BEHAVIORAL PATHS TO
A NEW WORLD ORDER**

Louis René Beres

> The essence of the question of what kind
> of society we may form—once we are
> freed from our past repressions and the
> hangover of our liberation feast—is what
> kind of material do we have to work with?
> As what we reshape is first of all our-
> selves, both as individuals and as a social
> combine, the question really is: What are
> humans like, what are they capable of, and
> what are their limitations?
> —Amitai Etzioni[1]

Man exists on an endangered planet. Everywhere he looks, there
is ample evidence to kindle his apocalyptic imagination and heighten
his despair. In response to such evidence, a growing number of international relations scholars have begun to develop a new orientation to
their investigations. To this orientation they have assigned the name,
world order studies. In the most general sense, the study of world
order is the study of alternative world futures. [2]

Unfortunately, the manifestly urgent character of our planetary
crisis has not produced a much needed change in the prevailing institutional strategies for world order reform. Now, as before, students
of world affairs seek solutions to global problems in new structures

---

This essay is based upon the author's earlier work, "Behavioral
Strategies of World Order Reform," International Journal of Group
Tensions 4, no. 2 (June 1974): 208–21.

for international regulation, leaving the essential human underpinnings of these structures unimpaired. Notwithstanding its multidimensional scope of concern (such as nuclear war, population pressure, food and energy shortages, ecological ruin, economic collapse) and its self-consciously future-oriented pattern of scholarship, world order studies perpetuate the long-standing reformist emphasis on changing social and political agencies. This emphasis is almost always limited to remedying the decentralized distribution of military force and sovereign authority in the world system. It amounts, therefore, to a continuing recommendation for the replacement of balance of power world politics with the centralized dynamics of collective security or world government.

In view of the serious consequences that are apt to ensue from misconceived or inadequate strategies of world order reform, scholars must begin to recognize that there are other, essentially noninstitutional, paths to be considered. These fall under the heading of behavioral strategies. By freeing their minds from the shackles of a strikingly unimaginative line of predecessors, world order scholars may turn their attention to man's individual nature and to the characteristic inclinations and activities of states. With this in mind, the following discussion represents a general introduction to the neglected idea of behavioral transformation in world order studies.

THE TWO BASIC BEHAVIORAL STRATEGIES

For world order scholars interested in augmenting institutional strategies with behavioral ones, two essential possibilities present themselves:

1. Transform man. Aware of Pascal's accuracy in demonstrating that the gap between man's aspirations and accomplishments inevitably produces "unjust" and "criminal" passions, the prospective global reformer can direct his energies to the task of individual human transformation. Homo homini lupus. Man is a wolf to man. To alter this condition represents the most primary behavioral path to global betterment.

2. Transform states. Recognizing the systemic underpinnings of every state's own interests, scholars of world order can explore ways of changing the characteristically competitive behavior of state actors. Whatever their particular requirements and nuances, these ways must be directed to a renunciation of the principle of "everyone for himself." This path to a new world order lends itself to an important subdivision: realignment of national interest.

Tied together in the consequences of a deteriorating world system, national leaders must learn to identify their preferences for their own particular states with the well-being of the entire global community. National self-interest and global community interest must become one. Here, national decision makers continue to act in accordance with judgments of national self-interest, but they are aware that what is best for the entire system is necessarily best for their own sovereignties. They recognize that there can be no policy of national gain that is at cross-purposes with the spirit of systemic well-being. To apply the vision of Pierre Teilhard de Chardin, this means that no state can prosper and grow except with and by all the others with itself.

Disappearance of national interest is next. In response to the bankruptcy of a private and competitive style of international interaction (a style that inevitably generates the very opposite of its intended result), national leaders must learn to act in the interests of systemic well-being for its own sake. Here, the self-interested character of state behavior is eliminated altogether. Rather than create a condition where state leaders believe that what is best for the system as a whole is also best for their own states, this path to world order reform renders the very idea of self-interest meaningless. Borrowing from Rousseau, it does so by a perfect and complete fusion of private and collective interests. Such fusion, it is hoped, would cause the very antithesis of Iago's "motiveless malignity" to prevail in international relations. Alexander Pope hints interestingly at this idea in An Essay on Man:

> Thus God and Nature link'd the gen'ral frame,
> And bad Self-love and Social be the same.

Transforming Man

In the philosophy of human affairs, far greater weight is cast on the side of man's base and unruly character than upon his intrinsic worthiness. Seldom do we encounter the sentiment expressed by the Swiss thinker Johann Kaspar Lavatar in his essay On the Nature of Man: "Of all earthly creatures man is the most perfect, the most imbued with the principles of life." More commonly, we discover the kind of sentiment expressed by Moliere in The Misanthrope:

> All are corrupt; there's nothing to be seen
> In court or town but aggravates my spleen.
> I fall into deep gloom and melancholy

> When I survey the scene of human folly,
> Finding on every hand base flattery,
> Injustice, fraud, self-interest, treachery . . .
> Ah, it's too much; mankind has grown so base,
> I mean to break with the whole human race.

Or even Eugene Ionesco's recorded memories of Paris:

> my mother could not tear me away from the Punch and
> Judy show at the Luxembourg Gardens. I stayed there,
> I could stay there, enrapt, for whole days. The spectacle
> of the Punch and Judy show held me there, as if stupefied,
> through the sight of these puppets that talked, moved,
> clubbed each other. It was the spectacle of the world
> itself, which . . . presented itself to me in an infinitely
> simplified and caricatured form, as if to underline its
> grotesque and brutal truth. 3

The animal called man is contemptible. He is loathsome. With
such an idea at hand, students of world order reform might direct
their attention to the prospects for transforming man. Without necessarily accepting Herbert Spencer's view that "It is certain that man
must become perfect," they might begin to consider the characteristic
ways in which human beings structure their interactions as well as
(or even in lieu of) the institutions and agencies of international relations. Such a changed orientation would signal a new regard for some
essential bases of global improvement.

But exactly what kinds of transformation might be considered?
In the most general terms, the ascendant leitmotif of these efforts
must be maximal individual development balanced by the demands of
interpersonal harmony. Or, in the words of Teilhard de Chardin in
The Future of Man, we must ensure that human populations "shall be
composed only of elements harmonious in themselves and blended as
harmoniously as possible together."

While a continuing antagonism seems to exist between the search
for personal progression and the requirements of social accord, it
need not be an irremediable sort of antagonism. Scholars might explore
productively the desirability and feasibility of certain compromise
tradeoffs between these competing claims and begin to set forth the
basic behavioral underpinnings of a new world order.

Indeed, the philosopher Heraclitus tells us that opposition is
the surest path to concert and that from things that differ and compete
comes the most beautiful and complete harmony. The unceasing dis-
cordance between individual and social fulfillment provides an exciting
area of exploration for scholars committed to heightening the chances

for survival on this endangered planet. Man must perpetually cultivate his sense of boundless aspiration and indomitable energy, but how can this be accomplished in the absence of unrestrained egoism? Man must conform to Goethe's dictum and strive to become something unique and incomparable, but how can he accomplish this without producing markedly antisocial effects?

To answer this question, the student of the human transformation route to world order reform must examine the means by which private wishes, once encouraged, can be tempered by public claims. He must seek to understand ways in which the competitive character of these claims can be transmuted into a relationship of protracted partnership based upon reciprocal awareness and complementary commitment. With such an understanding, he may extend himself beyond extant conceptions of a preferred world into a wondrously new vision of creative planetary improvement.

Like Faust before the sign of the Macrocosm, we know that it is not our fate to understand the universe. But we also know that it is not entirely unreasonable to try to cope with the human condition. The shortcomings of man are imprinted indelibly upon the works of our greatest thinkers. From Dante's Divine Comedy we have a remarkably comprehensive and coherent ordering of vices and virtues. From Swift's firm grip on the human creature in Gulliver's Travels we capture the essence of the odious Yahoos. And from Voltaire's Candide we discover an astounding truth: that of all the fantastic and horrible episodes in this tale—continuing rape, shipwreck, and slaughter—only the brief interlude in the harmonious society of Eldorado is fictitious. The venal behavior and constant brutalization that transpire in "the best of all possible worlds" are historically accurate and painfully real. Only a land in which congenial social interaction has been boosted to preeminence is fable.

What greater satisfaction can there be than to begin to unravel the hideous human roots of such accounts? What more productive approach to world order reform can the behaviorally oriented scholar claim for his efforts? In defiance of prevailing strategies for institutional reform, this scholar can be aware that the essence of worthy planetary life lies promisingly at its human beginnings. To grope constantly for this essence is one notable manner in which a new world system may be fashioned and sustained.

Transforming States

Realignment of National Interest

Recognizing that national survival now requires a firm renunciation of definitions of self-interest expressed in competitive terms, behavioral change might involve the creation of cooperative definitions. This means the development of conditions whereby national leaders abandon their characteristically egoistic course of national policy and begin to tie their own judgments of national self-interest to what they believe is best for the system as a whole. Here, national decision makers would recognize that the interests of their respective states and those of the entire system of states are necessarily congruent. Such recognition would stem from the understanding that states stand vis-a-vis one another in the manner of the best-known pairs of Beckett characters: Pozzo/Lucky, Vladimir/Estragon, Hamm/Clov: a condition of protracted enmity, albeit one tempered by the exigencies of mutual interdependence.

By supplanting competitive self-seeking with cooperative self-seeking (the basic self-interest dynamics of national behavior would remain unimpaired), this kind of behavioral transformation would permit national decision makers to escape from what Rousseau has described as "a kind of centrifugal force, by which they [national leaders] continually act one against another, and tend to aggrandize themselves at the expense of their neighbors, like the vortices of Descartes." No longer would national leaders continue to operate on the erroneous assumption that safety derives from a perpetual strengthening of their states' relative power positions. No longer would these leaders seek to ensure their states' security within an intrinsically unworkable pattern of terror and distrust.

But what must be done to bring about such a condition? Without retreating from their basically self-interested mode of behavior, how can state leaders reroute this mode to a global orientation? How can they begin to build upon the understanding that it is in their own states' best interests to develop strategies of interaction from a systemic vantage point?

The answer lies in a self-conscious attempt to create an alternative configuration of world politics with which every state's leaders can identify the support of their own major national preferences. As anyone can well imagine, this is no mean feat. Indeed, there is considerable temptation to say (with Schopenhauer, Tolstoi, and de Maistre) that such attempts at global design are only presumptuous nonsense. Can even the most gifted of men introduce an intentionally selected orderly movement into a world governed by a multitude of profoundly discrepant factors?

Clearly, in view of the heterogeneity of value systems involved, this kind of configuration cannot reasonably measure up to each state's optimal design. But it can still be acceptable to all of them. Scholars and statesmen can begin an expansive exploration of alternative configurations in an attempt to discover a suitable mix. Such exploration would be necessary since this kind of behavioral transformation must rest upon a broad variety of compromises between states.

To guide scholars and world leaders in this endeavor, a variety of basic design dimensions must first be articulated. As a start, these dimensions might correspond to: (1) the kinds of actors in world politics; (2) the structure of world politics (the prevailing polar pattern of global power); (3) the processes of world politics (the prevailing patterns of global war avoidance); and (4) the context of world politics (the prevailing weapons technology). By characterizing world system models along these four dimensions, the infrastructure of another sort of behaviorally transformed world might be blueprinted. Such a system would represent the outcome of large-scale tradeoffs between competing national preferences and would permit the kind of reoriented national decision making under investigation.

What this means, of course, is that institutional transformation must necessarily precede this particular kind of behavioral transformation. Until a new configuration is brought about with which every state's leaders can identify the preservation and advancement of their own major national preferences, no one can reasonably expect state actors to redefine their judgments of self-interest along systemic lines. It follows that this transformation of the characteristic behavior of state ac .ors is not a distinct alternative to institutional change but rather one step further along a continuous path to world order reform. (It should be pointed out, however, that this conception of institutional change is still far broader than the prevailing one. In effect, what has been described as the institutional strategy in this essay is almost always limited to recommending changes in the "process" dimension.)

And since institutional transformation might itself depend upon prior successes in transforming man, the transformation of states also may require individual human kinds of changes. Where this is the case, the alteration of national behavior under discussion represents a convergence of seemingly discrete strategies of planetary renewal. It reflects the culminating effect of transmutations at both higher levels of organization and lower levels of comprehensiveness.

Disappearance of National Interest

The sort of national behavioral transformation that has just been discussed requires judgments of self-interest to be realigned rather than eliminated. Transformed states would act in conformity with the best interests of the entire system, but only because these interests would be judged congenial to their own private interests. Self-interest would be defined in terms of systemic well-being.

Ambitious and fanciful as this particular behavioral route to world order reform might appear, there is a still more ambitious and fanciful behavioral path. This path would also impel states to act in behalf of systemic interests, but in this case they would value these interests for their own sake. Their actions would not derive from a presumed congruence between community and national interests. In fact, the very idea of national self-interest would be rendered inappropriate. As with the "rational beings" of Marcus Aurelius' Meditations, acting in the interests of the entire system would "delight for its own sake."

States in such a world system would resemble global analogues of what Charles Reich (The Greening of America) has called the "New Generation." By passing through a series of sublimations of national consciousness, states might overcome their characteristically egoistic behavior and achieve a condition wherein all are perpetually in pursuit of genuine relationships of mutual concern. This condition would follow upon a succession of self-transmutations directed toward a new vision of human community bereft of the old goals of power and deference and shorn of its competitive underpinnings.

Of course, this particular kind of behavioral change must appear monumentally impracticable. Could any other recommendation of philosopher or scientist more richly deserve Oswald Spengler's remark that "Men of theory commit a huge mistake in believing that their place is at the head of and not in the train of great events"? Can students of world affairs seriously entertain the prospect of international relations without individual states clamoring and scrambling for themselves? Do the present and historic forces of fragmentation and disunity portend anything else but a renewal of competitive world politics? And don't these forces remain inevitably ahead of the tides of consonance and unity?

Even if we must note that the prospects for this kind of transformation seem remarkably dim, Goethe's dictum should not be forgotten entirely: A perfect creation must transcend itself and go on to become something unique. Applied to states, this means an advance of national consciousness toward a condition whereby each state achieves its noblest expression in its collective existence. A wondrous key to more worthwhile international life, such an advance would represent—in Chardin's remarkable system of thought—the "ultrahominization" of world politics.

The beginning of such a transformation would come when significantly large numbers of individual men in positions of national leadership learn to push their extant mental powers toward more distant human boundaries. There exist much higher reaches of mind than we are currently prepared to accept and understand. These reaches must be continually cultivated. Only with the progressive perfection of these mental energies, with what Chardin calls "noogenesis," can such a far-reaching change of national behavior take place.

Such a change also is likely to require states to extend the radius of their affinity with other states to global proportions.

Undoubtedly, the satisfaction of this requirement would be contrary to the ongoing tide of conflict and revulsion and to the enduring inability to extend national "affection" to more than a few. The reasonable proponent of this kind of behavioral transformation therefore would be hard-pressed to argue convincingly that the universe of states may soon personify itself, creating an atmosphere wherein an elemental attraction of international harmony and selflessness will appear.

In any event, this particular kind of behavioral transformation is certainly not apt to spring full-blown from the present system of international relations. Rather, it would very likely require prior behavioral transformations of the two sorts already discussed. This means that, directly or indirectly, the behavioral route to world order reform always comes back to individual human beings and to the need for their cumulative improvement.

This idea was already hinted at by Francis Bacon's theory of man as microcosmos, a theory that saw man as a model of the entire world "as if there were to be found in man's body certain correspondences and parallels which should have respect to all varieties of things . . . which are extant in the great world." Where this theory is deemed fruitful, it is up to the world order scholar to focus once again on the directions and prospects of individual human transformation. Since the elements that combine to form the world system as a whole derive from the composition of individual men, an alteration of the latter inevitably affects the configuration and character of the former. Indeed, man is a "little world," a conception that signals almost unimaginably potent consequences for survival on this endangered planet. As Alexander Pope once put it:

God loves from Whole to Parts: but human soul
Must rise from Individual to the Whole.

Hence, if this form of behavioral transformation is to lead to an empyrean of the elect for the world's peoples here on earth, it must take as its starting point the reformation of man as a poor creature of mundane limits. In conformity with the preeminent theme of medieval civilization, this reformation must emphasize complete harmony between individual and society. And in keeping with the inestimable debt that we owe to the spirit of Romanticism, this reformation must take full advantage of the enormous possibilities resident in human nature, generating a growing awareness of the outer world of other men.

In a system of world politics founded upon the erroneous principles of a pax atomica, a system-directed pattern of national behavior appears remarkably distant. The ideal of sovereign states acting in behalf of their narrowly competititve judgments of self-interest remains as firmly entrenched today as it was back in the difficult times of the break-up of medieval Christendom. Indeed, the nineteenth and twentieth centuries have consecrated ever-increasing measures of commitment to certain principles of Machiavelli and Grotius.

At the same time, the cosmopolitan spirit of the eighteenth century has not disappeared altogether. Evidence of this spirit, nurtured by the visions of Marcus Aurelius, Dante, Cruce, Samuel Johnson, Lessing, Goethe, Veblen, and Chardin, can be found in various current forms of internationalism. Whether or not these forms can ever take hold of the prevailing drift of world politics and steer it in the holistic direction of systemic concern is apt to depend significantly upon the perceived urgency of the developing planetary crisis. Where this perception approaches the outermost limits of tolerance, and where the futility of competitive strategies becomes perfectly obvious, states may pass quickly through the prior sort of national transformation and ultimately become susceptible to the kind of behavioral change now under discussion. Ironically, the prospects for such successive transformation would require a near-fatal poximity to the brink of global despair.

Admittedly, in principle at least, the evolution of a state system comprised of "selfless" actors need not necessarily presume the imminence of worldwide calamity. In his own way, Goethe lifted himself above all prejudices of national identification without an apocalyptic leap, remarking that others might also strive for this stage where "one stands in a certain measure above all nations, and feels the happiness or the woe of a neighboring people as though it were his own."

Goethe, however, standing unmoved on the battlefield at Jena, offers an unlikely prototype for a new national consciousness. Presently, any realistic hope for transforming states in a manner that would render them "citizens of the world" would have to be based upon widespread perceptions of irretrievable disaster. Only then could we even begin to foresee the distant abandonment of the idee fixe that ties state behavior to the most narrowly conceived judgments of self-interest. With such perceptions, individual states might begin to reassess their constitutions from a systemic vantage point and ultimately learn to consecrate their efforts for the well-being of all states taken as a whole.

This judgment rests on the seemingly contradictory argument that the appearance of a most desirable system of world order would require an increasing proximity to a most undesirable one. Doesn't this demonstrate a strikingly illogical (not to mention dangerous) sort of reasoning? After all, can it be argued plausibly that to improve the world we must first bring it even closer to the very configurations of global calamity we seek to avert?

To answer these questions, one must remember that however odious they might be, various imperfections may actually contribute to long-run improvement. By itself, Tarquin's rape of Lucretia seems abhorrent. But how different it appears in the long view of history, for without this act there would have been no Roman Republic, no Roman civilization, no proper framework for an enduring Christianity, and so on. Thus, in the eyes of a significant portion of humanity, a crime had its place in the prior improvement of this world just as the growing threat of global disaster now has its place in the creation of a better one.

This is not to express concern for the truthfulness of this particular tale or to suggest that the growing threat of global disaster is in the nature of a crime. And it is not to suggest that this threat ought to be self-consciously aggravated to a point where its portentous direction becomes irreversible (a point where the prospective costs of this threat would clearly exceed its prospective gains). Rather, it is to suggest in parabolic mode that the prospects for national behavioral transformation require a steady worsening or deterioration of world politics to a point just short of uncontrolled breakdown, and that this suggestion is altogether reasonable.

Whether this means that these prospects are unworthy of their stated objective on account of the high risk involved depends upon a comparison with the degree of risk already built into the existing system. Where this degree of risk is believed to be similarly high, the incentive to transform states is entirely rational. While it is certainly true that the bridge leading from self-interest to benevolence must pass over some very troubled waters, there is certainly no greater safety in refusing to cross that bridge.

CONCLUSION

This essay has hinted at a number of behavioral paths to a new world order. Although these paths have been presented separately, their interrelatedness is marked and warrants emphasis. Indeed, it may even be useful to think of the two essential possibilities for behavioral transformation as successive phases of a single process of change, a process that represents a substantial and promising departure from the prevailing view of world order scholars that is articulated in a 1973 statement by the Institute for World Order in New York City:

This emphasis on institution building distinguishes world order from those approaches which stress the

importance of changes in attitudes and lifestyles and
focus on individual human beings as the creators of
worldwide social change.

Moreover, if we are interested in transforming behaviors within
the pluri-versum that now exists in world politics, it may be worth
noting that the fulfillment of the final phase might signify the disappearance of states altogether. In an international system where the
behavior of state actors is dictated only by the perceived interests of
the system as a whole, the very rationale of international politics is
removed. Here, political compartmentalization might be broken down
with far-reaching effects for a new personalization of planetary interaction. These effects might include a new spirit of worldwide organic
community stressing an unprecedented measure of mutual awareness,
complementary commitment, and collective concern.

To the extent that such a scenario of behavioral reform ever
does transpire, world order scholars will be reminded of the over-
reaching importance of individual human behavior to their inquiry.
At all stages of behavioral transformation, the individual human roots
of world order reform figure most prominently. Above all else, these
bases of an alternative world future require continuing study and
careful cultivation. To heed this plea is to reorient the present
direction of world order studies in a most auspicious manner and to
take a genuinely decisive step toward creative planetary renewal.

NOTES

1. See Amitai Etzioni, "Human Nature and the Transforming
Society," International Journal of Group Tensions 4, no. 3 (September
1974): 284.

2. For a full account of this developing orientation, see Louis
Rene Beres and Harry R. Targ, Reordering the Planet: Constructing
Alternative World Futures (Boston: Allyn and Bacon, 1974).

3. Eugene Ionesco, "Experience du Theatre," Nouvelle Revue
Francaise (Paris), February 1, 1958, p. 253. Cited in Martin Esslin,
The Theatre of the Absurd (New York: Anchor, 1961), p. 84.

CHAPTER 13

THE STRUCTURE OF
WORLD CONSCIOUSNESS
Francis A. Beer

THE STRUCTURE OF WORLD CONSCIOUSNESS

When we speak of global design, we refer in other terms to the structure of the world. The design or structure is complex and not yet well defined or well understood.[1] Nevertheless, one of its more important dimensions is implicit in the existence of communities of different scope. At the broadest level is the world, or the planet itself. Spread out below are the ranges of nations and the topology of various subnational systems—for example, the states of federal systems like the United States, various groups like political parties or ethnic aggregations, schools, work organizations, friendship groups, and family. Finally, living on this landscape are individual people.

Whatever its state of objective existence and its parts, this structure also is reflected in popular culture and psychology, where it is a kind of phenomenological skeleton, a framework on which to hang our attitudes.

Attitudes toward the structure may have a number of different elements or dimensions. They may be directed toward the community as a whole and its symbols; the regime or its institutions and processes; the government and its specific policies and programs.[2]

Attitudes also imply affective, cognitive, and conative dimensions.[3] Affect includes feeling or emotion. The cognitive component is relatively intellectual, comprising the degree of salience or information. Finally, the conative dimension of attitudes suggests that they lead to some kind of behavior or action.

We must be concerned with the structural relationships of all these aspects of consciousness. To deal with them in detail, however, would require more space than we presently have. We shall therefore concentrate on a smaller sample, the intersection of two relevant dimensions. We shall be particularly concerned with affective orientations to the symbols of communities.

We shall call such orientation identification, and we presume that identification may be either positive or negative. [4] When people are positively involved, we call their supportive attitudes loyalty or legitimacy. When they are disaffected, disgruntled, and otherwise negatively disposed, we speak of political, social, or psychological alienation. [5]

Identifications with different levels may fall in a number of different patterns. Our purpose is to suggest some of the ways they may be arranged, possible reasons for differential development, and the implications of our knowledge for change.

PATTERNS OF IDENTIFICATION

We may make three different assumptions about the way identifications are arranged:

1. Identifications are part of more generalized attitudes and therefore tend to fall in congruent patterns.
2. Identifications with different levels are not necessarily symmetrically related and may fall in divergent patterns.
3. Identifications are relatively unrelated.

Depending on which assumption we make, we are able to specify a family of models that follow from our original assumption.

Congruence Models

We have called models that show the first general pattern of symmetrical identification congruence models. The fundamental assumption is that identifications form overlapping sets with relatively consistent relations. Identification with one level of the system is a predictor of identification with others.

Perhaps the simplest of all are the models in Figure 13.1, in which loyalty and alienation are all or nothing, either completely pervasive or totally absent. These are cases of perfect congruence, where identifications are conjoint, generalized, and symmetrical toward all levels of the system. If we gathered evidence in such a system, there would be a perfect correlation between identification toward any one level and any other.

FIGURE 13.1

Patterns of Identification:
Congruence Models

Generalized   Generalized
Loyalty   Alienation

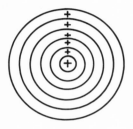   

Levels: individual, group, local, state, nation, world.[6]

    A looser construction of congruence suggests that there may
exist a symmetrical and mutually supportive relationship between
system identification at different levels without a perfect fit. Legitimacy at one level may go together with different degrees of support
for others, and there may exist a core of citizens with loosely coupled
"multiple loyalties."[7]

    Similarly, alienation from one set of structures may imply a
congruent disillusion with others, producing a diaspora of the disaffected, citizens with multiple alienation.

    A good deal of philosophy and social scientific theory and research
supports the assumption of congruence. To do it justice, we would have
to undertake a comprehensive survey of contemporary knowledge.
Nevertheless, we hope that two prominent examples will be enough.
First, the idea that multiple loyalties may be self-reinforcing finds a
handhold in the traditional literature of the group theory of politics.
Americans have traditionally been represented as a nation of joiners,
and it is assumed that overlapping group memberships will bind rather
than fragment the pluralist polities in which they occur.[8]

    Similarly, the psychological theory of cognitive consistency
suggests that identification with any particular institutional level should

represent part of an internally consistent field, one of whose characteristics should be identification with other levels.[9]

Congruent multiple alienation draws support from the same
sources. Those who are not or do not feel themselves part of the
overlapping group structure would presumably elaborate an opposite
and consistently negative pattern of attitudes.[10]

In spite of such support, the congruence model is not completely
satisfactory as a general description of identification. From a theoretical point of view, it suggests a kind of structural symmetry that
we suspect, from our own immediate experiences in the world, may
not always exist. Perfect congruence might be possible in the best
of all possible worlds; all or most of us do not necessarily live there.
Even if the congruence model were generally true, the claims of
different political levels under many kinds of circumstances may compete with each other, tugging the individual in different directions.
The multiplication of secondary identities can pose logically inconsistent or impossible demands. Empirically, patterns of identification
development do not always follow the neat pattern that the congruence
model implies.

Divergence Models

One alternative to congruence is divergence.[11] Like a direct
electrical current, congruence models rest on the principle of homogeneity. The divergence model is more like alternating current, constructed of polar opposites.

The divergence model suggests that a political order includes
a dialectical antagonism of suprasets and subsets.[12] Legitimacy at
one level may go directly against the grain of legitimacy at other
levels, and there may exist a plurality of citizen cores with mutually
exclusive loyalties and alienations.

The congruence prototype itself implies a divergent derivative,
where positive loyalties develop at lower levels and then either
weaken or are transformed into alienation at higher levels. Two
examples appear in models A and B in Figure 13.2, our common conceptions of essence of international politics and states rights within
larger federal systems.

Model A presents a scheme of international politics as it is
conceived by self-conscious scholars and practitioners of the "realist"
school as well as many others. In this model the individual develops
a relatively integrated identity and fairly strong positive identifications with the nation-state and its institutional infrastructure. For
some reason, however, the process stops at the national border,

FIGURE 13.2

Patterns of Identification: Divergence Models

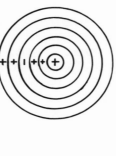

A. International Politics

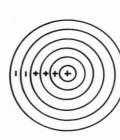

B. States' Rights

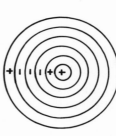

C. Political Leapfrog

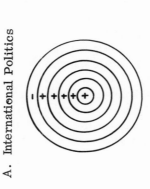

D. Minority Rights

E. Revolutionary Heroism

F. True Believers

Levels: individual, group, local, state, nation, world.

and the international level of the world system remains a kind of
Hobbesian state of nature. [13]

The pattern of states' rights, in model B, is similar. Again
the individual integrates and reaches out fairly well up to a certain
level, in this case the state of a federal system. Beyond this point,
however, he becomes suspicious of the claims and intentions of the
suprainstitutions of the system. Perhaps he does not preceive the
validity of the national claim because he still harks back to the days
before nationhood. For him, national politics may be just a variant
of international politics. On the other hand, he may be relatively
impotent in the system's higher reaches, and therefore redouble his
hopes and efforts at lower levels.

Although some of the implications of model C, political leapfrog,
are similar, the mood is different. The individual who engages in
political leapfrog accepts and supports most of the general structure
of the system. Nevertheless, there is a fundamental discontinuity at
some point, here in his identification with the state level. Perhaps
he is at a disadvantage within its idiosyncratic boundaries; if so, he
may use his resources in higher parts of the system, mostly likely
at the national level, in an attempt to change the rules within the state
itself in his favor. [14]

Model D is a case of a minority rights movement, perhaps
arising in opposition to a dominant states' rights political culture.
In this model there is strong individual identity and group solidarity
but a feeling of disadvantage within local and state political arenas.
In a kind of double leapfrog, minorities in such a system may attempt
to jump to the national level, perhaps in the name of fundamental constitutional rights, to rescue them from the inequities of state and
local jurisdiction. Apparently, profoundly alienated from their immediate surroundings they request increased federal assistance supporting
their demands for individual liberty and equality. [15]

Alternatively, model D also may describe the situation of
"cosmopolitans" who have migrated from a national center to a more
provincial setting. Unwilling or unable to cast off their prior identity,
they may feel alienated by their new environment. In this situation,
they are eager to maintain a distance between themselves and
"parochials." [16]

Model E presents one perspective on revolutionary struggle.
The worker with strong individual identity and class loyalty fights
against the long odds of local, state, and national structures in the
name of the world proletariat. [17]

Finally, model F is suggested by some of those who have
written about or been strongly influenced by the totalitarian regimes
of the 1930s or the McCarthy period of the American 1950s. [18] In the
true believer model, the individual who is unable to "make it" in most

of the world turns to the nation for salvation. Such an individual may be filled with internal conflicts that prevent the emergence of a strong individual identity. He or she may find no gratification in conflict-ridden interaction at different levels. Nevertheless, the emergence of a charismatic national leader, with media-amplified virtues, may provide a strong attraction. Such a leader may act out the negative fantasies of the individual against groups within the nation, as well as turning to enemies in the world outside. [19]

Null Models

Null models may assume any of the configurations we have already described. They are distinguished essentially by the underlying assumption that identifications with different levels do not occur as the result of regular forces but essentially at random. Identification at one level is not necessarily related to others. The development of political loyalty is a stochastic process with a connection existing only at random between loyalty at lower and higher levels of the system.

DYNAMICS OF CONSCIOUSNESS

The phenomenology of consciousness rests upon psychogenetic and psychodynamic bases. [20] Our description of the models themselves has already suggested some of the ways in which different patterns of identification may appear. In more general perspective, each family of models seems to depend on different kinds of assumptions about the way in which identification develops.

Congruent identification implies the importance of natural growth and unfolding the potential for which is determined by human biology. Consciousness begins to bloom early in life as the child gradually differentiates and generalizes.

The first stage would seem naturally to be the formation of a primitive ego or identity. As this occurs, other identifications presumably also develop with primary groups: family and peers.

Children gradually come into contact with the symbols of secondary groups, which are incorporated into the developing consciousness.

The classic formulation of this process is by Jean Piaget and A. M. Weil. They summed it up, saying that "the child's discovery of his homeland and understanding of other countries" was part of a broader "process of transition from egocentricity to reciprocity." [21]

This transition may take place successfully or it may not, and the resulting attitudes may be either positive or negative. Even if they achieve a relatively advanced state of reciprocity, patterns of identification are not necessarily stable. The gradual development of reciprocity "is liable to constant setbacks, usually through the reemergence of egocentricity on a broader or sociocentric plane, at each new stage of this development or as each new conflict arises."[22]

The variety of remaining models and supporting theory is so great that it is more difficult to specify a prototypic pattern through which such patterns of identification develop. Nevertheless, this variety itself seems more consistent with the thrust of much contemporary behavioral psychology, in particular the theory of operant conditioning, which places heavy emphasis on the importance of the immediate environment. The relevant implication for identification is that individuals tend to exchange loyalty for rewards and alienation for constraints and coercion.[23]

If this is correct, identification with one level of the system does not necessarily spill over into others. Rather, patterns of loyalty and alienation respond to more immediate patterns of the environment around them and to the manipulation of those who control society's rewards and punishments. Support for different levels of the structure depends in part on the degree to which they provide appropriate rewards and constraints.[24] If there is some order, as in the divergence models, it is because of underlying regularities in the structure of reinforcement. If not, it reflects the disorganization of society itself.

METACONSCIOUSNESS

In our discussion of identification we have been concerned with a small part of the total structure of world consciousness. Our attention has centered on positive and negative affect toward the central symbols of communities at different levels.

There are analogous cognitive variations. People may be aware or unaware, interested or uninterested, to different degrees. They may be concerned uniformly with almost everything or nothing; or they may be more selective, perhaps not paying much attention to world government but very much involved in women's liberation.

Individuals also may differ along the conative dimension depending on whether or not they are prone to act overtly on the basis of their knowledge and feelings, or whether they are more passively inclined toward the world.

Attitudes may differ not only with regard to the symbols of the community but also toward other dimensions such as the nature of the regime and its particular policies and activities.

We are not able to elaborate the multiple possible combinations of these dimensions. Nevertheless, the patterns and dynamics that we have discussed are relevant to the intersection of dimensions we have not considered. They too may fall into and contribute to complex congruent, divergent, and null patterns—and be influenced by genetic and environmental pressures.

As this rich web of combinations is elaborated, specified, and tested against empirical reality, our knowledge of the structure of consciousness expands. The development of our knowledge of consciousness itself represents an important addition to the structure of world consciousness—a kind of metaconsciousness, a new layer of awareness above what already exists.

Metaconsciousness is subject to the same kind of patterning and dynamic forces as the other dimensions of consciousness and has an important relationship with them. [25]

Metaconsciousness, for good or bad, must share the same genetic bases as ordinary consciousness. Yet it can draw environmental support from the existence of a growing body of shared knowledge and of groups and individuals devoted to its expansion and promulgation.

Metaconsciousness may act as a kind of lever on the larger structure of world consciousness itself. The attainment and expansion of metaconsciousness implies a substantial degree of activity. It can be a tool for increasing structural salience. Even though the structure of world consciousness is not currently understood very well in a comprehensive and detailed way, the self-conscious effort to gain greater knowledge brings structural elements into better focus and greater attention.

Metaconsciousness also implies structural support. Presumably we find some value in the existing structure we set out to uncover. If we are disturbed by a high degree of irregularity and a substantial potential for violence, we may wish to achieve a better alternative future.

A changed subjective consciousness may be a force for a change in objective structure. A new world consciousness is probably a necessary element of creating a new world politics[26] or a new world society. Hopefully a recognition of the importance and value of different structural levels will lead to renovation and revitalization of the many dimensions of our conventional life, perhaps an orderly, humane, and technologically advanced decentralization. [27]

We hope that a highly structured metaconsciousness will represent a force for the attainment of such values as peace, justice, and liberation. We have no guarantee that this will be so. Much contemporary violence is committed in the name of abstract commonalities. Metaconsciousness may be more a force for repression than for liberation. [28]

Yet we hope that we may eventually go beyond what we often mean by loyalty today—a kind of superficial conformist identification with structures at different levels—to include a much deeper dimension as well. We would hope to comprehend not only a feeling of identification with structure or organization but also a deeper empathy or compassion for all the life within its boundaries.[29]

Is this really beyond the possibilities of human nature or artifice?

NOTES

1. For a summary of contemporary structuralist thought, see J. Piaget, Structuralism, trans. Chaninah Machler (New York: Harper and Row, 1968). See also H. Gardner, The Quest for Mind: Piaget, Levi-Strauss, and the Structuralist Movement (New York: Vintage, 1972).

2. See D. Easton and R. D. Hess, "The Child's Political World," Midwest Journal of Political Science 6 (1962): 229-46.

3. See M. B. Smith, "The Personal Setting of Public Opinions: A Study of Attitudes Toward Russia," Public Opinion Quarterly 2 (1947): 507-23.

4. This is, of course, a crude distinction. Nevertheless, it reflects an important psychological dimension. See J. D. Barber, The Presidential Character (Englewood Cliffs, N.J.: Prentice-Hall, 1972), and particularly A. L. George, "Assessing Presidential Character," World Politics 26, no. 2 (January 1974): 234-82.

5. The classic exposition of the phenomenon of multiple loyalties is H. Guetzkow, Multiple Loyalties: Theoretical Approach to a Problem in International Organization (Princeton, N.J.: Princeton University Press, 1955). For general overviews of work on alienation, see F. Johnson, ed., Alienation: Concept, Term, and Meanings (New York: Seminar Press, 1973); W. C. Bier, Alienation: Plight of Modern Man (New York: Fordham University Press, 1972); A. W. Finifter, Alienation and the Social System (New York: Wiley, 1971); and R. Schacht, Alienation (Garden City, N.Y.: Doubleday, 1971).

6. We use these six levels as examples here; obviously, others also might have been included.

7. See Guetzkow, Multiple Loyalties.

8. See R. Dahl, Who Governs? (New Haven: Yale University Press, 1961); D. Truman, The Governmental Process (New York: Knopf, 1951).

9. See, for example, A. P. Ableson et al. , Theories of Cognitive Consistency: A Sourcebook (Chicago: Rand McNally, 1968); S. Fewman, Cognitive Consistency: Motivational Antecedents and Behavioral Consequences (New York: Academic Press, 1966); M. Rosenberg et al. , Attitude Organization and Change: An Analysis of Consistency Among Attitude Components (New Haven: Yale University Press, 1960); L. Festinger, The Theory of Cognitive Dissonance (Palo Alto, Calif.: Stanford University Press, 1954). Presumably the pressures of social status consistency provide additional support for congruence. See, for example, D. D. Nimmo and C. Bonjean, eds. , Political Attitudes and Public Opinion (New York: David McKay, 1972), Part III; E. S. Midlarsky and M. L. Midlarsky, "Some Determinants of Aiding Under Experimentally Induced Stress," Journal of Personality 41, no. 3 (September 1973): 305-27; Midlarsky and Midlarsky, "Additive and Interactive Effects on Altruistic Behavior," in Proceedings, American Psychological Association (1972).

Individual psychological "adjustment" also is part of the congruent pattern. Cf. Di Palma and H. McCloskey, "Personality and Conformity: The Learning of Political Attitudes," American Political Science Review 63, no. 4 (December 1970): 1054-73; R. E. Lane, Political Life (Glencoe, Ill.: Free Press, 1959).

10. See P. Sniderman and J. Citrin, "Psychological Sources of Political Belief: Self-Esteem and Isolationist Attitudes," American Political Science Review 65, no. 2 (June 1971): 401-17; H. W. Ransford, "Isolation, Powerlessness and Violence: A Study of Attitudes and Participation in the Watts Riots," American Journal of Sociology 73 (March 1968): 581-91; H. McCloskey, "Personality and Attitude Correlates of Foreign Policy Orientation," in Domestic Sources of Foreign Policy, ed. James N. Rosenau (New York: Free Press, 1967); Kenneth Keniston, The Uncommitted: Alienated Youth in American Society (New York: Harcourt, Brace, and World, 1965).

11. Many representations are possible in addition to the theoretical ones we elaborate here. Set theory would provide a more formal mathematical way to describe and map them. For a brief introduction, see J. G. Kemeny et al. , Introduction to Finite Mathematics (Englewood Cliffs, N.J.: Prentice-Hall, 1957), Chapter 2; H. Newcombe, "Venn Diagrams of Values: Peace, Justice, Freedom, Love," Peace and Change 2, no. 2 (Summer 1974): 45-50, provides an application. Analogous models exist in contemporary astronomy, physics, chemistry, and biology.

12. This is a primary insight of social conflict theory. See, for example, R. Dahrendorf, Class and Class Conflict in Industrial Society (Palo Alto, Calif.: Stanford University Press, 1959); L. Coser, The Functions of Social Conflict (Glencoe, Ill.: Free Press, 1956).

I also am indebted to R. N. Adams, "Power: Its Conditions, Strategy and Evolution," mimeo. (Austin, 1972).

See G. Sjoberg, "Contradictory Functional Requirements and Social Systems," Journal of Conflict Resolution 4, no. 2 (June 1960): 198-208; A. Gouldner, "Reciprocity and Autonomy in Functional Theory," in Symposium on Sociological Theory, ed. L. Gross (New York: Harper and Row, 1959), pp. 241-70, for a discussion of systems, countersystems, and their component parts.

13. See H. Targ, "Children's Developing Orientation to International Politics," Journal of Peace Research 2 (1970): 79-98.

14. M. K. Jennings and H. Ziegler, "The Salience of American State Politics," American Political Science Review 64, no. 2 (June 1970): 523-35; and Jennings, "Pre-Adult Orientations to Multiple Systems of Government," Midwest Journal of Political Science 11 (August 1967): 291-317, compare and relate natural and state identification and their correlates. One might elaborate a similar model of "tribal rights" reflecting segmentary dynamics developed by anthropologists dealing with "primitive" societies. It would display a negative transformation of identification beyond familial and tribal boundaries.

15. This is supported by the implications of recent studies of American disturbances, which found or implied a pattern of high individual and group efficacy associated with high political alienation. While the disturbances disrupted accepted political process, they also had political targets, of which an important one was the federal government. J. Citrin, "Comment," American Political Science Review 68, no. 3 (September 1974): 973-88; A. M. Orum and R. S. Cohen, "The Development of Political Orientations Among Black and White Children," American Sociological Review 38, no. 1 (February 1973): 62-73; J. Paige, "Political Orientation and Riot Participation," American Sociological Review 36, pp. 810-20; and Garrison and K. Keniston, Young Radicals: Notes on Committed Youth (New York: Harcourt, Brace, and World, 1968), pp. 86-92, 306-10.

16. See A. Gouldner, "Cosmopolitans and Locals: Toward an Analysis of Latent Social Roles," Administrative Science Quarterly 2 (December 1957): 281-306 and (March 1958): 444-80.

17. Or it may refer to the microrevolutionary deviants and their friends. See A. W. Finifter, "The Friendship Group as a Protective Environment for Political Deviants," American Political Science Review 68, no. 2 (June 1974): 607-25.

18. For a recent review, see H. Gabbenesch, "Authoritarianism as a World View," American Journal of Sociology 77, no. 5 (March 1972): 857-75; B. Bettelheim, The Informed Heart (Glencoe, Ill: Free Press, 1960); E. Hoffer, The True Believer (New York: Harper, 1951); H. Arendt, The Origins of Totalitarianism (New York: Harcourt,

Brace, 1951); T. W. Adorno et al., The Authoritarian Personality (New York: Harper, 1950); E. Fromm, Escape From Freedom (New York: Farrar and Rinehart, 1941); D. Bell, The Radical Right (Garden City: Doubleday, 1964); W. Kornhauser, The Politics of Mass Society (New York: Free Press, 1959); S. M. Lipset, Political Man (New York: Anchor, 1960).

19. The leader himself may have strongly negative components in his personality. See the pioneering work by H. Lasswell in Psychopathology and Politics (Chicago: University of Chicago Press, 1930); World Politics and Personal Insecurity (New York: McGraw-Hill, 1935); Power and Personality (New York: Norton, 1948). American variants are discussed in, inter alia, W. C. Bullitt and S. Freud, Thomas Woodrow Wilson (Boston: Houghton-Mifflin, 1967); A. L. George, "Power as a Compensatory Value for Political Leaders," Journal of Social Issues 24, no. 3 (1968): 29-49; Alexander L. George and Juliette George, Woodrow Wilson and Colonel House: A Personality Study (New York: John Day, 1956); B. Mazlish, In Search of Nixon: A Psychohistorical Inquiry (New York: Basic Books, 1972); and Mazlish, ed., Psychoanalysis and History (Englewood Cliffs, N.J.: Prentice-Hall, 1963).

20. It is beyond the scope of the present essay to review the literature or knowledge in this area. For an introductory overview, see A. L. George, "Assessing Presidential Character," World Politics 26, no. 2 (January 1974). Somewhat different perspectives—metapsychological and psychochemical—are summarized in R. E. Ornstein, The Psychology of Consciousness (San Francisco: W. H. Freeman, 1972); D. Hawkins and L. Pauling, eds., Orthomolecular Psychiatry (San Francisco: W. H. Freeman, 1973).

21. See J. Piaget and A. M. Weil, "The Development in Children of the Idea of the Homeland and of Relations with Other Countries," International Social Science Bulletin 3, no. 3 (Autumn 1951): 561-78.

Cf. J. Piaget's works: The Language and Thought of the Child, trans. M. Gabain (Cleveland and New York: Meridian Books, 1967); Six Psychological Studies, trans. A. Tenzer (New York: Vintage, 1967); The Moral Judgement of the Child, trans. M. Gabin (New York: Free Press, 1965); B. Inhelder and J. Piaget, The Growth of Logical Thinking from Childhood to Adolescence, trans. A. Parsons and S. Milgram (New York: Basic Books, 1958). See also G. Mercer, "Adolescent Views of War and Peace—Another Look," Journal of Peace Research 11, no. 3 (1974): 247-50; D. Statt, "The Influence of National Power on the Child's View of the World," Journal of Peace Research 11, no. 3 (1974): 245-47; R. M. Merelman, "The Structure of Policy Thinking in Adolescence: A Research Note," American Political Science Review 67, no. 1 (March 1973): 161-67; Merelman, "The Development of Policy Thinking in Adolescence," American Political Science Review 65 (December 1971): 1033-47. H. Tolley,

<u>Children and War: Political Socialization to International Conflict</u>
(New York: Teachers College Press, 1973) provides a good overview
and bibliography of related work.

The general thrust of the argument is also consistent with Maslow's theory of human development. See, for example, A. H. Maslow,
<u>The Farther Reaches of Human Nature</u> (New York: Viking Press,
1971), and <u>Toward a Psychology of Being</u>, 2nd ed. (Princeton, N.J.:
Van Nostrand, 1970).

22. Piaget and Weil, "The Development in Children," pp. 561-
78. See also E. H. Erikson, <u>Childhood and Society</u> (New York: Norton,
1950). Freudian terminology opens the window to an alternative view.
We mentioned earlier that the congruence model was supported by
the theory of cognitive and social consistency. This consistency may
rest on an unstable psychodynamic foundation.

In a sense the theory of consistency is Freudian in origin,
derived from the repression of the undesirable. In Freudian terminology, consistency can be achieved by repressing dimensions of experience, or reordering them, so that they fit in with the dominant
structure of the psyche. The consciousness of identification is the
consciousness of the superego. As it develops, the superego arranges
and orders the dimension of civilized political life.

The consistency of the adult develops to some extent from the
experiences of the child within the family. The greater the tensions
within the early family, the more limited such development and the
more fragile such consistency may be in later life.

Perhaps some of the clues to models E and F lie in the learning
implications of certain kinds of family structure for the development
of the individual psyche itself. The traditional German family, with
which Marx and Hitler interacted, presumably had at least some of
the characteristics that Freud observed. In Freudian analysis, the
individual psyche was sharply divided by bitter family politics. In
Freudian man there existed a continual struggle between the superego
and the id, but this battle was only a reflection of precedent family
division, exemplified in the famous Oedipus complex. The superego,
presumably an important element in adult reciprocity, represented
the permanent internalization of the hated father. As such it was in
constant struggle with the infantile impulses of the id, the residual
remnant of the natural child.

One wonders if much of the contemporary indifference to and
rejection of Freud is due to the fact that modern family politics are
more varied than his own experience. His analyses were probably
more valid for the Austria and Germany of his time than elsewhere,
and his analyses were less generalizable in their original form than
he had hoped.

For some fascinating recent discussions of the political implications of the post-Freudian family, see A. Mitscherlich, <u>Society</u>

Without the Father (New York: Schocken, 1970); R. D. Laing, The
Politics of the Family (Toronto: Canadian Broadcasting Corporation,
1969); P. Slater, The Pursuit of Loneliness (Boston: Beacon Press,
1970). See also L. S. Feuer, The Conflict of Generations (New York:
Basic Books, 1969); D. Jaros et al., "The Malevolent Leader:
Political Socialization in an American Subculture," American Political
Science Review 62, no. 2 (June 1968): 564-75.
          23. See B. F. Skinner, Beyond Freedom and Dignity (New York:
Bantam, 1971); and H. Wheeler, ed., Beyond the Punitive Society
(San Francisco: W. H. Freeman, 1973).
          24. The socialization literature has paid special attention to
learning experiences in the family and school as bases of later polit-
ical attitudes. Cf. R. W. Connell, The Child's Construction of Poli-
tics (Melbourne: Melbourne University Press, 1971); E. S. Greenberg,
ed., Political Socialization (New York: Atherton, 1970); H. Hirsch,
Poverty and Politicization (New York: Free Press, 1970); R. Dawson
and K. Prewitt, Political Socialization (Boston: Little, Brown, 1969);
D. Easton and J. Dennis, Children in the Political System (New York:
McGraw-Hill, 1969); R. D. Hess and J. V. Torney, The Development
of Political Attitudes in Children (Chicago: Aldine Press, 1967);
F. I. Greenstein, Children and Politics (New Haven: Yale University
Press, 1965); H. Hyman, Political Socialization (Glencoe, Ill.: Free
Press, 1959). Nevertheless, there have been a number of studies
suggesting that socialization experiences do not stop with puberty and
extend through the life of an individual. See especially O. G. Brim
and S. Wheeler, Socialization After Childhood: Two Essays (New York:
Wiley, 1966), p. 53; John C. Wahlke et al., The Causes of the
American Revolution (Boston: Heath, 1962), pp. 77-95; John Eulau
and John Sprague, Lawyers in Politics, a Study in Professional Con-
vergence (Indianapolis: Bobbs-Merrill, 1964), Chapter 3; Kenneth
Prewitt et al., Political Socialization: An Analytic Study (Boston:
Little, Brown, 1969). A comparative perspective is provided by
G. A. Almond and Sidney Verba, The Civic Culture: Political Attitudes
and Democracy in Free Nations, an Analytic Study (Boston: Little,
Brown, 1965), pp. 280-83, and G. A. Almond and G. Powell, Jr.,
Comparative Politics: A Developmental Approach (Boston: Little,
Brown, 1966), pp. 68-69.
          This is the clear implication of recent literature of political
violence and participation: L. M. Salamon and S. Van Evera, "Fear,
Apathy, and Discrimination: A Test of Three Explanations of Political
Participation," American Political Science Review 67, no. 4 (Decem-
ber 1973): 1288-1306; B. N. Grofman and E. N. Muller, "The Strange
Case of Relative Gratification and Potential for Political Violence:
Toe V-Curve Hypothesis," American Political Science Review 67,
no. 2 (June 1973): 514-39; E. N. Muller, "A Test of a Partial Theory

of Potential for Political Violence," American Political Science Review 66, no. 3 (September 1972): 928-59; I. K. Feierabend and T. R. Gurr, eds., Anger, Violence, and Politics: Theories and Research (Englewood Cliffs, N.J.: Prentice-Hall, 1972); T. R. Gurr, Why Men Rebel (Princeton, N.J.: Princeton University Press, 1970). See also S. Milgram, Obedience to Authority: An Experimental View (New York: Harper and Row, 1974); A. Mehrabian and S. Ksionzky, A Theory of Affiliation (Lexington, Mass.: D. C. Heath, 1974); A. H. Miller, "Political Issues and Trust in Government," American Political Science Review 68, no. 3 (September 1974): 951-72; J. D. Aberbach and J. Walker, "Political Trust and Racial Ideology," American Political Science Review 64 (December 1970): 1199-1219; R. M. Merelman, "Learning and Legitimacy," American Political Science Review 60 (September 1966): 548-61.

25. See C. Bolton, "Alienation and Action: A Study of Peace Group Members," American Journal of Sociology 6 (December 1972): 537-62.

26. See D. V. Edwards, Creating a New World Politics (New York: McKay, 1973).

27. See H. Targ, "Social Science and the New Social Order," Journal of Peace Research, nos. 3-4 (1971): 217-220.

28. See N. O. Brown, Love's Body (New York: Vintage, 1966); N. O. Brown, Life Against Death (Middletown, Conn.: Wesleyan University Press, 1959).

29. See W. Eckhardt, Compassion (Oakville, Ontario: Canadian Peace Research Institute, 1971); J. W. Sloan and H. Targ, "Beyond the European Nation State: A Normative Critique," Polity, Summer 1971, pp. 501-20.

14

**IMAGINATION AND
ALTERNATIVE
WORLD FUTURES**
W. Warren Wagar

TWO MODES OF KNOWING

Peace and world order studies fall, as a matter of academic course, into the province of the social sciences. Political scientists do most of the work, with contributions from sociologists, economists, social psychologists, and others. If the historian lends a hand, it is only to supply historical "background," or perhaps historical "examples" for the models and hypotheses of bright-eyed behaviorists. Students of religion, philosophy, literature, and the arts, and creative people in these fields, seldom become involved at all. In short, the humanities (in which I include history) have had little impact on peace and world order studies, and little on futures research in general. The results of humanistic learning may sometimes figure in the social scientist's labors; its ways of thinking, almost never.

May we conclude that imagination has won no place in peace and world order studies? This would be too strong. All the sciences, from physics to sociology, demand boldness of vision and imaginative powers of high intensity. But there are varieties of imagination that few students of the future tap, much to their loss. It will be the task of this essay to explore the possibilities for significantly enlarging the role of the humanistic imagination in peace and world order studies.

By way of a beginning, let us make sure of our terms. In the language of F. S. C. Northrop, the social and natural sciences produce knowledge in its "theoretic" component; the humanities, including literature and the fine arts, make most of their discoveries in the "esthetic" component of knowledge.[1] The scientific imagination pursues truth through the creation of mathematical and mechanical models. Its

conception of reality is abstract. The humanities—with the exception
of some schools of philosophy, the parent of all sciences—pursue
truth through the understanding or representation of concrete, directly
perceived or imagined reality.

The truth of a work of history or literature or art lies, then, in
its contact with the existential. The historian empathetically recon-
structs events that happened once and once only, to living men and
women. The novelist and the playwright conjure up fictitious worlds
inhabited by men and women who might have lived, representing the
events that happened, once and once only, in their personal histories.
The artist pictures the actual and the concrete, objectively or subjectively. The speculative philosopher or theologian sees directly
into the heart of things by acts of pure intuition.

Which of these two great categories of knowing has the greater
relevance for the study of futures—knowledge through theoretical constructs or knowledge through empathy and immediate perception? At
first blush, the answer is obvious. Since the future has not yet
happened, it must be predicted on the basis of a theoretical knowledge
of the structure of reality; it must be known through generalizations
about human behavior charged with prognostic power. One cannot
empathize with the unborn or perceive unhappenings or intuit the form
of the not-yet.

But look again. Although the positive sciences alone have filed
a formal claim of prophetic faculties, they cannot literally know the
future. They cannot even know the past and the present, since their
object is self-confessedly the abstraction from reality of general
statements about its "nature," rather than knowledge of existents as
they are in themselves. The models of positive science do not portray
reality; they represent the theoretically constructed relationship
between theoretically constructed qualities of the real world. All
Western natural and social science is ultimately Platonic. Through
its analysis, simplification, and idealization of reality, its knowledge
is always part-knowledge, incapable of true holism. It deliberately
excludes from vision the full range of forces that, together, make the
future. It is also deterministic to the core, incapable of conceiving
a realm of freedom in which intelligent beings may alter their futures
at will.

What the positive sciences "know" about the future is what, for
example, the scientists at M. I. T. headed by Dennis L. Meadows
"know" about the limits to growth. Quantifying five trends in the world
economy and their theoretical interaction, the Meadows team has built
a world model from which it computes alternative futures—not of the
real world but of the model itself. If only because such critically
relevant factors as "new forms of human societal behavior" could not
be modeled at all, "we would not expect the real world to behave like

the world model in any of the graphs we have shown."[2] The most that anyone can ask of such exercises is a list of possible components of a future world order.

The modes of knowing of the humanities also fail to provide knowledge, in the strictest sense, of the real future, but they can point to possibilities no less prolifically than the modes of the positive sciences. The humanities—or we might use Wilhelm Dilthey's term, the Geisteswissenschaften, the sciences of mind and spirit—concern themselves with mankind in its quintessentially human nature. The humanities view mankind not as a species of social insect doomed to repeat endlessly the destiny imposed on it by inheritance and environment, but as a family of conscious beings endowed with the power of transcending their animality, for better or worse.

The knowledge of the humanistic studies and arts has, above all, two qualities that set it apart from positive knowledge: concreteness and holism. It is concrete because, for the most part, it deals with real or imaginary people in their uniqueness and historicity. The person of the humanities is not an example but the picture of a real being, not quite like any other, situated in particular places at particular points in time. Or, as Johan Huizinga once wrote in regard to history, "The sociologist and the psychologist are concerned mainly that the facts of a case conform to a system of ideas; for the historian this conformity has little or no importance—indeed, the term 'case' does not belong in history at all."[3]

The knowledge of the humanistic studies and arts is also holistic because most of it offers not abstractions but people in their totality as thinking, willing, feeling organisms. The novelist cannot—if he is a good one—see his characters as anything less than whole men and women, living in life-sized environments. The historian must do the same with the people in his pages, and the theologian studies God or the Ground of Being, not abstract models of divinity. The concrete cannot properly be viewed any other way than holistically: Just because it is concrete and alive, it is whole.

In the next two sections, we shall take a closer look at some of the ways in which the humanistic imagination can best serve peace and world order studies. One is the reading, writing, and criticism of a literary genre devoted largely to futures—science fiction. The other centers on alternative pasts—the theory and practice of comparative world history. In a fourth and concluding section, we shall return to the question of how the humanist's methods help both to correct and to complement social science methodology.

SCIENCE FICTION

The most clearly valuable product of the humanistic imagination for students of peace and world order is the science-fiction novel. A few years ago, I might have felt constrained to offer apologies for such a suggestion, but science fiction has now come of age. It is recognized as one of the chief modes of serious fabling and myth making in twentieth century literature. Many universities offer academic credit for studying it, and there is a growing critical literature of weight and distinction.[4] To the already long established classics of Wells, Huxley, Capek, and Orwell have now been added the work of writers like Kurt Vonnegut, Jr., J. G. Ballard, William Golding, Anthony Burgess, and Stanislaw Lem, offering further confirmation of the respectability of science fiction as a literary medium.

Respectable or not, science fiction does not have the same purpose as "straight" fiction. It has only incidental value as a revelation of character or the eternal verities of the human condition. What sets science fiction apart and gives it a reason for being is the fundamental premise of every science-fiction story: that the world it explores is somehow—in one, two, or many ways—different from the real world. As everybody knows, science fiction specializes not in science per se but in speculation. It assumes that things are not as we know them, either because they are taking place in the future or because, even in the present, something has happened to change the rules of the human game.

In short, science fiction deals, more than any other kind of fiction, in ideas. Whenever a science-fiction writer visits an alternative world or an alternative future, he must build in his imagination all the structures that make life possible in that changed situation: the institutions, the values, the history, the biology, the psychology. Some things, for whatever reasons, may not really be different at all. Others will be vastly altered. The point is that, unlike the mainstream writer, the writer of science fiction can take little for granted about the context in which his characters act. He must invent the context, and indeed this may be the most important thing he does.

As often as not, the changed circumstances imagined in fullest detail are political. Some of the most powerful work in modern science fiction envisages new kinds of states, new forms of warfare, new techniques of behavioral engineering, new world (or galactic) orders. Years before totalitarianism had been perfected in reality by Stalin, Hitler, and Mao, H. G. Wells in When the Sleeper Wakes (1899) and Yevgeny Zamyatin in We (1921) had foreseen many of its essential features. E. M. Forster's "The Machine Stops" (1909), Rudyard Kipling's "With the Night Mail" (1905), and Aldous Huxley's Brave

New World (1932) gave us the psychology and politics of technocracy. Wells fought several world wars in his novels before the first real one arrived in 1914,[5] and Jack London in The Iron Heel (1906) brilliantly depicted some of the shapes of modern class warfare. The more recent classics of science fiction often provide us with glimpses, in no little detail, of our own political future (or so it may be). The visions of population and crime control in Anthony Burgess's The Wanting Seed (1962) and A Clockwork Orange (1962), of post-Armageddon medievalism in Walter M. Miller's A Canticle for Leibowitz (1959), of computerized warfare and peacemaking in D. F. Jones's Colossus (1967), of multinational corporations in John Brunner's Stand on Zanzibar (1968), of urban racial struggle in Alan Seymour's The Coming Self-Destruction of the United States of America (1969), are exercises in political thought. George Orwell's Nineteen Eighty-Four (1949) has become a landmark in modern political philosophy and supplies a provocative model of world order for good measure.

To be sure, happy futures are rare in the best science fiction, just as wholesome, well-integrated personalities seldom appear in the novels of the literary mainstream. The essence of comedy is error, and of tragedy, defeat. But there is much to be learned from the errors and defeats of science-fiction counterutopias. And occasionally matters turn out well. The Shape of Things to Come (1933) was only one in a long series of novels by H. G. Wells that brought a benevolent world order out of the jaws of global war.[6] Aldous Huxley's Island (1962), Arthur C. Clarke's Childhood's End (1953), and Robert Heinlein's Stranger in a Strange Land (1961) survey possibilities for human renewal through psychospiritual change. Of greater practical value, perhaps, are the numberless novels set in the far future when earth has a world government and belongs to a galactic federation or empire of civilized worlds. The federation may have its enemies and war may still thrive, but terrestrial unification is taken for granted. The political mythology of an eternal United States or Soviet Union sinks into the same oblivion as the dream of Eternal Rome. In some of the more distant futures, earth itself is lost to view or plays a shadowy existence as the half-forgotten "mother planet."

In this context, I can think of no more influential model of world order than the one supplied by Gene Roddenberry's television serial Star Trek. For four years, and in all the reruns that followed, Star Trek gave millions of viewers a lovingly detailed picture of a galaxy more or less at peace, yet full of perils and potentialities for change and progress. The men and women of the Starship "Enterprise" are soldier-explorers sent out by the United Federation of Planets, a polity that includes earth and many worlds with nonhuman inhabitants. The federation follows a policy of racial harmony, interplanetary peace, and noninterference in the affairs of cultures outside its pale. Against its chief rivals, the Romulan and Klingon empires, it maintains armed vigilance but sedulously avoids aggressive acts. It could be argued that the federation is only the United States in disguise, and that the Romulans and Klingons are Russians and Chinese. The alien science officer from Vulcan (Mr. Spock), by this analysis, becomes the token black man in an otherwise all-white crew. Nonetheless, I suspect that most of Star Trek's loyal following take its message literally: The earth will some day achieve political union and the human polity will fuse with its counterparts on the planets of other suns.[7]

Well and good, you might say. But what can the serious student of peace and world order do with the visions of science fiction? What can the science fictionist and the critic of science fiction tell him that he does not already know? The answer is quite simple. The best novels, stories, and films in the field are the work of resourceful intellects fortified with wide reading who have been able, in Dennis Livingston's words, "to take the myriad strands of data about man's potential available from experience and research and to weave them intuitively into coherent wholes."[8] Their imaginary worlds, which by now must number in the thousands, embody models of human interaction on all levels that can be valuable in themselves and also open new avenues of inquiry and thought in the mind of the social scientist.

In other words, the science-fiction writer develops images of the future that the researcher will find substantively useful, and at the same time the science-fiction writer's skillful employment of humanistic imagination prods the social scientist into thinking about problems from fresh perspectives. The social scientist who reads science fiction has more than ideas about the future; he has pictures of vividly imagined human beings and institutions acting in a world of their own that make the future come alive as surely as our records of historical people and things make the past come alive. The reader of Brunner's Stand on Zanzibar, for example, comes away with much more than ideas about international and corporate relations in the year 2010. He comes away with sharp impressions of the doings of the General Technics Corporation and the English Language Relay Satellite Service; of Common Europe, Yatakang, and Beninia; of Norman House, Donald Hogan, and Dr. Sugaiguntung. He has visited the future, seen some of its events, met some of its people. He may feel that Brunner has missed the mark, and yet if Brunner's vision is strong enough, he will have been moved to think about the future of mankind in ways that abstract treatises rarely move us.

Of course there is nothing to prevent the scholar from trying his own hand at the writing of science fiction, both to disseminate his ideas more widely and to have the brain-ventilating experience of transforming those ideas into concrete images. Predictably, he will find them changing and reordering themselves in the process, and he will learn more than a little about what he really thinks. In the field of world order studies, a modest example is Teg's 1994 by Robert Theobald and J. M. Scott (1969). B. F. Skinner's Walden Two (1948) is the best-known case in point. For that matter, anyone who has ever constructed a scenario of the future in the manner of Herman Kahn—and scenario building is one of the standard methodologies of futures research—comes close to being a writer of science fiction. What makes a scholar's scenario like Paul Ehrlich's "Eco-Catastrophe!"[9] a work of futurology and a novel like John Christopher's The Death of Grass (1956) a work of fiction? The formal distinction should not be allowed to overshadow their essential similarity in purpose, in method, and in substance.

SHAPES OF WORLD HISTORY

"History," writes Mario Rossi, "did not happen, yet the historian makes it happen—for his reader. History is created by the craft of the historian."[10] The alleged subjectivity of historical writing is a much-debated matter, although nowadays the champions of objectivity appear to be winning the debate. My sympathies lie with the losers. If some historical work consists of establishing who did what when and where and how much, in terms so hard that any investigator could duplicate the investigation and arrive at comparable or even identical data, other historical work eludes the methodology of the positive sciences in order to give the past a human face and form.

For J. H. Hexter, the rhetorical device peculiar to history is the narrative, the story that tells what happened in a series of reconstructions and explanations grounded in common sense.[11] Certainly history began as storytelling, infused with Hellenic respect for truthfulness and the critical use of sources. Alan Bullock properly reminds us of the similarity of historical method and the art of the novel.[12] A good specialized work in history today typically combines sociological analysis and narrative technique.

But overarching analysis and narrative alike is the historian's concept of the shape of world history. He needs his humanistic imagination (and common sense) to weave a credible narrative; he may need it even more to arrive at a notion of the world drama. What are the periods, the rhythms, the design of world history? What does history mean? How, understanding the form of the past, can we perhaps foresee or influence the shape of things to come? The "facts" themselves give us no clue: Selecting patterns of significance from the infinity of facts in order to draw a picture of world history is a project more for the imagination than for science, and the pictures so drawn are works of art or morality, or both. World history never happened in the way any merely human voice can tell it. The grand visions of the past that we assemble in our history books are visions of alternative pasts, exercises in speculation only a little less daring than those of the futurologist.

Seen in this light, the difference between well-informed imaginative forays into the future, as in science fiction, and large-scale essays in world history dwindles considerably. The student of world order reaps similar benefits from each. Again, the great advantage he gains is the sense of holism imparted by the humanistic imagination. He learns to view humankind whole and full, in the kind of wholeness and fullness that only an imaginative faculty centered on concrete human beings and their concrete acts in particular spaces and times can perceive. Yet for all its rootedness in the concrete, so vast and diverse are the facts of world history that there is no hope of world historians "agreeing" on their grand visions; each is unique and personal, like the futures imagined by writers of science fiction.

In terms of peace studies, one way of looking at the shapes of world history is to see the past as a series of world orders adjoining one another in space and time. More fascinating than the wars of other ages (although they, too, are instructive) are the long periods of civil peace, law, and cultural synthesis that characterize the histories of the major imperial civilizations, such as Confucian China, the India of Asoka and Harsha, Islam during the Abassid caliphate, the Rome of Augustus and Hadrian. There is no possibility of duplicating any of these dead civilizations in the future. Their social structures, economies, world views, and much more are gone forever. But they were complete human orders, with solutions good or bad to the problems of their time. The historian's art in understanding how they emerged, flourished, and declined, and how their peoples and cultures interacted, is worth close study if one wishes to construct models of future world orders.

At the same time, it is worth noting the contrasts between different historians' pictures of the same past world orders, and between different civilizations themselves, each with its own somewhat different way of solving its problems and its own somewhat different set of problems. The comparative study of civilizations developed by Herder and Spengler does much to stretch the imagination and preclude any simpleminded one-track prophecy of the future of humankind.

But Herder and Spengler, like most students of comparative civilizations, enclosed their contrasts in an imaginative concept of the structure of universal history, and I find it hard to think of any

large project in world order studies that would not benefit from emu-
lating them. The more clearly one articulates his vision of the meaning
of history (which is only another way of saying the meaning of life),
the richer and the more coherent and therefore the more credible will
be his models of possible world orders.

Such a vision may spring directly from one of those already
available to us. It may be taken from the philosophies of progress of
the Enlightenment, from Condorcet, Kant, or Herder himself. It
could be Hegelian or Marxian. It could be liberal, in the vein of Mill
and Spencer; or technocratic, in the vein of St. Simon and Comte; or
utopian socialist, in the vein of Fourier and Proudhon. With Spengler,
who mixed humanistic methodology with a quasi-scientific determinism,
it could insist on the incommensurability of cultures and the cyclical
rhythm of their rises and falls. It could adopt the prophetic hope for
human unification, above and beyond cyclical processes, of Toynbee
and Aurobindo, or the evolutionary mysticism of Bergson and Teilhard
de Chardin.

What all these established visions share is their intuitive grasp
of the meaning of human experience conceived as a process unfolding
in time, even if it may also point to realities above time, and as a
process that encompasses both past and future. A philosophy of history
does not necessarily predict the future, but it gives us hopes and fears
for the future, events to watch for, guard against, or encourage. It
motivates the search for a usable future. It helps us define the kind
of world order that we judge is worth struggling to build.

But it is better for the world order student if he can develop his
own philosophy of world history. I suspect that anyone seriously interested in world order studies already has such a philosophy lurking in
the nether regions of his consciousness, waiting to be brought up into
the light of rational analysis and integrated into his personal Welt-
anschauung. In a culture so historically minded as the modern Western,
few thinking people can fail to confront at least in their private intellectual lives the great issues of speculative historical philosophy.
Creating a philosophy of history requires no professional training in
either field—and less effort for most of us than writing our own science
fiction.

FACTS AND VALUES

Thus far I have argued that the humanistic imagination, in enter-
prises like the writing and criticism of science fiction and the study
of world history, can help the student of world order by giving him
examples and techniques of holistic thinking applicable to the discovery

of the future. Imagination sees interrelationships and fathoms human motivation in ways that are not open to the positive scientist.

But I have also been smuggling into our discourse other benefits of the humanistic imagination that transcend, if I may say so, the truth-seeking function of any scholarly pursuit, regardless of its methods. One of these is the impact of imagination on the scholar himself. An apt analogy could be drawn with the role of fantasy in lovemaking. Readiness for intercourse and orgasm for many people hinges on their success in conjuring up sexual fantasies that touch the deepest needs of their being. Fantasies are intangible. They are not glands and organs, they secrete no fluids, they feel no pleasure. Yet without them the genital apparatus is often powerless to perform. They open our circuits and dissolve our inhibitions. The wrong fantasies can just as quickly lock our circuits up again.

So it is, I think, with world order studies. Building models of world order is not only a work of knowledge; it is a work of faith. How can we build models convincing both to ourselves and to others if we cannot tap the resources and satisfy the needs of our subrational and superrational selves? Reason is not enough. Data are not enough. We need visions, powered and colored by imagination, that can undergird the findings of our sciences. At times we may discover such visions in a novel, a scenario, or an articulated philosophy of history—or perhaps in the symbols of a work of art. At other times, imagination may give us only a poetic phase, a powerful simile, or a shudder of joy or fear that is somehow translated into the language of our world order model. No matter. Our models cannot work, cannot persuade, without the support of imagination.

And beyond the affective domain lies the still larger domain of value creation and value clarification. It is always tactful when addressing scholars to speak of "study" and "investigation" and "research." As scholars, we are all presumably involved in the grim business of finding out that-which-is or that-which-was or that-which-will-be. The futures field is no exception. We "study" the future. In Bertrand de Jouvenel's term, we define that which is "futurible,"[13] that which is imaginable on the basis of current knowledge, which can be projected into the future step by step from the state of all our current arts and sciences.

Yet none of us really stops at fortune telling. Although we wish to know what is clearly possible and clearly impossible in a given segment of future time, our stronger interest (following Dennis Gabor) lies in inventing the future.[14] The construction of models of world order is an attempt, sometimes disguised as pure scholarship, to bring the future under human control, and specifically under the control of the modeler. As such, its principal stock in trade is not knowledge, although knowledge is indispensable to it, but values. The

point at issue is what the modeler wants to happen, within the limits
of what his scholarly intelligence tells him can happen.

It follows that the highest use of the humanistic imagination for
the world order scholar is its power to generate values. A science-
fiction novel in this light becomes a morality play of the future, a
revelation of the best (or worst) of all possible futures. A philosophy
of history becomes an ideology, a determination of what is good and
what is evil in the historical process, with an implicit or even explicit
program for winnowing the latter from the former in time future and
thereby realizing the purpose or goal of historical experience.

Unless you can bring yourself to believe that the good is a matter
of knowledge, and that a positive science of morality is available to
bridge the chasm between fact and value, nothing remains but to rely
on immediate intuition for your supply of values. The positive sciences
are helpless. The humanistic mode of perception alone avails. What
is good is what each of us, from the depths of his caring and feeling,
declares good.

This solipsistic ethical philosophy may seem, at first inspection,
to lead to the direct opposite of world order: to world anarchy. But
there are also social controls over thought, whether imposed deliberately by engineers of the public conscience or allowed to grow up
haphazardly. We manage to form orders of consensus linking our
private judgments of good in various more or less diplomatic compromises. The "truth" is diluted, but then it was never truth anyway,
as science understands truth. It was your will, my will, everyone's
will to power. Yet it had its beginning in an act of intuition, in the
humanistic imagination taking wing and rendering its judgment in its
own uniquely personal way. On such judgments in their thousands and
millions, perfectly or imperfectly fused in social compromises, the
world order of the real future will be founded.

The danger of overreliance on the methodology of the positive
sciences, by contrast, is their obliviousness to the whole problem of
values. The pure social scientist cannot avoid making value judgments,
but he does so quite often by pretending that he has no need to make
them. The "truth itself" will point the way to the happiest future.[15]
Once he has discovered what the truth itself commands us to do, the
issue of goals is closed and all attention promptly shifts to the manipulation of human beings and their environment to achieve the most
efficient implementation of truth's commandments. Efficiency is
something that the positive sciences excel in engineering. When goals,
however, are seen for what they are—products of the wills of men and
women—the issue of where to go next remains open, subject to negotiation, change, and the political process. We know that values are
not automatically provided, and that no moral question answers itself.
Models of world order become not blueprints for prisons but pathways
to unexplored lands.

I shall not conclude by shouting "All power to the imagination!" Imagination without knowledge is methodological fascism. But knowledge without imagination is surrender, the surrender of the scholar to all the powers in society that seek to make him their salaried agent and acolyte. It is the scholar's task, and above all the futurist's task, to refuse such service; not to "understand" the future but to make it.

NOTES

1. See F. S. C. Northrop, The Meeting of East and West (New York, 1946), Chapter 12, and The Logic of the Sciences and the Humanities (New York, 1947), Chapter 5.

2. Donella H. Meadows et al., The Limits to Growth (Washington, D.C.: Potomac Associates, 1972), p. 142.

3. Johan Huizinga, "The Idea of History," in The Varieties of History, ed. Fritz Stern (New York, 1956), p. 291.

4. See, for example, Bernard Bergonzi, The Early H. G. Wells: A Study of the Scientific Romances (Manchester, 1961); H. Bruce Franklin, Future Perfect: American Science Fiction of the Nineteenth Century (New York, 1966); Mark R. Hillegas, The Future as Nightmare: H. G. Wells and the Anti-Utopians (New York, 1967); David Ketterer, New Worlds for Old: The Apocalyptic Imagination, Science Fiction, and American Literature (Bloomington, Ind., 1974); Robert M. Philmus, Into the Unknown: The Evolution of Science Fiction from Godwin to H. G. Wells (Berkeley and Los Angeles, 1970).

5. H. G. Wells, In the Days of the Comet (1906), The War in the Air (1908), The World Set Free (1914). See also I. F. Clarke, Voices Prophesying War, 1763-1984 (New York, 1966).

6. See W. Warren Wagar, "H. G. Wells and the Radicalism of Despair," Studies in the Literary Imagination 6, no. 2 (Fall 1973): 1-10.

7. See Stephen E. Whitfield and Gene Roddenberry, The Making of Star Trek (New York, 1968).

8. Dennis Livingston, "Science Fiction of Future World Order Systems," International Organization 25, no. 2 (Spring 1971): 270. See also Livingston, "Science Fiction as an Educational Tool," in Learning for Tomorrow: The Role of the Future in Education, ed. Alvin Toffler (New York, 1974), pp. 234-56.

9. Paul Ehrlich, "Eco-Catastrophe!" (1969), reprinted in The Futurists, ed. Alvin Toffler (New York, 1972), pp. 13-26.

10. Mario Rossi, A Plea for Man (Edinburgh, 1956), p. 27.

11. See J. H. Hexter, The History Primer (New York, 1971).

12. See Alan Bullock, "The Historian's Purpose: History and Metahistory," in The Philosophy of History in Our Time, ed. Hans Meyerhoff (Garden City, N.Y., 1959), p. 298.

13. Bertrand de Jouvenel, The Art of Conjecture (New York, 1967), pp. 18-19.

14. See Dennis Gabor, Inventing the Future (New York, 1964).

15. "I have no desire to plant a standard other than the truth itself. It is to this that the wise and honest must repair." Kenneth Boulding, The Meaning of the 20th Century (New York, 1964), p. 199. Cf. my review of Boulding's book in The Virginia Quarterly Review 41, no. 1 (Winter 1965): 119-22.

CHADWICK F. ALGER is Mershon Professor of Political Science and Public Policy at Ohio State University. Director of the Program in Transnational Intellectual Cooperation in the Policy Studies at Ohio State, he was a founder of the Consortium on Peace Research, Education, and Development (COPRED) and is currently serving as co-chairman of COPRED's Task Force on Peace Studies Consultation and Exchange. Professor Alger has published extensively on the impact of the United Nations on the nation-state system, particularly in terms of intergovernmental communications and participants. He is currently directing a project on Columbus in the World: The World in Columbus that is developing procedures for discerning how metropolitan communities are linked to global systems.

FRANCIS A. BEER is Associate Professor of Government at the University of Texas. He is the author of The Political Economy of Alliances: Benefits, Costs, and Institutions in NATO; Integration and Disintegration in NATO: Processes of Alliance Cohesion and Prospects for Atlantic Community; and editor of Alliances: Latent War Communities in the Contemporary World. In addition to a number of journal articles, Professor Beer has written the forthcoming books, International Violence and How Much War in History? Definitions, Estimates, Trends, and Extrapolations.

LOUIS RENÉ BERES is Associate Professor of Political Science at Purdue University. He is the author of Transforming World Politics: The National Roots of World Peace (1975); World Peace Through World Federal Government (1975); Reordering the Planet: Constructing Alternative World Futures (with Harry R. Targ, 1974); The Management of World Power: A Theoretical Analysis (1973); and Learning Package in World Order Studies (1973). Professor Beres also has written numerous journal articles.

DAVIS B. BOBROW is Professor and Chairman, Department of Government and Politics, University of Maryland. In addition to numerous journal articles, he has written International Relations—New Approaches and has edited and coauthored Weapons System Decisions, Computers and the Policy-Making Community and Components of Defense Policy. Professor Bobrow has served as Special Assistant for the Behavioral and Social Sciences in the Office of the Director of

Defense Research and Engineering and as Acting Director, Behavioral Sciences, Advanced Research Projects Agency. He has also served as Senior Social Scientist at the Oak Ridge National Laboratory.

CHARLES F. DORAN is Associate Professor of Political Science at Rice University. His research specialties are foreign and domestic conflict analysis (events data and dynamic modeling), United States-small state relations, international political aspects of resource scarcity and environmental protection, and the implications of each question for alternative world futures. Professor Doran's publications include The Politics of Assimilation: Hegemony and Its Aftermath; Umweltschutz—Politik des peripheren Eingriffs: Eine Einfuhrung in die Politische Okologie; and several journal articles. Recently he has supervised the coding of Middle-East events data for a micro-analysis of the June 1967 War.

RICHARD A. FALK is Albert G. Milbank Professor of International Law and Practice at Princeton University. A close associate of the Institute for World Order, he is Research Director of the North American Team of the World Order Models Project and the author of many books and articles in the field. Professor Falk's most recent publications include This Endangered Planet; Regional Politics and World Order (edited with Saul H. Mendlovitz), and A Study of Future Worlds.

GEORGE KENT is Professor of Political Science at the University of Hawaii. He is the author of The Effects of Threats and many journal articles including "The Application of Peace Studies" in The Journal of Conflict Resolution, March 1971; "Plan for Designing the Future," Bulletin of Peace Proposals, 1972; and "Teaching Practical Policy Analysis," Teaching Political Science, October 1974. Professor Kent speaks widely before professional associations on topics related to world order and alternative world futures.

SAUL H. MENDLOVITZ is Professor of International Law at Rutgers University, and President of the Institute for World Order in New York City. The author and editor of many books and articles, and Director of the Institute's World Order Models Project, his most recent contribution is Regional Politics and World Order, edited with Richard A. Falk. Professor Mendlovitz also serves on the Social Science Advisory Board of the U.S. Arms Control and Disarmament Agency.

MARVIN S. SOROOS is Assistant Professor of Politics at North Carolina State University. In addition to two other articles on methods of future-oriented research in international relations, his published writings have included an analysis of the relationship between international involvement and foreign behaviors and comparisons of the International Processes Simulation to real world reference systems. He has been a frequent participant on panels at professional gatherings and recently has been the president of the Southern Regional Section of the Peace Science Society (International).

MICHAEL STOHL is Assistant Professor of Political Science at Purdue University. A specialist in the study of linkages between foreign and domestic policy, his most recent publications include "Linkages Between War and Domestic Political Violence in the United States, 1890-1923" in Quasi-Experimental Approaches, eds. James Caporaso and Leslie Roos; "Alternative Futures for Peace Research" in the Journal of Conflict Resolution, December 1972; and "Theory and Method in the Studies of the Relationship Between Foreign and Domestic Conflict and Violence," Fifth International Peace Research Association Conference, Varanasi, India, January 1974.

HARRY R. TARG is Associate Professor of Political Science at Purdue University. He is the author (with Louis Rene Beres) of Reordering the Planet: Constructing Alternative World Futures (1974). He has published several articles dealing with childhood political socialization and war/peace attitudes, regional integration theory, and alternative world futures in such journals as Journal of Peace Research, Polity, Peace and Change, and Teaching Political Science. Professor Targ is presently investigating the contribution of anarchist thought to world order design problems.

W. WARREN WAGAR is Professor of History at the State University of New York at Binghamton. He has written five books and edited five others, including The City of Man, Building the City of Man, and Good Tidings: The Belief in Progress from Darwin to Marcuse. Professor Wagar has held a Fulbright Scholarship, an American Council of Learned Societies Fellowship, and a Senior Fellowship from the National Endowment for the Humanities to undertake a study of visions of the world's end in modern secular literature.

A. MICHAEL WASHBURN has been the Director of the Institute for World Order University Program since 1970. In this capacity he has met and advised large numbers of professors, administrators, and students on matters concerning peace education. He has served as cochairperson of COPRED's Task Force on University Curriculum Development and is presently the chairperson of the newly formed Peace Studies Section of the International Studies Association. Now

Executive Vice-President of the Institute for World Order, his published writings include Toward the Study of Peace (with Paul Wehr, 1974) and Creating the Future: A Guide to Living and Working for Social Change (with Charles Beitz, 1974). Recently, he was guest editor (with Kathleen Newland and Brenda Steinmetz) of a special issue of Peace and Change, "Creating Undergraduate Peace Studies Programs."

THOMAS G. WEISS is closely associated with the Institute for World Order in New York City. Formerly Assistant Director of the Institute's University Program, his publications include "Toward Consensus: The Institute for World Order's Model World Order Project," with Saul H. Mendlovitz in Introduction to World Peace Through World Law, eds. Grenville Clark and Louis Sohn; and A Framework for Teaching International Politics (forthcoming) with Norman Walbek. He also is the author (with Saul H. Mendlovitz) of Shaping the Future, a forthcoming introductory textbook. He has worked for the International Labor Office, the United Nations Institute for Training and Research, and the Fund for Peace.

DEVELOPMENT ON A HUMAN SCALE: Potentials
for Ecologically Guided Growth in Northern
New Mexico

> Peter van Dresser

ORGANIZATIONS OF THE FUTURE: Interaction
with the External Environment

> edited by Harold Leavitt,
> Lawrence Pinfield, and
> Eugene Webb

THE VIDEO-TELEPHONE: Impact of a New Era in
Telecommunications

> Edward M. Dickson,
> in association with
> Raymond Bowers